Western Questions
Eastern Answers

Volume 3

Other books by Ashish Dalela

Semantic Atomism
Semantic Reasoning
The Journey of Perfection
Material and Spiritual Natures
Conceiving the Inconceivable
The Science of God
Time and Consciousness
The Balanced Organization
The Yellow Pill
Cosmic Theogony
Emotion
Mystic Universe
Uncommon Wisdom
Moral Materialism
Signs of Life
Is the Apple Really Red?
Sankhya and Science
Six Causes
Quantum Meaning
Godel's Mistake

Western Questions

Eastern Answers

A Collection of Short Essays

Volume 3

ASHISH DALELA

Western Questions, Eastern Answers —A Collection of Short Essays
Volume 3

www.shabda.com

Published by Shabda Press
www.shabda.co
ISBN 978-93-85384-20-2

Contents

PREFACE

The problems I write about have very broad ramifications. I'm referring to the questions of meaning and morality, the issues of free will and determinism, the problems of indeterminism in science, the issue of semantics in computing and mathematics, and the question of the origin of life and the universe. Much of the appeal for such problems often fades in the modern rush of life, when people believe the questions are merely intellectual curiosities and that even if we were to find those answers nothing much would change in our day-to-day lives.

Whatever little interest remains for such topics today, the prospective reader list is further slimmed by the choice of the viewpoint from which I write about these issues. First, my perspective is drawn from the personalist school of Vedic philosophy, quite different from *Advaita* or impersonalism, with which most people are familiar. Second, most people are naturally turned off by reference to a 'religious' philosophy. Third, by speaking of the problems that most academics are working on, outside mainstream academia, I rule out a large number of intellectuals who could have been potential readers. And yet, this is the viewpoint that I believe holds the greatest promise for answering the biggest outstanding problems. Having observed the utter failure of *Advaita* attempts to recast science in a new mold, as well as the materialist attempts to subsume new problems such as mind, meaning, and consciousness under the current physical worldview, I am convinced that a different view of nature is necessary, which is logical-empirical and yet not materialistic.

Over the years, I have written several books, the details of which you will find at the end of this work. To introduce these books, and as a result of the ensuing discussions with readers, I wrote several blog posts. This book collects these posts. Ideally, I should have inserted these discussions back into the books that originally led to these discussions. But given that revising a book is much harder, I have just collected the posts here.

The 'market' for such topics is incredibly small today, constrained both by a lack of interest and by unfamiliarity with modern science.

It includes those who have a good understanding of modern science and its problems, coupled with the awareness of the historical evolution of Western philosophy and the problems that caused that evolution, combined with an interest in understanding Vedic philosophy, and conjoined with the curiosity in the relevance of that philosophy to modern thinking. If any of the above prerequisites fails, the readership tends to reduce dramatically. Clearly, these books and posts are not therefore byproducts of economic considerations.

These books and posts were written for a very simple reason: I wanted to read such books and posts myself, but I could not find them anywhere. So, I studied, digested, and assimilated what I wanted to understand. Having reached a certain point, I also wanted to write it down, just because writing makes things clearer. Over time, however, I also thought that there might be some people interested in similar topics—knowing fully well that the likelihood of running into someone with that interest is almost next to zero. But, of course, the world is big! Next to zero chance multiplied by a very large number of people still produces a few interested souls. These are the readers who have constantly encouraged me through their appreciation, amazement, and kind words. That encouragement has kept me going on this journey.

Why did I choose to name this collection "Western Questions, Eastern Answers"? Philosophy and science in the West have largely been practiced with the aim to understand the present world. A number of theories have been propounded, none of which are free of problems. Philosophy and science in the East (specifically the Vedic tradition) has always been practiced with the aim to transcend the world. Vedic texts provide many theories, but always in answer to a transcendental question. On one hand, therefore, we have questions that haven't found good answers. On the other, there are very good answers that haven't been connected to the burning questions of mankind today.

Combining them makes a lot of sense from both sides, although I believe this type of approach to a 'synthesis' of religion and science hasn't been attempted before. Clearly, to repeat the same answer but in response to a different question, and the answer to still make a lot of sense, we must understand not just the questions and answers, but also the other answers that were earlier given for the same question, and how the new answer is better. That is not just a demand on the author; it is an equally difficult demand on the reader as well. But that's the price to be paid if there is indeed a long history of incorrect answers which have to be rejected before a correct answer would be accepted. After all, we might still do the right thing, if only as the option of last resort.

My aim is to provide the answers that were previously given in response to radically different questions, but now in response to the questions that currently remain unanswered. Many people have tried to marry the intellectual and ideological views of East and West, sometimes with hilarious and disastrous results. This attempt is therefore not without considerable risks, although the effort is worth the trouble.

The books and posts are my personal journey into a subject that is very difficult, and rare by modern standards. I do hope to make it a tad bit simpler for others by showing the path that I have treaded. If you would like to discuss this further, do reach out to me through email or other ways available on my website. I wish you a fruitful journey.

The Cycle of Guna and Karma

Published Date: 2017-04-08

Introduction and Overview

The term *guna* indicates what we *desire*, and the term *karma* indicates what we *deserve*; both exist as possibilities, but their combination in time produces the cycle of birth and death. This is the essence of the Vedic science in which *guna*, *karma*, and *kāla* combine to create the world. This article focuses on the unique role played by *karma* and its significance in the creation of experiences. The post also discusses the law of *karma* at length and describes how the consequences of our actions are produced through an interaction between *guna* and *karma*, which produce one another, and their interaction creates a cycle.

Role vs. Person

In the everyday world, we can distinguish between a *role* and a *person*. The *roles* are the "posts" such as kings and queens, presidents and secretaries, deans and students, employers and employees, parents and children, husbands and wives, etc. Each role has some rights and duties. The *persons* are the participants in the roles, who respond to the expectations of a role. The qualities of a person are described differently than that of a role; persons are called virtuous or immoral, kind or ruthless, happy or angry, talented or foolish, introvert or extrovert. While a role sets up bounds on a person's acceptable behavior, most people are either exceeding the bounds or falling behind them.

In Vedic philosophy, when a person exceeds or falls behind the bounds of a role, he or she produces *karma* due to an interaction between the person and the role. Vedic philosophy emphasizes that while each person is unique, their uniqueness has to be subordinated to the demands of their role. For example, when you take the role of a father or mother, you are expected to fulfill its requirements whether or not you find the role meaningful or pleasing. The role, as noted above, involves authority and responsibility. You may not desire the authority, and you might not love the responsibility, but you have to fulfill them, because not fulfilling the demands of a role, or exceeding it, produces *karma*.

In a sense, the person is the "particle" and the role is the "field" surrounding the particle. These "particles" are pushed into different parts of the "field" and this is called the changing role of a person. As the person moves into the new role, he creates more *karma* which then propels him into yet another role. In this way, there is a cycle of interaction between the person and the role, which keeps moving the person from one role to another. The understanding of *karma* constitutes a scientific description of how a person transmigrates through roles in life, enjoying or suffering through the vagaries of material existence, and how a cycle of repeated birth and death is created.

Time, Place, and Circumstance

In Vedic texts, we don't find words such as *role* and *person*. We rather find words such as *guna*, *karma*, and *kāla*, where *guna* is the individuality and personality of a person, *karma* is the moral consequences of their actions, and time controls both *guna* and *karma*. This description is not easily understood because while we can see the activity of people, it is not clear how *my karma* acts *through their* behavior (it seems apparent that my enjoyment and suffering often depend on others' activities so if I have to suffer or enjoy, my *karma* should act through the behaviors of other people). In fact, the notion that my destiny is enacted by the actions of others creates new problems of free will.

We can understand *guna*, *karma*, and *kāla*, through another triad called *deśa-kāla-pātra*, which is often translated as "time, place, and circumstance". Since *kāla* is used in both cases, there is no need to separately explain the term; it means time. In previous articles, I have described how matter in Sāṅkhya constructs a tree-like space from the three modes. The *gunas,* therefore, create space and each combination of the three modes is a unique ideological "place" in the universe. Consequently, we can equate the term *guna* with the term *deśa* or space and place; one of them says that the world is three qualities, while the other says the world is space; these two are identical notions when we understand how the locations in space are produced through the combination of three qualities.

The term *pātra* needs more explanation. It literally means a vessel, utensil, or pot. It is a container that holds some content. The question is: What is the content this *pātra* is holding? In the present context, the container is holding a body made of *guna*, and while we can perceive the *guna* we cannot perceive the container. The container is the "role" the body "occupies" just like water fills up a pot. The term *pātra* is also used in drama to describe a 'character' such as a King or Queen. This occupation is like a drama scene being populated by actors; the scene comprised of roles is the pot or the container.

Deśa-kāla-pātra means that *karma* creates the roles, the scenes of interactions, or circumstances (i.e. the "vessels"). These vessels are then filled up by material bodies who are placed into the roles. To understand *karma*, we have to see how the universe is produced as roles and the body is pushed into that role. The roles define rights and duties, and when the body occupies the role, there is a natural definition of *moral behavior*. Morality exists as the "vessel" in which we are situated. We are expected to obey the bounds of this "vessel"—i.e. don't exceed the rights and don't fall short of the duties.

Real and Imaginary Space

The universe as a whole is some possible locations (meanings). All the locations are not manifest at once; they are produced one by one due to time. However, which of these locations will *interact* with the other locations constitutes the observable scene. This interaction is produced by *karma* which connects events at different locations in space. For example, the chair on which I'm sitting and the table on which I'm writing, are not next to each other in conceptual space. They are conceptually far apart—because they are instances of different ideas (chair and table)—although they are *interacting* with each other due to my *karma* and that interaction creates the *impression* of physical proximity.

There is hence a *real distance* in space created by *guna,* which is permanent because it is the gap between two concepts, which always exist as a possibility. The distance between the "table" and "chair" never changes in the conceptual space, and in that sense, the material space is eternal. The temporary part is that some objects occasionally interact with the other objects in order to create a scene. These objects are not necessarily close, nor are they necessarily far apart. However, when they interact they appear to be close, and when they don't interact they appear to be far. The appearance of proximity and distance is an illusion produced due to their mutual interaction.

The interactions produce a phenomenal space that we experience as the three-dimensional world. The situations in this space are not real in themselves. Rather, they are produced from two things: (1) real objects which exist in their own place forever, and (2) temporary *karma* which causes their interaction to produce an effect. *Karma* is the cause of relationships or circumstances or roles and characters in which we are placed. There is distance and proximity in these relations too, however, each relation is also a possibility, because we are not permanently acting like a father, mother, child, friend, etc. The interaction between the bodies, under the restrictions of the role, creates the phenomenal proximity which is different both from the conceptual proximity/distance, and the role-based proximity/distance. *Karma* creates the scenes of the drama by connecting different participants, but the strength of this interaction decides the phenomenal proximity.

The Creation of Experience

One of the big mysteries of modern science is that atomic theory describes the world as a possibility but only one of those possibilities becomes a reality at any given moment. The situation is like tossing a dice in which all the faces are possible, but only one of the faces will turn up at any given point in time. The difference is that these faces in atomic theory are different objects. So, we interact with one object after another, but we cannot predict which object is going to be next. What we see is a product of that interaction.

Scientists have been asking how the succession of the interactions could be created because we are not able to find a "force" that can choose the next experience. The mystery is deepened because we think that in the physical space the atom and the measuring instrument are very close to each other. Then what causes the atom to "suddenly" emit and be detected by the measuring instrument? This problem is still unsolved at present.

The problem can only be solved when we understand that the electron and the measuring instrument are not close; they are two *types* of objects, and they are semantically far apart. However, they can interact due to *karma*. What atomic theory calls the "collapse" of a wavefunction is the interaction of two distant objects to produce a measurement event. The *cause* of this measurement event is not a physical property and not a force. It is a type of reality called *karma*. It exists in an unmanifest form and thus it cannot be measured until it creates an effect. It decides which detector (observer) gets to measure (see) which quantum (object). *Karma* is manifesting in time, but unless we understand how this *karma* is created, where it exists, and how it manifests, we cannot understand the atomic theory.

The Mechanism of Karma

If two objects—A and B—have to interact, then there are two kinds of uncertainties (at the two objects, respectively) to be resolved. The first uncertainty is that A can interact with any C, D, or E, not just B. Similarly, B can interact with any P, Q, or R, not just A. Thus any transaction needs to overcome the uncertainty on two sides: a sender and a receiver, because the sender can send to any receiver, and a receiver can receive from any sender.

For any transaction to occur, there have to be two sides with complementary *karma*: one is giving and the other is taking. The mechanism of *karma* involves the *pairing* of two instances of *karma* from two individuals, due to which when two people get into a close relationship (e.g. a marriage) we can say that their "destinies are tied". A strong relationship—e.g. marriage—requires that most of the *karma* a person receives or transmits should be exchanged with their partner. If their *karma* doesn't match, then they would forcibly be involved with other individuals, thereby loosening the marital bond.

Vedic philosophy describes that the pairing of two individuals is arranged by a third party—the demigods—who are higher nodes in the tree. Information cannot therefore directly travel from one leaf of the tree to another leaf. It has to climb up the inverted tree, find a branch where the leaves are joined, and then descend to the destination. Thus, the source and destination of *karma* are not the only two entities involved. There is always a third party involved in all interactions which mediates and creates it.

The three parties are called *ādidaivika*, *ādiatmika* and *ādibhautika*. The third party is *ādidaivika*; the first and second parties are *ādiatmika* and *ādibhautika*. The sender and receiver are not "equal" in a transaction; one of the two is higher—i.e. in a controlling position relative to the other, although the third party is even higher. Thus, *ādidaivika* is highest, and therefore *sattva-guna*. Between the remaining two, the *ādiatmika* is higher, and therefore *rajo-guna*. Finally, the *ādibhautika* is the lowest, and therefore *tamo-guna*. All material transactions involve these three players. A role has three parts—*ādidaivika, ādiatmika,* and *ādibhautika*. There are two instances of *karma* transacted between *ādiatmika* and *ādibhautika*, and their mutual interaction is arranged by the *ādidaivika*.

The Event and the Object Spaces

The resolution of the problems of morality and free will requires the separation of actors and actions. It results in two kinds of descriptions—one of the events and the other of the objects or actors that cause the actions. The event is an exchange, different from the objects or actors exchanging it. If you lend money to your friend, the event is money lending, but that exchange doesn't mean that you or your friend are money. The space of events is quite different from the space of objects.

The universe of events has three features (the "what", "where", and "when"); space, time, and matter here refer to events, not to the actors involved in the events. Similarly, there is another space, time, and matter that constitutes individual actors with three features ("who", "why" and "how"); space, time, and matter here refer to the actors, not to events. Now we have two kinds of spaces—one of the events and the other of actors. Both these spaces are "fixed" in the sense that the locations of events and actors are well-defined. What is not fixed is which scene will include which actors. This is decided by *karma*.

Karma is the agency that connects the actors to each other and to the events. In the space of events, the universe can be described as occurrences—e.g. money is lent, money is returned, someone is born, someone dies, a president is elected, a house was bought, etc. In the space of actors, the universe can be described as material bodies. All the bodies and all the events are predefined, but which body goes through which event is not. Thus the body hops through events, which we call material experience: e.g. I received the money, I lent the money, I was born, I died, I was elected as president, I bought a house, etc.

Karma reconciles these two different kinds of descriptions of nature; it allows us to say that underlying each event is a material object causing it. By selecting the components of interaction, *karma* defines (1) which objects will participate in an event, and (2) which event will be explained by which material objects. Since the events are always connected to some objects, behind every experience there is some reality. If the events and objects were not connected, we could have an experience without a corresponding reality.

In this interaction, the material objects are the *material cause* and *karma* is the *efficient* cause that joins objects into causal interactions. Modern science is the illusion of thinking that the material cause is the efficient cause. For example, if someone steals our money, we don't blame our *karma*; we blame the person who stole it. The person who steals it is indeed the material cause of the theft. However, they could have potentially stolen from another person and I would still be unaffected. The reason the thief steals from me is due to my *karma* and this *karma* is thus the efficient cause of theft.

Anatomy of a Role

Of course, theft is morally incorrect, and we judge that morality not simply by the action of taking money, but by the *role* of the person who is taking that money. Thus, *karma* can decide whether someone will take my money. But whether the person is involved in a legitimate duty or an illegal act is decided by the roles of the actors. The material and efficient causes are therefore adequate only to explain the occurrence of the event at present, but a role is additionally required to judge the morality of the event.

A role is comprised of three different aspects. First, each role has associated rights and duties. Second, these rights and duties are defined both for giving and for receiving. Third, the giving and the receiving are divided by the three modes of nature which in turn divide the six qualities beginning with knowledge. They can be described more fully as below:

- A role has rights and duties. We are expected to exercise the right and fulfill the duties to the extent expected and demanded by the role, whether we like it or not.
- The rights and duties involve both giving and taking. Thus, we have the right to both give and receive; similarly, responsibility also includes both giving and receiving.
- Each act of giving or receiving exchanges properties in three modes; for example, food can be bitter, sweet, or salty, color can be cyan, magenta, and yellow, etc.

While exercising the authority of a role, a person is *ādiatmika*—i.e.

higher—than the persons over whom he or she exercises authority—i.e. *ādibhautika*. While fulfilling the responsibilities, a person is *ādibhautika*—i.e. subordinate—to the persons who consume the responsibility, who now become the *ādiatmika*. A person in authority is a relative master over those affected by his decisions. The same person, while fulfilling a duty, becomes a subordinate to those who consume the responsibility. No person is an absolute master or servant, as each person has some authority and some responsibility.

How Three Modes Create Karma

Our personality and individuality are built from the three modes of nature—*sattva, rajas*, and *tamas*. The mode of *rajas* creates zeal and confidence and under this mode, a person exceeds their authority and responsibility. The mode of *tamas* creates laziness and inertia and under this mode, a person falls short of their authority and responsibility. The mode of *sattva* balances zeal and laziness and under this mode, a person does just what the role expects—neither exceeding nor falling short of its demands.

When we exceed or fall short, *karma* is produced which has three varieties called *sukarma, vikarma*, and *akarma*. The term *sukarma* indicates "good" *karma*; the term *vikarma* indicates "bad" *karma*; the term *akarma* indicates "no" *karma*. If we think of the role as a boundary on expected behavior, then the law of *karma* stipulates a person to neither be inside nor outside that boundary. Rather, the ideal behavior is to be just on the boundary.

The mode of *sattva-guna* is the ideal mode because in this mode we neither exceed nor fall short. When actions are performed under *sattva-guna* the activity is called *karma-yoga*, which dissolves your personality into the role: your unique tastes (what produce your unique meanings and pleasures in life) don't matter; what matters is the demands of the role. Under *rajo-guna* and *tamo-guna*, a person's personality and individuality become more important, which then results in either *sukarma* or *vikarma*.

We can think of the three modes as parent and children. The mode of *sattva-guna* is the parent. The mode of *rajo-guna* is the elder sibling, while the mode of *tamo-guna* is the younger sibling. The parent precedes the two siblings, but the elder sibling precedes the younger sibling. The two siblings are always fighting and the parent is trying to resolve the fight between them. They are three members of a family and at different times they get to make the decision that the family will collectively follow. Which mode is prominent or subservient when, is the function of time, which operates in cycles.

The Law of Karma

Based on the above distinctions, we can describe the "law" of *karma* through the following table. No such table is described in Vedic texts. However, such an understanding of morality can be easily gleaned from texts such as *manusmṛti*, which describe good and bad actions. Whether or we like it or not, these rules of morality are embedded in our society from time immemorial. The philosophical underpinning of these laws is now not well-known, but it is still not impossible to agree upon the laws themselves.

	Rights				Duties			
	Giving		Taking		Giving		Taking	
	Reward	Punish	Reward	Punish	Reward	Punish	Reward	Punish
Excess	Good	Bad	Bad	Good	Good	Bad	Bad	Good
Short	Bad	Good	Good	Bad	Bad	Good	Good	Bad

Below I elaborate the above rules using insights from everyday intuitions about moral behavior. The elaborations are numbered according to the numbering in the below table.

	Rights				Duties			
	Giving		Taking		Giving		Taking	
	Reward	Punish	Reward	Punish	Reward	Punish	Reward	Punish
Excess	1	3	5	7	9	11	13	15
Short	2	4	6	8	10	12	14	16

1. We all have a capacity to give good things to society and we are expected to give; when our charity exceeds our natural capability to provide, we create good *karma*.
2. When we have the capacity to give to others but we become misers and decline to help others even when we can or help below our capacity, we incur bad *karma*.
3. We are within our rights to reprimand others under our authority but this reprimand should be used sparingly—as

and when required—and mostly lower than the maximum permitted. Judicious use of reprimand is good *karma*.

4. Exceeding the limits of our authority to punish others—whether that extends to those beyond our jurisdiction or beyond the extent of the crime is bad *karma*.
5. When we employ people, we have the right to demand their services; however, an employer should aspire to demand less than what he compensates the employees for. Giving more and taking less is good *karma*.
6. When an employer exploits the employees and makes them work more than what they are compensated for, or defined by their job role, the employer incurs bad *karma*.
7. Everyone has some natural capacity or tolerable limit to suffering losses and harm for the benefit of others. When a person exceeds this capacity—i.e. performs a great sacrifice for others—he creates good *karma*.
8. When a person has the capacity to incur a personal sacrifice but doesn't make the sacrifice when required, or performs a lower sacrifice than capacity—he creates bad *karma*.
9. An employee is expected to perform their duties diligently; however, some employees go beyond the call of their expected duty and create greater value for their employer; they produce good *karma*.
10. An employee who neglects his or her responsibilities and does not perform their duties as expected in a job fails to create the value demanded and produces bad *karma*.
11. In certain jobs like that of a judge or police, one is expected to punish others as a matter of duty; when the person metes out a greater punishment than expected or required for the given crime, he creates bad *karma*.
12. When a judge or police correct the people in society by being kind and compassionate to them and awarding them less than the maximum possible punishment for a given crime, they create good *karma*.
13. Some employees—e.g. tax collectors—are expected to receive or collect valuables (e.g. money) from others; when they exceed the maximum limit that they are permitted for a given case, they incur bad *karma*.

14. When a tax collector is lenient in their demands for people who are in distress or difficulty and demonstrates mercy and compassion even while doing his job as diligently as he can, he or she creates good *karma* due to forgiveness.
15. A captain of a ship, or a soldier on a battlefield, or any leader in society, is expected to sacrifice as a matter of their expected duty. When a person sacrifices far greater than the expected limit, he creates good *karma*.
16. When a captain or soldier or leader is expected to make a sacrifice but runs away from the responsibility out of cowardice, or lets others make sacrifices on his behalf while saving himself, he incurs bad *karma*.

Karma is a Tight Rope Walk

The above table describes sixteen rules of how good or bad *karma* is created. However, if we just read through the above simple rules, three kinds of exceptions should be evident.

- All the rules don't apply to everyone; as we can see, some rules are prominent for leaders and warriors, while other rules are pertinent for ordinary workers, while yet other rules are relevant only for employers and businessmen. This entails that the rules of *karma* are different for the different types of people—i.e. the classes in the Varna system of social organization.
- The application of rules is based on a person's capacity. A poor man giving a small charity produces good *karma* whereas a rich man giving a small charity produces bad *karma*. A small sacrifice by an ordinary person creates good *karma*, but when people expected to sacrifice fall short of their duty, then the partial performance of duty results in bad *karma*.
- The rules have to be applied based on the situation involved. For example, a judge being lenient on a hardened criminal is a dereliction of duty, because the criminal performs more crimes against the innocent, and the judge can be held responsible for the shortfall. Similarly, a tax collector waiving taxes when the person has the capacity to pay is a party to a crime.

The application of these laws depends on a person's capacity to perform their duties and rights, which is often a result of their currently manifesting *karma*. The application of rules also depends on the judgment of the situation because both excessive and deficient application of the rules is bad *karma*. While the rules help us understand the guidelines, applying the rules can often be a tightrope walk, because the material situation is hierarchical, and therefore the rules too have to be applied in a hierarchical manner. Thus, based on the person, time, place, and situation, some rules become more important than others. A table of rules is not adequate to determine justice.

Owing to this fact attempts to create good *karma* can backfire and result in bad *karma*. For example, a zealous ruler can be extremely harsh in the application of laws, and thereby punish the innocent. Similarly, a compassionate lawyer can be very lenient in the application of laws, hoping for the best results, but that leniency can be interpreted as a weakness of the law. Thus, both alternatives of being overzealous or overly compassionate result in bad *karma*. Hence, Vedic texts advise a person to aspire to be free of the material roles, not to seek powerful roles.

The above table can be simplified to denote the modes of nature and their effects. The below table illustrates how good and bad *karma* is created which then affects the future roles.

	Rajas				Tamas			
	Rajas		Tamas		Rajas		Tamas	
	Rajas	Tamas	Rajas	Tamas	Rajas	Tamas	Rajas	Tamas
Rajas	Good	Bad	Bad	Good	Good	Bad	Bad	Good
Tamas	Bad	Good	Good	Bad	Bad	Good	Good	Bad

The essence of good *karma* is (1) giving greater value and lesser detriment, and (2) taking the lesser value and greater detriment. The law of *karma* is that as the good *karma* increases, the rights, authority, and power available to a person increases and hence the person rises in the material hierarchy; similarly, as the bad *karma* increases, the duties, responsibilities, and liabilities also increase and the person falls in the material hierarchy. As the good *karma* is finished (i.e. new good *karma* is not created), the person falls in the hierarchy, and as the bad *karma* is finished (i.e. new bad *karma* is not created) the person rises in the material hierarchy. The living entity is thus going up and down the material tree due to *karma*, sometimes enjoying at a higher position, and other times suffering at a lower position.

The Essence of Material Morality

Everyone in the material world is looking for a situation where they have far greater rights and far lesser duties. Rising in the material world means going up the tree of material hierarchy where we can find greater power, whereas going down the tree of material nature is when we have lesser power. It is worth noting that all situations in the world—higher and lower—can be enjoyed. For example, there is happiness in having the power and never having to use it, because everyone is obedient and lawful. There is also happiness in not having the power and therefore the responsibility because then the person doesn't run the risk of committing a mistake and therefore falling down.

The pleasure in higher segments of the universe is that of greater freedom and greater responsibility. The pleasure in the lower parts of the universe is in lesser freedom and lesser accountability. In higher regions of the universe, for example, pleasure means the respectful and responsible exchange of ideas. In lower regions of the universe, pleasure means sadomasochistic domination and subservience.

Neither the top nor the bottom is ideally suited for spiritual advancement. This is because if you are at the top, then you have so much power that giving it up is not easy. The soul, in such a situation, is enamored by the influence, control, and authority and shudders at the thought of losing it; even the demigods are thus insecure despite having tremendous power over the others. Conversely, if you are at the bottom, then you have very little power and freedom to do anything of your choosing. The soul, in such a situation, is overly bound by the surrounding circumstances and situations and is unable to think or act independently. The living entities at the top and at the bottom are enjoying different kinds of pleasures, but neither of them has what it takes to exit the universe easily.

The living entities in the middle of the universe have neither great autonomy nor great bondage. Accordingly, the pleasure enjoyed from the exercise of rights and the execution of duties is not great. In fact, given the circumstances, it is not obvious whether the best way to enjoy material life is to increase your rights and responsibilities or to reduce your freedoms and accountabilities. Thus, some people pursue a high-class life (the top businessmen and politicians), while others desire a middle-class life (white and blue-collar workers), while yet others are happy with a lower-class life (hippies, vagabonds, and gypsies). Who can convincingly say who is the happiest of them all?

The Vedic texts prefer life in the middle for spiritual advancement because it is easier to give up both *rajo-guna* and *tamo-guna* and pursue *sattva-guna*. As a person stops the creation of new *karma*, he or she finishes the business in this life and is free of the material roles. He or she can then think of non-material roles, and develop a personality for them.

The Cycle of Guna and Karma

The role is objective and not subjective. Hence, the law of moral judgments is also objective and not subjective. This fact allows us to formulate a natural theory of morality, and explain how the consequences of moral judgment are responsible for what we call "motion" or the transmigration of the soul. As we play our role well, we can either rise to a higher role or renounce all roles. As we play our roles badly, we are bound in constraining roles where we have limited freedom.

Guna and *karma,* therefore, constitute a cycle of causality. *Karma* creates circumstances. A living entity tries to comprehend these situations makes strategies for action in order to enjoy in the given circumstances, thus changing his *guna*. The new *gunas* now produce new activities and depending on whether these activities exceed or fall short of expectations, new *karma* is created. This causal cycle runs in a cyclic time where the universe itself goes through the same kinds of events over and over. The living entity in the universe is, therefore, going in circles: (1) due to the *guna-karma* cycle, and (2) due to the time cycle.

As the person creates good *karma*, he rises up the material tree and enjoys greater autonomy, power, and responsibility. As the person creates bad *karma*, he falls down the material tree and enjoys greater bondage, subservience, and determinism. There is pleasure in all kinds of material situations, provided one has adapted their taste of enjoyment according to the circumstances available. As the good *karma* is over, the living entity again changes their situation for the worse (depending on the taste of enjoyment they have developed so far). Likewise, when the bad *karma* is over, the living entity changes its situation for the better (depending on its taste). This type of back and forth produces a cycle called "transmigration" and it emerges from the *guna-karma* cycle and the time cycle.

The Problem of Scriptural Exegesis

Published Date: 2017-04-16

Exegesis, according to Wikipedia, is "a critical explanation or interpretation of a text, particularly a religious text". In the Vedic tradition, it exists as the commentaries by previous *āchāryās* who have explained the scriptures in various ways according to time, place, and circumstances. Such commentaries are essential for one key reason—the meanings of the words are continually evolving with time, and if we simply read the original text, we might interpret it according to the present-day meanings of the words, which might not be the meanings as were previously intended. This post discusses the consequences of changing meanings on the understanding of scriptural knowledge.

The Evolution of Words and Meanings

We are all familiar with the fact that every culture invents new words, and gives the old words completely new meanings. In the last few decades, for example, the words "cool" and "hot" have acquired completely novel meanings; depending on context both words can indicate something desirable and attractive. Modern society has also invented many new words such as "affluenza" and "bling" which previously did not exist. These words in due course of time might acquire additional meanings. Some of these words may disappear from our vocabulary and then be rediscovered with new meanings.

As we go through time, therefore, it is hard to say what the true meaning of something stated in the past was, unless we immerse ourselves into the time, culture, and context in which it was originally stated. Oxford Dictionary's online blog states that "On average, we add approximately 1,000 new entries to Oxford Dictionaries Online every year". A thousand new words every year! In contrast, the typical vocabulary of a native English speaker is about 5000 words, with twice as many words used in writing. That means that more words are added to a dictionary in 10 years than your entire vocabulary! Since our vocabulary is not continually expanding, many older words will gradually disappear from active use over time. Thus, active words in use change over time, and if you haven't updated your vocabulary over your lifetime, you might not be able to understand most of what the younger generation will be talking about by the time you get old.

This fact presents serious problems in understanding the meanings of the texts that were authored long ago. What meanings do you think people would give to the text being produced right now, a few centuries from now? Will they see strange words that they don't understand? Or will they bother to find out the meanings of the words from a dictionary that is contemporary to the text? What about phrases such as "couch potato" and "piece of cake"? If the words "couch" or "cake" acquired new meanings, what would these phrases mean then?

Wittgenstein's Language Games

Ludwig Wittgenstein, probably the most important 20th-century philosopher, brought to fore the key idea that words don't have fixed meanings. Rather, their meanings are dependent on the context of their use. He called these words "tools" meant to get a "job done". Wittgenstein gives the example of a mechanic working with an assistant in a workshop. When the mechanic says "screwdriver", the assistant hands him a screwdriver. When the mechanic says "sledgehammer", his assistant gets him a sledgehammer. If this same mechanic went to a pub or a bar later in the day, then the use of the words "screwdriver" and "sledgehammer" would get him cocktails rather than tools.

Wittgenstein's point is that words don't have fixed meanings. Depending on the context, the same word has different meanings. As the contexts change, new words are invented, and some of the old words are discarded. Some words don't make any sense in some contexts but are very meaningful in other contexts. Kissing a woman on the cheek might be considered a mark of respect in some cultures, and a mark of disrespect in other cultures. Patting the back of a person who is junior to you might be acceptable, but patting the back of someone who is older or more senior would be an insult.

In so many ways, what we called words or *vāk*—which represents the things that we can observe—have contextual meaning. Depending on the context, some actions are meaningful and acceptable. In other contexts, the same actions become unacceptable or meaningless. If you are talking about a "President" while standing in a football club, you most likely mean the president of the football club. If you are talking about a "President" in a news channel, you likely mean the president of that nation. The word "President" doesn't have a universal meaning; rather the meaning is context-sensitive.

The Tree of Meanings

This idea is enunciated in Vedic texts as an "inverted tree" of meanings. In this tree, the higher nodes represent abstract concepts, while the lower nodes represent details. We can think of the higher and lower nodes in a tree as the outline and the details in a picture, respectively. The outline precedes the details and it cannot be erased before erasing the details. Therefore when the universe is annihilated, the details are removed before the outline. Similarly, when the universe is created, the outline appears before the details. During the partial annihilation of the universe, some of the lower planetary systems are destroyed while the higher planetary systems still exist; this means that some of the details are wiped out while the outline of the picture exists. Later, the details are again filled within the outline.

The outline is the "context", the details are the "words", and the meaning of the word is the relationship between the "context" and the "word". Since the meaning is the relation between the word and the context, the meaning is the "position" the word has in relation to the context.

In the above example, the "workshop" and the "bar" are *contexts*. The sounds "screwdriver" and "sledgehammer" are *words*. The context (workshop vs. bar) is the outline, and the sound (screwdriver vs. sledgehammer) is the detail inside that context. The meaning of the sounds is given in relation to the contexts. This "meaning" can be objective if space were a tree in which the workshop and bar were higher nodes, and the words "screwdriver" and "sledgehammer" were details of these higher nodes. The branch connecting the detailed nodes to the abstract nodes would now represent the meaning.

The Problem of Exegesis

I went through the above description to illustrate one key point, which is that the meanings of the words change with the contexts because the meanings depend on context. The same words therefore can potentially have multiple meanings depending on the context. The word "Hari" for example, sometimes means a "monkey", at other times means a "lion", and at yet other times means a "thief".

We can observe the variance between the words and meanings empirically in the everyday world. This idea has been formally articulated in Western philosophy. And this idea is the bedrock of the semantic worldview in Vedic cosmology as well. That should, hopefully, leave no doubt in our minds that it is impossible to know the meaning of a text—e.g. a scripture—unless one puts oneself into the same context, culture, environment, ethos, and belief system as the speaker or author.

Given this problem of meaning, the interpreter or commentator of a scriptural text has only one key job: he must put the audience or the readers into the same context as the author of the scripture. This is, however, not as easy as it sounds, because the context is everything that joins a leaf or fruit to its root. How can you become aware of this entire context before you read the first word? After all, we expect that all this context will only be built up over time as you understand more and more about the scripture, and you can then return to the same text with this new contextual build-up and find new meaning in the old text. The problem, however, is that if you start reading without the full context, then you obtain an incorrect understanding of the text, which is then used to interpret the next text which too turns out to be incorrect, and so on, *ad infinitum*. You must somehow magically arrive at a perfect understanding of something based on which you can then interpret the next thing correctly and after that, all the interpretations fall into line.

The question is: How do you get a perfect understanding of even *one* verse or text? If you can obtain a perfect understanding of just one text or verse, then it might be sufficient to provide the context which can then be used to understand the rest. But there is no way to know if *any* of your understanding is correct because you can never be sure if you are actually placed—even for a brief moment—in the same context as the author itself.

Of course, the problem would get much worse if there are many authors of the text. For example, if the Veda were authored by many authors instead of just *Vyāsadeva*, then the problem of understanding Veda would be much harder because you don't know which part is authored by which person, and therefore you don't know which context to put yourself into, and therefore the true meaning of anything. Even with a single author, the problem is hard because you cannot know if you are in the same context as the author. The problem is unsolvable if there are multiple authors, and you don't know who wrote what.

The Meaning of Revelation

It is for this reason that Vedic knowledge is considered inaccessible to "outsiders"—i.e. those who are not properly following a spiritual master who can place you in the same context as the author. Of course, the problem is not unique to Vedic texts but can be found in any area where a single term can be given many meanings. For example, an equation X + Y = Z can also be given many meanings—e.g. X = people below 50, Y = people above 50, and Z = all the people. The meaning depends on the context in which this claim was made, and if you know the context you can give this claim numerous meanings.

Vedic knowledge is revealed, which means that the person who is writing a commentary has to exist in the same context as the author by which he can understand the intended meaning. The words of a text do not by themselves fix the meanings because meaning is the relation between a word and its context—which, quite interestingly, happens to be another sound. Therefore, being in the right context to translate the text means having some sound, following which other sounds can be given meaning.

The Interpretation of Technical Terms

Vedic texts contain numerous words which have no equivalent translation, but some translation has to be provided when the scripture is translated into English. For example, we frequently translate the word *prakriti* into the word "nature" although there is no equivalent word in English. When the word 'nature' is used as a replacement for *prakriti*, it evokes certain kinds of images. It could evoke the image of forests, trees, rivers, mountains, and such, or it could mean the entire universe around us, including our own bodies, in which case it effectively amounts to assuming that nature equals atoms and molecules. There is no good way to express *prakriti* in English because it comprises not of molecules and atoms, but of three logical states called *sattva*, *rajas*, and *tamas*. *Prakriti* is not the environment around us, nor is it trees and birds. And yet, all these things are produced due to *prakriti*. The term *prakriti* is actually a unique scientific concept, which has no counterpart in English today. And yet, the number of such terms in the Vedic texts is so large that if we stop providing equivalents then the text would be mostly Sanskrit. In that spirit, *prakriti* is translated into "nature" but given that there is no precise definition of "nature" in English itself, everyone is freely supplanting this word with personal imagery in unique ways.

Thus, attempts to avoid a translation (because it might be inaccurate) end up creating a bigger problem, namely, that someone else is providing an unauthorized translation anyway, which the rest of the world would read anyway, and whatever is said in that translation becomes the final word on the scripture because there is no alternative presentation given that those who try to provide an extremely accurate translation of the original text are unable to find the equivalent words in the new language. Given that problem, it is better to provide a translation (even if imprecise) than not provide anything.

There are also many words in Vedic texts which have counterparts in English or other languages, but the meanings of these words have no similarity to the Vedic meanings. Such words include terms like "space", "time", "object", "cause", "motion", "atom", "field" etc. Therefore, when scriptures are translated into English, equivalent words may be used, but the *understanding* or *meaning* of these words has no similarity.

For example, most people today think of "space" as a very big box when in Vedic philosophy it is like a tree. Most people think of "time" as a straight line when it is a circle in Vedic philosophy. Most people think that "objects" are things that lie outside the observer when an "object" is a concept in the observer's mind in Vedic philosophy. Most people think that objects are "moving" in space when the motion in Vedic philosophy is a phenomena not reality. We commonly think that "atom" is a physical particle, when the "atom" in Vedic philosophy is a symbol of information called "sound". We commonly think that meanings are in our minds, but in Vedic philosophy, meaning is the location in space. We think of a "field" as a force that surrounds us, whereas in Vedic philosophy "field" is the role in which a person is placed that gives them and others rights and responsibilities to act.

Practically every technical term in Vedic texts has a different meaning than we think. Even word-for-word translations of the Sanskrit text into English are therefore not adequate, because, for example, when the Vedic texts describe "space" how do you understand that it means a tree rather than a box? Vedic knowledge cannot be acquired just because we have the books which we are able to read. This knowledge can only be acquired after we understand a new set of concepts. But the new set of concepts cannot be acquired unless we wash away the concepts that have been imparted to us from childhood.

How Materialism Influences Thinking

A common example of how modern education has influenced our thinking in significant ways is the idea that the three-dimensional world we perceive through our eyes is the real space. However, if we closely study Vedic philosophy, we can see that the phenomenal world that we experience—i.e. the three-dimensional space—is actually not real. It is rather a *construction* produced from a reality that we never perceive.

The material reality is a tree with God as its root, which unfolds and enfolds its branches due to time, and while the soul wanders on the tree, he finds new experiences because the branches of the tree are interacting with each other due to previous *karma*. This is the summary of the reality in Vedic philosophy with five components—God, soul, time, matter, and *karma*—that produce an experience in which we cannot see God, soul, and *karma*. While time is seen as change, its cyclic nature is not understood and we see only see a linear progression. Finally, most of the subtle material reality beyond sensation (mind, intellect, ego, and morality) is not seen. Thus, we can understand that we are definitely not seeing three out of five categories. We experience time, but we totally misjudge its nature. And we do experience only a fraction of the material categories.

With so little being perceived, we still have a tendency to claim that the world is just like we perceive it. The most ostentatious example of such an illusion is the idea of proximity. For example, if I am holding someone's hand I think that the person is very close to me. I may have no clue that the person whose hand I'm holding may hate me, and therefore is mentally very far away, although the two objects which are very far away are made to interact *creating* a sense of proximity. Allured by the physical sense of proximity, we are unable to see how the minds are different and distant. We get physically attracted and enter relationships and then suffer through them because our minds are nowhere close.

Barriers to Spiritualization Today

Today we can find key Vedic texts translated into many languages across the world. However, the mission of spreading Vedic knowledge remains incomplete because language is not the only barrier to understanding. A far bigger barrier is deeply ingrained ideas and concepts drawn from the cultures, education, and the society we live in presently. As we come to grips with the message in the Vedic texts, we are often faced with numerous contradictions between what the scripture states, and what we are able to accept based on our prior education, current society, and the cultural environment all around us. Spiritual knowledge cannot spread widely if its message contradicts deeply ingrained ideas in society. In fact, religion today is in rapid decline because its values, ideas, and aspirations are in contradiction with those of the modern world. In this environment of ideological conflicts, we have to ask the following question: Given that we already broke the language barriers, which barriers are next?

We can see that even though people read the books, the books are not understood for two reasons. First, because ordinary words such as "space", "time", "object", "cause", "motion", "atom", "field", etc. have radically different meanings. Second, there are numerous words such as *prakriti, mahattattva, ākāsh, jala, vāyu, agni, prithivi, prāna, karma, guna*, etc. which simply have no counterpart in the English language.

As a result of the above two reasons, even ordinary phenomena—e.g. motion and perception—have a radically different explanation, which we cannot understand unless we (1) grasp new meanings of the words that English already uses, and (2) understand the original meanings of the words that don't exist in English. The translated books that we can see are not sufficient if the words in them mean something different than what everyone is used to, or if the books contain words which don't have an English counterpart, but some words have to be chosen in order to complete the translation.

The Atheistic Legacy of Scriptural Translation

To translate texts from one language to another, a dictionary is required. In the case of Sanskrit to English translation, a Sanskrit-to-English dictionary is required. These dictionaries were originally produced by German and British translators during the colonial era although (a) they had no spiritual inclination or initiation, and did not study under the tutelages of an enlightened master, and (b) they had explicit motivation to denigrate the Vedic culture, texts, and civilization as being "inferior" to the modern European civilization. Since the Europeans could no longer claim that Europe was the "cradle of the civilized world" as the Vedic culture seemed much older, there were explicit attempts to undermine the importance and relevance of Vedic knowledge in modern times. Vedic texts were only of *historical* interest, but not of scientific, cultural, linguistic, philosophical, or socio-economic interest.

The dictionaries that we are using for translation today were created in the colonial era by Europeans, and their purposes were not entirely genuine. As a result, today we have words such as *ākāsh, jala, vāyu, bhūmi, agni* etc. being translated as "Ether", "Water", "Air", "Earth" and "Fire". The immediate problem arising from such a translation is that Vedic thought seems primitive relative to the table of chemical elements created by modern science. It appears that while science is telling us about electrons and protons, Vedic philosophy is indicating that the world is a mixture of tap water and stove fire. You don't have to say much more after you provide such a translation and the original culture accepts it, because with such a translation, the people in the Vedic culture would begin to loathe themselves.

The problem here is that scientific concepts using ordinary words have been translated without a context so as to look like ordinary things. Modern science too uses ordinary concepts such as "energy", "momentum", "charge", "force", "color", "spin", etc. but we would be fools to think that the meanings of any of these terms is just how these words are used in physics. Every term in physics has a precise meaning—given by a mathematical formula and a measurement procedure—quite different from the meanings of these words in English. The reuse of the same words for an entirely different purpose is not the problem. The problem is that we don't know the context in which it is used.

It helps to remind ourselves that "screwdriver" and "sledgehammer" have different meanings in a workshop and a bar. Sounds are not meanings by themselves unless we know the context. Unfortunately, we don't have that understanding today. We are not giving a precise logical, mathematical, or conceptual definition to the terms in the scriptures. We use them loosely and we don't understand their meanings. As a result, we can breed a new generation of poets and litterateurs but not scientists and philosophers. Just as an ordinary man doesn't become a soldier by wearing the soldier's dress, similarly, using the same words doesn't make us knowledgeable in Vedic philosophy unless we know the word's meanings.

Spirituality Begins in New Concepts

The biggest barrier to understanding Vedic texts today is new concepts. We already have books in many languages but we lack the concepts to understand them. Enamored by our sense perception based thinking, we consider the illusion to be reality, and thus we cannot understand reality. When this reality is presented in Vedic texts, people think that this presentation must be a fantastic poetic imagination. Our urgent mission should be to explain the meanings of words, because the meanings we currently attach to such words are clearly unreal or false, while the new meanings that can help us understand this knowledge are totally unknown. This is quite like words such as "energy", "momentum", "charge", "force", "color", "spin", etc. have radically different meanings in physics and everyday use.

Unless we understand the meanings of words such as "space", "time", "object", "cause", "motion", "atom", "field", etc. in a new way, we can never understand other words such as *prakriti, mahattattva, ākāsh, jala, vāyu, agni, prithvi, prāna, karma, guna,* etc. Consequently, the words such as "soul" or "God" would not be understood according to the Vedic texts. Indeed, most people today think that when they walk on the road, their "soul" is going along because the soul is in their heart, and the heart is moving. Consequently, the soul's transmigration through different bodies—within this life—is never understood because they are always thinking about "motion" instead of transmigration.

Vedic texts cannot be understood without a complete overhaul of modern thinking. The translations of Vedic scriptures don't make sense because we are using words whose meanings we don't understand. We can read books any number of times, but that is not going to make us enlightened because we conjure false imagery imparted by modern education. We have to find a way to explain these books to everyone.

Did Ācharyas Not Foresee This Problem?

We can ask ourselves: if the problem is so serious, why haven't the *ācharyas* talked about it? This question is somewhat naïve because the *ācharyas* have indeed asked us to "study" the books not merely "read" them. And, furthermore, the problem is evident even at a distant glance because the descriptions of texts such as Śrimad Bhāgavatam are not comprehensible. So, to claim that *ācharyas* did not foresee the problem is incorrect. They have foreseen, but the alternatives to the problem are far worse.

Given that translation is a hard problem should we not translate the texts into English and other languages because they don't have the equivalent words and the words in many cases have different meanings? This turns out to be a nonstarter because it entails Vedic knowledge remains inaccessible to most people due to a linguistic barrier. The translations lift us out of the older linguistic barriers and then present to us the next problem of the conceptual and semantic barriers.

Overcoming the Barriers

The real solution requires the development of a true scientific understanding of the texts accompanied by the presentation of the real meaning of words such as "space", "time", "object", "cause", "motion", "atom", "field", etc. followed by the clarification of the words such as *prakriti, mahat, ākāsh, jala, vāyu, agni, prithvi, prāna, karma, guna,* etc. which can then lead us to the true understanding of words such as "soul" and "God". The journey is not easy, but what are the alternatives?

With such an understanding, many modern words (e.g. "spin", "mass", "momentum", "charge", "quark", "lepton") would become meaningless and cease to exist. And several new words such as *prakriti, guna, karma, manas, prāna, vāk,* etc. would be added to our vocabulary. Acquiring Vedic knowledge means acquiring a new vocabulary to describe the world.

The next barrier to spirituality is *understanding* the books that the *Āchāryas* have given us. We have enough material at hand to realize that there is something to be understood. Just because we can read it, however, doesn't mean we know it. We are actually reading a scientific text without scientific training. Just as a book on advanced physics, mathematics, cosmology, or biology can be written in English, but the meaning of that book cannot be grasped until we immerse ourselves into science itself, similarly, Vedic texts too cannot be understood just because they are now written in our native languages. Familiarity with the language is not enough. One also needs a familiarity with the concepts and such a familiarity necessitates a scientific explanation of the Vedic words.

The Unity of Vedic Philosophy

Published Date: 2017-04-26

At present, most people view Gauḍiya Vaishnavism as one among the many sects of Vaishnavism, with the others being Viśiṣṭādvaita, Dvaita, Dvaitādvaita, and Śuddhādvaita. Vaishnavism is itself considered one of the three sects—namely, Shaiva, Shakta, and Vaishnava. The three sects are together believed to constitute personalism as opposed to impersonalism: the claim being that the four Vedas and Upanishads portray an impersonal truth while personalism (Shaiva, Shakta, and Vaishnava) is a later development. Together, the personal and impersonal are considered different views of Vedānta. Vedānta itself is regarded as only one of the six schools of theistic Vedic philosophy, with the others being Sāṅkhya, Yoga, Mimānsa, Vaiśeṣika, and Nyaya. Looking through this lens of diversity, some people conclude that Vedic texts cannot be divine knowledge because they express divergent ideas. One response to this critique is to describe Vedic knowledge as a tree in which unity is found as we go from the leaves to the root. A different response is that the leaves only manifest the diversity preexisting in the root. If diversity is a problem we are trying to overcome, then as we move from the leaves to the root we find unity. But if we have reached the root then a more pertinent question is: How did all the diversity emerge from the unity? The essence of Vedic thought is that diversity was *enfolded* in the unity from which it was subsequently *unfolded*. Diversity is no longer a problem to be overcome. It is rather the means to enhance our understanding of the unity which produces it.

The Possibility vs. Reality Distinction

Vedic texts describe that originally the Absolute Truth exists in an unmanifest form—i.e. as a *possibility*. This possibility has three aspects—*sat, chit,* and *ananda*—i.e. choice, knowledge, and happiness. There was a choice but it wasn't exercised to choose anything, there was the ability to know but it wasn't used to know any meaning, and there was the capacity to enjoy but it wasn't used to enjoy any pleasure. Everything existed in a state of possibility ready to spring forth into a reality. But what could convert the possibility into reality? There are different answers to this question, but before we consider these answers, it is imperative to understand the fundamental difference between possibility and reality.

What is reality? Reality in Vedic texts is experience—or what we commonly call "phenomena". There is, of course, something that exists "behind" this phenomenon, although we don't call it "reality". Rather, it is called "possibility". The technical terms are *unmanifest* (before experience) and *manifest* (at the point of experience). Clearly, you cannot know the unmanifest, although this unmanifest creates the manifest. However, this inability to know the unmanifest doesn't create a problem if the unmanifest is a possibility because once you can see the reality, you can *posthoc* know the possibility.

This idea is very unintuitive in Western philosophy where "reality" is that which exists independently and outside of our experience, and our experience is a phenomenon, not reality. Therefore, we never call the phenomena a reality in Western philosophy because we think that reality exists materially and objectively outside our minds. However, if you extend this idea to its logical limit, then reality must also be outside God's mind—i.e. exist even before God's experience. How can then God be the origin of reality if this reality is outside God's experience, and He only becomes aware of this reality? Atheism thus follows naturally from the idea that there is some reality outside the observer.

Vedic Answers to Epistemological Problems

The Western philosophical stance gets us started quickly in terms of telling us that there is a phenomenal experience produced by some external reality. However, this soon creates four problems. First, that we cannot ever experience reality; we can only experience phenomena. Therefore, even if reality exists outside experience, there is no way to know it. Second, it leads to the problem of mind-reality interaction: How can reality be evicted from the mind and then enter the mind? After all, aren't they supposed to be two fundamentally different things? Third, if the mind-body problem is not solved, then how can I claim that God created reality because it also involves a mind-body interaction? In this case, we are suggesting that the world is God's body and God is the mind that creates it. Fourth, if reality is outside our experience, then it must also be outside God's experience. How can God be said to be omniscient if this reality is outside experience and we only have access to phenomena?

The inversion of thinking in Vedic philosophy is that experience is not produced from reality but from possibility—the possibility of choice, knowledge, and pleasure. And when this possibility is converted into reality, the reality exists as an *experience*, although the experience is within the observer, and therefore the reality is also within the observer! There is hence never a situation where there is a mind separate from matter. In fact, matter is not even a substance or object; matter is simply an experience. Both matter and spirit are, therefore, "inside" experience, and they are "parts" of reality—i.e. when the reality is the totality of experience, then matter and spirit are parts of that experience.

The reasoning for this philosophical inversion is that whatever lies "behind" experience is before experience and it can thus never be experienced. We cannot, therefore, consider it a "reality" in the sense of something that can be known or understood. Instead, we have to consider it as something that always exists although in an "unmanifest" form or as a possibility. In short, what people call "reality" in Western philosophy is a "possibility" in Vedic philosophy. And what people call "phenomena" in Western philosophy is actually called "reality"—i.e. that which can be understood. When this inversion is made, the four problems of Western philosophy mentioned above simply disappear.

Now, phenomena are a reality, and when we experience phenomena, we know reality. There is no mind-body problem because matter is inside experience; there is no substance or "stuff" outside the observer. Since there is no mind-body problem, there is no problem in how God creates the universe; the short answer to that question is that God creates the universe by creating His experience. Finally, God is omniscient because the universe is His experience and inside His consciousness.

Advaita Vedānta vs. Vaishnava Vedānta

Given this inversion of thinking, the essence of Vedānta is how the possibility becomes the experienced reality. It is here that the debates emerge. It is noteworthy that these debates are unlike many debates in Western philosophy on the nature of reality and its experience. The debates come *after* all the questions of Western epistemology and ontology (the mind-body problem) have been addressed.

There are many schools of Vedānta philosophy—of which two are dominant. The *Advaita Vedānta* position says that all phenomena are temporary and therefore the so-called "reality" or experience is manifest temporarily. The cause of this manifestation is *māyā*. However, if we remove *māyā* then the phenomena disappear, and we return back to the state of possibility. The *Vaishnava Vedānta* says that material phenomena are indeed temporary and therefore material experience is indeed manifest temporarily. However, beyond the material experience is another kind of experience that is eternal. While this experience is produced from the same unmanifest possibilities as the experiences of the material world, the "transcendent experience" is actually not temporary.

The debate comes down to one issue—namely, is there an experience beyond the material experience? The *Advaita* philosophy—propounded originally by Shankarāchārya—is largely silent on this question although Shankarāchārya indirectly hinted towards a transcendent experience by composing glories of Lord Kṛṣṇa in works such as *Bhaja Govindam* and *Jagannathastakam*. His followers, however, abandoned that path and insisted that there can be no experience beyond material experience. This denial is a flaw because by denying a new kind of experience, they only deprive themselves of it. The Vaishnava position is actually inclusive of the Advaita position but goes beyond it. Those who see a conflict between the personal and the impersonal schools only need to understand Shankarāchārya.

The Genesis of Vaishnava Vedānta Interpretations

Once we recognize that there is a transcendent experience, and we know that we at present don't have that experience, the natural conclusion is that experience is produced by another observer. We can call this observer "God" although in Vedic texts He is called the Absolute Truth. Similarly, we can call the individual observer who aspires to a transcendental experience but might not have it, the "soul". By accepting that there is a transcendent experience, one is naturally led to the conclusion that there is soul and God, although the relation between soul and God is not yet clear. The multiple schools in Vaishnava Vedānta arise in the attempt to address one simple question: What is the relation between the soul and God? Since reality exists inside God's experience, is the soul part of God, or separate from Him?

If the soul and God were different, then the interaction between the soul and God would result in a similar kind of problem as the mind-body interaction problem we saw earlier. The problem of interaction entails that the soul must have existed before God knows about the soul, and therefore the soul's relation to God is incidental to their interaction. When this interaction is in question, then we cannot claim that their relationship must be a necessity. In short, all four problems related to an observer and reality now arise in the context of a soul-God relationship. Thus, when Vaishnavism speaks about Dualism or Non-Dualism, it is in the context of the soul-God interaction, not in the context of the mind-matter interaction. However, there are clear parallels between the two problems.

We can see that if the solution to the mind-body interaction is unmanifest creating manifest, then the soul too must be the creation of God—and, in fact, must exist *inside* God just as His other experiences. All the Vaishnava positions are unanimous in this view—the soul is *part* of God's experience. In making this judgment they have only carried forward the thinking that previously led to the notion that reality is part of the observer, and created as the experience of the observer. Nevertheless, the mind-body and the soul-God relationship problems are not identical because the body has no free will while the soul (we suppose) has free will, because of accountability of the soul's choices entailed by *karma*.

The question of free will thus leads to a problem: if the soul is part of God's experience, and created by God's will, then how does it contradict God's will? Is the fall down of the soul into matter caused by God's will—since the soul is part of God's reality? But if that were the case then the soul could not be responsible for its transgressions. We have to accept that the soul has free will to allow for responsibility or *karma*. The central question of Vaishnavism, therefore, reduces to the following: How did God create the soul such that the free will of the soul can contradict the creator's free will?

The Theory Underlying Vibhu and Anu

In *Advaita Vedānta* there is only one reality—*Brahman*—and the individuality of the soul dissolves in the *Brahman*. In *Vaishnava Vedānta*, individuality never finishes totally, although it can exist as a possibility in the *Brahman* waiting to spring forth. The soul and God are therefore like part and whole. The whole is not the sum of the parts. And the part is not dissolved in the whole. In that way, both part and whole are individually real. But how is the part created from the whole, within the whole? This is the essence of the theory of the "big" or *vibhu* and the "small" or *anu*. The variety of the Vaishnava Vedānta positions is all hinged upon describing the relationship between the part and the whole. Again, before we dive into the disagreements, we must understand what is already agreed upon. In this case, there is an agreement that (a) there is God and the soul, (b) that God and the soul are individuals, and (c) that the soul is part of God (not merged inside God, and not standing outside God to form a relationship).

To understand *vibhu* and *anu* we have to imagine a tree of ideas in which the root is the abstract concept and the leaves are the instances. In between the root and the leaves are trunks and branches, which have some properties of the root (i.e. they can spawn branches) and some properties of the leaves (i.e. they are spawned from the trunk). The meaning of *vibhu* and *anu* is that God is the root, trunks, and branches (i.e. everything that can, in turn, spawn some branches and thus be the creator) but the soul is the leaves (i.e. it cannot create anymore because it is the final leaf, fruit, or flower on the tree).

The meaning of *vibhu* is that He is "big" in the sense that He can have parts. The meaning of *anu* is that the soul is "atomic" and it cannot have any parts, although can be a part of the *vibhu*. In short, God is one with parts, and the soul is one without parts. Thus, the soul can never equate with God. However, the soul is never divorced from God because it exists as one of the parts of God.

The Description of Three Trees

Relationships are of six types—selfishness, gratitude, servitude, friendship, parental, and conjugal—and the tree of relationships is produced from the combination of the six types of relationships. Meanings are also of six types—knowledge, beauty, power, fame, wealth, and renunciation—and the tree of meanings is produced from the combination of these six qualities. These two trees are entangled in the world when different types of meanings are exchanged in different contexts.

The *Vishnu-tattva* living entities are the root, trunks, branches, and twigs of the trees of meaning, and when meaning is more important than pleasure and relationships then this hierarchy of meanings also becomes the hierarchy of relationships and pleasures. That is, the root of the tree of meanings is also the person in the highest role. The

Jiva-tattva living entities are the leaves, fruits, and flowers of this tree. In other words, the soul cannot create more parts or instances from itself because it is the most detailed concept and the most atomic role. Therefore, the soul remains the eternal servant of God.

The tree of pleasures, however, is based on the kinds of pleasures and not on the meanings exchanged in the relationship. In this tree, the highest pleasure is not necessarily the highest meaning. For example, gold may be more meaningful than a flower, but the ornaments of flowers can be more pleasing than the ornaments of gold. Therefore, when pleasure is prioritized over meaning, then an ordinary living entity can rise in the tree of pleasure—by pleasing God more than others. The soul is, from the standpoint of meanings, still the leaf, fruit, or flower of the tree, but this leaf, fruit, or flower can be offered in a way that produces much more happiness than the big trunks or branches.

The Soul Has an Eternal Form

Since Vaishnava Vedānta recognizes a transcendental experience beyond the material experience and *Brahman* is the state devoid of experience, the totality of experience—i.e. reality—is divided into three parts: *antaranga-śakti* or transcendental experience, *bahiranga-śakti* or material experience, and *taṭasthā-śakti* or the possibility of experience. The soul is the possibility of experience. When it comes into contact with the *antaranga-śakti,* it has the transcendental experience. When it comes into contact with *bahiranga-śakti,* it has the material experience. And when it is situated in *Brahman* it remains a possibility waiting to become a reality or conscious experience.

Different Vaishnava Vedānta Interpretations

There are several Vaishnava Vedānta interpretations, and the prominent ones are:

- 11th Century - Sri Ramanujacharya's Vishishtadvaita Vedānta
- 13th Century – Sri Madhavacharya's Dvaita Vedānta
- 13th Century - Sri Nimbārkacharya's Dvaitādvaita Vedānta
- 16th Century - Sri Vallabhacharya's Shuddhadvaita Vedānta
- 16th Century – Sri Caitanya's Achintya Bhedabheda Tattva

Each of these Vedānta traditions recognizes that God can choose many things at once while the soul can only choose one by one, due to which God is called *vibhu* and the soul is called *anu*, and hence God and soul are not identical. We have also seen above that the soul is part of God's experience—i.e. that God knows the soul—as the specific part of God's total experience. However, the soul doesn't always know God—e.g. he doesn't understand that he is part of a totality of God's experience.

Given this understanding, how do we describe the relationship between the soul and God? Should we call the relation between part and whole Dvaita (duality) because a part is not equal to the whole? Or should we call the relation Viśiṣṭādvaita (non-duality in a specific sense) because the part is, after all, a member of the whole, so it cannot be considered entirely separated? Should we say that the part and whole are Dvaitādvaita (duality and non-duality) because God is like the elephant and the soul is like the elephant's trunk and tail, and the elephant (as the mind) exists even when the elephant's trunk and tail (as the body) don't. Or should we say that the part and whole are Śuddhādvaita (have the same essential quality—i.e. *sat*, *chit*, and *ananda*) because they are just like spark and fire?

The understanding of how the soul is the leaf, fruit, and flower of a tree in which God is the root, trunks, and branches, helps us see the unity in these diverse descriptions. Given that the root, trunks, and branches are different from the leaf, fruit, and flower, God and soul are never similar—Dvaita. Given that the leaf, fruit, and flower are part of the same tree as the root, trunks, and branches, God and soul are not truly separable—Viśiṣṭādvaita. Since the root, trunks, and branches emerge before the leaf, fruit, and flower, therefore, we can say that God can exist when the soul doesn't exist, although the soul cannot exist without God—Dvaitādvaita. Since the trunks and branches are also emanations from the root as the leaf, fruit, and flower, we can consider them both similar—Śuddhādvaita.

The varied Vaishnava Vedānta descriptions are meant to emphasize different facets of the same reality, not different realities. In *Śuddhādvaita*, the common qualities of God and soul (*sat*, *chit*, and *ananda*) are emphasized. In *Viśiṣṭādvaita* the whole-part relation between the soul and God is emphasized. In *Dvaita* the fact that God is supreme and the soul is small is emphasized. And in *Dvaitādvaita* the idea that God is prior to and therefore independent of the soul is emphasized. These are not contradictory descriptions. These are differences of philosophical emphasis. Therefore, the Vaishnava schools are not mutually contradictory, although they are often superficially presented as contradictory.

The Gauḍiya Vedānta Description

I deliberately did not discuss the Gauḍiya Vaishnava position thus far, because it is important to first see how the prior Vaishnava positions are consistent before we see how the Gauḍiya position advances the understanding of Vaishnavism. The advancement in Gauḍiya Vaishnavism is that there are *three* trees—of pleasure, meaning, and relationship. The advancement is also that the pleasure tree is more important than the meaning tree, and the meaning tree is more important than the relationship tree. This means that the pleasure created through the act of giving and taking is more important than what is given or taken. Similarly, what is given and taken is more important than the relationship in which it is given or taken. Thus, it is possible to please God even through simple acts, and it is possible to perform great acts even outside of empowered roles.

This thesis is clearly advanced in Gauḍiya Vaishnavism by describing two forms of God—*Kṛṣṇa* and *Balarama*—as the masters of the two trees: *Kṛṣṇa* is the master of the pleasure tree (as the highest enjoyer) and *Balarama* is the master of the meaning tree (as the highest meaning). *Balarama* is "older" to *Kṛṣṇa* because the living entity has a personality of meaning before such meaning is exchanged for pleasure. Nevertheless, *Kṛṣṇa* is supreme because pleasure is more important than meaning. The inner paradox in Gauḍiya Vaishnavism is how God is in two forms, and the younger form is the higher form. Understanding Gauḍiya Vaishnavism means understanding the nature of these two forms, and how the logically prior form is subordinated to the logically subsequent form.

We had, at the beginning of this post, asked how the possibility (unmanifest) becomes a reality (manifest). The answer is that *sat*, *chit*, and *ananda* are combined to create reality. Recall that *sat* is the possibility of choosing, which isn't yet exercised—i.e. it hasn't decided what to choose. *Chit* is the possibility of knowledge and activity, which hasn't been exercised—i.e. nothing is known. *Ananda* is the possibility of pleasure, which hasn't been used—i.e. nothing is enjoyed. To create reality, four decisions are made:

- I want happiness
- I want knowledge and activity
- I want specific pleasures
- I want specific meanings and actions

With these decisions, the possibilities are transformed into reality: they now become phenomenal experiences and can, therefore, be known and enjoyed. In the process, "choice" acquires a specific meaning—it is the choice *between* meaning and happiness, which implies that one of pleasure or knowledge would be prioritized. The result of prioritization is that there are two separate decisions—one of the decisions is to know specific ideas, and the other decision is to enjoy specific pleasures.

When "choice" acts on the possibility of knowledge, it divides knowledge into *knower* and *known.* Similarly, when "choice" acts on the possibility of pleasure, it divides pleasure into *enjoyer* and *enjoyed.* Thus, before the action of choice, there is "knowledge" and after the action of choice there is "knower" and "known", in addition to "knowledge". Similarly, before the action of choice, there is "pleasure" and after the action of choice there is "enjoyer" and "enjoyed", in addition to "pleasure". The "enjoyer" is called *Kṛṣṇa* and the "enjoyed" is called *Hara*. The "knower" is called *Rāma* and the known is called *Ramā*. Thus, from that unmanifest possibility of *sat, chit,* and *ananda,* two pairs of realities are created. The first pair—of *Kṛṣṇa* and *Hara*—is the subject and object of pleasure. The second pair—of *Rāma* and *Ramā*—is the subject and object of knowledge.

The Description of Spiritual Cosmology

The domain of meanings and pleasures are respectively called *Vaikunṭha* and *Goloka*. The God of *Vaikunṭha* is the God of big meanings, while the God of *Goloka* is the God of big pleasures. Since the soul is always the leaf, fruit, or flower of the tree, it is always the servant of Lord Vishnu in *Vaikunṭha* and it has no other servants (because no one's meanings are higher than others). Everyone in Vaikunṭha is therefore at an equal level, except for one ruler—Lord Vishnu. *Vaikunṭha* is the role model for an egalitarian society in which everyone serves Lord Vishnu and nobody is higher or lower.

In *Goloka*, however, the soul who loves God more can please Him more, and he rises up the tree of love, and thus supervises others whose love might be lesser (although they have the same meanings). *Goloka*, therefore, is the role model of a hierarchical society in which a person becomes the servant of the servant of the servant of God. In *Vaikunṭha*, everyone is directly the servant of God. The soul's love for God is variable; it can love God deeply and be in Goloka; it can subordinate love to meanings and be in *Vaikunṭha*; it can silence both love and meaning temporarily and be in *Brahman*; it can turn love into animosity within the material world. Even in Goloka, the same person can sometimes be friendly and then become protective like a parent and then appreciate the qualities of God silently.

Thus in *Goloka*, knowledge is still necessary, which means the six qualities of *Bhagavān* (knowledge, beauty, power, wealth, fame, and renunciation) exist but they manifest according to the need of the relationship between the subject and object. In another realm—called *Vaikunṭha*—knowledge is prioritized over pleasure. In this realm, pleasure is required, which means the six kinds of relationships (self, reverence, servitude, friendship, paternal, and conjugal) with *Bhagavān* exist, but these relationships manifest according to the type of quality being exchanged. For example, we can find Vedic texts describing philosophical conversations between Lord *Viṣṇu* and *Lakshmi* regarding the nature of reality, but we cannot find any such conversations between *Kṛṣṇa* and *Radha*. Conversely, there are numerous descriptions of amorous pastimes between *Kṛṣṇa* and *Radha* but there is no description of amorous pastimes between Lord *Viṣṇu* and *Lakshmi*. In other words, a couple in *Vaikunṭha* engages in philosophical discussions while a couple in *Goloka* indulges in amorous pastimes. They are both couples, but they act differently.

Thus, *Kṛṣṇa* is the supreme enjoyer in Goloka while *Rāma* is the creator of all conceptual objects. The creator produces all the types of meanings—names, forms, qualities, activities, etc. *Hara* then fashions these concepts into objects for different kinds of pleasures. In a sense, *Ramā* creates all the bodies, and *Hara* creates all the pleasures. The body defines the kinds of meanings a person can offer and accept. The role defines the nature of the soul's consciousness by which it is connected to the consciousness of God and it defines the kinds of meanings expected out of a person based on their specific part.

The Description of Pañca-Tattva

The five forms mentioned above—the four forms of *Kṛṣṇa, Hara, Rāma,* and *Ramā* and the soul—together are called the *pañca-tattva* or the five forms of reality. In the pastimes of Lord Chaitanya, *Kṛṣṇa* appears as Sri Chaitanya, *Hara* appears as Gadadhara, *Rāma* appears as Sri Nityānanda, *Ramā* appears as Sri Advaita Acharya, and the living entity or the soul appears as Srivāsa. These five fundamental "elements" constitute the Supreme meaning and pleasure, the object and the happiness, and the soul.

Gauḍiya Vaishnavism is somewhat unique in distinguishing between meaning and pleasure as separate forms and energies of God in such an explicit manner than other forms of Vaishnavism. These are further described as *material* and *efficient* causes:

- CC Ādi 6.16 — Lord Viṣṇu Himself is the efficient [nimitta] cause of the material world, and Nārāyaṇa in the form of Śri Advaita is the material cause [upādāna].
- CC Ādi 6.17 — Lord Viṣṇu, in His efficient aspect, glances over the material energy, and Śrī Advaita, as the material cause, creates the material world.
- CC Ādi 6.18 — Although the Sāṅkhya philosophy accepts that the material ingredients are the cause, the creation of the world never arises from dead matter.
- CC Ādi 6.19 — The Lord infuses the material ingredients with His own creative potency. Then, by the power of the Lord, creation takes place.
- CC Ādi 6.20 — In the form of Advaita, He infuses the material ingredients with creative energy. Therefore, Advaita is the original cause of creation.

The *efficient cause* of activity in the material world is *guna* (the desire for pleasure) and *karma* (the consequences of previous actions). When *Karanodakaśāyī Viṣṇu* glances over material nature, He injects the soul with his previous *guna* and *karma*. However, the manifestation of *guna* and *karma* is controlled by time or *Saṅkarṣaṇa*—also called Lord Shiva—who controls the events. The two forms of God involved in the early creation—*Karanodakaśāyī Viṣṇu* and *Saṅkarṣaṇa*—act as the efficient and material causes.

The Unity of Shaivism, Shaktism, and Vaishnavism

Historically, one of the most contentious issues in Vedic philosophy has been the separation of Shaiva, Shakta, and Vaishnava traditions. Most outsiders look at the Vedic tradition and struggle to understand which of the three traditions is greater. We cannot expect an unbiased answer to that question from any of the sect practitioners as such questions can only elicit one of two possible answers. First, they will blindly describe their tradition to be the best without adequate justification. Second, they might argue that all these traditions are ultimately untruthful, and only the original Being is the truth: this Being exists as a possibility that is yet to have converted into any kind of reality.

The Gauḍiya Vaishnava explanation offers useful insights into this contentious issue. The first contention is between the efficient and the material cause. In the material world, Lord Shiva as the time of the universe causes the manifestation of material phenomena and in this process, Lord Shiva is the *material cause* of the creation. Similarly, Lord Viṣṇu is the master of the soul and of the *guna* (desires) and *karma* (consequences) attributed to the soul in the material world. He is, thus, the *efficient cause* of creation because the universe exists for the soul. These two forms are not contradictory but complementary. Lord Shiva is the creator of the material universe, but Lord Viṣṇu is the master of the soul.

The debate between Shaiva and Vaishnava philosophers is, therefore, superficial to an extent because both are masters in the material creation although of different things. Nevertheless, the material cause—Lord Shiva—is "lower" than the efficient cause or Lord Viṣṇu. Similarly, in the spiritual world, the efficient cause—Lord Kṛṣṇa—is "higher" than the material cause or Lord Rāma, who manifests Lord Viṣṇu and Vaikunṭha.

Once the difference between efficient and material causes is understood, and the contentious debates between Lord Shiva and Lord Vishnu are resolved, then we can see how their consorts Parvathi and Lakshmi—who are worshiped as the female divine forms—are similarly related as material and efficient causes. Their relation to Lord Shiva and Lord Viṣṇu is that of being the object of the subject. There is fundamentally no contradiction between the Shaiva, Shakta, and Vaishnava traditions because there are two masculine and feminine forms—representing the subject and object of meaning and pleasure.

I opened this post with the Vedānta Sutra conclusions and the differences between *Advaita Vedānta*, the four dominant schools of *Vaishnava Vedānta*, and then how Gauḍiya Vaishnavism advances the philosophy of the ultimate truth. We have seen how these systems of philosophy describe the same truth, although emphasizing different aspects of it. We have now also seen that by understanding Gauḍiya Vaishnavism, we can see a deeper form of unity between Shaiva, Shakta, and Vaishnava traditions. They might appear superficially different, primarily because their practitioners have emphasized their differences rather than attempted to understand their inherent unity.

The Unity of the Six Theistic Schools

This brings me to the question of Vedānta being only one of the six orthodox systems of philosophy—the other five being *Mimānsa*, *Sāṅkhya*, *Yoga*, *Vaiśeṣika*, and *Nyaya*. A detailed discussion of these schools will double the length of this post, so I will make some brief points and then pick up this topic in a later post. My basic point regarding the six systems of thinking is that they are describing different aspects of material and efficient causes.

The philosophy of *Mimānsa* is about the efficient cause or *karma*, how the *karma* is earned, enjoyed, or suffered. The worship of demigods in the *Mimānsa* system is not actually the worship of a person, but that of a *role*—the demigods change in every age but the *mantra* of the worship remains the same. How can we worship the same demigod if the demigod is a person rather than a role? The study of *Mimānsa* corresponds to the study of the *efficient cause* of the creation. Similarly, the study of *Sāṅkhya* and *Yoga* systems is the study of the *material cause* of the creation—the tiers of matter.

The study of *Vedānta*, *Mimānsa*, *Yoga*, and *Sāṅkhya* schools is inadequate unless we understand that the universe is comprised of material atoms, and everything—from gross matter to mind, intellect, ego, morality, *prāna*, pleasure, etc.—is atomic. There are many kinds of atoms, which are ultimately produced from the three modes of nature (*sattva*, *rajas*, and *tamas*), the three parts of the soul (*sat*, *chit*, and *ananda*), and the six qualities that modify each of the three parts and modes. *Vaiśeṣika* is the study of atomism, and *Nyaya* is the premise that these atoms are *logical* components.

Vedānta, *Mimānsa*, *Yoga*, and *Sāṅkhya* set up the conceptual background for Vedic thought, but *Vaiśeṣika* and *Nyaya* transform this "philosophy" into a "science". Sri Chaitanya was a formidable *Nyaya* philosopher of His time and *Nadia* where He was born was formerly the seat of *Nyaya* philosophy. It is due to the legacy of *Nyaya* that Bengal produced many formidable scientists and philosophers in the recent past. Unfortunately, most of *Nyaya* and *Vaiśeṣika* are now lost and somehow need to be rediscovered through modern science and philosophy. Together, *Nyaya* and *Vaiśeṣika* constitute a form of "Logical Atomism" that Bertrand Russell, Ludwig Wittgenstein, Rudolf Carnap, Alfred Whitehead, and David Hilbert—all prominent logicians and mathematicians—attempted in the early 20th century but failed because of failing to incorporate concepts into reasoning.

By understanding the efficient and material causes and their respective roles we can understand the unity of *Vedānta, Mimānsa, Sāṅkhya,* and *Yoga*. The unity of *Vaiśeṣika* and *Nyaya* in this system stems from the realization that these trees are comprised of trunks, branches, leaves, fruits, and flowers which are atomic objects and the atoms are created by logic. Just as numbers are used to reason, similarly, under a better understanding of logic (free of the current problems of incompleteness and semantics) atoms can be described logically. This is the area of Vedic philosophy that is the hardest, least supported at present and requires the greatest focus going forward if we are to understand and present the Vedic system of thought in a modern, logical, and scientific manner.

Preserving the Unity of Vedic Thought

With growing interest in Vedic philosophy, there are also wide-ranging attacks on the Vedic traditions in modern times. One of the academic strategies of attack is to argue that Vedic philosophy lacks unity and cannot be considered a single system of thought: it is an aggregation of contradicting ideas.

Critics obtain support for their thesis in the fact that the Vedic system comprises diverse sects and practices. They also try to date the Vedic texts implying that these texts are not of divine origin but were written by different authors at different times. The central idea is that if Vedic texts were presented as individual books authored by different people with different ideas at different times, then the unity of the Vedic system would be undermined. As this unity is undermined, one can "divide and conquer"—i.e. selectively use one idea against another, and arrive at those ideas that one wants to adopt while discarding the other ideas that one might not like. This is a standard procedure by which one ideology is slowly "digested" into another whereby some select ideas which are culturally compatible with the seeking culture are incrementally adopted while the rest of the sought culture is rejected.

In this post, I have attempted to show why the fundamental premise of such "patrons" of Vedic knowledge is flawed: (1) the branches of the Vedic tree are not contradictory because they emanate from a single root, and (2) the branches only unfold the enfolded diversity within the root. Selective appreciation of one branch may be a good starting point. Understanding why some ideas are higher than others is an even better conclusion. However, the knowledge is incomplete unless one recognizes that unless something exists in the root, it cannot magically manifest as leaves or fruits. The different fruits of the Vedic tree are therefore only expressing the diversity in the seed from which the tree has sprung. This diversity is not a distraction, and it is not unnecessary. It is rather a vehicle for one who wants to understand the root from which the tree has sprung forth, more comprehensively.

Diversity Doesn't Mean Disunity

It is undoubtedly true that the Vedic system has diverse sects, practices, and philosophical ideas. However, it is also true that diversity doesn't necessarily imply disunity. Understanding Vedic knowledge isn't about understanding one branch, but actually the root of everything. And that root cannot be understood unless we appreciate how it produces many branches. The disunity of Vedic systems is a modern phenomenon due to two reasons—(a) the gradual demise of the true knowers of the Vedic system who could adapt its teachings in different ways according to time, place, and situation, and (b) the replacement of true knowers by rigid and ignorant sectarian institutions who fail to look beyond their sect into the deeper purpose of the Vedas, the origin of diversity, and the unity itself.

Diversity can be the strength of a tradition because people with different understandings can participate in it. Diversity can also be a weakness if it is used to divide, fuel a conflict, and weaken traditions. Much of the modern academic Vedic "research" views the Vedic system, not through the lens of a thoughtful tradition that has survived millennia of affront due to its innate truth and consistency. Such studies rather try to extend the present disunity into the past to claim that the Vedic system was always discordant, superstitious, and excessive. In other words, the ultimate goal of such academic studies is not to strengthen the Vedic system through a better understanding. It is rather to weaken it.

Such academic studies may do little harm to those who are already living the Vedic tradition and are not bothered about the opinions of those who prefer to lick the bottle of milk from the outside. However, they unnecessarily confuse genuine seekers through numerous clandestine critiques, masquerading as "translation" and "commentary". The genuine seekers are not interested in this or that sectarian branch, but in the root from which all the branches have emanated. The study of diversity is meant for those advanced seekers who find such a study affording a far better appreciation of unity.

Guru and Non-Locality

Published Date: 2017-04-30

Many people currently view a guru as a classical particle, which interacts with other classical particles through *physical contact* like a billiard ball colliding with another billiard ball. The advocates of such a theory claim that it is necessary for a person to be physically in touch with a guru, in order to seek instructions, obtain advice, and receive knowledge. This conception of guru is not entirely wrong because billiard balls do indeed collide with other billiard balls and cause them to move. And yet, this conception of interaction becomes very limited when we understand a new kind of cause called "quantum entanglement" in which two distant objects can interact instantaneously.

What is Local Causality?

Locality is the idea that the cause and effect are *local*—namely that something must push (or pull) an object in order to cause a change. In the case of billiard balls, the ball itself is the push and pull. But such a model would not explain remote causation such as "gravity" in science, or even the effect of planets on human life in astrology. To address such problems, science evolved the notion of a "remote locality" in which an object emits a particle which then travels towards a destination and collides with it to produce a change. The emitted particle is the "ambassador" that changes the objects after it collides with them.

The *localist* (by that I mean a person who believes in local causality) claims that the *guru* is the ambassador of God because he brings the message to us, and he must be in physical contact with us in order to deliver the necessary message. Sometimes, God, Himself comes in physical contact, and at other times, God sends a messenger to make physical contact with us. Such a messenger or ambassador is the local presence of God like *photons* are the local presence of the remote Sun.

A localist must also presume that the messenger is *traveling*. One day he is here, and another day he is gone. Once he is gone, the effect has ceased, and to renew the effect, another messenger must travel. So, there has to be a continuous stream of messengers without which the message would be lost.

What is Non-Local Causality?

Non-local causality is one in which two objects are "entangled" in such a way that changes to one automatically cause changes to another regardless of the distance between them.

In physics, this means that an "ambassador" particle doesn't have to *travel* to a destination in order to create an effect, and indeed, since the effects are being created instantaneously, such travel becomes physically inconceivable: How can something travel at an infinite speed violating the speed of light?

Non-locality has appeared as a problem for the localists in atomic theory, where the classical physical assumptions about traveling causes have come under question. There are numerous experiments now that show that causes can propagate instantaneously, without a traveling particle.

Understanding Non-Locality

Non-locality can be understood if we incorporate two notions of "distance"—physical and semantic. Consider two tables that are kept far apart from each other. Physically, there is a considerable distance between them. But semantically, they are both tables and hence very "close" if we were to measure the differences in their *types* rather than physical *instantiation*.

There is a sense in which the tables are physically far apart, and another sense in which they are very close. The problem of non-locality arises for the localist because he or she discards the semantic proximity between the two tables, and considers only the physical distance. If, however, we were to look at the semantic proximity and attribute causality to it, then the causal interaction would not seem non-local, because the two objects are indeed very close to each other semantically.

In simple terms, if the guru and disciple are two separate bodies, which are far-flung, then clearly the communication between them requires some physical messages—e.g. letters, phone calls, or face-to-face conversations. However, if the guru and disciple are two distinct minds, and these minds have similar meanings, then the guru and disciple are not far from each other. The minds can interact *locally* because they are indeed very close, and the problem of non-locality doesn't arise.

Non-Locality is the Real Causality

Now, should we treat causality as physical or semantic? Should we worry about the physical distance between the guru and disciple, or the semantic difference between their minds?

If the minds of the teacher and the student are very different, then meanings emitted from the teacher's mind take a long time to be absorbed in the student's mind, even if the student is physically very close. Conversely, if the student and the teacher are semantically similar (i.e. have similar thinking) then the meanings from the teacher are quickly absorbed into the student, even if the student and teacher are physically apart.

The time taken for the message to travel from the teacher to the student is therefore not based on the physical distance, but based on the extent of their semantic difference. If I'm trying to teach advanced physics to a novice, then the ideas will take a long time to be understood. But the same ideas can be quickly grasped by someone who knows intermediate physics. The "speed" at which the cause creates an effect is therefore not a function of their physical distance but their semantic difference.

Learning, therefore, is about absorbing the message and bringing about a change to our *thinking* and this change is not faster or slower depending on the physical distance. If we have developed our thinking and brought it closer to the thinking of the teacher, then even more meanings can be quickly absorbed. The rate of education of the student, therefore, depends on how quickly the student can absorb the ideas, and that does not depend on the physical distance between the student and teacher.

To the extent that physical proximity results in more meanings being transmitted (e.g. the teacher and student can talk more face-to-face), physical proximity is helpful. But if the message has been fully delivered and yet not absorbed, then the only alternative is repeating the lessons.

What is Dīkṣā and Śhikṣā?

Dīkṣā is the first instance when we absorb the message, while Śhikṣā is every time it is repeated. If the student is intelligent, then only Dīkṣā is needed, because the message doesn't have to be repeated. If the student is unintelligent, then the same message has to be repeated many times.

The message repetition can be done by the same person who provided the message the first time, by a different person who only repeats the message, or by oneself repeating the message to ourselves. Notably, the message itself isn't different, and in that sense, the Śhikṣā and Dīkṣā guru are not different *semantically* because they only repeat the same meaning. And yet, there can be a difference between the person who provides the message the first time, and those who repeat it.

We can be our own guru by repeating the message to ourselves. We can receive repetitions of the message from friends, elders, or subordinates, and all these are Śhikṣā gurus. The Dīkṣā guru is the person from whom we absorb the full and authentic message the first time. The process of absorbing the full and authentic message *once* is thus called *Dīkṣā*. If we are intelligent, we don't need to repeat it another time. But if repetition is required, both Dīkṣā and Śhikṣā guru may provide it.

The Tree of Spiritual Development

The process of *dīkṣā* provides the *seed* of the spiritual tree. This seed is the original *attraction* for the message, and it is received at a deep level that alters our consciousness and makes us want more and more of the message. Thus it is said, "guru-krishna prasade paye bhakti-lata bīja", where the *bīja* is the "seed" from which the tree can be grown. Once the initial attraction to the message develops, the person can seek to learn more about the message. As the seeker invests more time, energy, and focus, the seed develops into a fuller understanding.

In the material world, which is described as an *inverted* tree, the deep seed is called *mahattattva* which represents *moral values*. To be attracted to something, we must begin to *value* it morally—i.e. as a source of material happiness. Every seeker has to feel original happiness to seek more of that same happiness. The principle for spiritual development is similar although the new moral value is not personal gratification but service to God. The meaning of bhakti-lata bīja is that a deep level of moral value is imparted to the disciple, which causes him to feel unprecedented happiness. Once such happiness has been experienced, a person's intents, beliefs, concepts, senses, and sensations are automatically modified. This process of modification has the same hierarchy as in Sāṅkhya.

The moment when a profound attraction and conviction is felt, which then alters the course of a person's life forever, is the time when *Dīkṣā* occurs—i.e. the seed has been received. In previous times, the guru imparted a secret mantra into the ears of the disciple and that imparting was considered the first instance of the knowledge transfer, and therefore called *Dīkṣā*. The disciple's body and mind were then considered to have been purified due to the reception of this seed. The pure disciple's body may even tremble and shake due to happiness from this reception.

But simply uttering the *mantra* in the ears of the disciple is not adequate if the disciple does not actually develop the attraction for this message. Therefore, the true moment of *Dīkṣā* is when we have felt that happiness which makes us want more and more of it again and again. The *Dīkṣā* is therefore not simply a ceremony or even the hearing of knowledge. It is that moment in which we first feel the happiness that convinces us to seek it again and again—because that happiness indicates that a new kind of moral value (God's knowledge is a separate moral category) has been received. This is the real *seed*.

The Process of Watering the Seed

Many people will receive the knowledge, but will not develop the attraction for it. They might be hearing or even understanding it, but that's about it. The knowledge is not going deep enough to touch a person's morality; the knowledge receives superficial at the level of senses or the mind. They are not to be considered to have received *Dīkṣā*. Many people will develop an attraction and may temporarily forget about it, only to return to it again and again as the only source of their ultimate happiness—they have received *Dīkṣā*. The term "Dīkṣā" therefore only indicates our *conviction* to pursue that happiness whose glimpse we have seen once, which is enough to motivate us forever after.

Dīkṣā-guru shows us a glimpse of happiness in order to *convince* us. We may begin the process of spirituality after this glimpse, and the process may not be complete. As we continue the process after many stops and starts—or, in a new life—a new *Dīkṣā* is not required, although the repetition of that same knowledge through *Śhikṣā* can be employed. The process of watering the seed is repeating the

Śhikṣā—by listening to others, reading the message, and repeating it in our mind.

The *Dīkṣā-guru* is that person who gives us unshakeable conviction in the message due to which we can never let go of the happiness of God that we originally see, even if we temporarily forget about it. We may encounter people that give us some knowledge that is later forgotten or reversed. But *Dīkṣā* is the point of irreversible attraction, and *Dīkṣā-guru* is the person who provides that irreversible attraction. There is hence only one *Dīkṣā* in the entire material journey of the living being—the point at which the living being found that irrevocable conviction. There can be innumerable instances of *Śhikṣā*.

Dīkṣā is, therefore, the seed while *Śhikṣā* is the watering of the seed. If you don't have the seed, pouring the water repeatedly isn't going to produce any results. But if you have the seed, and you are not watering it, the seed still lies dormant. In that sense, once the seed has been acquired, a living being has obtained a phenomenal achievement—the greatest that can be hoped for—which is that the journey to perfect happiness has begun. The journey may take a long or short time, depending on how much water or *Śhikṣa* he can pour and how fast one can grow the seed of spiritual knowledge into a full-blown tree.

What is Proximity to the Guru?

If you are a localist, you can think that reducing the physical distance to the guru is real proximity. If, however, you have a scientific understanding of causal interactions, then you will realize that the real proximity is making the mind similar to that of the guru, because that allows a person to be continuously in touch with the guru, through non-local entanglement. We cannot see this connection in the phenomenal world, and that's why such phenomena are still considered mysterious, or what Einstein called "spooky action at a distance". The term "non-locality" is in fact simply an unfortunate usage, because there is proximity and locality although it is semantic and not physical. Therefore, the entanglement appears spooky to one who believes in physical causality. It is not spooky to one who truly knows how a mind can entangle with another mind such that the thoughts in one mind automatically become the thoughts in another mind.

The local and non-local causality are respectively called *vāpu* and *vāni*—or physical body versus the guru's instructions. Being close to *vāpu* means physical proximity and being close to the *vāni* is semantic proximity. The *vāni* is more important to *vāpu* because the real space in nature is semantic and not physical.

Physical proximity is a sensory illusion produced from an interaction. When two things interact strongly, they *seem* close. When they interact weakly, they *seem* far. Generally, this interaction is created by *karma* and time for material interactions. For a spiritual contact—e.g. the contact with a *guru*—this contact is arranged by God's grace. The key important factor is that whether the contact exists or not, neither the guru nor the disciple is actually "moving" in space. They are fixed in their ideological states. What we experience as contact is because the two interact. In the case of the guru too, when we see him, it is because he wants to interact with the disciple. Similarly, when the guru is not seen, it is because the guru doesn't want to interact with the disciple. The physical distance (or proximity) is created by a causal interaction.

It is therefore false to presume that the guru has "died" and is unavailable due to which we cannot experience his presence. The truth is that the guru can directly interact with the disciple face-to-face, in exactly the same manner as before when he was physically present because both physical presence and physical absence are appearances produced from causal interaction.

The guru is not physically far now, and he was not physically close earlier. These notions are symptoms of ignorance about how perception is created from a subtle reality. If and when a true understanding of perception is acquired, we can understand that neither the guru nor the disciple is moving in space. Their interaction is based on the guru's will to impart knowledge to the disciple. If the guru wishes, he can impart the knowledge and that appears as a physical presence. If the guru does not wish, he may not impart knowledge and that appears as a physical absence.

The Balanced Organization

Published Date: 2017-05-01

Introduction and Overview

Vedic philosophy describes the body as a universe and the universe as a body. Since the world is intended for life, there is no fundamental divide between "physical sciences", "life sciences", and "social sciences". The cosmic structure, the social structure, the biological structure, and the psychological structure are isomorphic parts of a single continuum. Given this continuum, we can presume that what lies in between the categories that Vedic texts already describe can also be described in the same way as the other types of entities on the continuum.

I will use this article to illustrate the application of Vedic principles to sketch the foundations of an *Organizational Theory,* borrowing from the principles of material organization found in other areas such as Ayurveda, Aśtanga-Yoga, Vedic Cosmology, and Sāṅkhya philosophy. Such a study is useful not just in comprehending the nature of organizations, but also helpful in comprehending other kinds of organizations such as the universe and the living body.

A Quick Recap of Three Modes

Vedic philosophy provides a description of matter comprised of three modes of nature. There are many ways to understand these three modes, and one of them is called *manas*, *prāna*, and *vāk*. The term *manas* means the mind or an idea. The word *vāk* means a word or sound that expresses that idea. The connection or the process by which the idea is converted into a word is called *prāna*.

I'm quite certain that these are not easily understood ideas, so other ways to understand them are not likely to hurt us. The world in Vedic philosophy is symbolic—i.e. it expresses the meanings that the soul wants to enjoy. The universe is therefore comprised of *symbols.* A symbol has a meaning, or what Ferdinand de Saussure called *signified.* The symbol also has a physical embodiment that refers to the meaning, which Saussure called the *signifier*. This would have been adequate enough for symbolism if we were only talking about text in books, and not trying to describe how such texts were produced by the activity that converts ideas into symbols. When we try to describe how things are created from ideas, or how ideas are learned from things, we run into conventional mind-body problems.

Saussure's division into *signifier* and *signified* is inadequate. To make this complete, we have to add a third component into this—let's call this *signifying*—which is the act of converting an idea into a symbol. A symbol can thus be broken down into *signifier* (*vāk*), *signified* (*manas*), and *signifying* (*prāna*). Thus, matter is a symbol, in which the mind is the signified, the body is the signifier, and the connection between the mind and the body (created through *prāna*) is the act of signifying. When the person dies, the *prāna* detaches the mind from the body, carries the mind to a new location, and then creates a new body. *Prāna* is the activity, *manas* is the idea, and *vāk* is the thing. A symbol has three aspects—an idea, an activity, and the thing produced by the activity which represents the idea.

The Building Blocks of an Organization

Based on the above description of material nature (*manas*, *prāna*, and *vāk*), we can find a synonymous English description for organizations. I will use the words "idea", "process", and "product" to translate *manas*, *prāna*, and *vāk*, commensurate with the fact that *manas* is the concept, *vāk* is the physical expression of the concept, and *prāna* is the process by which this concept is converted into the product. Many organizational theorists speak of these as the *vision* (which denotes the mission or purpose for which the organization exists), *strategy* (the path, trajectory, or methodology the organization will follow to achieve its vision), and *execution* (the actual products or services that the organization will provide to its consumers).

The words *vision*, *strategy*, and *execution* are much abused and variously nuanced. Therefore, I will employ a much cleaner terminology here—*idea*, *process*, and *product*—which have relatively cleaner interpretations and therefore subject to much less confusion arising from current theories.

If we want to quickly see an illustration of how this maps into a real-world organization, then we can think of a market-driven business organization where the new ideas are produced by the "field" teams such as sales and marketing, the "operational" teams define processes for execution and quality to convert ideas into products, while the "engineering" teams follow the processes to create a product. Therefore, the sales get the "ideas", the operations define "process" and engineering creates "products". An organization must have these three parts in order to qualify as a complete organization.

The field teams create the requirements—the "what" and "why"—for the organization. The operational teams create the processes and procedures—the "how" and "who"—for the organization. Finally, the engineering teams create the actual product—"where" and "when"—for the organization. It is important to answer the "what" and "why" before we answer the "who" and "how" questions: we must know what we are going to do and why before we discuss how it should be done and by whom. Similarly, it is important to answer the "who" and "how"—i.e. the methods of working and the qualified people who can follow these methods must be known—before these people would create the product (each product has parts with individual trajectories—the "where" and "when").

Thus, a natural hierarchy or priority between idea, process, and product exists in all organizations. However, this doesn't necessarily mean that all ideas would be freely created prior to products. It just means that some ideas must be converted into products because products can be used to create new ideas. In fact, there are both top-down and bottom-up processes as we shall soon see.

The Structure of an Organization

Every system requires some *idea*, *process*, and *product*. Whether all these things are done by a single person—e.g. a person expressing their ideas through speech—or they are executed by a team of people (which divides people into different functions) or they are embodied into the functions of a large organization, the logical components and their logical priority remains unchanged. In fact, by understanding this logical order and priority, we can construct complex hierarchies in which the product (output) of one level becomes the idea (input) for another level in the organization..

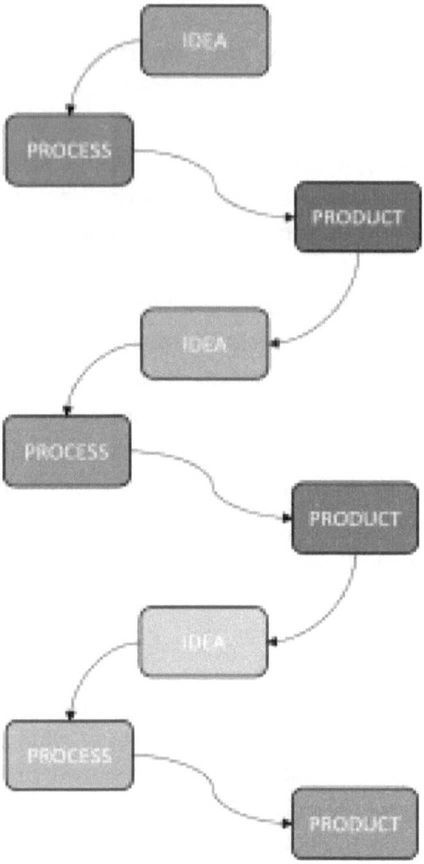

For example, in a business organization, a top-level executive can provide an idea as a brief to her subordinates who can then transform this synopsis into a detailed document of requirements, which even lower subordinates can elaborate into individual feature functionalities. The abstract idea thus begins at the top, but through processes and products, gets more and more refined. At the top, one might just have a crude idea. As this idea trickles down, it obtains a better and better definition. In fact, the top-level idea division can in turn be divided into the idea, process, and product, and then each of these divisions can be further partitioned into three parts.

The functionality of such divisions is defined in relation to the higher-level entity. For example, if a division of "product" is under a division of "process", which is under a division of "idea", then the function of such a "product" division is to produce a document, which outlines the "process" by which new "ideas" will be created. Similarly, if there is an "idea" under a "process" under a "product", then the meaning of such hierarchy is to provide an "idea" about a new "process" to create "products".

Hierarchical Tiers of an Organization

Sāṅkhya philosophy describes how the infinite variety in the universe can be reduced to three categories—idea, process, and product—and variety is created by structuring them into hierarchies. Each symbol has three parts—*manas, prāna*, and *vāk*—but its full meaning is given in relation to the entire hierarchy of symbols. In that sense, the universe is constructed as a diversifying tree of symbolic meanings.

As the symbols emerge from higher symbols, at the top of the tree are 3 trunks, which then divide into 9 branches, which then produce 21 twigs, and so forth, at each layer multiplying the divisions by 3. The tree grows exponentially in complexity, however, it still has a finite number of levels, which constitute the "space" of that level. The top-level space has 3 parts, the next lower level space has 9 parts, the next lower space has 21 parts, and so forth. The top-level concepts are *abstract* or "big" ideas. Their subdivisions are *detailed* or "small" ideas. The small ideas are created inside the big ideas, due to what I have called the *has-a* hierarchy of containment which creates parts inside wholes. Each of these tiers, from top to bottom, exists like a space stacked on top of the other spaces like a spindle.

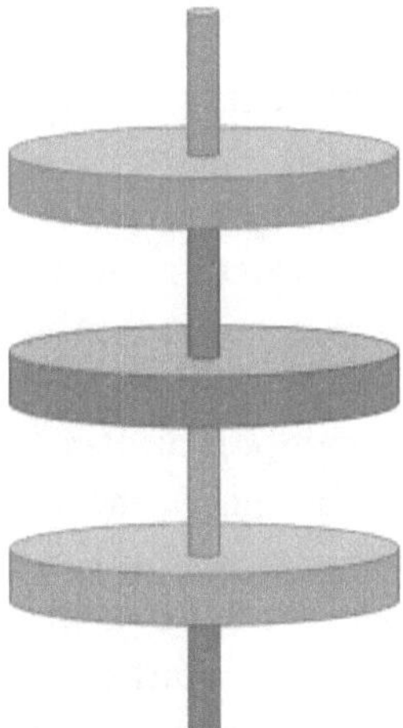

The result of such partitioning is that the organization is now crafted into multiple tiers, such that each tier has three components—idea, process, and product—and each tier connects to lower tiers. At each tier, a good organization expects collaboration or cooperation between the idea, process, and product tiers. And at each level, a good organization expects a good command over lower levels. In that sense, each organization has "command and control" from top to bottom, and "collaboration and cooperation" from east to west. Organizations fail when there isn't enough collaboration at a given level, and when an organization loses control over lower levels and the lower level is disconnected from the higher level.

Similarities to Biology and Cosmology

One of the key goals of this post is to illustrate that in discussing organizational theory, we are not talking about a new model that applies only to organizations. Specialization is dominant in modern academia which divides knowledge into separate departments where each department speculates independently on its particular domain oblivious to what implications such theories have on other parts of the system. For example, economists have little understanding of the sociological impacts of theories such as capitalism, because sociology is a separate department from economics. The sociologists, similarly, have little understanding of the impact of social organization on people's psychology because psychology is a separate department from sociology. Similarly, every department operates independently, creating models that have little to no similarity to other departments. Vedic knowledge is different. It describes a model of organization that can be applied to every kind of system—cosmology, organization, and biology. Here are some similarities between the models.

An idea is higher than a process which is higher than a product, and yet these are aspects of a single symbol produced from a higher symbol (which too has the same three aspects). This means that there is a hierarchy *between* the symbols and *within* a symbol. The different parts of a symbol are therefore not at the same level, and the different symbols at a given level too are not at the same level. Rather, there is a slight hierarchy within each level too, which means that the "level" is not flat or uniform on all the sides. Rather, one side (denoting the idea) is higher than the opposite side (denoting the product).

In Vedic cosmology, the two sides are called *Uttarāyaṇa* and

Dakshināyana as the Sun goes up and down a tilted circle. The connection between the idea and the product is made by a process, and there are two parts of this process—one that slants downwards and the other that slants upwards.

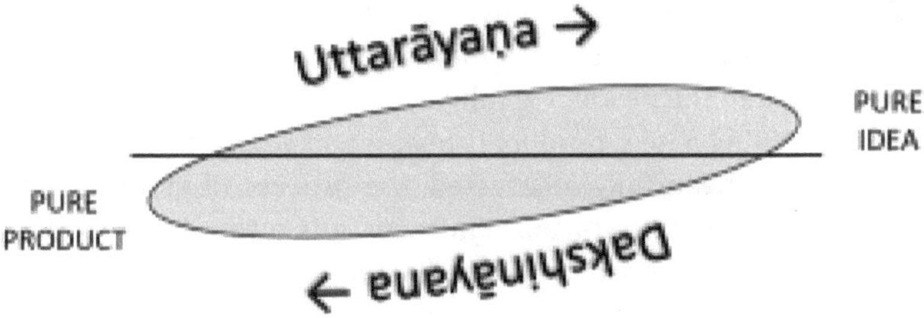

As the Sun goes downwards, the path is called *Dakshināyana* and as the Sun goes upwards, the path is called *Uttarāyaṇa*. The key point is in one half (called *Dakshināyana*) the ideas are converted into products using a process while in the other half (called *Uttarāyaṇa*) the products are converted into ideas using a process. The downward path defines products from ideas, while the upwards defines ideas from products. We can think of these two paths as synthetic and analytic respectively: the synthetic part constructs a product from an idea, while the analytic part extracts the idea from a product.

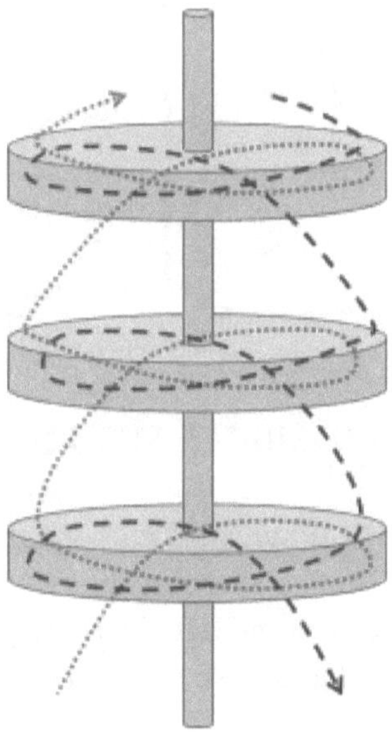

However, the synthetic and analytic processes don't just execute within a circle. Instead, the process cascades across multiple levels as shown in the above figure. The upward process covers one side of the circle while the downward process covers the other side of the circle. In this way, the upward and downward processes cross each other. These opposite processes are joined at the top and bottom, which means that when the product is fully developed, immediately the process of conceiving a new product is begun and when the new conception has finally been fully abstracted, the process of creating a new product is immediately started. Thus, there is a top-down loop, and there is a sideways crisscross loop. This kind of loop is best understood through the depiction of *yoga-nādi* in the body.

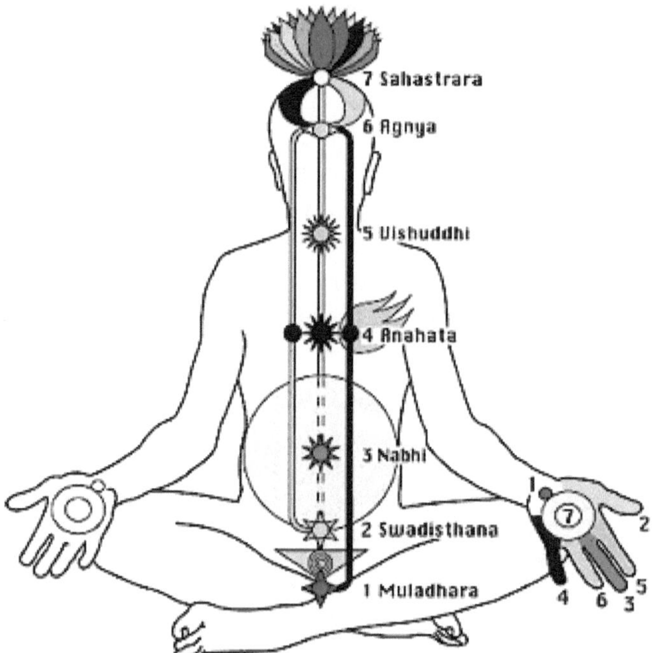

THE SUBTLE SYSTEM

In *yoga* philosophy, the downward path is called *idā* and the upward path is called *pingalā*. The *idā* starts at the left nostril and then moves to the right and then back to the left alternately. Similarly, the *pingalā* starts on the right nostril and then moves to the left and then back to the right alternately.

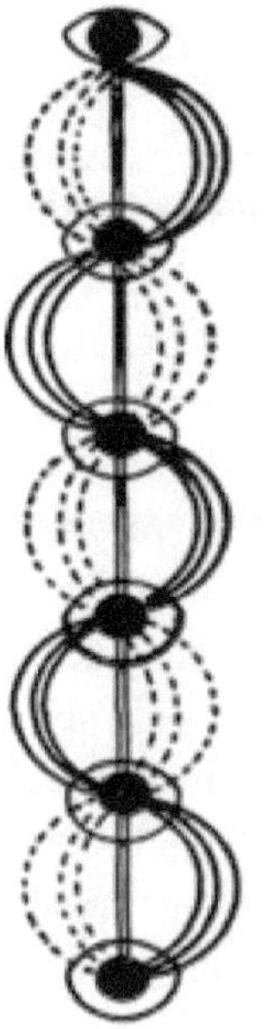

It is also noteworthy that the downward path goes clockwise (similar to how a screw is tightened and moved downward) while the upwards path goes anticlockwise (similar to how a screw is unscrewed and moved upwards). Owing to this screw-like behavior, the *idā* and *pingalā* are said to be "coiled" and hence called *kundalini*. The coiling of the *kundalini* is often compared to a coiled snake. They constitute two opposite paths—upward and downward—but these paths are not actually straight lines. Rather, they are like spirals—move clockwise to go down and move anticlockwise to go upward.

The upward and downward paths are not active simultaneously. Rather, there is a time when the screw is tightened and the pressure is applied from the top to the bottom to convert ideas into processes and then into products. Then the pressure is released and the products are converted back into processes and then into ideas. The top-down motion is detailing, and the bottom-up motion is abstracting. These two processes are not applied simultaneously but occur one after another. Thus, the person who dies during *Uttarāyaṇa* ascends to higher planetary systems—because they are able to leverage the upward movement to transfer themselves to higher planetary systems. Similarly, the person who dies during *Dakshināyana* will be carried downward by the downward movement.

The true *yogi* doesn't rely on the alternating *idā* or the *pingalā,* but on the central nerve called *sushumnā* that rests at the origin of the spindle and everything emanates from this origin. This central nerve is energized when the *idā* and *pingalā* are no longer alternating paths; instead, they become simultaneous paths. Thus, the *yogi* doesn't depend on the upward and downward alternating process. He rather directly ascends or descends through the central nerve.

The key import of this description is that for most people creativity and learning are alternate jobs. Initially, everyone creates something and sees whether it works; the fact is that most of the time it doesn't work. Then they use the failures of the created system to learn new processes and ideas, and these new techniques and ideas are then used to refine the product iteratively. This is called the process of theory and experiment in which one observes the world and through an analytic process extracts the ideas out of material objects, and then tests these ideas by creating new objects. Thus, one goes through the cycle of creativity (constructing a product) and learning (analyzing a product).

The constructive process is *anabolic* and the analytic process is *catabolic*. Due to this nature, the top-down process is that of the Moon or *creativity* and the bottom-up process is that of the Sun or *learning*. Since the top-down and bottom-up occur alternately, the process is described as a cycle in which there are alternating phases of Moon and Sun—which are then compared to the periods called "day" and "night". Of course, they are not actual day and night; they are alternating periods of new analysis and new creativity.

While most individuals, organizations, and the universe go through the periods of creation and analysis, the true *yogi* called *stitha-prajna* situates himself at the center and away from the alternating cycle where he is not constrained by the cyclic movements to go up and down. Such a *yogi* can move up and down whenever he wants, which means that there no period for creativity and analysis. The person who has understood the cycle of creativity and analysis exits this cycle and places himself in the center which never changes—i.e. doesn't go through the cycle. This fixed position helps them continually rise and not be affected by the ever-changing cycle of rising and fall in the *idā* and *pingalā*.

The central path preferred by a *yogi* offers insights into how an institution or organization can end its "experimental learning" processes where it tries to implement a half-baked product, which inevitably fails, and then uses it to learn something new, and naturally, the learning is about what was missing previously. Now, this missing ingredient is again implemented in another half-baked product to avoid the shortcomings of the previous product, but the new product is now lacking in what existed previously. Thus, the new product also fails, and one goes back to the analysis phase of what is missing. In this way, organizations keep going round and round in circles repeating the same mistakes through a cyclic path. The exit for them is to realize that there is a "middle path" that is outside these cyclic paths. This middle path involves the creation of a "balance" between the various extremes. If any of the previously mentioned facets—idea, process, or product—is overemphasized, then an imbalance will be created. The "middle path" is therefore the path of balancing the three different tendencies to end the up-down cycle.

Two Models of Innovation

The perfectly balanced system is situated in the middle of the space shown above. The imbalanced systems are situated away from the center. As a system moves towards the center—i.e. obtains greater balance—the changes involved over a cycle continually reduce, and the system tends towards stability. The products created by an organization that is close to the center live very long and require minimal changes. The ideological churn in such organizations is minimal and the organization repeatedly produces the same product using the same process, instantiating the same idea. Ultimately, when the organization touches the center, its cycle of learning and creation ends; it can now evolve or rise to the next level where it can start delivering a whole new kind of product and/or service that it was not delivering earlier, closely aligned to what it was previously doing.

Conversely, as an organization moves outward from the center, the cycle of change becomes bigger and bigger. In each cycle, the greater and greater number of products have to be created or modified, which requires a continuous generation of new ideas and new processes. Modern management theorists call this "innovation".

The essential fact underlying "innovation" is that things are not working. If they were already working, then why would anyone require "innovation"? But if things are not working, then certainly there is a need to improve things. However, there are two modes of innovation—a real mode and an illusory mode. The real mode of innovation is that an organization produces very few products which don't need to be changed. The illusory mode of innovation is that one produces too many products which need too many changes. In the former mode, the organization tends towards stability. In the latter, the organization quickly reaches instability due to radical, wide-ranging, and continuous changes, arising out of trying to do too many things—all of which are imperfect and therefore require frequent revisions.

Modern management theory exhorts organizations to move towards instability in which everyone has to try to do many things which might all be imperfect in the beginning but they have to be quickly revised and improvised through experience, and the ideas or products discarded if they are not working. There is even a term for this illusory innovation model—"fail fast". The central flaw in this model is that nobody is prepared to give any reasonable amount of thought and time to understand the real problems in order to build what is right. The goal is simply to build what one needs right now, test it against what little opportunities are available, and make a quick decision without understanding the pros and cons. In short, impatience and short-sightedness are the techniques for innovation and the unique value you can bring is to dazzle your consumer with a new shiny contraption such that it would be worthless soon, and you would now be required to prepare one more equally worthless contraption pretty soon.

Organizations that seem to profit from such a model of innovation don't realize that as they do more and more faster and faster, they are running a huge risk of making many simultaneous mistakes, which can be hard to correct, and if they are not corrected, they can eliminate the organization. Intelligent consumers realize that they don't need the latest and greatest innovations. They rather need something that works reliably and can be obtained at a lower cost relative to the value. Therefore, to fuel their model of innovation, the fast movers have to resort to "marketing" and "advertising" which are euphemisms for deluding the consumer into thinking that such "innovations" are necessary.

The Problem of Balance

As an organization iterates faster and faster, there are greater and greater opportunities for imbalance simply because some part of the organization will slack and not keep up with the pace of the rest of the organization. We cannot expect multiple distinct parts to move synchronously and harmoniously. Attempts to push organizations to run faster and faster can backfire as they can break the organization into disjoint pieces which are out of sync with each other. There is simply no way that humans can work faster and faster because there is a pace at which humans are designed to work. The aim of all organizations should be to stop the churn in the anabolic and catabolic parts of the cycle. That is, what we create and what we learn is stable and the organization operates smoothly, not making big ideological, process, or product changes. It just must be close to the center, ideally right at the center so that its products are widely appreciated, cost-optimal, and long-lasting.

As an organization picks pace, one or more of the three modes become dominant or weak, thereby resulting in anomalies. The table below describes eight cardinal anomalies.

	Manas	Prāna	Vāk	Notes
1	Dominant	Weak	Weak	Many new ideas, but no practical realization of these ideas
2	Weak	Dominant	Weak	Same idea produces same things by following many different processes
3	Weak	Weak	Dominant	Many products from the same idea and process with minor differences
4	Dominant	Dominant	Weak	Many new ideas and new processes but the end result is the same as before
5	Weak	Dominant	Dominant	Old ideas but new processes used to create several different products
6	Dominant	Weak	Dominant	New products created using new ideas, while following the same processes
7	Weak	Weak	Weak	No new ideas, processes, or products; the system appears to be dead
8	Dominant	Dominant	Dominant	Too many new ideas, processes and products; the system seems chaotic

Of course, these aren't the only anomalies for two main reasons. First, these anomalies are sequenced one after another in a circular fashion within a given level. Second, the levels themselves are stacked hierarchically. Each symbol in the material tree can be anomalous in 8 different ways, and the result on the branches of such anomalies are exponentially higher. In other words, the chances of anomalous behavior are far greater than the chances of stable behavior. And as the system become anomalous, it risks being broken apart and destroyed. There are many typical failures by which organizations can die which include its members deserting the organization and its products losing the quality.

The Question of Organizational Longevity

Everybody wants to lead a longer life. Every organization, similarly, wants to exist perennially. However, just as living bodies can die sooner than later, similarly, organizations too can cease to exist sooner than expected. Forbes, for instance, notes that "Half a century ago, the life expectancy of a firm in the Fortune 500 was around 75 years. Now it's less than 15 years and declining even further." Similarly, Forbes also notes that "In total, Fortune 500 companies represent two-thirds of the U.S. GDP with $12 trillion in revenues, $840 billion in profits, $17 trillion in market value, and employ 27.9 million people worldwide." These are amazing statistics because they tell us that on one hand the share of the large organizations is 2/3rd of the largest economy. On the other hand, they also tell us that the average lifetime of such an organization is now less than 15 years. The combination of the massive share and the rapid destruction of such large companies represents a crisis in Organizational Theory.

Those who argue that such "creative destruction" is good for society are probably blinkered economists who may have never opened a book on sociology, psychology, politics, or medicine. In other words, they have no clue on what effect such destruction has on society at large, and how it changes people in ways that are counter to the promise for which economics was invented in the first place—happiness.

Every society will build institutions and organizations because humans act collectively and consensually. We don't have to explain to anyone why teamwork is important, because the fact is that no man is an island unto themselves. People have to organize themselves into collective activities. But they cannot become happy as part of these collections, nor can they achieve the purposes of such organization, unless we formulate accurate theories of such organization. What are the essential parts of an organization? How many layers must an organization have? How big should an organization be, relative to how nimble it has to be? Clearly, organizations that have to be nimble must be small, and organizations that have to be long-lived must be large and stable. But where is the theory that explains why large organizations cannot be nimble and why nimble organizations must be small?

Organization Theory, like the other "social sciences" such as economics, sociology, politics, etc., is actually not different from natural sciences because the principles of structure, function, and organization are common across natural and man-made systems. The natural systems are not created randomly, and the man-made systems are not simply ideas in our heads. There are real principles of organization by which energy flows both top-down and bottom-up, and only by understanding the principles of such energy flow can we craft and design organizations that are suitable for the given purpose, achieve what they were meant to achieve, and live for the duration that they are expected to survive. A theory of organization is natural science—like cosmology and biology—and all these domains share common structural and functional principles.

Sāńkhya and Modern Atomism

Published Date: 2017-05-06

Introduction and Overview

Sāńkhya has a theory of atomism, which is quite different than the theory of modern atomism. The modern description of atoms is based on the distinction between matter and force whereas the Sāńkhya description is based on the distinction between words and meanings.

The key question is: Can we study what modern science calls atoms and molecules using Sāńkhya? If yes, how would this study be different from the study of atoms and molecules at present? This article answers many such questions, including why the particles of modern atomism—i.e. quarks and leptons—are contrived physical interpretations of waveforms. It is possible to give the same waveforms a semantic interpretation in which all dynamical properties (e.g. position, time, angle, direction, momentum, energy, spin, and angular momentum) denote meanings and all material properties (such as mass and charge) are no longer required. These waves are now "words" that denote "meanings".

The Hierarchical Tree and Modern Atomism

In some previous articles, I have discussed how Sāńkhya describes the world as symbols, which are organized into a hierarchical tree-like structure. I have also discussed the three components of symbols—*manas* (meaning), prāṇa (process), and *vāk* (word). In an earlier article, I described these three as the *signified, signifying*, and *signifier* components of a symbol, following the work of Ferdinand de Saussure who describes a symbol as *signifier* and *signified* (neglecting the process of creation of such symbols, which I have termed as *signifying*, and which Sāńkhya calls the activity or prāṇa).

The atoms that modern science studies—e.g. Oxygen or Copper—should be understood (from the standpoint of Sāńkhya) as symbols of meaning. A symbol has three parts—a meaning, a word, and activity.

The activity is required in order to convert the meaning into a word; for example, if you have to express the meaning in your mind, you have to spend some energy while speaking your mind.

The key difference between Sāṅkhya and the modern description is that what modern science considers different subatomic particles (such as quarks and leptons) are simply different *modes* of vibration of space. Space is, thus, as a musical drum, and different particles are sounds produced from this drum. Depending on where a drum is hit, a different kind of sound is produced, which physics describes as different kinds of particles. Since quantum theory inherits the classical physical legacy of materialism, it interprets these sounds as material "particles" rather than thinking of them simply as *modes* of vibration of space, which could then be described as words representing meanings.

The Principle of Superposition

The vibrations of any membrane are supposed to be *additive* and *linear*. This means that if the membrane can vibrate in modes A and B, then it can also vibrate in another mode of A + B. This additive property of different types of motions is called the Principle of Superposition.

Consider, for example, the linear rolling motion of a wheel, which is a combination of two motions—(1) the translational motion in a straight line, and (2) the rotation of the wheel about its axis. If you brake the wheel, it might still drag forward due to the translation motion. Conversely, if your wheel is stuck in the mud, it might rotate about its axis without moving forward. The linear translation and the circular rotation are therefore two orthogonal *modes* of motion of the wheel. Since these two motions are possible separately, their combination—i.e. the normal rolling motion of a wheel which combines the linear translation and the circular rotation is also a *mode* of motion of the wheel. In the case of the rolling motion of the wheel, we can say that the wheel is in a *superposed state* of two motions—rectilinear and rotational. There are other modes of motion possible too. For example, you can have a sideways motion of the wheel due to which a wheel is spinning, moving forward, and moving sideways. Similarly, you can have the car climb up an incline and add an upwards mode to this motion. In this way, the car's motion can be broken down into several *orthogonal modes*, which are then *superposed* in the car.

Similarly, if you hit the drum in the middle, it will vibrate in one way. But if you hit the drum on the edge it will vibrate in another way. Depending on where you hit, and how hard you hit, the drum will vibrate differently. The unique property of the drum—because of which it constitutes a *linear* system—is that you can hit the drum simultaneously in two or more places and the resulting vibration would be a linear sum of those separate vibrations. Just as the wheel in rolling motion combines rectilinear and rotational motions, similarly, the drum also has the property of superposition and linearity.

This is an important consideration in atomic theory, which is also a *linear* theory. That is, you can think of the atom as a drum, and the subatomic particles as the vibrations of the drum. Each such particle is created from the drum when the drum is hit at some location. We can distinguish between three things—(1) the drum, (2) the act of hitting, and (3) the resulting vibration. These are respectively called *manas*, prāṇa, and *vāk*, where the *manas* is the drum, which is hit by a force called prāṇa, and the result is a vibrational mode that we can perceive. If the force is removed or dissipated, then the sound stops, but that doesn't mean the end of the drum. This means that there is a reality that exists independent of observation—which we can call "idea"—but it cannot be perceived unless it is excited by a force. To study atomic physics, we have to study the different kinds of drums and how these drums are variously beaten by different kinds of forces. This is the essence of atomic theory in Sāṅkhya.

The Possibility of Infinite Particles

Modern particle physics experiments bear out this approach to particle creation because these experiments bombard matter with energy, requiring powerful particle accelerators. Effectively, the particle physics experiments hit a drum harder and harder to produce newer kinds of sounds. There is no end to this hitting, or to the number of particles that can be created by such a process. Particle physics is, therefore, infinite, just as the number of sounds and rhythms that can be created by playing arbitrarily shaped drums are also infinite.

The only reason we consider it finite is that we are beating a specific kind of drum found on Earth. In Sāṅkhya, space in different parts of the universe is different; as a different kind of drum hit by different kinds of strokes, it produces different kinds of sounds. We can never complete particle physics because we can never obtain all the drums.

Particle physics is a catalog of what we see here and now.

A more accurate approach to study the particles is to think of the ways in which they are produced. This involves four factors. First, we must understand the varieties of drums that can be played. Second, we can talk about how hitting the drum differently produces a new vibration. Third, we must understand the kinds of drums that are presently available and the various ways in which they can be vibrated. Fourth, we must study how the drum *should* be played; just hitting the drum in whatever way we like is not science; true science is learning to play the drum according to some rules. This will be the primary methodology by which I will try to explain a new kind of atomic physics.

Fermions and Bosons

Since the time of Newton's mechanics, physics has used matter and force to describe nature. They were subsequently termed particles and fields in classical physics. Later, in atomic theory, these are called *fermions* and *bosons*—after Enrico Fermi and Satyendra Nath Bose. The fermions are the matter particles that comprise the nucleus and the shell of the atom. The forces by which these particles interact with each other are called bosons. The Standard Model of particle physics describes six quarks, six leptons, and four fundamental forces.

In modern physics, a certain type of boson (e.g. photon) is associated with a certain type of material property (e.g. charge). In Sāṅkhya, there are no fundamental physical properties such as mass or charge; there are only symbols that can represent different kinds of meanings. The symbol that means "heavy" is not a fundamentally different physical property from a symbol that means "bitter". The material world is thus not physical properties at all; it is just words whose *meanings* denote a whole bunch of physical properties. In that sense, we are never going to seek physical forces such as gravity, electromagnetism, strong, and weak forces with corresponding physical properties like mass, charge, color, and flavor. We are rather going to seek an understanding of the forces involved in the creation of words and sentences.

Matter-Energy Equivalence

The idea of matter-energy equivalence is well-known since Einstein's theory of special relativity articulated the formula E = mc2. The *m* in this equation is *mass* which implies that the equivalence holds only for mass. We might then ask: What about other properties such as charge, color, and flavor which are responsible for electromagnetism, strong, and weak forces? Are these not equivalent to energy? The short answer is that all the other properties (charge, color, and flavor) come in two opposite polarities—positive and negative. Therefore it is possible to create and annihilate these particles in pairs without violating conservation laws. Mass is the only property in current physics which doesn't have an opposite polarity (as there is no such thing called "negative mass" at present). Thus mass-energy equivalence is required because mass cannot disappear by combining with anti-mass, but other properties can appear and disappear in this way.

Why is negative mass a problem? Negative masses require negative energy which requires negative time. To talk about negative mass, we have to speak about two kinds of time—(a) that is moving from past to present, and (b) that is moving from future to present. The latter kind of time is possible if we could imagine something called a "destiny" that comes from the future to the present—i.e. it exists in the future (implying that the future is fixed) and is then realized in the present. Destiny-based thinking has been impossible in modern physics because it raises questions such as: How are such destinies created? To answer this question, we have to change the causal model from cause and effect (which involves the past and present) to one that involves cause, effect, and consequence (which then requires past, present, and future). The consequences build the destiny, which lies in the future, which arrives into the present and constitutes a *negative* time.

With such negative time, it is possible to conceive negative mass, which means that energy doesn't convert into mass; rather energy creates a *pair* of mass and anti-mass particles. I bring up this issue of mass-energy equivalence for two main reasons. First, mass is an outlier in today's physics because every other particle has an antiparticle, but mass doesn't. If mass were to have an antiparticle, then it wouldn't be an outlier. Hence, the issue of negative mass is pertinent to the problem of thinking about the world purely in quantum theoretic terms. Second, when we speak about the world as symbols of meanings, we can only speak of them in opposites—e.g. hot vs. cold, bitter vs. sweet, black vs. white, etc. Therefore, the particle and antiparticle pairs become *symbols* of opposite meanings moving in opposite directions.

The Existence of Opposite Waves

Now we can enhance our previous picture of a hand hitting a drum in which the drum produces two vibrational modes which are opposite to each other. These opposite waves are created because a drum is a finite object, and it *reflects* the wave from one end to the other, causing the second wave to move in the opposite direction. Thus, it appears that one wave is moving left to right, while the second wave is moving from right to left. Since the two waves are identical in all other respects, in modern atomic theory, they are called the Ψ and Ψ* waves. In a representation that separates time and space components, these two waves are identical except that they move in opposite directions.

The standard formulation of quantum theory multiplies Ψ and Ψ* waves, and this multiplication is supposed to create a *probability* of finding a particle in a certain place. In classical physics, the same two kinds of waves were multiplied and together they constituted a *Standing Wave*. The sound in all musical instruments is produced due to such standing waves; i.e. these waves are not *propagating* or moving in space. Since they have a specific location, they are just like particles. Since they are vibrating, they are just like waves. And yet, they are not point particles, nor are they infinitely extended fields. There is fundamentally no paradox—e.g. wave vs. particle—in thinking about reality if we think of it as vibrations *of* space. All paradoxes arise by forcing a classical physical picture on a new observation.

The prāṇa is that energy that hits on the drum and creates two opposite waves, which then represent two opposite *sides*. By creating sides within an idea, we convert it into an object. The purpose of energy is to convert the symbol of an abstract idea into two (or more) symbols of detailed ideas. These details now become *parts* of the original idea. For example, the "coin" is an abstract idea. But when energy is added to the coin, the coin gets a "head" and a "tail", which are opposite sides of the coin. Every system of parts is comprised of such opposites—e.g. a dice of six faces has three pairs of opposites. Of course, we have to bear in mind that I'm using the term "opposites" to illustrate a point about how different parts are created, although it is not necessary that an object only has an even number of parts; a pentagon for example has 5 sides; we will see shortly how this basic idea about different sides (that begins in opposites) can also be generalized.

Opposite Sides vs. Opposite Particles

While discussing mass-energy equivalence we saw the creation of a particle and antiparticle and compared it to opposite ideas such as hot vs. cold, bitter vs. sweet, etc. We also saw above that an object has opposite sides—e.g. head vs. tail, front vs. back, top vs. bottom, etc. The opposite sides of an object are not the same as opposite objects. But since we call both opposite sides, and the opposite objects, particles, we can—depending on the context—use the terms particle and antiparticle to talk about them. We just have to be careful what we are really talking about. Modern physics, of course, use the term antiparticle to describe the opposite object, not the opposite side.

When we describe the world as meaning, opposite meanings are at opposite "ends" of space. There is hence a "top" and "bottom" of the universe, which have opposite meanings. The opposite ideas cannot co-exist as they will annihilate each other, and hence we never observe the antiparticles in the present world, except in collider experiments. Even in such experiments, we see that when the particle-antiparticle pair is created, the two move in opposite directions. If the universe was built from such opposites, such particles will exist in far-flung regions of space.

The opposite parts of a Standing Wave, however, are completely overlapped and this overlap is the cause of new phenomena. In the exchange of a quantum particle, one wave goes from the emitter to the absorber, and this is how we think of a transaction from source to destination. The surprising part, however, is also that there is a wave going from the destination to the source. In Sāṅkhya, both parts are called *karma* due to which two entities exchange information, and the exchange cannot occur simply because a source emits a particle; the destination must also be prepared to receive it. The ability to emit and absorb is due to *karma.* Since the emission is triggered by the source, there is also a choice involved at the source. Similarly, there may be a choice involved at the destination which is called *guna.*

The *guna* is the unmanifest desires—which were created in the past—and manifest in the present as thought or action. Karma is the consequences of previous actions—which lie in the future as destiny—and manifest the present circumstances. Both *guna* and *karma* are unmanifest in that they are in the past or in the future. But this "past" and "future" are not *physical* but semantic. That is, the past exists in the present as *memory,* and the future exists in the present as *destiny*. The past and future are in the present, but unknowable.

Each quantum is therefore comprised of two opposite parts: *guna* and *karma*, which appear as opposite waves inside the quantum. Similarly, each quantum also has an antiparticle and there are opposite parts (*guna* and *karma*) inside the antiparticle too. The opposite particles and the opposite sides follow the same principles but they are different. The process for the creation of a single quantum involves the production of a particle and antiparticle—i.e. the opposite particles. However, the creation of a material transaction involves the combination of opposite sides. The opposite particles are due to different modes in *guna*. The opposite sides are due to the different roles in a transaction. The result of *guna* and *karma* is that transactions can cause the emission or absorption of a particle or an antiparticle.

The Dynamics of Parts

Once we understand how a whole is being divided into parts, then we can generalize this idea in a few different ways. First, we can think of a process by which a system of N parts acquires an additional part and thereafter it becomes N+1 parts; this process is called prāṇa or the addition of parts. Second, we can think of a process by which a system of N parts loses a part and then becomes N-1 parts; this process is called *apāna* or the removal of parts. Third, as parts are added or removed, the new set of parts must take on the functionality of the whole through a process of responsibility reallocation which is called *samāna* or the balancing of different parts by allocating them different jobs.

The prāṇa, *apāna*, and *samāna* are the primary forces that control what happens inside a system boundary. In addition to this, there is the *vyāna* force which carries symbolic information from one system boundary to another. For example, when we eat food, the ingestion is caused by prāṇa, following which the ingested food is broken into parts by the process of *samāna*. Once the food has been broken, the parts are ejected from the digestive system using *apāna*, carried by the circulatory system using *vyāna* to the other parts of the body where it can be ingested again through prāṇa. The prāṇa, *apāna*, and *samāna* are therefore intra-system forces, while *vyāna* is inter-system force.

Finally, there is the force called *udāna* which involves *cloning* the symbols to prepare them for externalization. For example, if you have an idea in your mind, and you want to express this idea to the world, then there is an act of cloning involved. The force called *udāna* is not the same as the force called *apāna* because *apāna* means eviction or expulsion, while *udāna* means copying and transmitting the copy. Thus, a teacher emits the meaning to a student, but it is not considered a "waste", and by transmitting the knowledge, the teacher doesn't become ignorant. If the transmission of knowledge involved *apāna* then after educating the student, the teacher would be ignorant. Therefore, the *udāna* process is also emission but it involves the act of cloning a drum into a second drum, and the second drum is then ejected.

Other than the transmission of knowledge, DNA replication is another example of *udāna* due to which the ideas are copied and transmitted. This ability to copy becomes the property of all living beings by which they can reproduce and educate each other. The *udāna* is advanced in humans reflecting in their ability to produce music, art, literature, and science, as compared to other species such as fishes, birds, beasts, and trees which can only reproduce. The "reproduction" is not just biological; the mind is also reproducing ideas into other minds.

The key point is that these forces are not uniformly present even on Earth. The different forces are dominant in different life forms, so the idea that nature is uniform is completely false.

The terms prāṇa, *apāna, udāna, vyāna,* and *samāna,* are collectively called prāṇa and often translated as "life breath". A close scientific equivalent of this term is "force", provided we understand that these forces are not associated with physical properties (e.g. mass or charge) as in modern physics. The fact is that there is no accurate translation for prāṇa in English. By understanding the dynamics of a system as composed of parts, and the role the five prāṇa play in this dynamics, we can give a new definition to the word "force" that is different from the current scientific usage and everyday usage.

Prāṇa and the Modern Forces

We cannot create an equivalent mapping between the forces of modern physics and Sāṅkhya because in modern physics a "system" is not a *theoretical construct*. The word "system" is just used pragmatically as a way to eliminate outside influences and study an isolated phenomenon (assuming that it can be isolated). Within this isolated picture, everything is described in a flat space-time—i.e. without boundaries. Sāṅkhya, on the other hand, has an explicit notion of a system with boundaries. Therefore there are "forces" of ingestion, digestion, elimination, transportation, and replication. We cannot find equivalences between these approaches unless physics is redefined to deal with systems grounds-up. This definition necessitates the induction of the idea of a *boundary* in nature.

Quantum theory emerged from the study of blackbody radiation in which a blackbody is heated to the point where it emits particles. This process is very but due to oversimplification, we cannot predict when the energy would be absorbed and when it would be emitted. The real process is that when a black body is heated, there is the involvement of prāṇa (the addition of energy). When this energy is absorbed, there is the involvement of *samāna* and *vyāna* (the digestion of energy and its redistribution within a system). And when energy is emitted, there is the involvement of *apāna* (the excretion of energy). What quantum theory is trying to describe as one force—e.g. electromagnetic radiation—is actually four different kinds of forces. Conversely, what quantum theory considers different forces such as electromagnetism, gravity, weak and strong forces don't exist in Sāṅkhya. These are orthogonal methods of describing the observations.

These forces become far more evident as complexity increases—e.g. in a living body. And therefore the forces are described in analogy to ingestion, digestion, assimilation, excretion, and duplication, which are prominently seen in the body. That doesn't mean the living body is something unique. It rather means that physics is flawed due to which biology is incompletely understood.

The Problem of Reductionism

Scientists widely suppose that the forces within the atom adequately describe the formation of molecules (and other more complex constructs) which is a false idea according to Sāṅkhya and arises due to a non-system-oriented approach to the study of matter. Accordingly, if we just focus on the study of what is inside the atom, we would ignore all the 5 forces which cause the motion of molecules across boundaries (prāṇa), the breakdown of molecular structures inside a boundary (*samāna*), the motion of molecules from one part of the living body to another (*vyāna*), how such molecules are cloned (*udāna*), and how such molecules are evicted from a system boundary (*apāna*).

According to Sāńkhya, these five forces are *fundamental forces* and not epiphenomenal behaviors of subatomic particles.

The empirical observations of chemistry and biology are true. But their theoretical explanations based on particle physics and its forces are wrong. Chemical bonding in modern science, for example, is due to electromagnetic forces which results in electrovalent and covalent bonds. The bonding is due to *samāna* in Sāńkhya which divides and rearranges matter into logically distinct parts. So, we can loosely equate *samāna* with electromagnetism in this context. However, in a different context—e.g. within the atom—the force that adds vibrational modes to a silent drum is prāṇa rather than *samāna.* Present science describes the attraction between electrons and protons in the same way as the molecular bonding process, but these are actually different kinds of processes. The result is that both descriptions become flawed.

Chemical bonding studied in chemistry and the linearity of subatomic particles in atomic physics are both due to *samāna* and this has hence proven useful in science whereby the same force that makes up the subatomic particles linear also makes the chemical bonds. However, the process of *samāna* is not adequate to describe the processes of prāṇa (by which matter is added) or *apāna* (by which matter is removed). To address these problems, new forces are added, such as the strong and weak forces. Modern physics doesn't describe these forces as acting between a particle and a boundary. They are rather described as forces between particles. In that sense, the theories are quite different.

The "boundary" is also a particle, but it is a "higher" level particle. It is not that one particle participates in electromagnetic force while another particle will only experience the strong force. Rather, all particles can experience all kinds of forces—e.g. of ingestion, digestion, and elimination—and the difference is not based on particles but on the nature of the force. Sāńkhya thus has a theory of matter and force, but their conceptions are so different that we must either use different words or redefine the ideas in a completely new way.

The Study of a Single Atom

Once we understand the five forces in Sāńkhya, then we are better prepared to understand how to describe a single atom. As noted earlier, the atom is like a drum, and energy is added to a drum due to prāṇa and causes it to vibrate. The linearity of the different *modes* of vibration is *samāna*. Similarly, *udāna* is when a vibrational mode is cloned and externalized—e.g. when one drum causes another drum to vibrate due to what we call "resonance". The force called *apāna* is when we remove a vibrational mode from a drum, and *vyāna* is when this removed mode or the externalized mode is carried to another drum where it can be absorbed due to prāṇa (in the new drum).

The fact that something is ejected (*apāna*) or expressed (*udāna*) doesn't mean that it will automatically arrive at a destination. The process called *vyāna* takes the ejected or expressed symbol to a new drum. Similarly, the fact that such a symbol arrives at a system doesn't mean it will be absorbed. And if it is absorbed, it doesn't mean it would be digested (it could be eliminated too). In this way, there are varieties of *uncertainties* in nature, which are overcome by the forces. Each force overcomes a specific uncertainty and becomes necessary in nature.

In our case, the mind or *manas* is the drum; the prāṇa is the hand hitting the drum at some specific point or points, and the resulting sound that we hear is the body or the *vāk*. The drum, of course, is not necessarily a flat circular surface. It can be any three-dimensional surface. The form of this drum determines the various kinds of vibrations it can produce. However, unless the drum is hit, its existence is not perceivable (i.e. you cannot hear the drum) although the drum exists. In that sense, there is a reality but it has to be 'activated' for sensual perception. The process of activating is also the process of *selecting* some part of the possibility. So, the prāṇa is a force that activates, and it is also the *choice* of some specific activations.

The drum in question is just space. Different locations in space are individual drums. Prāṇa imparts energy at a location, which causes that location to vibrate and appear as a perceivable particle. In fact, when the energy is imparted, at least two drums (representing the particle-antiparticle pair) will be simultaneously activated. Each drum vibrates in a specific mode at a specific energy. Therefore, if the energy doesn't match the energy required for a specific mode, it would not be absorbed. The meaning of prāṇa is therefore that we provide what is required or what can be absorbed. Prāṇa is not just energy; it is that specific energy applied to a specific drum in order to make it vibrate in a specific manner. The specificity of the relation between the energy "packet" and the drum being vibrated is what we call prāṇa.

A Brief History of Wave-Particle Duality

Before the advent of modern quantum mechanics, Louis de Broglie had proposed a wave-particle duality in 1924. The basic purpose was to explain the fixed orbits of electrons that Bohr had previously envisioned. Louis de Broglie postulated that the fixed orbits were standing waves (comprised of two opposite waves) that carried the particles. This standing wave was called the *Pilot Wave* since it piloted the particle in space. The particle did not have energy; the energy was in the Pilot Wave.

This system works quite well—in fact, as well as modern quantum mechanics—but it was abandoned in favor of Schrödinger's Wave Mechanics in which there is no particle until you make a measurement, at which point the particle appears magically (the magic is called "collapse" of the wavefunction into a measurement alternative). Both systems are equally imperfect because it is a question of either admitting both particle and wave in a theory (as de Broglie did) or wave in the theory and particle in the experiment (as Schrödinger did). For aesthetical reasons, physicists thought that the wave-only model (in the theory) is superior to the wave-particle duality model that de Broglie had proposed, and de Broglie's model was abandoned in favor of the Wave Mechanics proposed by Schrödinger.

The real issue with de Broglie's approach is that in a complex system, there are many waves, which, according to the Principle of Superposition, must add up linearly. Once you add something linearly, you can also divide it linearly and the Superposition Principle allows you to divide the superposed state in many ways. In other words, you cannot insist that there is indeed one set of Pilot Waves that are piloting different particles because factually the system can be described using an alternative set of waves, without changing any of the particles. The wave thus becomes an addendum to the particles, and the explanation hinges on a particular choice of waves in a system.

This flaw exists even in modern quantum theory where the wavefunction can be expressed through many different *bases* which correspond to different *sets* of waves. The total energy of these waves, and the energies of the individual waves, remain the same. However, the *form* of the waves changes. Thus, the problem in both systems is that we require a method of wave selection. This method of wave selection—in addition to the particles—came to be later known as "local hidden variable theories" which were forbidden by Bell's Theorem.

In other words, de Broglie's approach has a problem, but the solution to that problem is theoretically forbidden (just like in Schrödinger's Mechanics).

I noted above that the person playing the drum applies a force, but also applies it at a location on the drum. This means that there is an energy being transmitted by the hand, but there is a specific point on which the hand hits the drum, which in turn constitutes the selection of the specific type of wave to be created. Therefore, where we hit and how hard we hit may be separate questions, but they have a single answer. Nobody plays the drum in which you first hit the drum and then try to define where it is to be hit. The energy and the location of the energy are decided at once in the same event. In that sense, we cannot *add* new variables into the system—as Bell's Theorem tells us—because there is only one variable that carries two kinds of information. We have to find how to enhance our variable to contain two parts.

Quantities vs. Qualities in Atomism

In current quantum theory, we can describe how hard to hit the drum but we cannot specify where to hit it. We can distinguish between the waves that are produced by a soft hit or a hard hit, but we cannot distinguish between hits in the middle of the drum versus its edge.

If you are playing the drum, each hit performs two functions—a choice of where to hit, and an energy transfer through the hit. But what do you do if the drum is so small that you don't know where it is being hit? Prāṇa addresses this problem because it is not just energy, but also a *choice* of target. *Prāṇa* carries the choices of consciousness, which means that it transfers choice and energy.

The difference between prāṇa and modern forces—e.g. a photon—is that the former has a specific target from the beginning, but the latter doesn't. An example of this fact is seen in cosmology where light is emitted by the Sun but it is not *meant* for a destination; whatever object falls in the "path" of the light happens to receive it. The same light, in Sāṅkhya, has both energy and a choice; it is meant for a destination, just like the hand which hits the drum is going to hit it at a specific location in order to produce a specific kind of vibration.

If you hit the drum at point A, then it produces a wave A, which is the word A. If instead, you hit the drum at point B, then it produces a wave B, which corresponds to the word B. So, now, we have two different kinds of words—A and B—produced by the same energy.

If the transactions are performed based on energy, then the difference between A and B would never be known. The situation is similar to drawing different letters using the same drop of ink. The size of the drop of ink only tells us whether the letter is big or small. It doesn't tell us what *symbol* the ink was used for. Similarly, the quantum of energy is a drop of ink, which can be used to write different letters. Which drop is used for which alphabet is unknown as we have no control over the so-called "microscopic" properties of matter. Our senses can't hit the drum at a specific place and cannot write a specific letter. We can only know how hard the drum was hit or how big the drop of ink was. We have no idea where the drum was hit and how the ink was used. In short, we know *quantities* rather than *qualities.*

We can see how we have come to the end of the road in physics where science was done using quantitative properties rather than qualities. The *quality* in this case is not some esoteric non-physical property. It is simply the waveform that has the same energy as many other waveforms. Likewise, it is the alphabet that consumes the same amount of ink as a lot of other alphabets. The energy is quantized, but just knowing that it is quantized doesn't tell us what that energy was used to symbolize or represent.

The Physical Interpretation of Waveforms

Quantum theory is incomplete because we are weighing different letters—A and B—by the amount of ink in them. If we understood that they were letters with font size, then we would know both quality and quantity. Therefore, we don't have to reject physical properties from the study of nature. We rather distinguish them as a letter and a font size. A letter has a font size, and these two properties cannot be divorced. In fact, we can say that the *manas* is the letter and the prāṇa is the font size. The resulting *vāk* is a combination of the letter and the font size.

Once the *vāk* has been created, we can physically measure it and convert everything into quantities. But the *vāk* was produced from *manas* and prāṇa which are not measurable: we cannot separately measure a letter without a font size, or a font size without an actual letter. That doesn't mean that the letter or the font size is not objective. It just means that they are objective and yet not perceivable.

According to quantum theory, all subatomic particles are just different waveforms. Quantum theory allows an infinite number of waveforms, so it is natural to ask how all such waveforms could be created from the first principles. To achieve this goal within the materialist paradigm, physicists postulate properties like mass, charge, color, flavor, etc. If the postulated property predicts a waveform not yet seen, scientists make attempts to "measure" these waveforms by bombarding particles with energy—i.e. hitting the drum harder and harder to hear a new sound. Since this drumbeating is random (we are not targeting a specific part of the drum), it is only a matter of time before you will detect every imaginable sound. When some such sounds are found, there is much euphoria about the advancement of science but the entire process is so naïve—once we adopt a semantic viewpoint—that it is surprising that we continue to spend so much time on it.

Recall that Schrödinger's Wave Mechanics evicted all particles from the picture (although de Broglie had particles before Schrödinger's mechanics). So, when particle physics talks about quantum particles, what is it really talking about? The short answer is that particle physics is trying to give these waveforms a physical interpretation—i.e. that the wave is an illusion and the particle is the reality—when according to Schrödinger's Wave Mechanics, the wave is the reality and particle doesn't exist. Mathematics says one thing and English another. According to the mathematics, particles are epiphenomena of waves. But in English, waves are epiphenomena of the particles.

The Semantic Interpretation of Waveforms

We cannot succeed in this manner, because there are zillions of waveforms that we haven't yet seen. The fact is that we are not even searching for these waveforms, because our theories have *conditioned* us into thinking that if we have found what our theory has predicted, then we don't need to look for anything that the theory hasn't predicted. This is the bias of a theory in which we stop looking for things that a theory doesn't predict and hence we don't find them. Furthermore, the sounds of a drum depend on the nature of the drum too, and all possible drums are not available to us. In so many ways, our descriptions of waveforms as indicating physical particles are wrong.

We have to move to a new way of describing waveforms in which the physical interpretation—called quarks and leptons—is an illusion. Rather, these waveforms are words, whose meaning is given in relation to another word—*higher* in space. The notion of higher and lower requires a hierarchical space, in which *distance* and *direction* are indicators of meaning. Each waveform will only occur at a specific location in space, so, even though we cannot know the waveform, we can know the location, and location becomes an indicator of meaning.

Quantum Meaning: A Semantic Interpretation of Quantum Theory—discusses this reinterpretation of *physical properties*. In effect, we discard material properties (e.g. mass, charge, color, flavor, etc.) and reinterpret waveforms as meanings. This requires one new theoretical construct—that of the hierarchical space-time—in which space and time are trees.

This is not merely an attempt to *reinterpret* the mathematical formalism of current quantum theory. It is rather the effort to interpret the formalism in a way that we can see its flaws and move towards a new theory of atomism in which both forces and objects are conceived around meanings. Such a description doesn't violate any predictions of current quantum theory. But it overcomes all its problems.

The Universe in a Lotus Stem

Published Date: 2017-05-08

One of the most enduring images in the Vedic scriptures is that of Lord Brahma sitting on a lotus the stem of which goes down to the navel of *Garbhodakaśāyī Viṣṇu*, who is also praised as *Hiranyagarbha*. The fourteen planetary systems in Vedic cosmology are described to reside inside the "stem" of this lotus, which is kind of perplexing because the universe is three-dimensional—and described as a sphere—but the lotus stem is one dimensional. How can we squeeze three dimensions into one dimension? This post discusses this question and shows how the three dimensions are reduced to one dimension by "twisting" the single dimension using a process like the "curved" flow of *kundalini.* The post discusses parallels between the body and the universe, the process of primary and secondary creations, and how these are connected to Sāṅkhya as well as the forms of Lord Viṣṇu who are "controllers" in the material universe.

Hierarchical Space is Curled

The material universe in Vedic philosophy is comprised of ideas; the table you touch, the food you eat, the flowers you smell, and the house you live in, are all ideas. All these ideas exist eternally in the universe as *possibilities* but sometimes they are converted into *actualities.* The conversion of the possibility into actuality involves adding some *energy* to the idea, in order to create a sound vibration or *word.* Accordingly, the idea is called *manas*, the energy is called *prāna*, and the word is called *vāk*.

These three ingredients are also classified according to the three modes of nature—*sattva*, *rajas*, and *tamas*—which respectively denote an *idea*, an *activity*, and an *object*. When we use this description to conceive of semantic space, space requires three dimensions, in which the vertical dimension represents *ideas* while the two horizontal dimensions represent *objects* and *activities*. But there are some peculiarities of this space due to which this three-dimensional space is not three-dimensional; it can rather be reduced to a single dimension.

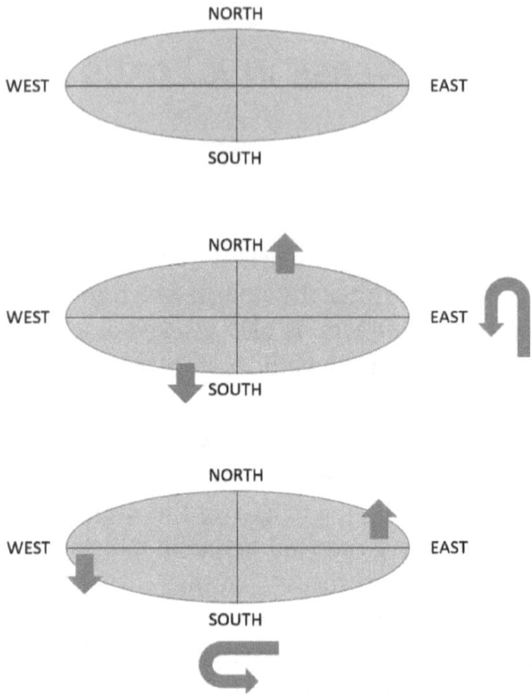

The main reason is that what we consider the "horizontal plane" is actually not horizontal. Rather, the plane is twisted along both East-West and North-South directions as shown above. The result of this twisting is that North is higher than South, and East is Higher than West. When we combine these two twists, we find that the four cardinal directions are not at the same level. Rather, North is the highest and South is the lowest; between North and South, are East and West, East being higher than West.

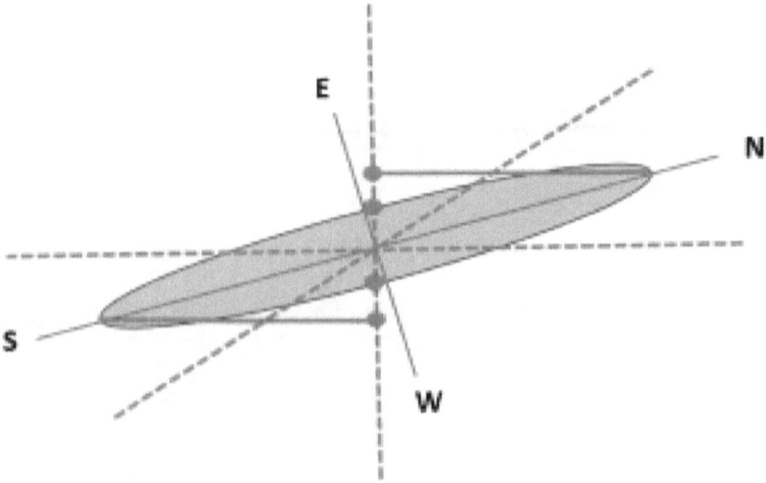

This fact can be seen in the above figure where the circle has been twisted in a way as to lift the North above South, and East above West. In the above figure, the blue color denotes the "horizontal plane" while the green color denotes how we see this "horizontal plane" from an actually horizontal perspective. When we project the four directions into the center, we can see how the four cardinal directions are actually hierarchically positioned along a central line with North at the top, followed by East, followed by West, and finally followed by South. The result of tilting the planar surface of four cardinal directions is that the four directions are not at the same level.

We can further understand the tilted structure, by removing the circular plane and drawing the cardinal directions as arrows jutting out of the center. The figure below illustrates the directions without a plane. With this picture, we can see that the four directions are not in a plane but arranged hierarchically, such that we can draw an "S" shaped curved path through them.

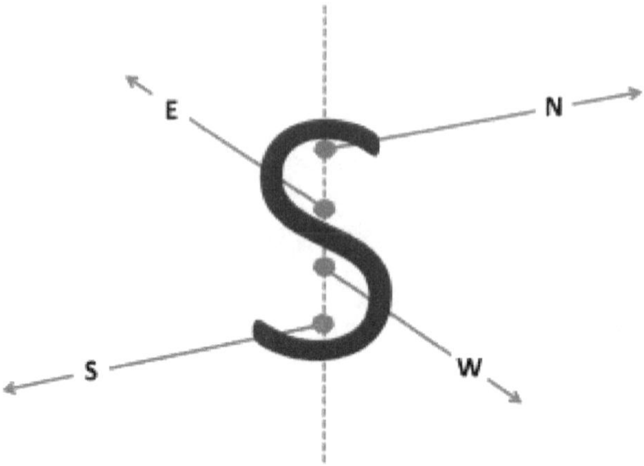

Conversely, if we exchanged the positions of East with West, and the position of North with South in the above picture, we can obtain a hierarchy in which South is highest, followed by West, East, and North. The figure below illustrates this.

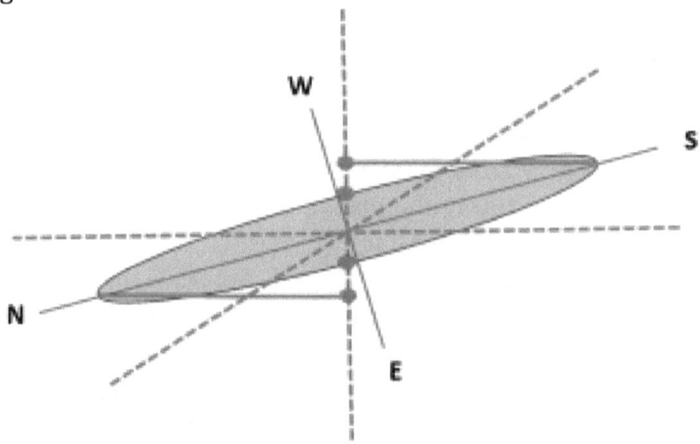

The interesting feature of this hierarchy is that it is exactly inverted to the first hierarchy. Therefore, if we drew a top-down path as North-East-West-South, then we can again draw a bottom-up path as North-East-West-South. This inverted bottom-up path is the mirror image of "S".

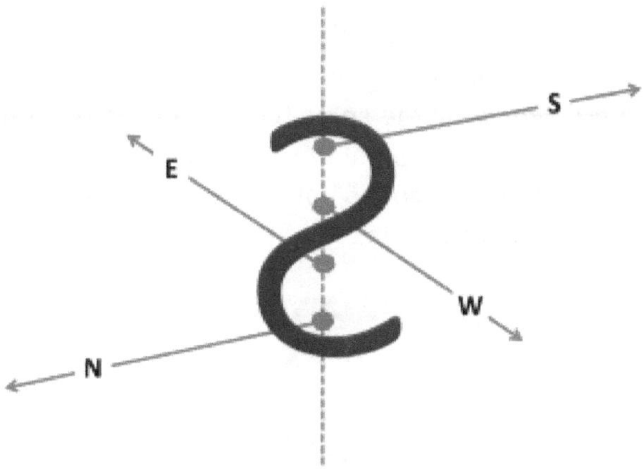

We can think of the two as paths that go from top to bottom, and from bottom to top. If we combine such paths over multiple levels, we will construct a top-down and bottom-up entwined path. There are many ways in which to think of such entwined paths, but the simplest way of thinking of them is as two opposite waves that can be combined to create a Stationary Wave. The entire vertical dimension can now be thought of as a vibrating string in which there are two waves: one that moves top-down, and the other that moves bottom-up.

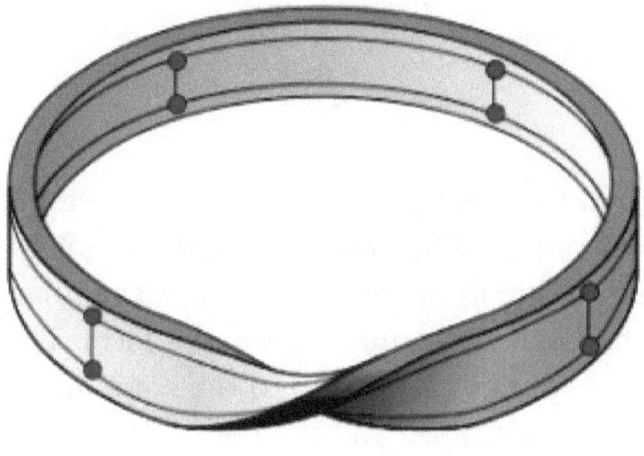

Ironically, both waves (top-down and bottom-up) are moving in the same order (North-East-West-South) but once they reach the end, the hierarchy is inverted and the path again moves in the same order (although in the opposite direction). This is an example of a Mobius Strip in which the path moves in a loop but at the end of each loop the directions are inverted.

Relation to the Yoga System

The bottom-up and top-down paths construct—at the level of the universe–what is called the *kundalini* in the body. The stem of the lotus is like the *Meru Danda* or the spinal cord which is one dimensional, but from it, a three-dimensional world is manifest because this single dimension is actually "coiled" or "curled". We can call this single dimension a "curled dimension".

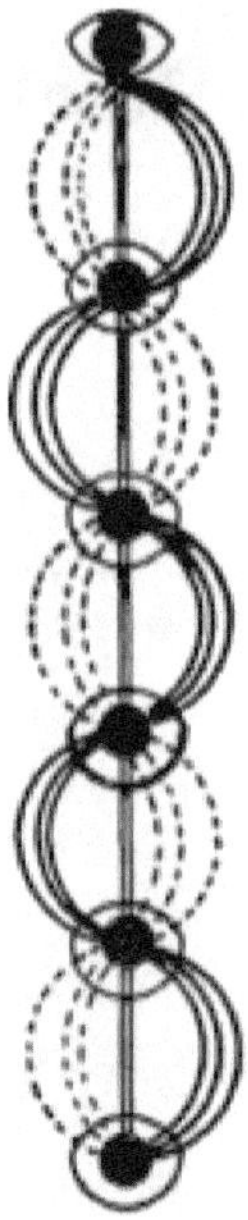

The central column helps us compare the universe to a living body and grasp the meaning of "universe in a lotus stem". In the below figure of the seven *chakra* in the body, the central column and the crown at the top of the head construct a lotus-like form. The lotus and the stem in the body are like the lotus and the stem in the universe. The lotus represents *mahattattva* and the body of Lord Brahma is constituted of *mahattattva* or moral principles—also called *dharma*. This *dharma* has four directions—East, West, North, and South—and the four Vedas (Rig-Veda, Sāma-Veda, Yajur-Veda, and Atharva-Veda) are uttered by the four "mouths" of Lord Brahma facing the four sides.

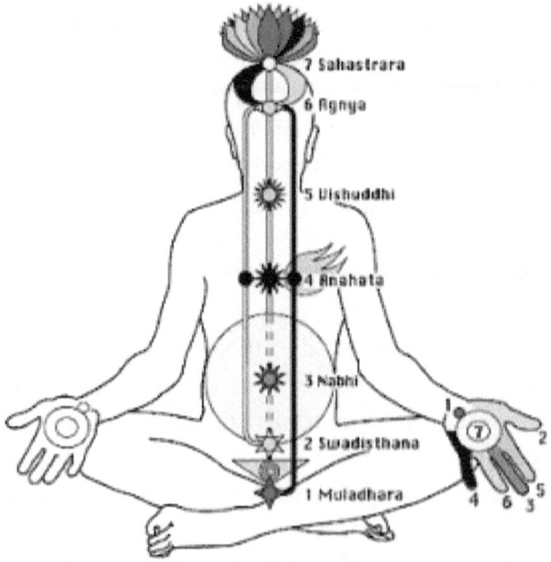

THE SUBTLE SYSTEM

If we exclude the lotus from this stem and the lotus form, we are left with the six *chakras* as shown in the figure above. Through these chakras, the energy alternates from one side to another. This alternating energy has two parts: (1) a right-handed part that moves anticlockwise and upwards, and (2) a left-handed part that moves clockwise and downward. The right-handed path is like unscrewing a screw and is called *pingalā* in the human body. The left-handed path is like screwing the screw and is called *idā* in the human body. The downward path is creativity where an abstract idea is converted into details, while the upward path is cognition where details are merged into an abstract idea. Thus, when the universe is created, it is top-down. When the universe is annihilated it is bottom-up.

Generally, the *idā* and *pingalā* are alternating energies, which means that creation and destruction are also alternating movements. The process of *yoga* is to make the energy flow in both *idā* and *pingalā* simultaneously which causes the *sushumnā* to be awakened, and this is called the awakening of the *kundalini* in the *Aśtanga-Yoga* system. The key point is that a person who has transcended the creation and annihilation movements is not part of the material universe's cyclic transformations.

The Creation and Destruction of the Universe

We have discussed above that matter exists in an unmanifest form called *manas*. When energy is added to it, a vibrating sound is produced. This vibrating sound is generally studied as a Standing Wave, which comprises two opposite waves. These opposing waves represent desiring and deserving, the two conditions required to perceive anything. Due to deserving, something becomes accessible for perception. But due to desire, we can choose not to access it. Perceptions are the combination of desiring and deserving.

In the same way, the entire universe can be understood as existing in an unmanifest form inside the stem of the lotus; in this state, the universe can be called *manas*. When energy flows inside this stem top-down, the universe is created through a creative process called *idā*. When energy flows inside this stem bottom-up, the universe is destroyed through a destructive process called *pingalā*. In Vedic cosmology, this top-down flow of energy is described as the flow of "water" from the top of the universe, which trickles down to the bottom in the *Garbhodaka Ocean*; the water is said to originate from outside the universe in the *Karana Ocean*. Similarly, the Vedic texts describe that at the time of destruction, a massive "fire" arises from the bottom of the universe which destroys the universe and the lower planets merge into the higher planets, everything finally merges into the body of Lord Brahma, who then along with *mahattattva* merges into the body of *Karanodakaśāyī Viṣṇu*.

The *idā* is compared to the moon or water, while the *pingalā* is compared to the sun or fire. Thus the top-down flow of water is the creative process, and the fire from the bottom to the top is the destructive process. In this way, the alternating flow of water and fire represents alternating creation and destruction. The process is just as *idā* and *pingalā* alternate in the body.

Primary and Secondary Creations

Vedic texts describe that the universe is created in two parts—primary and secondary. The primary creation comprises of the creation of all material elements—i.e. sense objects, sensations, senses, mind, intellect, ego, and morality. The secondary creation is that of different planets, species, living beings, etc. The primary creation is performed by Lord Viṣṇu, while the secondary creation is so done by Lord Brahma. These two types of creation can now be better exemplified through the above understanding.

The primary creation is the creation of the perfect sense objects, sensations, senses, mind, intellect, ego, and morality, and can be said to constitute the *sushumnā* which flows at the center and independent of the *idā* and *pingalā* from bottom to top. The rising energy constitutes the "ascending process" of development in which nature is created from visceral to abstract, by adding higher and higher levels of organization. In other words, first, there is a form that would appear as a self-sufficient independent object. The universe cannot be created from such independent objects, so the first organizing principle is created which can organize these independent objects. This principle is also atomic and appears as an independent object. However, since the principle is inadequate, the second organizing principle is created to organize the first organizing principle. This is a bottom-up creation and is carried out by *Garbhodakaśāyī Viṣṇu* which is why the lotus grows from His "navel" upward. In this creation, many kinds of independent objects are created which are useful to *organize* at higher levels.

The bottom-up creative model is similar to the present scientific conception of creation. For example, modern science thinks that after the Big Bang, there was a soup of atomic particles which then randomly aggregated into complex atoms, which then formed molecules, which then became unicellular living beings, then onto multicellular beings, which then acquired brain, thinking ability, and ultimately moral principles and religiosity. The process of *Garbhodakaśāyī Viṣṇu* creating the stem is not different except that the stages in this creation are not random. The creation is indeed bottoms up, but each stage in this creation involves the production of a new kind of organizing principle.

All these organizing principles exist originally as a form of Lord Viṣṇu. When a *yogi* is enlightened, and energy flows through the *sushumnā*, he can see the original process of creation in elemental form, or how *Garbhodakaśāyī Viṣṇu* had created the universe—i.e. the organizing principles. All these organizing principles appear as different "controllers" in the universe. Their "control" is not like our control because they are the *principle* of a specific kind of control, while we are *instances* of principle. In that sense, all these other controllers are manifest from the original principle, and therefore the original principle is called the Supreme Controller or *Īśvara*. An enlightened *yogi* sees the *principles* of control, thereby understanding the science of how nature is controlled—i.e. organized into a systematic structure.

The creation of all these principles—along the central *sushumnā*—constitutes the *primary creation*. It flows from bottom to top, manifesting higher and higher organizing principles, until the highest organizing principle of morality or *dharma* is manifest. The first instance of this principle is Lord Brahma, and when Lord Brahma has been created, the primary creation has now come to an end. Hereafter, the *secondary creation* begins which involves Lord Brahma creating the individual living entities, planetary systems, social models, and various other things top-down—*employing* the previously created principles. In other words, the primary creation is that of principles or organization, while the secondary creation is the *application* of these principles to produce various kinds of organization.

Unlike the bottom-up process carried out by *Garbhodakaśāyī Viṣṇu* which constitutes the *sushumnā*, the top-down process by Lord Brahma constitutes the *idā*. Finally, when there is time to destroy the universe, *Saṅkarṣaṇa* emits a fire that rises bottom-up and engulfs all secondary creations. The primary creations still remain intact, which means the organizing principle is still present as "ideas" but they are not being applied to create organized systems. In the Vedic texts,

Garbhodakaśāyī Viṣṇu is called the "maintainer" because He produces the principles or the science of how to organize. He is therefore the reason why the universe appears to be organized. Lord Brahma is the "creator" because he applies these principles to create structure and organization. Finally, Lord *Saṅkarṣaṇa*—also sometimes called Lord Shiva—becomes the destroyer. The maintainer and the destroyer are acting bottom-up while the creator acts top-down.

Mythical or Mystical?

Vedic texts appear mythical at first glance. But they are actually comprised of a model of organization, a science of the principles of organization, and a philosophy of nature, consciousness, and God. At the simplest level, we can try to comprehend the model—e.g. that the entire universe exists inside the stem of a lotus-like structure. Then we can understand how the three dimensions can be reduced to a single *twisted* dimension. That twisted dimension helps us see the similarity to the yogic model of the body, which opens the door to a synergistic understanding of the universe as a body and the body as a universe. So far, we are in the domain of models—the body and the universe.

Beyond this, lies the science of the organizing principles of nature—which are amply described in Sāṅkhya as constituting different levels of hierarchical organization. All these principles can be applied repeatedly which means they exist in atomic form, and their repeated application implies the combination of atoms. The combination is created by the next higher principle so, at each level of organization, a new order is created. All this process of organizing—and the organizing principles or forms of Lord Viṣṇu—constitutes science. Beyond this science is the philosophy of consciousness, how it has a meaning and pleasure-seeking ability, although that ability is covered by illusion due to which the universe is created as truths and illusions, pleasures and pains. This constitutes the philosophy of life.

If one is patient, it is possible to gradually proceed through models, science, and philosophy in order to understand the profound knowledge found in Vedic texts.

The Philosophy of Masculine and Feminine

Published Date: 2017-05-10

Introduction and Overview

A soul has three tendencies called *sat* (consciousness), *chit* (meaning), and *ananda* (pleasure), and its choices draw a compromise between meaning and pleasure. The original *sat-chit-ananda* Absolute Truth creates five forms—*Kṛṣṇa, Rāma, Hara, Ramā,* and *Jīvā*, called the *pañca-tattva* or five categories. Two of these are masculine (*Kṛṣṇa* and *Rāma*) while the other two are feminine (*Hara* and *Ramā*). Each masculine form is paired with a feminine form.

The form of *Kṛṣṇa* and *Hara* are the subject and object of pleasure, while the forms of *Rāma* and *Ramā* are the subject and object of meaning. In this article, I will use these descriptions to outline a philosophical view of feminine and masculine. It is noteworthy that masculine and feminine are not just material bodies in Vedic philosophy; they are spiritual archetypes or forms. This philosophical understanding can then be used to discern the basis of gender roles in society, and why some modern roles (for both men and women) are rejected.

Masculine-Feminine vs. Male-Female

Given that the soul has a choice between prioritizing either meaning or pleasure, in Vedic philosophy, *masculine* is defined as the preference for meaning, while the *feminine* is defined as the preference for pleasure. The person in pursuit of meaning seeks higher and more abstract ideas—ultimately culminating in one or more of the six original ideas of knowledge, beauty, renunciation, power, fame, and wealth. The person in pursuit of pleasure, instead, seeks pure and unalloyed relationships, in one of the six original forms as relation to the self, and to others as reverence, servitude, friendship, parental affection, and conjugal love. Accordingly, the pursuit of the six original qualities (knowledge, beauty, renunciation, power, fame, and wealth) is defined to be masculine, while the pursuit of the six original relationships (to the self, and to others as reverence, servitude, friendship, parental affection, and conjugal love) is defined as feminine.

The terms *masculine* and *feminine* are somewhat different than the terms *male* and *female.* The definition of the *male* is a *subject* who seeks meaning or pleasure, while the *female* is an *object* who is sought as meaning or pleasure. Thus, the *male* is the seeker or the pursuer of meaning and pleasure, while the *female* is defined as the sought or the object of these pursuits.

According to these differences, *Kṛṣṇa* is a *feminine-male*—He is the seeker of pleasure; as the seeker, He is male, but due to the preference for pleasure, He is feminine. Conversely, *Rāma* is a *masculine-male*—He is the seeker of knowledge; as the seeker He is male, and due to the preference for meaning, He is masculine. Similarly, *Hara* is the *feminine-female*—She is the ultimate object of the quest for pleasure; we can say that She is the pleasure sought; as the sought, She is female, and due to the preference for pleasure, She is feminine. Conversely, *Ramā* is *masculine-female*—She is the object of the quest for meaning; we can say that She is the meaning sought; as the sought, She is female, although due to the preference for meaning, She is masculine. The four original forms are summarized in the below table.

	Masculine	Feminine
Male	Rāma	Kṛṣṇa
Female	Ramā	Hara

Manifestations of the Original Forms

We can see many typical examples of the above four original forms in the present world too.

- By conventional definitions, a man is a "masculine-male", which means that he is predominantly inclined towards the quest for meanings—knowledge, power, wealth, fame, splendor, and renunciation. Such a man is honorable, responsible, intelligent, diligent, powerful, disciplined, moral, and reliable. In most cases, he is also boring, aloof, uptight, abstract, serious, introverted, and irritable. He takes care of his family but is not amiable or fun-loving.
- Conversely, there is also a "feminine-male" who is irresponsible, disorganized, and unambitious, who seeks

thrill instead of meaning, who is humorous, delectable, out-going, extroverted, and joyful. He is likely an artist, a musician, or a writer, who can't be pinned down into a place or relationship; he roams and explores the world, seeking excitement and love. He won't have a steady job or a profession. He does whatever pleases him.

- In most literary descriptions, a "woman" is a "feminine-female"—mysterious and seductive, she seeks risky and dangerous situations to find pleasure. She loves with great passion, but she cannot be possessed; she looks for the thrill, excitement, adventure, and fun, and doesn't want to be bogged down by pragmatic questions of livelihood, responsibility, discipline, and reliability. She is the ultimate erotic object, or what is ordinarily known as *femme-fatale.*
- Conversely, there is a "masculine-female" who people call the "girl next door". She is shy, quiet, peaceful, dutiful, responsible, respectful, organized, and disciplined. She will love deeply, but it won't be passionate; she will tolerate difficulties for her family demonstrating patience and forbearance; she will seek home and hearth, health and security; most times she would be well-educated and well-read; she will not be worldly, because she is worldly-wise.

The above are cardinal examples of the original male and female forms. The "girl next door" is the representation of *Ramā*—the consort of *Rāma*—who makes the ultimate dutiful wife, the most responsible mother, and a partner for good and bad times. The *femme-fatale* is the representation of *Hara*—the lover of *Kṛṣṇa*—who is the personification of erotic pleasure, exploration, and adventure. Similarly, the "mature and responsible man" is the representation of *Rāma* who seeks knowledge, power, wealth, and transcendence; he makes a responsible father and husband but is not humorous, fun-loving, or outgoing; he would most likely be a bad singer or dancer! Finally, the "artistic and passionate man" is the representation of *Kṛṣṇa* who leads a carefree life of abandon; he has many friends and girlfriends, but no dedicated profession, and does whatever he feels like.

The Union of Male and Female

I noted above that the male and female are like subject and object; since this is not an easy idea, I will try to illustrate this now in a better way. In a previous article, I described how the material world is comprised of sounds which can be described as the music produced from the act of playing an instrument. The original male and female forms are like the player and the instrument, respectively. The player is the *male* and the instrument is the *female*. The instrument is the possibility of any kind of sound and She exists in an unmanifest form—i.e. unknowable—until the instrument is played. The player is also the possibility of playing any kind of sound, and He too exists in an unmanifest form—i.e. unknowable—until He plays the instrument. The union of the male and female is when the instrument is played. The "children" produced from such a union are the sounds that we admire as musical compositions.

The instrument is generally not the instigator of music; the desire to play originates in the player, although the player is often excited into playing just by looking at an instrument. In this way, the male generally pursues the female, although the female can also attract the male. The male is, however, in a superior position, because the final act of playing has to come from the player and not the instrument. The instrument can attract and inspire the player, but the choices of playing are in the male. In that sense, the player is superior and the instrument is inferior, although they are also complementary because the music is a combination of the instrument and the player. The desires of the player cannot be fulfilled without an instrument and the instrument cannot be complete if it is never played.

The male and the female, therefore, have desires, but of different kinds. The female desire is to be used or played in a certain way, and the male desire is to use or play in a certain way. They are both incomplete without the other, and they crave a union in order to complete themselves. In many Vedic texts, therefore, the male and the female are described as the *creator* and the *creatrix* who combine to produce a *creation*. The combination is like that of a player and an instrument to create music.

In Vedic philosophy, there are innumerable forms of male God always accompanied by a female Goddess. The male is always the player and the female is always the played. The choice of the female is to define the limits on what is possible; for example, the form of the instrument defines what kinds of sounds can *potentially* be produced. The choice of the male is to pick from what is available; for example, the choice of the player defines the played sounds. Because the female sets the bounds on what can be chosen, the female is sometimes said to be superior to the male. Similarly, because the male chooses from among the available options, the male is said to be the decision-maker.

Both the male and female are actually decision-makers, although in completely different ways. The female decides the menu, and the male decides what to eat. The male cannot ask for what is outside the menu, and the female cannot stop the male from choosing what is within the menu. In the spiritual world, the male and the female are closely matched, which means that the female makes a menu that has exactly those things that the male relishes; they are thus unified in their intent and purpose. In the material world, there is great discord because the desires are outside the menu, or the menu is not exactly desirable.

The Archetypes of Consciousness

The essence of the personalist philosophy is that consciousness has *form*—i.e. it has the properties of masculine and feminine, male and female. The essence of impersonal philosophy is that consciousness has no form—i.e. it has no properties. Vedic personalist philosophy manifests itself into the above four archetypes of *Kṛṣṇa, Hara, Rāma,* and *Ramā*. These four archetypes are the "original forms" of meaning and pleasure, from which all other meanings and pleasures are created. In the *pañca-tattva* philosophy, these archetypes are the four forms called *Chaitanya, Nityānanda, Advaita,* and *Gadādhara*.

The soul is situated among the four archetypes but has the option to emulate any one of them. Some souls choose to emulate *Kṛṣṇa* and become "artistic and passionate men". Some other souls decide to emulate *Rāma* and become the "mature and responsible men". Some souls find the archetype of the "girl next door" very attractive and they like to emulate *Ramā*. Finally, there are souls who find the archetype of *femme-fatale* very attractive and they are inclined to emulate *Hara*.

In *Vaishnava* philosophy, these four archetypes are the only unique and distinctive forms; every other form—man or woman, masculine or feminine—is produced from these archetypes. For example, there can be men who are responsible in their careers but also seek thrill through women or sport. Similarly, there can be women who secretly seek thrill, excitement, and seduction, but overtly appear to be shy, dutiful, and responsible. The archetypes are therefore not mutually exclusive; rather, the soul has the choice to emulate and follow them in different ways. The important point is that the soul cannot create a new or original archetype apart from *Kṛṣṇa*, *Hara*, *Rāma*, and *Ramā*.

Austerity – The Ideal in the Material World

One of the key ideas in Vedic philosophy is that while the soul has the capacity and freedom to prioritize between meaning and pleasure, in the material world the natural preference is for meanings over pleasures whereas in the spiritual realm the natural preference is for pleasures over meanings.

In both cases, *choices* are involved, which means free will always exists. However, the material world is described as a temporary place in which the quest for pleasure with abandon only leads to misery and suffering. One is thus advised to exercise great restraints in the enjoyment of pleasure. There are, conversely, far fewer restraints on the pursuit of meaning in the material world; the general guideline provided by Vedic texts is that knowledge and renunciation are the most important meanings; all other meanings are acceptable so long as they serve the purpose of knowledge and renunciation.

In other words, the archetypes of *femme-fatale* and the "fun-loving lover" are summarily rejected in the material world. Quite notably, these two archetypes are the highest forms in the spiritual realm. This distinction is articulated in the Vaishnava philosophy by describing two forms of *bhakti*—*vaidi* and *ragānugā*. The *vaidi-bhakti* is a life in which men are the "boring, intelligent, and responsible caretakers of family and society" while the women are the "girl next door"—i.e. quiet, shy, tolerant, forbearing, unassuming, responsible mothers and wives dedicated to their family. Conversely, in the *ragānugā-bhakti*, the men are the playful fun-loving explorers, while women are the demanding, entitled, assertive, risk-taking, mysterious, and seductive embodiments of passion and love.

It is noteworthy that the archetypes of the "playful explorer" and the "mysterious seductress" are not always rejected; indeed, they are described in Vedic texts as the highest form of spiritual existence. They are, however, forbidden during material existence—also called the practice of *vaidi* or "disciplined" life.

The meaning of *vaidi* is "according to rules and regulations" and it embodies a life that pursues meaning over pleasure. The reason is that each soul has an eternal form of meaning (the six qualities described above) which has to be discovered through a regulated process before the soul can engage in a life of playful abandon. The regulated life is, however, not eternal; rather, the life of playful abandonment is eternal. Nevertheless, the regulated life has to be practiced in order to discover one's form of meaning, before this form can participate in roles or relationships that involve the exchanges of playful abandonment.

The Divine Origin of Gender Roles

The traditional gender roles—for both men and women—come from the strictures of *vaidi-bhakti*. They are, in fact, emulations of *Rāma* and *Ramā* or Viṣṇu and Lakshmi. While it is quite possible that men can be "fun-loving lovers" and women can be *femme-fatales*, this life of careless enjoyment is rejected in *vaidi-bhakti* unless one discovers their true forms of meaning. Owing to this fact, society is expected to be designed in such a way that all men are "boring, intelligent, and responsible caretakers" and the women are "dedicated, forbearing, plain Janes". This is the life of austerity and simplicity designed to cleanse a person of the varieties of ill-conceived relationships for false enjoyment.

Many people suppose that the traditional gender roles are designed to favor men and that they were produced due to patriarchal societies. This idea is flawed because the man and woman in the material world are asked to emulate Lord Viṣṇu and Mother Lakshmi—God and Goddess. Their choices, as we have seen above, are different: the female is free to define the limits on the male's possibilities, while a male is free to choose from among the available alternatives. Thus, a female binds a male with a limited menu, and a male binds a female by asking her to provide whatever he chooses in the menu. The affection or love between them is that the male will not want to breach the boundaries that the female has set, and the female will not try to deny the male what he wants to be on the menu.

The divine relationship becomes materially polluted when this love is lost. In such a situation, the woman becomes a dominating controller who tries to limit the options and choices of the man to a point that the man becomes dissatisfied. The man then breaches the bounds set by the woman and seeks another woman who can fulfill his desires. Alternately, a man may try to obtain from a woman what the woman cannot provide, and this inability to make the man happy may force the woman to seek another man who appreciates what she can provide much better. These frustrated alternatives between a man and a woman are barely the glimmers of the original male-female divinity.

The Process of Spiritual Advancement

The world is created from ideas with the original idea being the most abstract. In this origin, the female is the limit on everything that is possible because that is all that She will allow, while the male is the limits on everything that He wants to choose, and therefore has the desire for. These original forms are not just higher, they are also the "biggest" forms—size being defined semantically rather than physically. In the semantic notion, the form of "knowledge itself", "beauty itself", "glory itself", "power itself", etc. are the highest and the biggest ideas; every other idea is a limited possibility within it.

Spiritual perfection for both men and women is to get as close as possible to the divine couple—e.g. Lakshmi and Viṣṇu. For a woman, the proximity to Lakshmi means that she tries to stretch the limits of possibilities—as she stretches these limits, she comes closer to Lakshmi who is the fullness of all the possibilities. Similarly, the man tries his level best to elevate his desires from narrow parochial ideas to higher and broader cravings—culminating in "knowledge itself", "beauty itself", "glory itself", etc. and in broadening he comes closer to Viṣṇu.

The affection between a male and a female is that the female tries to fulfill all of the male desires, while the male never breaches the bounds defined by the female. As a male raises his desires to original ideas, the female becomes the instrument of realizing these desires. But if the female is incapable of fulfilling the desire, the male gives up such desires. Recall that the male and the female are like the player and the instrument; they advance when the player wants the original sound, and the instrument expands to produce the new kind of sound. But if the instrument cannot produce the expected sound (e.g. we cannot expect a drum to produce the sounds of a wind or string instrument), then the player withdraws the expectations of such sounds. This is the principle of divine partnership. While men and women can never become God and Goddess, by emulating Lord Viṣṇu and Mother Lakshmi, both men and women can realize their original forms.

The feminist idea that women have been forced to serve men due to a patriarchal society is ignorant about the philosophical underpinnings of the conventional roles in which a man and woman are expected to play the transcendental archetypes of Viṣṇu and Lakshmi, whereby the marital relationship between man and woman is a reflection of the transcendental relationship between the Eternal Couple.

Enlightenment via Marriage

The idea underlying the marital arrangement—with the traditional gender roles—is that the temporary matrimony between man and woman itself can become eternal through a loving bond between husband and wife. When a man dies, and he has been purified, he will transfer to the *Vaikunṭha* planets in a form similar to that of Lord Viṣṇu, while his wife (assuming she has also been purified) will also similarly transfer to *Vaikunṭha* in a form similar to Lakshmi. If one of the two is not purified, they will take birth again as husband and wife and assist each other's spiritual advancement. The traditional gender roles have thus a profound basis in spiritual archetypes due to which men and women will continuously follow each other—life after life—until they liberate each other into *Vaikunṭha*.

We should therefore understand that the traditional gender roles are not about which gender is in a greater position of power, nor are they subject to whimsical adjustment in time or place. Rather, the conventional gender roles are due to the fact that in the material world men and women are expected to emulate the archetypes of Viṣṇu and Lakshmi or *Rāma* and *Ramā*—rather than the archetypes of *Kṛṣṇa* and *Hara*. The strictures of gender roles are designed to take a person to the point of liberation where they know their true form of meaning—i.e. their inclination and capacity towards the six qualities.

Marriage is thus not a material bond. It is meant to be a divine and eternal relationship and is expected to be made into one. As the man and woman try to emulate Viṣṇu and Lakshmi, all false notions of pleasure are removed, and one sees oneself as that thing-in-itself. Such a state is called *mukti* or liberation. Once a person is liberated, and they have seen their form or the thing-in-itself that they are, then they would be transferred out of the material world into the realm called Vaikunṭha. Once the soul is enlightened about its true form, then he or she can seek relationships of pleasure. Through such relationships, one can now begin to emulate the archetypes of *Kṛṣṇa* and *Hara* if he or she wants. The road to that destination, however, passes through *vaidi-bhakti*—i.e. traditional gender roles.

Men Are From Sun, Women Are From Moon

Published Date: 2017-05-11

Introduction and Overview

"Men are from Mars, Women are from Venus," says that bestseller book from John Gray. This book has become a classic, although it stereotypes both men and women, disregarding the fact that each person has both masculine and feminine tendencies in them to varying degrees. We can clearly speak about the masculine and feminine as ideas, concepts, or archetypes, but we cannot speak of ordinary people as purely feminine or masculine.

This article extends the previous one (where I described masculine and feminine as archetypes of consciousness in Vaishnavism) into *yoga* philosophy where the masculine and feminine are combined to produce a human body—the masculine being the upward flow called *pingalā* (also called the sun) and the feminine being the downward flow called *idā* (also called the moon).

This gives a scientific orientation to the gender debate. But more importantly, *yoga* philosophy teaches us that we are not men or women; to extricate ourselves from the false sense of manhood or womanhood, we have to combine the opposing tendencies in a very specific sense. That specific sense represents the simultaneous quest for knowledge and devotion.

Gender in the Human Body

Let's begin with the fundamental basis of everything—consciousness—which is described in Vedic texts as *sat* (consciousness), *chit* (meaning), and *ananda* (pleasure). The soul's choice is whether it prefers meaning over pleasure, or pleasure over meaning. For example, if you are working to solve the problems of world hunger and disease, you might have to undergo many hardships, but you would accept them simply because you prioritize meaning over pleasure.

Conversely, when you lie to a friend about an uncomfortable fact because the fact might affect your relationship with them, you prioritize pleasure over meaning. Each person has personal priorities—sometimes you prefer meaning over pleasure, and at other times pleasure over meaning—which change many times during a day.

This fact is described in *yoga* philosophy as the upward and downward flow of energy called *pingalā* and *idā*, which I will briefly describe now. In the human body, the *chit* or meaning-seeking tendency is present in the head, while *ananda* or the pleasure-seeking tendency is present in the groin. For the most part, most people have a predominant pleasure-seeking tendency, which means that their consciousness is in the groin. As their consciousness drifts towards meaning, it shifts into the head.

Accordingly, there are two paths in the human body. The top-down path involves going from meaning to pleasure—i.e. prioritizing pleasure over meaning—which is called *idā*. Similarly, there is also a bottom-up path that involves going from pleasure toward meaning—i.e. prioritizing meaning over pleasure—which is called *pingalā*. The top-down path, or the pleasure-prioritizing path, is called the *feminine* tendency. Similarly, the bottom-up path, or the meaning prioritizing path, is called the *masculine* tendency. It is worth noting that "feminine", "masculine", "male" and "female" are technical terms with a spiritual origin as discussed in the previous article. These have no relation to "man" and "woman", which are words I will reserve for describing the body types as we see them in the present world. They are summarized succinctly below for ease of understanding

Masculine = Meaning
Feminine = Pleasure
Male = Seeker
Female = Sought

The Autonomous Working of the Body

It's also important to realize that *idā* and *pingalā* exist inside all human bodies—both man and woman—because the search for meaning and pleasure is originally a property of the soul, later incorporated into the material body. The soul, however, has the choice to *prioritize* between meaning and pleasure. All of us have been making these priority calls over many lifetimes, due to which they have now become *habits*. That is, these calls are often made automatically without even a conscious intervention by the soul. The autonomous working of the body is now well-known; this operation is effected through the *Autonomous Nervous System* in the spinal cord. The *yoga* philosophy doesn't contradict this fact, but it gives it a new kind of meaning: the autonomous working is due to past habits due to which sometimes the energy is dominantly flowing downwards prioritizing pleasure over meaning, while it is at other times dominantly flowing upwards thereby prioritizing meaning over pleasure.

As long as only the upward or the downward flow is present, the operation is autonomous and doesn't involve conscious intervention. The problem bubbles up for executive decision by the soul when there is a conflict—i.e. both upward and downward tendencies are contending for superiority. The soul now gets involved to resolve this contention and make a priority call, which then aids in the formation of a new habit, which then works autonomously until the next contentious situation arises.

The material world is described in Sāṅkhya as the world of opposites or duality. This means that contention is the rule rather than the exception. You might have a preference for pleasure over meaning, but you realize that sometimes neglecting meaning can cause pain. For example, if you are too lazy, then you might lose your job, which would then take away many pleasures. Therefore, while laziness might seem pleasurable, you realize that rejecting it is important even to maintain some of the pleasures. As situations change, the preference for meaning or pleasure also changes automatically because there are predefined rules—i.e. habits—that automatically trigger a reaction.

Why Humans Are Superior to Animals

Animals are inferior to humans because their habits are so strong that all contentions are automatically resolved by previously formed habits without significant conscious intervention. The dominant habit in all animals is to seek pleasure. When they appear to be involved in altruistic activity—e.g. loving their children, or protecting the herd—it is not because of a fundamental sense of purpose by which a living entity wants to connect their lives to the purpose of the universe. It is simply an instinct to avoid pain and increase pleasure. Altruism—or the quest for meaning—dominates in humans.

The autonomous nervous system in animals therefore mostly

works independently of the soul, and very rarely it might bubble up a decision or two for the soul to make. In humans, there is far greater potential for conscious intervention because the habits are more or less equally balanced. That is, humanity is defined by its growing need for meaning, as opposed to the need for pleasure that already exists in animals. As the meaning component gains prominence over the pleasure tendency, a natural contention between the two is created. The contention creates a problem that has to be solved through explicit intervention by the soul. As the soul gets more and more involved in such decisions it realizes that there is actually a choice. As the soul recognizes the choice, it comes to the conclusion that it is different from the autonomous working of the body—and hence separate from the body.

The realization that the soul is different from the body arises due to contention, which emerges when a person has habits of pursuing meaning over pleasure. This is the primary reason that spiritual advancement cannot happen unless one asks about the questions of meaning in life. It is also the reason why I have focused much of my work on the question of meaning in science. Unless we start seeking meaning, there would be no contention with pleasure. And if there is no contentious issue, then consciousness has nothing to deliberate on. If there is nothing to deliberate, then the soul considers itself the material body. And when that belief is prominent, one descends into animal life.

Autonomous Operation and Choice

This was a worthy deviation to take while discussing gender roles because it helps us see how humans too are hard-wired to behave in certain ways—preferring either meaning or pleasure most of the time. While the relative proportions can vary at different times, most men and women are not *consciously* making preferential choices of meaning or pleasure most of the time. The perfection of life is when automation is destroyed and every decision is bubbled up for executive approval by the soul. That is when human being becomes perfectly aware of everything that is going on in their lives. The Vedic scriptures thus exhort the soul to "wake up, rise and be aware of everything" because the soul is in fact sleeping most of the time, rarely making a decision, and letting life run in autopilot mode.

The feminine and the masculine should not be seen as two material bodies. They should be seen as two tendencies in the body—upward and downward—which are always contentious. The battle of sexes is actually a battle inside us, and this is a good battle because it forces conscious intervention. Thus, there is an unconscious part of the body and mind which works autonomously and there is a conscious part of the body and mind which involves choices. The unconscious becomes the conscious when there is a conflict. Most people abhor these conflicts and mock people who are always thinking about what is right and wrong. They might urge them to just make a decision and move on with their life. However, we must note that these conflicts are the turning points in life where every decision is very important.

The Dominance of Masculine and Feminine Traits

Many women have a stronger *idā*—i.e. a preference for pleasure over meaning—which drives them towards thrill-seeking, or the tendency to be a *femme-fatale*. Conversely, many women have stronger *pingalā*—i.e. a greater preference for duty and responsibility—which drives them towards a dutiful, organized, and responsible life, or what we term the "girl next door" behavior. The *femme-fatale* is boisterous, demanding, entitled, and fun-loving. The "girl next door" is quiet, shy, intellectual, unassuming, giving, tolerant, and forbearing. These differences in their personalities arise due to the stronger tendencies from the top-down and bottom-up flow of alternating energy.

Similarly, many men have a strong *idā*—i.e. they have the passion to explore the world, enjoy its offerings, do what pleases them, not be bogged down by profession, homemaking, and responsibility; they are the creative and artistic people, who enjoy life with abandon, not worrying about tomorrow. Conversely, there are men who have a strong *pingalā*—they are serious, responsible, organized, caring, accountable, and professional, and they make good husbands, fathers, and caretakers of society. They might be boring, irritable, introverted, and sticklers for rules, but the world relies on them to make sure that trains run on time, that a country is secure, and that there is food on the table every day.

The *idā* exists as feminine energy in both men and women, while the *pingalā* exists as masculine energy in both men and women. The *idā* is like the moon while the *pingalā* is like the sun. The meaning-seeking tendency is fiery, hot, and corrosive; the pleasure-seeking tendency is nourishing, soothing, and cooling. These traits are commonly associated with masculinity and femininity so it is neither hard to understand this description nor difficult to experience it within and around us.

The Strength of Manly Qualities

Men naturally have an edge in the pursuit of meaning relative to women. The male body is better capable of subduing *idā* and enhancing *pingalā* than the female body where there is a natural tendency for *idā* to be stronger and the *pingalā* to be weaker. Again, note that these are statements about typical tendencies and not facts about every man or woman. There will certainly be men in whose body the desire for pleasure is far greater than the quest for meaning. There will also be women in whom the quest for meaning is dominant over the desire for pleasure. These are, hence, not generalizations. However, they are indeed statements of the *best case scenarios* in both men and women.

If both men and women were inclined towards the realization of their eternal form of meaning, and both men and women were provided a similar kind of pure upbringing (in other words, if there were no discrimination of circumstances), the men would still have a higher ability to reach into the abstract, understand the nature of reality, and pursue greater than life quests. Similarly, even when women are given a pure upbringing, their body and are mind are still preoccupied with the immediate surroundings rather than with the questions of the origin of life, death, and rebirth, and tend to delve more into the observable and the measurable rather than the abstract and the incalculable.

The dominant upward movement of *pingalā* in men gives them bodily strength, intellectual capacities, the desire to transcend their present material circumstances, and the conviction to accept hardship and austerity—all concerned with greater meaning. Similarly, the downward movement of *idā* in women is responsible for physical fragility, but contributes to a decline in capacity for abstract thought, moral judgment, or distilling vast amounts of data into insight; due to the dominance of *idā*, most women are more concerned about this life than life beyond the present one, and about their bodily comfort here and now than the possibility of self-discovery in the future.

The Strength of Womanly Qualities

It is important to realize that while men might have a greater capacity for abstract thought and greater physical strength to bear hardship and austerity due to the rising *pingalā*, they are also generally more deficient than women in receptivity, surrender, warmth, sharing, patience, and tolerance, which are essential qualities for spiritual advancement. Therefore, despite their ability to think clearly and take hardships in purification, men fall prey to arrogance, individualism, ruthlessness, impatience, and intolerance.

Conversely, due to the downward flow of *idā*, the women have a natural superiority in many traits such as receptivity, surrender, warmth, sharing, patience, and tolerance, which can aid in their spiritual advancement. They might not have a comparable capacity for abstract thought and physical hardship, but their avoidance of arrogance, independence, ruthlessness, impatience, and intolerance are in themselves strengths that can make their road of spiritual progress far easier and smoother.

Which Combinations are Pertinent?

Recall from the previous article, the four cardinal archetypes of *masculine-male, feminine-male, masculine-female,* and *feminine-female.* The man (i.e. the body) who aspires for the *masculine* traits (i.e. meaning), also becomes quickly enamored by the *male* role—i.e. the "intelligent but boring caretaker". Conversely, the woman (i.e. the body) who aspires for the *feminine* traits (i.e. pleasure), also becomes quickly enamored by the *female* role—i.e. *femme fatale.* We had also discussed how male and female combine to create two pairs in the spiritual realm, although more combinations are possible, we do indeed see them in the present world. However, all combinations are not good.

The below table summarizes these combinations with the horizontal and vertical rows representing the archetypes in different individuals. The first letter (M/F) denotes masculine vs. feminine. The second letter (m/f) denotes male vs. female. Their definitions are as per the previous article. There are some combinations of qualities that constitute lesbianism and homosexuality. Due to lack of space, I will not discuss them presently. There are also some relationships that will be incompatible opposites and cannot be useful between two people. Finally, as we discussed in the previous article, only the spiritual combination is ideally recommended.

	M-m	M-f	F-m	F-f
M-m	Homosexual-ity	Spiritual Combination	Homosexuality	Incompatible Opposites
M-f	Spiritual Combination	Lesbianism	Incompatible Opposites	Lesbianism
F-m	Homosexual-ity	Incompatible Opposites	Homosexuality	Hedonistic Relationship
F-f	Incom-patible Opposites	Lesbianism	Hedonistic Relationship	Lesbianism

The masculine traits fail unless they are paired with the female traits. In that sense, the person who pursues the path of meaning must also acquire tolerance, patience, kindness, surrender, and receptivity. Similarly, the female who has these virtues cannot progress unless the virtues are aligned to the quest for higher meaning. In fact, one who patiently tolerates or surrenders to pleasure with abandonment, also slowly forgets their true form of meaning due to entanglement in many kinds of material relationships and transactions. Therefore, the womanly qualities of receptivity and surrender can easily be misguided, and the primacy of a higher meaning is essential to spiritual life. This again underscores the need for combining masculine traits with female traits.

Combining the Masculine and the Female

While the conflict between pleasure and meaning is important (it forces awareness) ultimately conflict is not a comfortable situation. While everyone can prioritize between meaning and pleasure at different times, in most cases, we know the decision involves a difficult tradeoff—we are losing something important while gaining something we think is even more important. Anyone who has dealt with such choices inevitably asks: Why do I have to choose between one of the two alternatives? Why can't I have both alternatives at once?

This is hard to conceive because conventionally choices only allow one of the alternatives. Also, once the choice has been presented, we have to choose one of the alternatives; we cannot reject both alternatives. In classical Aristotelian logic, these two principles are called *Mutual Exclusion* and *Non-Contradiction*. Suppose you were given the choice to pick either vanilla or chocolate ice creams. Mutual Exclusion says that you must pick between vanilla and chocolate; you cannot choose mango or strawberry flavors, because between vanilla and chocolate we exhaust all the available options. Non-Contradiction says that we cannot ask for both vanilla and chocolate at once.

In the case of pleasure and meaning, Mutual Exclusion applies, because consciousness only has these two properties to choose from (*chit* and *ananda*). Since there isn't a third alternative, we don't need to look for strawberry and mango flavors outside the choice between vanilla and chocolate. However, one is likely to still ask: Why can't I obtain meaning and pleasure simultaneously? Why can't I be happy, loved, and recognized by others, while doing the most meaningful thing for my satisfaction?

This is what I mean by balancing the masculine and the female. The sun is enlightening and demanding, and those who follow the sun can shine bright, but also burn themselves and others. Conversely, the moon is nourishing and restful and those who follow the moon may remain stable and gentle, but they also risk succumbing into sloth and ignorance. It is worth noting that neither side is perfect. Owing to this problem, there is a fundamental need to balance the opposite sides of the choice.

The Balancing Act in Yoga Practice

The true *yoga* practitioners balance *idā* and *pingalā* in their body to give rise to the *sushumnā* which is the liberating force that arises only when there is the *simultaneous* flow of *idā* and *pingalā* (in all human beings normally the flow alternates between *idā* and *pingalā*). The simultaneous flow of *idā* and *pingalā* constitutes the option of picking "both" instead of "either-or".

Knowledge alone is inadequate for spiritual advancement because the practitioner has the potential to fall down due to pride and individualism. Time and again we find examples of those who have renounced pleasures, but are unable to give up anger, pride, and egoism. Their practice of spiritual life is like the brightly shining sun which eventually burns them out because there is no cooling and nourishing moon-like force in their lives. After going through this process for many years, such renouncers realize that their lives are so dry that they need to seek the company that soothes and cools them.

Interestingly, the Buddha also came to the same conclusion after years of performing austerities. He realized that these austerities are punishing the body and the mind to an extent that there is no happiness. Conversely, the path of sense gratification—which he had led previously as Prince Siddhartha—was also ignorant and oblivious to the truths of death, old age, and disease. The Buddha, therefore, propounded the "Middle Way" that avoided the extremes of hedonism vs. renunciation, and abstraction vs. ignorance. His rejection of these extremes and following the middle path constitutes the rejection of the choice as conceived through the lens of Mutual Exclusion and Non-Contradiction. In both Vedic and Buddhist thought, therefore, new logical categories called "both" and "neither" are admitted constituting the *Catuṣkoṭi* or "four vertices" as we have seen previously.

Mystical *yoga* emerges from the realization that our conventional choices are not adequate; we have to transcend the limitations of choice without rejecting choice itself. The path that rejects choice is called impersonalism and voidism—as it discards all variety—including masculine and feminine differences. The path that accepts the choice and yet transcends it is called *personalism* as it accepts masculine and female but recognizes that they are just two sides of the same coin; they must co-exist, they must nurture each other because they are *simultaneously necessary* for us. The path of impersonalism and voidism is the alternative called "neither"; personalism is the path of "both".

Meaning and pleasure are conflicting choices, and therefore masculine and feminine cannot be reconciled. The male and female are like the player and the instrument, and they are simultaneously necessary and complementary. Therefore, we cannot reconcile the masculine with the feminine, but we can reconcile the masculine with the female. The reconciliation is that one side pursues meaning while the other side practices surrender. This is not a choice; this constitutes "both".

Purifying the Idā Tendency

The *pingalā* is uplifting and the pursuit of higher meanings, therefore, needs no curtailment. However, the *idā* can be degrading, as it can suck a person into hedonism. Without *idā*, of course, *pingalā* has the tendency to burn a person. Looking at the available options, we can see that individually choosing one path (upward or downward) is not acceptable. Rejecting all choices means renouncing choice. We need to combine both paths, and yet we don't yet know how to overcome their natural contradiction and reconcile their inner conflict.

The short answer is that the top-down path need not necessarily represent hedonism; it can also represent the path of descending knowledge through grace, mercy, and compassion. The upward path is that of personal striving and the downward path is that of receiving grace and showering mercy. The upward path is masculine while the downward path is female (not the hedonism of the feminine path). In the upward path, a spiritualist makes the greatest endeavors for spiritual progress. In the downward path, the spiritualist knows that their efforts amount to nothing without the grace of God. While performing the greatest austerities and cultivating the highest knowledge, the spiritualist becomes helplessly surrendered in the realization that the results of any of his efforts are not in his hands.

Just as a *yogi* tries to bring the *idā* and *pingalā* simultaneously to life, similarly, a transcendentalist simultaneously cultivates sun-like brightly shining knowledge and the moon-like pleasing happiness from complete surrender. This surrender is called "bhakti" in the present world, and some people call it "faith". It denotes a person's helplessness, vulnerability, and a sincere cry for guidance. Typically, those who are endeavoring vigorously are not feeling helpless. And those who are feeling helpless are not endeavoring vigorously. In that sense, the *idā* and *pingalā* are alternating. Their concurrent enactment in our life means vigorous upward endeavors with utter downward helplessness. This sounds paradoxical, and it is indeed so. But only in this mode can a spiritualist avoid the possibility of fall down.

Understanding Gender Differences

Men and women are as different as the sun and the moon. Men have (generally speaking) an upward tendency but they rise and then fall due to pride and arrogance. Women have (generally speaking) a downward tendency and they will rise after a fall due to feeling helpless. Both genders are deficient in their own way. Men can easily grow into tall and strong trees—only to be uprooted by strong winds. Women can grow long as creepers—which are not uprooted by winds—but the creeper doesn't rise very high. Spiritual advancement means rising higher and yet not getting uprooted. It involves the height of the rising tree and the suppleness of the ground-hugging creeper.

In Vedic texts, thus, we can find that spiritual advancement is not limited to a particular gender, or a stage of life—e.g. married or renounced. As we saw in the previous article, men and women can unite in marriage, understanding their different roles, and achieve transcendence. If such a union is not possible, or not working out, each person can rise by uniting the female and the masculine inside themselves. In the case of men, this means cultivating more surrender and humility, because knowledge and austerity may come naturally to them (if the men are actually *masculine*). In the case of women, it means cultivating greater knowledge and austerity, because surrender and humility may come naturally to them (if the women are actually *female*). The key point is that wherever one is, there is no point in debating about which of the two—men or women—are better. The key goal should be to find the shortest path to perfection, and that involves a suitable combination of social complementarity between female and masculine, as well as the inner balancing act between female and masculine.

The Debate is Misplaced

While a lot is said about gender differences today, the science and philosophical understanding required to conclude the debate is missing. The debate is also often based on what is *worst* in both men and women, rather than what is *best* in them. The men are portrayed as dominating, aggressive, and ruthless, while women are portrayed as deceptive, selfish, and materialistic. We should make an attempt to change the debate and focus on the best in both men and women, rather than the worst. Once we understand the best sides of men and women, we would be better equipped to deal with the worst.

The Sun in Vedic philosophy represents the intellect, while the Moon represents the mind. The intellect perceives the language while the mind perceives the sentences. Both are necessary simultaneously. What is the point of having sentences if we don't know the language in which they are made? Similarly, what is the point of a language if we cannot frame sentences?

The intellect and the mind—the Sun and the Moon—are both needed as a whole in society and within each person. The intellect is superior but dependent on the mind. Similarly, the mind is inferior but irreplaceable for the intellect. Whether a person creates a balance in a relationship with the opposite gender in the *Grihastha* and *Vānaprastha*, or one creates a balance in oneself by cultivating both kinds of strengths in *Brahmacharya* and *Saṃnyāsa*, there is simply no getting away from the need to combine the masculine with the female. If anyone is thinking that they can advance in spiritual life just by the moon-like faith and grace, without the sun-like blazing fire of knowledge and personal endeavor, they are mistaken. Similarly, if someone believes that they can attain perfection through the sun-like fire of knowledge and austerities, without the moon-like surrender and devotion, they are misguided.

As long as the gender debate is about the body types, rather than the scientific principles of masculine, feminine, male, and female, the debate will remain superficial. So long as we don't understand how these types combine to create all bodies, we would be victims of stereotyping. And unless we recognize how a combination of masculine and female is essential, we will continue through the cycle of birth and death—again and again undergoing situations not entirely of our choosing.

Vedic Knowledge and Modern Education

Published Date: 2017-05-13

Introduction and Overview

Vedic knowledge was previously imparted in a systematic manner, covering the nature of spirit and transcendence, social duties and moral responsibilities, as well as vocational education based upon a person's role in society. For example, *Mahabharata* describes how the *Pāndava* and the *Kaurava* were sent for education to *Dronacharya* where they were taught spiritual topics, their duties as kings, and the science of warfare and weaponry. This principle—i.e. spirituality, duties, and vocation—still holds good. However, much by way of duties and vocations has now changed. This article argues that the traditional *Gurukula* system—with its rigorous emphasis on the chanting of Vedic *mantras*, the performance of *yajñas*, and the rigorous mastering of Sanskrit to understand the Sanskrit texts—is no longer necessary and in many cases impractical. We should instead view the *Gurukula* as centers of scientific education of reality based on Vedic principles. That requires Vedic knowledge to be transformed into modern subjects, alongside the replacement of their flawed ideas with the truth.

State of Current Education

The Basic Principle of Education

The material world is like an inverted tree, and each person has a position in that tree. At any position in the tree, you can easily see downward, but it is very hard to see upward. This means that if you are sitting at a particular leaf, you will only know about that leaf. If you climb up and come to a twig, then you would see the twig and all the leaves that are directly emanating from the twig. As you climb up further, you can see a branch that emanates many twigs which then emanate many leaves. Our knowledge grows through this process.

This growth can be described in two words—broadening and deepening. By broadening I mean that as we climb up the tree, a greater number of branches, twigs, and leaves come into our vision; our *knowledge* is *broadened* by rising. Similarly, as we climb up the tree, we find a new kind of unity that reconciles the aforementioned diversity; our *understanding* is *deepened* by the unity that reconciles a greater amount of diversity. The broadening of the knowledge and the deepening of the understanding always tend to go hand-in-hand.

The State of Primary Education

Realizing this principle is extremely important to grasp the problem of modern education. At present, we ask children to broaden their knowledge by cramming many subjects without deepening their understanding of the truth or even how all this fits together.

If you examine the teaching patterns in present-day schools, you will find middle grades imparting education in many diverse and unrelated areas—algebra, geometry, arithmetic, biology, chemistry, physics, civics, geography, history, languages, literature, computers, art, sports, dramatics, etc. Not only are these subjects taught by different teachers—who have a very limited understanding of the other subjects—but there is also no attempt to show how civics and geography are parts of the same tree of knowledge as physics and biology. Nobody today has the understanding of how algebra and linguistics, or biology and computers, can be unified as branches of a single knowledge tree.

The result is that children cram lessons, spit them out from memory during an exam, and erase them from memory after the exam. Most children come out of the education system hating it, but as they grow up, they push their children into the same system again.

The State of Higher Education

Children hope that the situation will get better when they narrow their focus to one or two specific subjects when they enter a university program, but it actually gets worse. This is because theories taught by narrowly focused programs are more disconnected from each other, from the real world, and they increase the difference in the understanding of truth between students undergoing different programs.

As a child progresses through the education system, the number of subjects they are taught naturally decreases. School children are taught arts, social sciences, physical sciences, life sciences, and logical sciences. By the time of high school, students limit their focus either to physical sciences, life sciences, or social sciences; art students detach from science; and so forth. As one enters college, each of the physical, life, or social sciences are further divided, and one picks a specialization. For example, there are separate departments for physics, chemistry, and mathematics in all universities. If one pursues a master's program, the focus is further narrowed within a department. If one goes into a doctoral program, a very specific topic, within a very narrow area, is assigned for investigation. And this trend continues later in life through post-doctoral studies and research. In short, the education focus is very broad in school and rapidly narrows subsequently.

Education Fails the Basic Principles

As time passes, and we become more educated, our expertise narrows, because the education system teaches us more and more about less and less. In the logical limit of this ongoing educational effort, we know everything about nothing. The modern education system goes from diverse branches towards leaves, rather than from those branches toward the root. The modern system neither broadens our thinking nor deepens our understanding; it rather narrows and shallows. As you enter the specialized fields of modern science you begin to see enormous amounts of data generated in each field, but very little understanding of how to parse and comprehend this data variety.

There are also many difficulties in broadening the knowledge because it is divided into departments that remain incommunicado. And we cannot build bridges because attempts to unify diverse areas are viewed as a threat to current individualities. Thus, knowledge is not a single tree with many branches. It can at best be called a forest of many trees, which have grown haphazardly, although they coexist in the same ecosystem. Just as you can get lost in a forest, similarly one can get lost in the dizzying jargon of the diverse departments of education.

Flaws in Current Education

Problems in Modern Education

I could have begun with discussing how to impart Vedic knowledge, but I have begun by describing the problem in modern education. This is because we cannot replace an existing system with a new one without knowing what to replace, why to replace it, and how to replace it.

The essential problem with modern education is that it is not broadening and deepening. We cannot see how diverse branches are part of a single tree. The human mind cannot hold large amounts of data. And since we cannot obtain an understanding of the whole, we focus on the leaves on one branch—thereby overlooking the roots. As we forego the study of the higher parts of the tree, there is a decline in intellectual sophistication, emotional acceptance of others, and moral judgment of our duties based on context. The world is seen as many fragmented and conflicting ideologies, which no center holding them together. Desolation and immorality follow as natural consequences.

Modern education is beset with cynicism about the potential for unification because you cannot find any academic pressure to unify diverse departments, or even emerge with a unified understanding of their diverse theories. Nobody in a university believes that one day there would be one department that would be regarded as the supreme department to which every single student has to enroll, regardless of what they are studying, because this department unifies all other departments. Nobody in the modern education system actually practices a hierarchy of the departments—even though they profess reductionism over and over—because the fact is that they are unable to reduce.

Anyone seeking the truth about reality is quickly lost in the forest of many trees. If one examines these trees, we can find that they propose contradictory ideas and theories, and while they demonstrate some convergence within their own domains from leaves to roots, ultimately there are so many trees that you can never conclusively answer any of the fundamental human questions. In fact, many people now mock these questions, calling them a waste of time. It is now fashionable to disregard deeper questions and focus on superficial details.

Such an education system serves no ultimate purpose; it can, however, create employable specialists. Thus, education is now entirely about vocations, not about a true understanding of reality, which can then be used to convincingly decide the nature of truth, right, and good. As society heads towards greater confusion due to ignorance, we can expect more unhappiness, more disruptions, and more decadence.

Flase Dogmas of Modern Education

Most children dislike education because it is not relevant to their interests. What does the study of soils, mountains, and seas have to do with one who is interested in art? What does the study of varied species of animals and plants have to do with one who wants to be a soldier?

The basic premise underlying the modern system of education imparting knowledge of diverse subjects is that children are born blank slates, rather than with innate proclivities. Since they don't know anything at birth, they cannot be inclined toward anything. Therefore, if we expose them to everything, then over time, perhaps they will decide what they are eventually interested in. This forces children to undergo courses and examinations that they don't consider relevant or useful to their interests. They hate the education system and fail to gain from it.

Yet another dogma about the modern education system is that if children learn everything, they will find a use for it later in life. This is actually more problematic because even if you know some biology it is worthless unless you know the details. A little knowledge can be very dangerous. You are not going to cure your diseases with a high school biology education. You will still need to go to a real doctor who knows the full science, not just a few parts that you were taught rather superficially and simplistically during your primary education.

Most modern education is also completely at odds with the kinds of questions that naturally arise in a child owing to their gradual psychological development. For example, children naturally ask their parents and teachers about where they came from. Parents mostly trivialize the question (e.g. that a stork delivered the baby) or provide a materialistic explanation (e.g. that the child is produced by a sexual union), when this question can be the beginning of an investigation into who we are, why we are here, and how we came here.

The dogmas of blank slate minds being exposed to a lot of oversimplified and superficial information during early childhood to generate some interest in them render the entire education process pointless. Then by suppressing and mocking the natural curiosities of a child, and diverting their attention to subjects unrelated to those curiosities, they exaggerate the irrelevant and undermine the important. The net result is that the majority of children hate their subjects, teachers, and schools, and always dream of escaping to other things.

Academic Presentations of Vedic Knowledge

Vedic knowledge is taught in modern universities as part of the department of religion, with religion being only one of the dozens of departments. This approach to Vedic knowledge treats it as yet another subject to be crammed just like the other subjects. What could be the use of such cramming? We have to view Vedic knowledge as the *center* of education—i.e. that there is a tree that has something at the root and something at the leaves. With that understanding, we can go from leaf to root, and then grow more branches and leaves.

When Vedic knowledge is taught as yet another subject in yet another department as yet another specialty, the education loses all meaning. Vedic knowledge is not another *subject* of knowledge—like civics, geometry, or chemistry. Vedic knowledge is that which can unify all other subjects. The Vedic method of teaching also views different departments as parts of a single tree. Acquiring it means understanding the root idea, the trunk ideas, and the branch ideas until one can explain everything based on these ideas. All things in this world are modeled using ideas; we just don't understand the process by which they are diversified. Education means seeing the idea hierarchy, understanding how it is produced from a root, and producing the most useful new branches, twigs, and leaves on the tree for everyone's consumption.

Vedic and modern education obviously differ in many ideas that they impart. But before we examine and understand that difference, we have to recognize that they differ in the notion of education and the concept of knowledge itself as a single tree vs. a forest of trees.

Solving Education's Problems

Making Education Relevant to Children

There are two prominent problems that a theory and methodology of education must solve—(1) making the education relevant to a child based on their natural proclivities, because the child is not born a blank slate, and (2) adapting it to their developmental stages.

We cannot impart the same type of education to every child because there is no universal definition of a human child. Children are all different. We also cannot expose them to ideas incongruent or misaligned with their current stage of psychological development. Finally, we cannot teach them disconnected subjects that are never going to get unified, even as they progress later in life, and they will just have to abandon those subjects as they grow up, making the entire time spent during primary education a complete wastage of time.

We can solve all these problems by focusing on one word: *relevance*. What is relevant to everyone? What is relevant to a specific child? What is relevant at a given age? What will be relevant later on? What is necessary for everyone for us to create a productive and moral society?

If we know how a human is different from animals, then we can answer the question: What is relevant to everyone? If we know the specific proclivities of a particular child, then we can answer the question: What is relevant to a specific child? If we know about the stages of psychological and spiritual development, then we can answer the question: What is relevant at a given age? If have a good understanding of what is to come later in life, then we can answer the question: What will be relevant to a person as they grow up? And if we understand that nobody can be happy by breaking nature's laws, then we can answer the question: What will create a morally productive society?

Reforming Modern Education

Education theory is a huge area of modern study that lies at the intersection of developmental psychology, the questions of what constitutes education, the pragmatic needs of modern society that drive vocations, and the methodologies by which education must be imparted.

We cannot do justice to any of these in a post like this, and we don't aim to. The intent is to make enough points about the Vedic system of knowledge and education that it can help us see how this system is dramatically different than modern education, and how it overcomes the numerous problems of the modern system, including, but not limited to, broadening the knowledge and deepening the understanding, unifying the diverse fields of knowledge into a single theory of nature, and making education relevant and interesting to children to motivate them to get educated not just because they consider it a necessary evil, but because they find the knowledge relevant to who they are.

A formal theory of education needs many things. These include a grasp of how we picture the world through ideas in our mind, how changing those ideas changes both the mind and the world, how these ideas are organized in an inverted-tree structure, how different branches of knowledge are different branches of this tree, how they cover different aspects of the world, the differences between primary and vocational knowledge, the developmental stages of psychological development, and how education can be relevant, just, competitive, and fair.

Education Needs a Philosophy

The current education system is modeled after a single idea: *industrialization*. Children are trained in subjects that will aid the advancement of industrialization. Industrialization in turn depends on a mechanical view of nature and life. In this view, a child is a combination of chemicals, and by education and training, we transform this adaptive machine into something useful for an industrial society.

Therefore, it doesn't matter what the child likes or not. The only thing that matters is what the industrial system needs. The child has to be trained to become useful for the industrial system. The industrial system needs many things, which are often disconnected. But since this system is man-made, therefore, we don't need a philosophy of humanity, a philosophy of nature, and the purpose of human life.

We cannot change education unless we change the idea underlying education, namely, industrialization. Survival is not an end in itself. It is a *means* to an end. Then what is the end? It is a spiritual goal of life, which requires us to discuss the nature of spirit, how that spirit is caught in matter, how it must behave while under the control of matter, and how it can get liberated from the laws of matter controlling it.

This is what I mean by "philosophy". If we cannot answer these questions, then we cannot formulate a theory of education. Education is the most urgent need at present. If we had only one thing we could change in the world, it would not be politics, environment, economics, healthcare, or national boundaries. It would be education that shapes the new generation which shapes everything else. But shaping education needs a philosophy about the nature of ideas, the structure of the tree of ideas, and how it grows and expands.

Education and Sāṅkhya Philosophy

Primary vs. Secondary Knowledge

Vedic texts describe the process of the creation of the universe, as it progresses through two distinct but important stages. That process offers us useful insights into the progressive education process. Lord Brahma—the first created being—is described in Vedic texts to be the person who undergoes education before he applies his knowledge to the creation of the planets, species, universal administration, etc. The universal creation is divided into two parts—called *primary* and *secondary*. The primary creation is about the essential universal principles that apply to everything at all places and times. The secondary creation concerns the specific applications to some in some places and times.

Garbhodakaśāyī Viṣṇu creates the principles—from bottom to top—and manifests Lord Brahma as the embodiment of the topmost principle (*mahattattva*) on a lotus (space in which the petals are directions with unique meanings). Lord Brahma attempts to understand the universe top-down by climbing down the stem of the lotus for 10,000 celestial years but fails to find the bottom of the universe—i.e. the origin from which the lotus has sprung. He then climbs back up, sits on the lotus where he hears the sound 'tapa' and performs austerities.

Climbing down the lotus is looking deeper. Lord Brahma initially executes the same process of investigation as modern materialistic scientists who think that the universe must be comprised of the smallest parts, which will be known by digging deeper into material objects. Lord Brahma finds that as he digs deeper and deeper—by climbing down the lotus—he cannot find any foundation. Going down the stem means dividing something big into smaller parts. There is no limit to how much you can divide. For example, you can divide 1 by 2 to get 1/2, 1/4, 1/8, 1/16, etc. At each step, you create two branches out of each node. But by such division, you can never reach the origin—i.e. the number 0—although you can get closer and closer. If you actually understand the process of division, you know that there is no logical limit to it. The origin is assumed in everything, including the process of division, and yet, you cannot reach this number by division.

The lesson is that the foundation of the material world is not the smallest atom. The foundation is the biggest idea. The universe originates in the biggest idea, not the smallest atoms. The universe is sandwiched between two ideas—everything and nothing. The idea 'everything' is at the top of the universe (above Brahma) and the idea 'nothing' is at the bottom of the universe (the root of the lotus). If one tries to seek the origin downwards, neither can one reach this origin, and even if someone got close to it, their conclusion would be that the foundation is 'nothing'. Looking deeper inside matter is an infinite process, and it ultimately ends with the conclusion of definitive nothingness.

This is the essence of Lord Brahma's education before he becomes the secondary creator. This can be a child's education before the child becomes a productive person. The understanding of the universe as an inverted tree—in which we begin with the idea of 'everything' and go on dividing it into smaller parts to obtain 'nothing' is the primary knowledge. Both 'everything' and 'nothing' have forms, and the things between them also have forms. What we call sociology, economics, management, physics, chemistry, biology, cosmology, medicine, law, etc. are secondary knowledge—i.e. in between the extremes. Lord Viṣṇu creates the limits and lets secondary creators create things in between and within these limits. Some are thus running upwards towards everything and others are running downwards toward nothing.

The meaning of primary and secondary creations applies to primary and secondary education. Primary education must explain the root of the tree, and this education is relevant to everyone because there is a common root. Secondary education can then explain one of the many branches, twigs, and leaves emanating out of this root, based on the proclivities of the children. Even as they will learn different subjects, they don't lose the sense of unity and coherence in knowledge. But as they learn different subjects, they are forced to learn about every branch, twig, and leaf; they have the primary knowledge of the root, and they can select one of the secondary types of knowing.

Four Great Qualities

The term *mahattattva* means the "essence of greatness". Ultimately, Lord Viṣṇu is the essence of greatness, but in Him, all the great qualities are combined. The same qualities are divided and separated as *mahattattva,* creating many different ideas about greatness. None of these ideas is the greatest because they lack the other qualities of greatness. And yet, even perfecting one of these qualities is a wonderful thing.

These great qualities are divided into four parts: (a) truth, (b) austerity, (c) cleanliness, and (d) kindness. Austerity and kindness are related: Sacrifice your happiness (austerity) and give others happiness (kindness). Truth and cleanliness are also related: Pursue the highest knowledge (truth) through a systematic and disciplined life (cleanliness). Then they are collectively related: Sacrifices must be made in the pursuit of truth and in the practice of a disciplined life, but even as you make sacrifices, be kind by not demanding them from others.

This is the essence of greatness and it constitutes primary education. We can also call it *character development*. It doesn't matter if you ultimately become a teacher, researcher, soldier, politician, businessman, or professional. If you embody the four essences of greatness, then you will be a *great* teacher, researcher, soldier, politician, businessman, or professional. Being a great person is the primary necessity, and being a teacher, researcher, soldier, politician, businessman, or professional is a secondary necessity. The purpose of education is to create great people, who will then create a great society. To achieve it, children must be taught about greatness right from childhood.

Before a child's mind is crammed with information that may be practically useful later in life, they must be told stories about great kings, great sages, and great devotees. A child will remember these stories for the rest of their lives, and he or she will become an ideal citizen, who will then make others ideal citizens of a society. By imbibing the principles of greatness in childhood, we ensure that they become great people later in life, regardless of their chosen vocation or profession. This education is the most essential primary education.

Sāṅkhya's View of Developmental Psychology

Dissemination of knowledge depends on the mental and intellectual development of the child. For example, we cannot impart the understanding of *karma* to a young child because the discussion of hell will conjure up images of ruthless punishments, painful torture, and immense suffering. This is not suitable for a young child, but it is appropriate information in the late teens. Similarly, we cannot teach them logic unless they understand the nature of concepts, how all concepts are produced from opposites, and how these opposites create principles of mutual exclusion and non-contradiction. Everything has a time and an order. If this order is violated, knowledge can't be grasped.

Sāṅkhya is a theory of matter, but also a bottom-up theory of a child's development. It begins in sense objects and proceeds into sensations, senses, concepts, judgments, intentions, morals, the consequences of actions, the nature of our desires, and finally the spirit soul. One of the great facts about Sāṅkhya is that we are not trying to understand things irrelevant to us; we are trying to understand how we perceive and conceive the world. There is nothing of greater relevance to us than the understanding of how our experiences are created.

Therefore, there is nothing boring about this education; education is a description of who we are, how we experience, and why we experience certain things as opposed to others. This is not theoretical because we have various kinds of experiences to test the theory. Sāṅkhya is a theory of experience, which begins in the objects we experience and culminates in the subject who experiences. There are many additional material stages that lie between the objects and the subject. All these stages are relevant to our understanding of the mind-body complex; they are relevant to understanding other people, cultures, and societies, and they are imperative to grasp the laws of nature.

The Developmental Stages in Sāṅkhya

Sāṅkhya can be viewed as the different developmental stages of a child, which proceed from ordinary objects to sense and mind apparatus to the self beyond these. These stages are briefly highlighted here. There is of course much more to Sāṅkhya than this brief summary.

- First, there are sense objects—e.g. you can see apples, trees, houses, etc. Accompanying these sense objects is also the perception of change—e.g. that if you eat an apple, it disappears, and time changes things. There are also sensations of pleasure and pain.
- Second, there are properties—e.g. you realize that there is something called color, shape, smell, taste, etc.—which are in the objects, and yet not purely objects. For example, you can show people red and blue, but you cannot show them the idea of color.
- Third, you understand that you have many kinds of senses—e.g. taste vs. smell vs. sight—and therefore there are other people who can also see, taste, touch, and smell. A child begins to understand that just as I can experience, other people can also experience.
- Fourth, we understand that concepts apply to many objects; for instance, apple is a concept, and the red, round,

sweet thing in my hand is actually one of many apples. This is the beginning of mental development beyond the sensual experience of the world.

- Fifth, we understand that the diversity of concepts is produced from a few concepts: this is the dawn of scientific thinking, in which a child realizes that conceptual diversity can be reduced to a few essential ideas, which constitute a *theory* about nature.
- Sixth, the child begins to understand that all such theories are *motivated* due to goals, or solving some specific problems; different people are interested in trying to solve different problems; they can have different goals, and hence prioritize different subjects.
- Seventh, the child realizes that these differences must be resolved by constituting moral principles of right and wrong, good and bad, which have to be applied to society at large. Society cannot be governed simply by my goals, but by moral principles.
- Eighth, the child can see that even though there are moral principles, not everyone is acting according to these principles. What are the consequences of not acting morally? This leads to an understanding of *karma* and transmigration through different bodies.
- Ninth, once transmigration is understood, the child can see how other living beings—i.e. animals—are living different kinds of lives (they have different capacities for perception, sensations, and emotions) but they cannot understand how they got that life.
- Tenth, the child sees that humans can realize the nature of birth and death, and this is the main problem of life; the goal of life is to exit this cycle; everything else we do has to be done with the goal of ending the cycle. The purpose of life is transcendence.

In Sāńkhya, these stages are called *bhūta* (sense object), *tanmātra* (properties), *indriya* (senses), *manas* (mind), *buddhi* (intellect), *ahamkāra* (ego), *mahattattva* (morality), *karma* (consequences), *guna* (innate qualities), and *jīvā* (the soul). If a child is systematically taught these ten topics over ten grades, then children out of school will know everything that needs to be known by everyone. If schooling is begun at 6, and a child undergoes systematic education over the next 10 years, then by the age of 16 he or she would understand the highest conclusion of life—*athāto brahma jijñāsā*—now (that you are in human life), therefore, you must inquire into the nature of the self.

Principles of Vocational Education

Preparing for the Real World

Once the child has acquired this conclusion, the next 2 to 9 years can be spent in vocational education, according to one's *guna* and *karma*. It is essential that the child is informed about the nature of *guna* and *karma* before they enter a particular type of vocational training because without this knowledge they will never understand what types of work they are capable of and how they can become great in their chosen vocations. Prior school education, therefore, is essential to make a child understand what they should choose as a vocation in life.

A great problem in modern times is that children go through school without a good understanding of what they need to do after school. All children look at the latest fads, do some personal research, consider what their friends are doing, where they can make the most money, etc., and then make a decision, without understanding themselves. This is a flawed approach to picking a vocation—which is called *Brahmana*, *Kshatriya*, *Vaisya*, and *Sudra*—because you cannot be successful (materially or spiritually) just by looking at the fads, what other people are doing, where the most money is to be earned, etc. The best route to one's success is their *guna* and *karma*. Unfortunately, there is absolutely no guidance today on this front. As a result, the choices that children are making are no better than a coin toss—i.e. random.

An understanding of *guna* and *karma* is necessary to realize what kinds of professions are most viable for a person, but also understand how embodying greatness in their chosen vocation is the path to the ultimate aim of life, i.e. transcendence. When children understand that the greatest vocational guide in their day-to-day life is their *guna* and *karma* rather than their research and random discussions with friends, they can pick the right kind of vocation themselves. Formerly, wise teachers were capable of understanding a person's *guna* and *karma* in order to engage the students in the right kind of vocational activity. This is not impossible today either. One needs an understanding of the material modes because based on those modes one can see a person's previous life, and based on that one can know *karma*.

Types of Vocational Education

By vocational education, I mean secondary knowledge. This can mean arts and crafts for the *Sudra*, economics, management, production, trading, and finances for the *Vaisya*, sociology, law, military, diplomacy, and governance for *Kshatriya*, and linguistics, logic, and philosophy for the *Brahmana*. The essence of this education is to prepare a person to become a secondary creator. They need to be trained in the specific things that they will create. This corresponds to the modern system of pre-college, vocational diplomas, and college education.

Vocational education can be short (typically for workers) or long (typically for intellectuals). If one has gone through school until the age of 16 years, then they can complete their vocational education anywhere between the ages of 18 to 25 years. Most workers would be capable of contributing to society by the age of 18, while most intellectuals would be ready to contribute to society by the age of 25. This is the time by which they can be considered sufficiently qualified and capable to formally begin practicing the vocation of their own choosing.

Vocational education gets a person constructively engaged in society. We expect the education of the *Brahmana* to be more arduous and extensive than the education of the *Sudra*. Thus, only those who are capable, interested, and qualified will venture into such vocational roles. Since society is structured hierarchically, attaining a higher position in society also entails attaining a higher level of qualification. The value of a social stratum is recognizable only when the hurdles in attaining that stratum are significantly higher than the previous strata.

Forms of Higher Education

Typically, the education of the *Kshatriya*, *Vaisya*, and *Sudra* ends by the time they get vocationally occupied. Of course, they can become apprentices to learn more. But beyond an initial education, they grow in expertise and experience, not in knowledge. That is, they learn how to apply the knowledge in better ways, but they don't grasp new ideas.

However, for the *Brahmana*, education is a lifelong process. It includes educating others, but also to be on the lifelong path to the study of Vedic texts and the elucidation of Vedic knowledge to others.

The tree of knowledge is infinite because it can always grow new branches, twigs, and leaves. *Brahmana* can also be the creators of new forms of knowledge. One of the key lessons of modern science is that completely new fields of knowledge that were heretofore unknown have been created. For example, until a few centuries ago, subjects such as particle physics and organic chemistry did not exist. The organizational theory was unheard of, as was the subject of psychoanalysis. All these are not entirely new areas of knowledge because they are created from the same original principles. Nevertheless, society has to continually produce new forms of knowledge to engage the intellectuals.

Intellectuals relish entering, exploring, and understanding new areas of knowledge. Intellectuals also like to debate and discuss; they like to write treatises and split hairs often on very minor points. This is not a bad idea at all. In fact, the six systems of theistic philosophy in the Vedic tradition—namely, Sāṅkhya, Yoga, Mimānsa, Vedānta, Nyaya, and Vaiśeṣika—are byproducts of intellectual activities *based* on Vedic texts. These fields are not directly Vedic texts. But what are the intellectuals going to do if not expound on Vedic philosophy?

The Vedic tradition has been alive for millennia because of its ability to support and encourage literally infinite intellectual work within the ambit of life's basic goals. As long as the principles of greatness are not violated, intellectual work is not scorned. We can expect that those interested in Vedic philosophy will not only explain its conclusion but also create new forms of knowledge based on Vedic principles, quite like modern science has created many new departments. Their conclusions will not diverge from each other. All these departments of knowledge will simply be the many trunks, branches, twigs, and leaves of an ever-expanding tree of knowledge with a single root.

Modernity and Tradition

Considerations of Daivī Varṇāśrama

We must note that the classical Vedic system—called *Varṇāśrama*—doesn't support the education of *Sudra*. In other words, the children of the *Sudra* were not allowed to go to a teacher, obtain any education, and then determine whether they are qualified for any higher roles in society. This is the fundamental reason that over time some *Sudras* felt that they were left behind in society because the upper three classes—*Brahmana, Kshatriya*, and *Vaisya*—got educated, and by that education, they could change their roles. The classic *Varṇāśrama* system allowed social mobility between the top three classes but excluded the children from the lowest class. This class can be a disenfranchised and disenchanted population that revolts against the higher classes (especially as its size grows) to dismantle the classful hierarchy.

The *Daivī Varṇāśrama* system is different. In this system, there is primary education for all classes—regardless of their birth—bringing them to the point where they can make informed vocational choices. In the modern age, the differences in *guna* and *karma* between the four classes have declined rapidly and most of the population is therefore *Sudra*. If we follow the classic *Varṇāśrama* system, there would be hardly anyone to educate! The *Daivī Varṇāśrama* system, therefore, envisions that the social classes are based on a person's eternal form, not their present conditioned state. For example, there are certain things that each person naturally relishes doing; some people may like administration, while others prefer business; some may like intellectual knowledge while others prefer art. These traits are real and eternal; the temporary and illusory are the numerous modifications of these traits by the three modes of material nature—e.g. a person interested in reading devours fiction rather than true knowledge, or a person perceptive in art considers ugliness as beauty. Under the guidance of the right teacher, our native tendencies can be encouraged, practiced, and realized.

Primary education is meant to give all children a chance to excel. The message to such children is similar to what modern society gives to its children—study well so that you can lead a higher life later. In other words, education is not limited to any class, and every class has the option of full social mobility across any other class. This system of *Daivī Varṇāśrama* has been taught and practiced by the *Vaishnava Acharyas* in recent times. One must bear in mind that it is not the classical *Varṇāśrama* system that forbade education for the *Sudra*.

The Traditional Gurukula System

The *Gurukula* were residential schools in which children studied under the tutelage of an enlightened teacher and helped him in running the school by collecting alms, firewood, fruits, and growing whatever minimal was feasible within their modest means. Śrimad Bhāgavatam describes how *Kṛṣṇa* and *Balarama* went to Sāndipani Muni for education where they mastered 64 arts in a very short period of time, indicating how a single teacher had mastery over all branches of knowledge and he was a complete educational institution in himself.

The *Gurukula* system was focused on the development of *Brahmana*—and the role of the *Brahmana* in traditional Vedic society was teaching and performing *yajña*. Extensive mastery of Sanskrit was required both for the performance of *yajña* as well as for teaching Vedic knowledge to disciples because the tradition was based on the oral transmission of knowledge. With the dawn of *Kali-yuga*, the oral tradition was converted into a written tradition and all prominent *Acharyas* have written extensive commentaries on the Vedic texts.

The traditional system of *yajña* has disappeared because people are not capable of performing complex procedures accurately and inaccurate performances produce no results. This yajña is no longer viable because most of these procedures do not produce expected outcomes.

In this sense, all the key functions of the traditional *Gurukula* are now unnecessary: (1) the system of *yajña* is now ineffective, (2) the accurate pronunciation of the Vedic *mantras* is not viable for most people, and (3) the preservation of Vedic scriptures by learning an oral tradition has been replaced by printed books. Since the *mantra*, *yajña*, and the preservation of the oral tradition are no longer necessities, the learning of Sanskrit and exclusive reliance upon it may be personally interesting to people, but is not essential in today's world.

A Modern Gurukula System

The purpose of the Gurukula is to impart three things: (1) knowledge of transcendence beyond matter, (2) understanding of matter and its laws, and (3) moral and theistic vocational education to create a stable and peaceful society. For such a system to be successful today, it has to educate a person in the same kinds of fields that modern education offers—e.g. economics, sociology, management, biology, medicine, mathematics, architecture, etc.—but by using a different set of concepts. These concepts have to be drawn from Vedic philosophy.

Thus, when we speak of a *Gurukula* in today's times, we should not conjure images of children reciting Vedic *mantras*, performing *yajña*, or mastering Sanskrit so that they can preserve an oral tradition. We must rather envision Vedic knowledge as being used to answer the questions that are relevant today, such that education can replace materialistic and atheistic ideas. It is said that the inquisitive soul must inquire from a teacher by submissively asking questions. The questions being asked today are quite different from the questions that were previously asked. The answers to these questions can be based on Vedic ideas, but they have to be answers to different questions.

For example, people at present want to discuss whether capitalism is better than socialism, whether women and men are equal or unequal, whether rationality is more important than emotionality, whether the universe is stable or expanding, whether time flows one way or two ways, how the species were created one by one, how fossil records tell us about the past, how old is the universe and how long will it live, are we alone in the universe or are there others, what is the origin of language, does the mind think in a language or is thought separate from language, how can machines do what the minds to today, why is nature mathematical, how do our minds know the world, how our dreams created, what is the ideal organization structure, does the structure create a function or does function create structure, etc.

The list of questions is endless, and the questions vary from the previous ones. We cannot pretend that people are the same as those in the past because their concerns, requirements, problems, and needs have changed drastically. This change creates new kinds of questions.

The purpose of education is to answer one's questions. The purpose is also to take one to the final conclusion. With these two in mind, we have to reinvent education—not by changing the ideas—but by answering a new set of questions using the same principles. The *Brahmana* previously had education and *yajña* as their main responsibilities towards society. Now, *yajña* is no longer their sole prerogative. Similarly, we have printed translations of the Vedic texts available in many languages. The key requirement is to make the knowledge accessible in a modern way—i.e. by answering the questions that people are asking now, not the questions that they were asking previously.

The Freudian vs. the Vedic Unconscious

Published Date: 2017-05-14

Two Descriptions of the Unconscious

The initial thesis of Freudian psychoanalysis and that of Vedic philosophy are similar—that our surface behaviors are the result of a deeper "unconscious" reality. The person in both cases is described *hierarchically*—e.g. as an iceberg, with only the tip visible, while most of its reality is submerged. But there are numerous differences in the process of how the unconscious is created—the process is *repression* in Freudian theory and it is *expression* in Vedic philosophy.

The biggest difference lies in their description of fear and desire. In Freudian theory, desire is internal and fear is external. In Vedic philosophy, fear is even deeper than desire, and causes that desire. But even deeper than fear is envy due to which we don't want to accept that we are parts of a whole and we must act our part. The Vedic description of how desire is created from fear, and fear from envy, provides a practical contrast to theories of the Freudian unconscious, besides a guide on how one can overcome the feeling of fear and desire by giving up envy.

The Id, The Ego, and the Superego

If we're looking for similarities, we don't have to look very far. Freud's conception of the id-ego-superego is nearly identical to the Vedic conception of *sat-chit-ananda* with some rearrangement. The Id in Freud's terminology is the collection of all uncontrolled desires. The Superego is the conscience, the moralizing and analyzing tendency. There is constant clash between the Id and the Superego, and therefore these two have to be balanced and mediated by a third agency called the Ego.

What Freud calls the Ego is called *sat* in Vedic philosophy; it is the active agency which makes *choices*. Since *sat* is choosing something, we can ask: What are the alternatives it is choosing from? The answer is that there are two alternatives—*chit* (meaning) and *ananda* (pleasure)—from which the consciousness chooses. I have earlier discussed choice as the need to *prioritize* between meaning and pleasure. Sometimes we think meaning is more important, and at other times we give greater importance to pleasure. The pleasure-seeking tendency is therefore the Id, while the meaning-seeking tendency is the Superego. Their continuous clash and the resolution of such clashes by the soul's choices represents the dynamic called id-ego-superego. Subsequently, we discussed how pleasure creates the *feminine* while meaning creates the *masculine*; we can say that the Id is *feminine* and the Superego is *masculine.*

Be careful not to equate masculine to male or man! Similarly, do not equate feminine to female or woman. These are technical terms, not to be confused capriciously. Thus, there can be a feminine-male, who is pleasure seeking and lives without care. Conversely, there can be a masculine-male who is responsible and analyzes situations carefully to avoid mistakes. These two kinds of men are dominant in Id and Superego, respectively. That is, their Ego or their choice making ability prefers pleasure over meaning, or meaning over pleasure, respectively.

In an earlier article, I described how the pleasure and meaning seeking tendencies exist in all living bodies as the downward-moving *idā* and the upward-moving *pingalā*, respectively. Similarly, the Superego or the moralizing and analyzing tendency takes one from impulsive pleasure tendencies to well-reasoned and meaningful objectives. Conversely, the Id or the uncontrolled desires push a person down towards pleasure, even disregarding what kinds of harms might come one's way as an outcome. There is, hence, considerable initial conceptual synergy between the id-ego-superego and the *sat-chit-ananda* descriptions.

Man is an Animal in Freud's System

One of the flaws in Freud's thinking was to equate the Superego to something which society imposes upon us, and which we have imbibed and internalized to conform to social expectations. Freud's idea is that the Ego is partial towards the Id or the pleasure seeking tendency—quite like the animals. However, unlike the animals, which are able to live a life of unrestricted and unconstrained pleasure, humans are constrained by the laws and norms of good behavior defined by society. Freud doesn't delve into why society would come up with such norms in the case of humans, when the animals haven't done the same. In other words, he doesn't seek the origins of human morality. And by not asking this question, Freud leaves the door open to the idea that man is just like animals—with some extra rules.

The primary legacy of Freud's work is that most people emerge from his psychoanalytic approach believing that humans are animals who have been caged by society and all psychological problems are the result of putting the animal in a cage. It's surprising that so many people have come to this conclusion when Freud did not seem to have explicitly articulated such a view, although he did not do anything to prevent the incidence of such a view either. I make this point because Freud (1856 – 1939) followed Charles Darwin (1809 – 1882) who had pronounced the judgment that man is an ape. By not resisting the idea, Freud appears to have upgraded the view to "man is a sick ape".

Freud's flaw lies in using the study of mental sickness to define the working of a healthy mind, rather than using a grasp of the healthy mind to diagnose the nature of the sickness.

The Creation of the Unconscious

Another big difference between Freud's ideology and the Vedic description lies in the creation of the unconscious. In Freud's view, the unconscious is created primarily due to the *repression* of desires. In Vedic philosophy, the unconscious is created due to the *expression* of desires. The difference between the two arises due to a different understanding of the unconscious.

In Vedic philosophy, the unconscious is the *guna* or the three modes of nature which exist as the *habits* of meaning and pleasure. Every time a habit is expressed, the habit is reinforced. If, therefore, one has to overcome the effects of the unconscious, one has to stop the expression of habits, so that their effect will eventually wane away. Every time a desire to express a habit arises, if the habit is suppressed, then after some time a new habit will be formed. In fact the best way of overcoming past bad habits is the formation of new good habits.

In Freud's view, the unconscious is the byproduct of repression of what was previously in the conscious. For example, if society looks down upon extramarital relationships, the desire would be suppressed and then later expressed as sexual activity in other forms. Freud called this *transference*. His recommended approach to curing mental problems is first to discover all repressions through dream analysis and free association in which you are prompted for a symbol and you explain its meaning. Once the unconscious has been discovered, Freud argues, it should be given a free reign in order to heal a person.

There is truth in Freud's ideas about the suppression of desire, because ultimately a living entity has desires—primarily of meaning and pleasure. The question is: How should these desires be expressed? There are legitimate expressions of desire, and there are illegitimate expressions of desire. Overcoming the unconscious involves sublimating the desires from illegitimate to legitimate ways, thereby forming new habits such that the old habits would automatically die down. If, however, the desires are given a free reign in illegitimate ways, they would be strengthened and create additional problems.

The difference between Freud and Vedic philosophy therefore originates in their different views of the unconscious. If we have desires, why are my desires different from yours? Vedic philosophy offers an answer: the desires are *habits*. That is, the material desires are not native properties of the soul. However, they are habits which have been acquired due to past repetitions and can be given up if those repetitions were stopped.

These habits exist in an *unmanifest* form—i.e. as possibilities for choice—and they manifest as choices. If these desires are suppressed they will manifest in other ways, as Freud correctly diagnoses. However, the solution to that transference is not to give all desires a free reign, but to find the correct avenues for expressing one's desires. For example, a desire for violence has some legitimate expressions—such as in a nation's defense or law enforcement. There are also partially legitimate expressions of this desire—e.g. in playing contact sports. Finally, there are illegitimate expressions of this desire in domestic and civilian violence. No desire is invalid, but there are correct and incorrect avenues for the expression of desires.

The Misinterpretation of the Unconscious

Many so-called spiritual teachers have employed the principles of psychoanalysis to teach people that it is okay to let go of one's "inhibitions" imposed "artificially" by society. These views have dominantly arisen in the West where the need for individualism is prioritized over the rules of socially acceptable behavior. People have been taught that these social rules are coming from religious traditions which created social norms in order to subjugate the population according to God's commandments, although that God is not helping them find the happiness they need. Therefore, to become happy—without the constraints of religious rules—one has to reject social norms.

People have forgotten that the rules of moral behavior enshrined in religions have a basis in the theory of *karma*—which is a natural law of cause, effect, and consequence. God doesn't directly participate in the natural law, however, the consequences of actions are delivered through *demigods* who administer the universe. These administrators are quite like the bureaucrats in a government who punish those who violate the laws of a country. The difference is that a criminal may escape the punishment of a government, but no criminal goes unpunished by the natural moral law.

It is therefore incorrect to presume that social norms are just cultural restrictions. They may have been expressed previously according to the culture (and some of these rules may be irrelevant now), but there is indeed a natural law that determines the legitimate and illegitimate expressions of desire. Letting go of one's inhibitions and doing whatever one wants invites *karma,* the result of which will be that a person would be placed under even more severe restrictions such that their desires would be even less fulfilled, thereby causing even more repression and transference. The problem of repression and transference therefore originates in giving desires a free reign.

The Genesis of Material Fear

The origin of what Freud considers social hemming of individual desires is actually a consequence of *karma* due to which a person is unable to fulfill their desires. Living entities are not free to do whatever they want. There are, of course, social strictures which *normatively* prohibit a person from doing many things. But quite aside from such norms is *karma* which creates the *opportunities* in which one can fulfill their desires. If the relevant *karma* is missing, the opportunities are not available.

We can blame social laws for the lack of such opportunities, but the laws are only normative and not preventive. That is, they are telling you that it is *bad* to do something; they are not *preventing* you from actually doing it. *Karma*, however, prevents a person from fulfilling their desires by limiting the opportunities in which such desires can be fulfilled. For example, a person's desire to find a loving partner may be frustrated when he or she only meets incompatible prospects due to previously created *karma*.

There is, hence, *desiring* and *deserving*, where the latter is produced as a moral consequence of our actions. One of the main causes of repression of desire is the frustration of desire. For example, if someone has experienced failed marriages, they would naturally imbibe a fear of marriage. Though they have the desire to find a loving partner, they would tread cautiously, not expose themselves to yet another disaster, and thereby not avail of any opportunities even when they are knocking at the door. The fear that stops us from exercising our desires is not just social norms but also bad experiences arising from *karma*. Indeed, the dominant cause of repression is bad encounters due to *karma*; the social conformance exists too, but is not dominant.

It is noteworthy that *karma* will frustrate your desires only if you have frustrated other's desires in the past. *Karma* is retribution for what one has done in the past. Therefore, if you have instilled fear in others, nature will arrange circumstances by which fear would be struck in your heart. Thus a person suffers through the cycle of hurting others, getting hurt themselves, suppressing the desire, transferring it elsewhere, which is then manifest in convoluted and illegitimate ways, creating more pain and suffering. Freud's understanding of this process is non-existent, because he sees neither *guna* as preformed habits, nor *karma* as the consequence of illegitimate enactment of habits.

The Genesis of Material Desire

The term *guna* is translated as a "rope" which binds the soul. This binding is like a leash on a dog, by which the dog can be controlled and dragged by its master. Lord Shiva is called *Paśupati*—the master of the animal. The term *paśu* indicates an animal, which is tied by ropes or *guna*, and then dragged by the master. The master in this case is Lord Shiva—the personification of time. Thus, time is the master, *guna* is the leash, and the soul is the animal tied by the leash and dragged by time. This is a powerful imagery to understand the condition of the soul in the world, and how the soul develops new desires.

The basic process is that when the rope of the *guna* is tightened, the soul feels suffocated, which gives rise to the fear of death and destruction, because the soul is already small, and when the leash is further tightened, the soul develops the fear of extinction. To overcome that fear, the soul becomes impatient and acts impulsively, which is called desire. So, the trigger for all material desires is fear (of which death is the most dominant), and therefore fear and desire are simply two sides of the same coin. Owing to this fact, psychoanalysts have examined some deep connections between fear and desire.

The *tantra* scriptures describe that a soul feels constrained in five ways due to *guna*: *niyati*, *kāla*, *rāga*, *vidyā* and *kalā*. *Niyati* is the feeling that the soul is in a particular place and that it cannot be in all the places. The limitation of *kāla* is the feeling that the soul is in a particular time and cannot be in all times. The limitation of *rāga* is the feeling that the soul can only accept a few things and not whatever is offered by the circumstances. The limitation of *vidyā* is the feeling that the soul can only know a few things and even if perfect knowledge were offered it is impossible to know that perfection. The limitation of *kalā* is the feeling that the soul has certain abilities and cannot be asked to do things that are beyond the capabilities. These five constraints are subdivisions of *māyā* which is the idea that "I am not that"—which means that I'm limited, incapable, bereft, and deficient in something.

It is a fact that the soul is limited, which is why it is called *anu* or atomic rather than *vibhu* or complete. But being limited itself cannot be the cause of unhappiness—if you feel secure and happy in the protection of God—just like a child feels safe in the lap of a mother or father and rests peacefully. The source of unhappiness is that the soul is small (like a baby) and it is also alone (without the mother and the father, having rejected their protection). The combination of being small and feeling lonely under fear leads to a deep sense of unhappiness. The unhappiness is therefore not just in the tightening of the leash (which makes the soul feel small) but also in the sense of loneliness (due to isolation from God) because one feels helplessly alone.

The problem is that material nature mocks and teases the soul for its powerless situation, by reminding it again and again about how small it is, how incapable it is, and how deficient it is. The soul is baited by material nature through provocation and incitement and this creates anger and fear in the soul. Once the fear and anger is created, the soul is motivated to get up and fight these limitations, as if to teach those who are mocking it a lesson. This passion and anger to get up and fight against the mocking and teasing is called *material desire*.

The Mechanism of Desire

This process is described in Vedic texts as comprised of two stages:

āvaraṇātmikā which means "covering" and *prakṣepātmikā* which means "throwing". The soul is like a dog bound by a leash called *āvaraṇātmikā*. When the leash is tightened, it angers the dog and it starts struggling to become free of the leash, and that tightening is called *prakṣepātmikā*—the desire to get up and fight the oppression of the leash. If the dog is sitting peacefully, then nature will tighten the leash in order to provoke the dog, and hence this tightening is called "throwing" because it causes the dog to become restless and run around in order to free itself from the leash. When the leash is loosened somewhat, the dog feels comfortable: "Ah, finally, I have proven my superiority over the leash, and now I am independent, so I can do whatever I want". The tendency to feel comfortable in life is called "covering" or illusion. In short, *āvaraṇātmikā* is the loosened leash and *prakṣepātmikā* is the tightened leash. Both are leashes, and hence two different aspects of the *guna*.

Time goes cyclically—which means sometimes the leash is tightened and at other times it is loosened. Accordingly, there are periods of restless activity, followed by relaxed satisfaction and enjoyment. The restless activity is "throwing" when the leash is tightened. The relaxed enjoyment is "covering" when the leash is loosened. Thus, it is said that happiness is nothing but the cessation of suffering because the soul suffers like the dog whose leash has been tightened. When the leash is loosened a bit, the dog feels relaxed that it can move around a little bit and that causes it to go back to sleep again.

The tightening and loosening of the *guna* are like a piston. If you have seen steam engines, the pulling and pushing of the piston makes the wheels go round and round. Time is that force which causes the piston to push and pull. Like a horse rider who pulls and relaxes the reigns on a horse in order to make it run in a race, similarly, time pulls and relaxes the *guna* of a soul to make it run. We can also think of the soul as a puppet orchestrated by strings in the control of a puppeteer—time. Sometimes the puppeteer pulls the strings and then at other times it relaxes the strings. These are powerful analogies but there is also an equally vivid science underlying these analogies.

Ultimately, we can see that even in Vedic philosophy the living entity is an animal. The difference is that in Freud's thinking the animal is wild, while in the Vedic thinking the animal is domestic. That is, the animal has a leash and is under control, not free to do whatever it desires, and however it desires it. That minor difference, however, changes the understanding of the unconscious and how desires (consciousness) emerge from it.

Fear and Desire Originate in Envy

The soul is fully aware of its limited situation. I mean, who doesn't know that they are in one place and not in all places, that they can know very few things, that they cannot like everything, or that they have limited abilities? And yet, the soul has innate envy of God who is complete—i.e. He is in all places, He is in all times, He can like anything, He knows everything, and He is capable of anything. We use words such as omnipresent, omnipotent, omniscient, etc. to describe God. God is complete or *vibhu* and the soul is limited or *anu*. But the soul doesn't want to be reminded of this limitation due to its envy of God. Time reminds the soul repeatedly of its limitations and provokes it.

In other words, either the soul has to accept that God is superior and thereby surrender to God. Or nature will keep tightening and loosening the leash periodically due to which the soul would be repeatedly reminded that it is actually bound, constrained, small, and incapable. Superficially, it appears that by baiting, material nature is actually instigating the soul to get up and fight. At a closer look, however, we can see that material nature is only reminding the soul that it is very small and it has to surrender. Material nature is therefore also a spiritual energy—but it is spirituality meant for the envious.

The spiritually advanced person realizes that fear and desire would never arise if they did not have the envy. If the soul is cognizant of God, then when material nature reminds the soul of its small position, the soul would simply nod its head in agreement, and accept that it is very small and helpless. Where is the need to be provoked on being told the truth? If the provocation is that you are small, then accepting that idea as a fact of life is the cure to the material problems. In fact, if the soul truly accepts that it is limited and small, then it will cry out like a baby seeking the shelter of a mother or a father.

Similarly, when a spiritually advanced person undergoes suffering, he simply nods his head in approval. He doesn't feel bad about the fact that he is helpless against circumstances, nor does he resent the circumstances, because he accepts that he is small and at the mercy of the complete. Anger and frustration at suffering is the sign that a person hasn't accepted their smallness, and that they feel entitled to a good life when the circumstances they are in are just outcomes of previous *karma.*

The Folly of Not Recognizing Envy

Psychoanalysts have correctly recognized that fear and desire are the deeper underlying problems in all humans; the desires are suppressed due to fear. However, their diagnosis of fear is incorrect because they don't go deep enough to recognize envy as the root cause of fear. Their opinion is that fear is coming from outside—the social constraints—when the fear is created inside a person when they are forced to feel inadequate, insufficient, and incapable. The fear and anger is not that the world is oppressing me, and therefore I don't have to revolt against the oppression of the world. The fear and anger is that I am so limited that I'm unable to fight the worldly limitations.

The oppression and suppression from the external world is simply an ignition for our internal insecurity. When we feel helpless against the oppression and suppression it makes us angry and fearful. But we must recognize two things. First, that we feel fear and anger because we know that we are helpless; if we had the power to change the world, then we would not feel fear and anger; we would rather feel excited about the opportunity to show our power; fear and anger are thus due to insecurity and helplessness. Second, we must recognize that all souls are helpless in the ultimate analysis; they might appear to have some relative strengths and power for the time being, but even they are barking like a ferocious dog precisely because there is fear and insecurity inside them. The root cause of our suffering is therefore not outside—caused by other people—but inside, originating in our insecurities.

The origin of the insecurity is envy. The psychoanalytic attempt to look deeper and deeper into the psyche is incomplete if we simply look at anger and fear and then immediately run outwards into the external world and blame society for creating that anger and fear in us. This is a cop-out where you begin an inward journey and after going to some depth you refuse to go further in. Vedic philosophy teaches us that the fear and the anger in us (which outwardly appears as desire) is only a surface symptom of envy. We are small and helpless, but we have refused to accept the One who is big and helpful. Every time when problems arise, we should remember that the worldly situation would not be perceived as a problem if it were not for our inner fear and anger—ultimately caused by envy. When our fear and anger is seen as originating internally, then we can become free of it.

The Oedipus and the Electra Complexes

There are areas in Freudian psychology where psychoanalysis becomes psychogymnastics, when extraordinarily convoluted explanations of quite simple phenomena are sought. A classic case of such explanatory gymnastics is the Oedipus and Electra complexes which represent a boy's preeminent attraction to his mother and a girl's natural fussing about her father. Below are some excerpts that describe the convoluted thinking.

"The psychodynamic nature of the daughter-mother relationship in the Electra complex derives from penis envy, caused by mother, who also caused the girl's castration; however, upon re-aligning her sexual attraction to father (heterosexuality), the girl represses the hostile female competition, for fear of losing the love of her mother." — Wikipedia on Electra Complex

In the phallic stage, a boy's decisive psychosexual experience is the Oedipus complex—his son-father competition for possession of mother. It is in this third stage of psychosexual development that the child's genitalia are his or her primary erogenous zone; thus, when children become aware of their bodies, the bodies of other children, and the bodies of their parents, they gratify physical curiosity by undressing and exploring themselves, each other, and their genitals, so learning the anatomic differences between "male" and "female" and the gender differences between "boy" and "girl". — Wikipedia on Oedipus Complex

In previous articles (here and here), I described how consciousness has four basic archetypes—feminine, masculine, male, and female—which are paired together as complementary companions. I also discussed how every human being is a combination of the two opposites, and an enlightened soul therefore creates this internal union between opposites in order to advance in spirituality. Any male therefore needs a female, and vice versa. The Oedipus and Electra complexes are simply manifestations of the idea that a child—if he or she doesn't have the unity of opposite archetypes will feel incomplete and therefore aim to unite with the opposite. This unity, however, is not due to a boy's envy of his father or due to a girl's envy for her mother. It is possible that if a boy has greater feminine tendencies while the mother is more masculine relative to the father, then the boy would be attracted more to the father.

Freudian psychoanalysis is symptomatic of the problem that Freud carefully observed numerous human psychological phenomena and then contrived their explanations in a way that most of them turn out to be excessively complicated and false, while the simplest explanation that could actually demystify a number of difficult phenomena is neglected.

The Relation to Impersonalism

The impersonalist philosopher recognizes that the root of our suffering is fear, anger, and desire. But he refuses to see that these arise due to envy. Of course, the impersonalists don't immediately run outward like Freud looking for an excuse for our fears and repressions. In that sense impersonalists are better than psychoanalysts because at least they recognize that the fear, anger, and desire inside us is an innate problem, not a problem caused by external circumstances. Nevertheless, the impersonalist's inward journey is also incomplete because they aren't able to realize that the origin of fear lies in envy.

The impersonalist therefore recognizes that fear, desire, and anger are the root causes of suffering and he practices freedom from them. The impersonalist also imagines that when he becomes free of fear, desire, and anger, he has become God—because God too is free of fear, anger, and desire. In that sense most impersonalists believe that upon freedom from material desires they will merge into God and become identical with God.

The problem is that even if you temporarily give up fear, desire, and anger, there is no guarantee that you won't get it again, because while pretending to give up fear, desire, and anger you don't become equal to God, who is always *vibhu* (complete) and we are always *anu* (atomic). God is indeed free of material fear, desire, and anger, but the reason is that He is the master of the material nature. He doesn't need to fear something that He fully controls. So, if the soul also conquers their inner fear, they have just conquered themselves, and not the world. And yet, the impersonalist confuses the two; he thinks that by conquering ourselves we have transcended the material world just like God.

Owing to the tendency to portray themselves as powerful conquerors—who slay the demons of inner fear, desire, and anger—the impersonalists often take shelter of psychoanalysis. But ultimately there are no answers in psychoanalysis, which goes inwards and then takes a U-turn outwards. Impersonalists are not therefore followers of the Vedic tradition because the journey inwards is completed when fear, desire, and anger are rooted out by recognizing that we are atomic and God is complete.

The Meaning of Yajña

Published Date: 2017-05-16

Introduction and Overview

In all Vedic texts the term *yajña* is used, translated as a "sacrifice". The performance of *yajña* is the means by which one advances spiritually. For most people, *yajña* is seen as a fire lit in a pot into which food grains are offered with a *mantra*. While this is by no means an aberration, it is not the only sense in which the term *yajña* is used. For example, the Bhagavad-Gita (BG) describes how the processes of *Aśtanga-Yoga* and *Jnana-Yoga* are also *yajña*. Then we have terms such as *Sankīrtana-yajña* which seem to have nothing in common with a fire sacrifice, *Aśtanga-Yoga*, or *Jnana-Yoga*. In what way are all these practices connected? What is the meaning of *yajña* that unifies these diverse practices into a single holistic understanding of *yajña*?

Three Components of Yajña

The Rig-Veda describes three components of a *yajña*—a "fire" or *Agni* into which the offering is made, a "food" or *Soma* which is offered, and a "process" or *Vāyu* for pouring the *Soma* into the *Agni*. In order to understand the meaning of *yajña*, we have to discern the meanings of these components, and their mutual relationship, which is easily achieved by comparing the *vāyu-agni-soma* to the three different kinds of offerings we can make which are represented by *sat-chit-ananda*, or our opportunities, meaning, and happiness.

Pleasure is dear to everyone, so in one prominent scenario, the *Soma* or the offering is *ananda* or pleasure; it is because we offer our pleasure that the *yajña* is translated as a "sacrifice" because giving up pleasure is indeed a sacrifice. But if we are sacrificing pleasure, then what are we sacrificing it for? The *Agni*—into which the *Soma* is offered—can be the *chit* which represents meaning. The significance of the term *yajña* in this case is that we are sacrificing our pleasure for meaning. For example, if you endure pain to defend a country (and that country stands for a higher principle) then you are offering your happiness for a higher principle and that offering constitutes a *yajña*. Naturally, however, a country's defense is not the only place you can offer your happiness, because there many other possible avenues. Some of these avenues are better than others, and the selection of the avenue for which happiness should be sacrificed represents *sat* or *Vāyu*.

Now, it is quite possible that instead of sacrificing happiness for meaning, you could have sacrificed meaning for happiness. For example, when it is time to defend your country, you could decide to stay at home thinking about how you might enjoy the rest of your life better by avoiding a battle. In such cases, you have prioritized pleasure over meaning, and "sacrificed" a higher purpose for personal happiness. Now, the *soma* is the meaning, the *agni* is your pleasure, and the act of staying home to avoid the battleground is *vāyu*.

Various Kinds of Yajña

The meaning of "sacrifice" is that you cannot get everything, and so you have to choose. When you make a choice, you prioritize some things and sacrifice others. We can call this prioritization "choice", and there are many ways in which we can perform these sacrifices.

However, all these sacrifices are not *yajña*. In a very generic sense, the act of prioritizing involves sacrificing something else, but to constitute *yajña* one must make sure that we are sacrificing a lower principle for a higher principle. For instance, sometimes, your duty may demand that you sacrifice your meaning and happiness for the meaning and happiness of others. In this case, the duty is the *agni* and your meaning and happiness are the *soma*. The process by which this sacrifice is made is the *vayu*. Similarly, you could also sacrifice one kind of meaning to obtain another kind of meaning, or one kind of pleasure to get another kind of pleasure. All of us make different choices or priority calls, and hence we are always sacrificing something or other. As long as the *agni* is the higher principle, and *soma* is the lower principle, the process can be termed *yajña*. By this *yajña* we can uplift our lives, perform our duties, and get the benefits of austerity.

Depending on the different methods of sacrifice, there are different kinds of *yajña*, produced from various kinds of prioritization.

- BG 4.25: Some yogis perfectly worship the demigods by offering different sacrifices to them, and some of them offer sacrifices in the fire of the Supreme Brahman.
- BG 4.26: Some of them sacrifice the hearing process and the senses in the fire of the controlled mind, and others sacrifice the objects of the senses, such as sound, in the fire of sacrifice.
- BG 4.27: Those who are interested in self-realization, in terms of mind and sense control, offer the functions of all the senses, as well as the vital force [breath], as oblations into the fire of the controlled mind.
- BG 4.28: There are others who, enlightened by sacrificing their material possessions in severe austerities, take strict vows and practice the yoga of eightfold mysticism, and others study the Vedas for the advancement of transcendental knowledge.
- BG 4.29: And there are even others who are inclined to the process of breath restraint to remain in trance, and they practice stopping the movement of the outgoing breath into the incoming, and incoming breath into the outgoing, and thus at last remain in trance, stopping all breathing. Some of them, curtailing the eating process, offer the outgoing breath into itself, as a sacrifice.

Lord Kṛṣṇa describes in the Bhagavad-Gita how different people create various kinds of *yajña* when they sacrifice one thing for another. Note some interesting alternatives such as "sacrificing the hearing process in the fire of the controlled mind". This is very difficult to understand unless we realize the meanings of "offering" and "fire". The "fire" represents what you have prioritized, and the "offering" is what you have deprioritized. Therefore, if you want to attain a controlled mind, you have to stop listening to the cacophony of the world, although this cacophony can be very pleasurable.

Thus, there is a *yajña* which involves stopping hearing in order to attain a silenced mind. In this process, the mind becomes the fire (i.e. the *Agni*), and the sense of hearing becomes the offering (i.e. the *Soma*). Similarly, there is a *yajña* in which one hears everything and becomes fully alert about their surroundings, thus raising their consciousness. In this process, the sense of hearing becomes the fire (i.e. the *Agni*) and all the sounds around them become the offering (i.e. the *Soma*) in the fire.

In many Eastern religions, such as Zen Buddhism, there is a simultaneous emphasis on silencing the mind and yet perceiving everything. Those practicing martial arts, for example, practice this contradictory form of meditation, which Lord Kṛṣṇa alludes to in BG 4.26. It is amazing how we can advance our consciousness both by perceiving everything, and by stopping all perceptions!

We are all familiar with the adage: "What are you prepared to give up to get the life you want?" The description of *yajña* elevates this idea to a natural principle in which one thing is sacrificed for another, and by making better choices about what we sacrifice and what we aspire for, we can perfect our lives. In other words, the perfection of *yajña* is understanding the hierarchy of meanings, pleasures, and opportunities by which one can sacrifice something (which is lower) for something else (which is higher). Everyone may be involved in some sacrifice, but everyone's sacrifice is not perfect and hence cannot be called *yajña*. Therefore, *yajña* means perfection of sacrifices.

Descriptions of Material Yajña

In the material world, meanings are regarded as generally higher than the quest for mundane sensual pleasure. Therefore, meaning or *chit* is generally considered the fire, and it constitutes the upward rising flow of energy called *pingalā*. Similarly, pleasure or *ananda* is generally considered the offering, and it constitutes the downward falling flow of energy called *idā*. Thus, in the material world, one generic description of *yajña* means sacrificing pleasure for meaning. *Yajña* can also mean the sacrifice of a lower meaning for a higher meaning, or the sacrifice of a lower pleasure for a higher pleasure. All references to "higher" and "lower" are based on a hierarchy.

The Vedic marriage is an example of the concept of *yajña*. When a man represents the upward flowing *pingalā*, and a woman represents the downward flowing *idā*, then the woman becomes an "offering" to a man, and a father who performs this offering is said to have performed a great *yajña*—the *kanyā-dāna yajña*—or the "sacrifice" of a girl. Most people today may find this idea reprehensible because it conjures up images of women being "sacrificed" at the altar of marriage. These imaginary notions are far from truth. The basic idea is that as long as a woman is unmarried, the male in her life is her father. When she gets married, the male in her life would be her husband. The father who gives away the bride in marriage thus makes a sacrifice by parting away with this daughter. If we treat the marriage as a *yajña* or sacrifice, then the husband is the *Agni* and the wife is the *Soma*. The choice of the *appropriate* husband for the girl made by the father constitutes the *Vāyu* in the offering. In other words, the girl's hand is given to a boy who is most appropriate for the girl—chosen by the father.

Similarly, the *guru* is the higher meaning in the material world, while the disciple is the lower meaning. The disciple is expected to sacrifice their meanings for those of the *guru*, which means that the disciple accepts the *guru's* goals as their goals. Similarly, the disciple sacrifices their happiness for the fulfillment of these goals. In that process the *guru* becomes the *Agni* and the disciple becomes the *Soma*. The process of spiritual initiation is one in which a disciple commits to deprioritize his or her happiness and meaning relative to the *guru*'s which means that the disciple takes a vow to prioritize the *guru*'s desires over one's own desires. Breaking that vow—i.e. taking back a commitment—is tantamount to lying. However, if this commitment is always upheld, then the promise is itself the highest *yajña*.

Descriptions of Spiritual Yajña

The situation in the spiritual world, however, is quite different, even though there is *yajña* there too.

The difference is simply that pleasure is higher than meanings. Furthermore, the preference for the *type* of pleasure shifts—the mental or intellectual pleasures (which are "higher" pleasures) are rejected in favor of the sensual pleasures (which are "lower" pleasures). Therefore, the *Agni* in the spiritual world becomes a lower pleasure, whereas *Soma* becomes a higher pleasure or any meaning.

The principle of *Agni* and *Soma* doesn't disappear. It only changes form such that *Soma* in the material world is pleasure and *Agni* is meaning, while *Soma* in spiritual world is meaning and *Agni* is pleasure.

Both worlds have *yajña* although they are quite different.

Comparison of Material and Spiritual Yajña

A contentious issue often arises in performing these trade-offs. For example, should the commander of an army give up his life in order to save the life of a foot solider, and jeopardize the effectiveness of the entire army? Or, should a father with many children sacrifice his life to save one child, and thereby leave all children to fend for themselves? Clearly, if the army commander saves himself and sacrifices the foot soldier, one could interpret this action as prioritizing one's pleasure over someone's pleasure. We could also interpret it as a sacrifice of greater meaning for a smaller pleasure. This complicates the decision process because of the myriad interpretations one could offer for the same kind of act. What is then the right kind of decision that can be considered *morally correct*—or in other words *right*?

Soma → Agni ↓	Higher Meaning	Lower Meaning	Higher Pleasure	Lower Pleasure
Higher Meaning	–	Material	Material	Material
Lower Meaning	Spiritual	–	Material	Material
Higher Pleasure	Spiritual	Spiritual	–	Material
Lower Pleasure	Spiritual	Spiritual	Spiritual	–

The table above summarizes the decision matrix. An example of "higher meaning" is the concepts in the mind, while an example of "lower meaning" is the concepts of senses, sensations, and sense objects. Similarly, "higher pleasure" means the pleasure of the subtle senses, while the "lower pleasure" means the pleasure of the gross senses. This table has some peculiar characteristics. For example, in the spiritual realm, Higher Pleasure becomes *Soma* for the *Agni* of Lower Pleasure. Similarly, Higher Meanings become the *Soma* for the *Agni* of Lower Meanings. This means that the senses are given more importance over the mind. The pleasure of mental and intellectual pursuits is thus rejected over sensual pleasure. This is the basis of the claim that *bhakti* should be free of *jnana* or knowledge.

Note, however, that this claim can only be made in the context of the spiritual *yajña* and not the material *yajña.* Many people misinterpret this as the rejection of knowledge in *bhakti* even in the material world—effectively converting *bhakti* into a sentimental or fanatic process. This is wrong because in the material world one must sacrifice ordinary pleasures for the pursuit of knowledge. Only when this knowledge has been perfected to include the understanding of God, can the mundane processes of knowledge acquisition can be sacrificed.

The material and the spiritual *yajña* are opposite in their choices. The mind and intellect are preferred from the material standpoint, but the senses are preferred from the spiritual standpoint. Of course, from the standpoint of precedence, the mind is still prior to the senses. However, in the spiritual realm, the soul's *choices* prioritize sensations over ideas, ideas over judgments, and judgments over morals; in other words, all morality can be suspended if there is a gross sensual pleasure to be obtained in relation to God. This is completely counterintuitive and is the main reason why *bhakti* is often criticized as being meant for the "less intelligent" because in the ultimate analysis, it indeed deprioritizes the mind and intellect over sensual pleasure (although only in the spiritual world). This is also a reason why some people (called *sahajiya*) prematurely prioritize sensual pleasure over knowledge in the material *yajña* itself.

There are many misconceptions about *bhakti* ranging from *sahajiya* who become sentimentalists, to the fanatics who accept everything on "faith" without an understanding of the deeper principles, to those who take such fanatics and sentimentalists to be the cardinal representatives of the *bhakti* tradition and reject the entire process to be unintelligent and faith-based. All religions who have a personal God, and who espouse devotion and faith suffer from the same problem due to which religion has earned a bad name today as the "opiate of the masses". The problem originates in a misunderstanding of *bhakti* in the material world versus its nature in the spiritual world.

There are indeed two mutually opposite kinds of *bhakti* in the material and the spiritual worlds. The process of *bhakti* in the material world is called *vaidi-bhakti* in which knowledge is emphasized over pleasure, and abstract is preferred over detailed. The process of *bhakti* in the spiritual world is called *ragānugā-bhakti* which is when knowledge is forgotten and sensual stimulation is considered the highest form of *yajña.* When the *vaidi-bhakti* and *ragānugā-bhakti* are confused, then people start believing that because one has to ultimately give up *jnana* or knowledge in *ragānugā-bhakti*, there is no point in acquiring this knowledge in the first place. And thus the notion of a fanatic, sentimentalist, and ignorant devotee of God is born—which is the dominant category of religious people everywhere.

Yajña is Dharma or Prescribed Duty

The term *dharma* has two aspects in Vedic philosophy—*descriptive* and *prescriptive*. By descriptive I mean statements of facts; for example the *dharma* of fire is to be hot, and the *dharma* of winter is to be cold. By prescriptive I mean statements about expectations; for example, the *dharma* of a police officer is to catch the culprit, and the *dharma* of a citizen is to obey the country's laws. We don't expect the descriptive *dharma* to be violated, but the prescriptive *dharma* can be violated with consequences, such as the creation of good or bad *karma*.

Yajña constitutes the prescriptive *dharma* or the expected behaviors. If we don't obey these prescriptive principles, the actions constitute the violation of *dharma* which in turn invites *karma*. As discussed in an earlier article, *karma* is produced when one exceeds or falls short of expectations; depending on whether rights or duties have been exceeded or left unfulfilled, new *karma* would be produced. But if the *dharma* or expectations are fulfilled exactly—neither exceeding nor falling short—then no *karma* would be created.

Yajña and prescriptive *dharma* are therefore identical. Since the expectations are defined relative to situations, the *yajña* is not same for all times, places, or roles. The expectations change with each situation, and we have to know the expectation for that time, place, and role, to perform *yajña*. Accordingly, there can be many religions, which constitute the time, place, and role-specific *dharma*. There can also be religions independent of *some* time, place, role constraints such that they can be applied to all places at a given time, or to all times at a given place, or to all times and places for a given type of role, etc. And there is an absolute religion—which applies to every time, place, and role.

A religion or *dharma* means "expectations" or duties prescribed according one's role and situation in relation to others in society. In a semantic description, the best expectation is to move toward the center of the semantic space. One who knows the center, and sees the current location, can guide people toward the center. The path that connects any location to the center is the *dharma* for that location. It is therefore incorrect to assume that all *dharma* are universal, just as it is incorrect to suppose that all *dharma* is contextual.

Vedic texts describe many kinds of *dharma*. The universal principle or *dharma* for the material world is preferring meaning over pleasure. However, there are also time-specific *dharma* for each age—i.e. *Satya-yuga*, *Dvāpara-yuga*, *Tretā-yuga* and *Kali-yuga*. Similarly, there can be place specific *dharma* for each age, and role-specific *dharma*. However, *dharma* is objective rather than subjective.

Aspects of Dharma and Yajña

In a *yajña*, the fire is lighted in a square area, with four sides of that area occupied by four *ritvik* or priests—*hotā*, *udgāta*, *adhvaryu*, and *brahmā*. Each priest recites one of the four Vedas: the *hotā* chants the Rig-Veda *mantra*, the *adhvaryu* follows the procedures of the Yajur-Veda, the *udgāta* sings hymns from the Sāma-Veda, while the *brahmā* oversees the *yajña*, following the Atharva-Veda.

The *Agni* or fire—which represents the higher purpose—therefore has four "sides" or *aspects*. When the *Agni* represents meanings, these four sides are called *Vasudeva*, *Saṅkarṣaṇa*, *Pradyumna*, and *Aniruddha* and they represent *mahattattva*, ego, intellect, and the mind, respectively. I have discussed previously how our meaning cognition has four aspects—concepts, judgments, intentions, and morals. The mind represents all the meanings, the intellect represents the the judgments of truth and falsity, the ego represents the goal or purpose for which truth is being used, and the *mahattattva* represents the moral value fulfilled by the accomplishment of the goal. Similarly, there are four aspects of pleasure, which appear as happiness in the mind, intellect, ego, and *mahattattva*. Accordingly, there are also duties to be performed by the mind, intellect, ego, and *mahattattva*, which means that they should employed or used correctly.

Within these four sides, the *Agni* is lighted and the *Soma* is offered using *Vāyu*. Vedic texts describe a further five-fold division within the *Agni*, *Soma*, and *Vāyu* which is shown in the below table.

Vāyu	Agni	Soma
Prāna	Pāchaka	Bōdhaka
Udāna	Alochaka	Kledaka
Samāna	Ranjaka	Śhleshka
Vyāna	Sādhaka	Tārpaka
Apāna	Bhrājaka	Avalambhaka

Yajña means finding the best use of our life and time and executing that mission. The best use is not to be decided whimsically and it is not merely our choice. There is indeed a best use for life, although we are free not to follow it. When we follow the best use, we gradually become free from *karma* because we follow *dharma*. When we don't follow *dharma* we gradually become entangled in *karma*.

How Guna and Karma Create the Body

Published Date: 2017-07-21

Vedic texts describe how the body of a soul is created due to *guna* and *karma*. This seems unintuitive if we think that the body is created by eating food. But how do we eat food? Food consumption is, in Vedic philosophy, influenced by two factors, called *guna* (plural) and *karma*. This post discusses how *guna* are the *nature* by which we enjoy consuming certain types of things, and *karma* is the *nurture* due to which we have access to certain types of things. Just because we enjoy certain things (*guna*) doesn't mean that we will get them, because the environment we are situated in (*karma*) might not enable access to them. Similarly, just because the environment enables certain things doesn't mean we will take them, because we might not enjoy them. Our eating is controlled by *nature* and *nurture* where the environment provides certain things, and we enjoy certain things. Their combination causes the food consumption, which builds the body.

The Nature vs. Nurture Debate

The nature vs. nurture debate goes back to the dawn of empiricism when John Locke proposed the idea that the mind is a "blank slate" or tabula rasa on which the external world impinges ideas and all knowledge is acquired as a result of that interaction. Effectively, Locke reduced the entire process of human development to *nurture*. The problem with this view is that many of us are born with innate inclinations towards music, art, science, nature, or sports.

As we encounter situations in our environment where these traits can be expressed, other people can see our innate tendencies. But if we reduce all human development to ideas acquired from the environment, then we can never explain why two people raised in the same environment have different inclinations from each other. In order to explain the differences between people, we need to postulate an innate nature which represents a person's desires.

The reverse problem of trying to attribute everything to an innate nature also turns out to be false because a person's desires cannot be fulfilled unless supported by the environment, and everyone seeks happiness by fulfilling their innate desires. So, a person adapts their desires according to what is offered and enabled by the environment, which will allow them to be happy.

As a result, many of our desires are acquired in the process of dealing with our environment, which constitutes the "ghetto" behavior where the environment deprives one of the desired opportunities, and the person then decides to start desiring what their surrounding offers them. The nature vs. nurture debate is flawed. We have to think of their combination where the human behavior is an outcome of nature *and* nurture, and each one modifies the other.

The Guna vs. Karma Complementarity

In Vedic philosophy, *guna* represent a person's personality or what they enjoy, such as the preference for a type of food, clothing, leisure, work, creativity, and so forth. There are three *guna* called *sattva*, *rajas*, and *tamas* which represent different kinds of pleasures; for example, *sattva* represents the pleasure of knowledge, renunciation, and self-realization, *rajas* represents the pleasure of being famous, powerful, and rich, while *tamas* represents the pleasure of hurting, killing, and destroying. The three *guna* cover the soul's innate need for pleasure.

To fulfill these needs, we must be situated in the correct type of situational opportunity, which then also define the *expected* behaviors. As the expected behaviors are fulfilled, exceeded, or unfulfilled, good or bad *karma* is created, which then produces new opportunities. Good *karma* means greater opportunities to fulfill one's desires. Bad *karma* means reduced opportunities, which then limit the fulfillment of one's desires.

For example, if I relish the scientific study of nature, and I have good *karma*, then I will find the situations where I can obtain good books or meet people who can impart me such knowledge. Conversely, if my *karma* is bad, then even though I enjoy the process of learning the truth about nature, I would simply never find the right books and the people to learn. If my *guna* were different—e.g. I enjoyed wealth and power, then good *karma* will give me the opportunities and abilities for fulfilling those desires, and bad *karma* will frustrate my desires.

The Role of Guna and Karma in Perception

Guna represents what we desire and *karma* denotes what we deserve. The desiring and deserving act differently on the senses of knowledge and action. For the senses of knowledge, the desire is sense pleasure, while deserving is (1) whether we obtain the relevant sense objects and (2) whether we can perceive them after obtaining them (e.g. the person is not blind). For the senses of action, desire is the manner in which we want to act, while deserving is (1) the ability in the senses to act (e.g. the person is not lame or dumb), and (2) the opportunities to act.

Due to the abilities enabled by *karma*, the soul is put into a different type of body. And due to the opportunities enabled by *karma*, this body comes into contact with other kinds of bodies. In this way, the soul's body and the soul's opportunities are decided due to *karma*.

However, this still doesn't preclude the role of free will. For the senses of knowledge, while *karma* determines whether we obtain the sense objects, and whether we can perceive them, *karma* doesn't determine whether we enjoy or suffer this perception. Our happiness or distress based on the sense perception is entirely caused by the *guna*. Thus, an animal might eat terrible things, and yet consider it a great pleasure; the *karma* causes the ability to eat those terrible things and the opportunity to find such things, while the *guna* leads to the pleasure or suffering from that consumption. Similarly, due to *karma* we obtain the abilities and opportunities to act in certain ways but due to *guna* we might not use such abilities and opportunities.

Karma and Fatalism

Vedic philosophy appears to be fatalistic unless we understand this complementarity. The action of *karma* is inevitable, but it doesn't completely fix our experience. In the case of the senses of knowledge, it fixes what sense objects will be received and if they can be perceived, but it doesn't fix the happiness or sadness. Similarly, in case of senses of action, *karma* fixes the abilities and opportunities, but the abilities are just tools—e.g. knives and guns—which can be used in many ways. We are given tools and opportunities, but our action is not decided by those.

Thus, our life is free in spite of *karma* in two ways—(a) we can control our happiness regardless of our situation, and (b) we can change the application of our abilities to what is possible in the opportunity.

The ability to control our happiness and do what is morally right is our free will.

Since this free will is conditioned by *guna*, or the past habits of choices, the key purpose of life is not to become free of *karma* but of *guna*. In essence, the goal is not to have good *karma* so that we can be happy. The goal it to change the *guna* such that we will be happy even in adverse conditions. Likewise, the goal is not to become powerful and capable before we do something worthwhile. Rather, the goal is to do something worthwhile with whatever abilities we have. The goal is not to obtain the best opportunities where we can experience the most pleasurable objects and do the most desirable things; the goal is to do the best the opportunity affords.

This is likely to make many people uncomfortable because they believe that if we had free will then we will obtain the best enjoyment, live under the best opportunities, and be free to do whatever we like. The fact is that they aren't able to do achieve such goals, or the achievements are far from satisfactory, which leads them to the denial of free will. Such a denial amounts to a "sour grapes" mentality because free will is never about the abovementioned things.

The Importance of Karma to Religion

When religion is described as the pursuit of desirable circumstances (in which we can be happy) or powerful abilities (by which we can do what we desire), it is obscenely misrepresented. Since both desirable circumstances and powerful abilities are produced due to *karma*, the creation of good *karma* is not regarded as true religion. Historically, all practices related to *Karma-Mimānsa* which produce good *karma* have been rejected since the time of Shankarāchārya. Ever since, the focus is entirely on the purification of *guna*—i.e. on how to be happy even in adverse conditions, and how to act morally even with limited abilities and under given opportunities.

As the focus of religion shifted from *karma* to *guna*, the proper scientific understanding of *karma* and how it produces bodily abilities and circumstances also dramatically declined. Then onwards, the knowledge of how the body is created, and how it enters different situations, was replaced by "material science". The important lesson of history is that as religion defocuses on the understanding of *karma* (in order to prioritize freedom from *guna*), a materialistic science takes over the description of the living body and why it enters particular situations.

The rise of materialism can be attributed directly to the decline in the understanding of *karma*. While the ultimate goal of religion is not the creation of good *karma* (but the purification of *guna*), without understanding *karma*, the gaps in understanding our body and the situations around us are being filled by materialism, which defeats both good *karma* and pure *guna*. In that respect, even to revive the goal of *guna* purification, there is a need to institute the scientific knowledge of *karma*, because focusing on *guna* purification while neglecting the advancement of *karma* works only when the person has already advanced into very good *karma*.

The rejection of *Karma-Mimānsa* in favor of *Advaita*, and the rejection of *Advaita* in favor of a personalism are viable only when we understand that good *karma* is *necessary* but not *sufficient* for religion. The rejection of *Karma-Mimānsa* is not the rejection of *karma* itself; it is rather the rejection of the idea that our life must be devoted to nothing other than acquisition of good *karma*, rather than freedom from *karma* or the cycle of birth and death. When we neglect the understanding of *karma*, we don't obtain freedom from *karma*; we rather fall into the ditch of bad *karma* because we are not careful in avoiding the creation of consequences.

The Currency Exchange Analogy

The action of *karma* is quite like currency exchange where you can earn money in one country as Dollars and spend it in another country as Yuan, Kroner, or Rupee. Every currency has an exchange rate with other currencies, owing to which we can convert the *karma* earned in one situation into the *karma* spent in another situation. For example, pious people perform charity and sacrifices on Earth and they can enjoy the resulting *karma* in heavenly planets. It is not necessary for them to enjoy on Earth, due to the currency exchange between locations.

However, once you move to the new country, you have to abide by the unique laws of that country. The laws of the country where you made the money don't apply in the new country, and what was considered good while earning the money may not be considered good while spending it. This means that the laws of Earthly behavior don't apply in the heavenly planets and vice versa. The diligent person, therefore, uses the heavenly planets to make further sacrifices and create even better *karma* so that they can rise to even higher heavenly planets.

The foolish person, however, uses that new opportunity to enjoy and spend their earnings and when the money is finished, they are deported back to the original place for further earning.

The most intelligent person, however, is one who doesn't earn good or bad *karma*. He or she just spends whatever good or bad they have previously earned and avoids creation of further *karma*. This means that if they are in good situations, they just do their duties without influenced by lust or greed. Similarly, if they are in a bad situation, they tolerate it without anger or fear.

The Body Combines Guna and Karma

The material mind and body of the soul is a byproduct of its *guna* and *karma*. The soul is placed in the womb of a particular type of mother—i.e. the environment at birth—due to *karma*, which affords choices of consumption. The soul chooses from the possible alternatives (ability and opportunity) based on *guna*. The role of *guna* lies in determining (1) whether we engage or withdraw the senses from participating in the bodily activities and (2) whether we enjoy or suffer through such participation. The combination of ability, opportunity, participation, and pleasure, creates the experience of the soul. In this experience, the ability and opportunity are caused by *karma* while the choice of participation and the pleasure or pain is due to *guna*. The ability can also be created by *guna* when by repeated effort we can enhance our abilities because we like doing something and despite limited opportunity we can enhance the ability by our effort.

Consider the extreme example of someone who is being tortured for misdeeds. It might appear to the outsider that the person has no choice except to suffer from pain arising from this torture—which has been caused by previous *karma*; *karma* has created the ability to perceive, and produced the circumstance in which the person is caught. But the choice still exists because the person can withdraw their mind and senses (not the body) from that experience, and the resulting pleasure and pain from that experience would be different than if the senses were engaged.

I use this example to illustrate the fact that worldly situations don't preclude choice, nor do they entail suffering. However, to attain that freedom from worldly situations one must understand how the soul can withdraw the senses—just like a tortoise who draws its limbs inwards—and focuses them on something other than outward experiences. When the *guna* are impure, the soul is incapable of withdrawing from the activities of the mind, senses, and the body. But when the senses are purified, the soul pays no attention to the unwanted acts of the mind or senses.

The purification of *guna* is not meant to improve the bodily circumstances or increase bodily abilities. It is rather meant to withdraw from the material activities of the mind and the senses. Of course, that state is difficult to achieve, and I don't mean to trivialize its attainment. I only mean to highlight the fact that free will is never lost even when the situation seems predetermined. However, to realize that one is free even in predetermined situations one must be spiritually advanced.

As the soul is gradually purified of the *guna*, it has greater ability to disengage itself from the body and its circumstances. Therefore, such disengagement is a measure of spiritual progress. The situation is often compared to the difference between a ripe and a tender coconut. When the coconut is tender, its shell and core are attached. The shell is the *karma* and the core is the *guna*. Their attachment makes the soul enjoy or suffer every experience. But as the coconut dries up, the core separates from the shell, and that entails cessation of material experience. The separation means that the soul can be happy within itself even when the exterior is painful.

The Novelty in the Description of Matter

This notion of the body changes our understanding of matter. Matter is not a *thing*; it rather exists as a *possibility*: in the human body it is the *ability* to exploit the *opportunities* in the environment. Therefore, the description of matter as 'possibility' is a vista to understanding the body as ability and the surrounding as opportunity. However, in modern science, these possibilities are studied as *probabilities* because we are unable to imagine how something exists as a possibility. The description then becomes incomplete due to loss of predictability.

Sāṅkhya describes all matter as *ideas* rather than things or quantities. An idea is the possibility of being converted into a fixed thing, and yet it is not a fixed thing. The idea is also *objective* and yet it is not an *object*. This is the basis on which we can solve the problems of probability—e.g. in atomic theory—when the body is described as a *possibility* or *idea*. In short, the body we see is an idea, although it is definite. But that definite idea is produced from an abstract idea, which is relatively more indefinite as compared to what we can perceive by the senses. The 'abstract' reality is *objective* but it is not an *object*. These are called "subtle" and "gross" matter.

My pleasure personality, my material body, and the opportunity in which I'm situated, cannot be observed by themselves—they are all "unmanifest". The manifest world is created when these unmanifest properties start mixing. For example, my need for pleasure combines with the bodily ability to seek pleasurable "food" in the environment; or, the environment offers something which mixes with the bodily ability (e.g. hunger) and we consume it to create satisfaction. The world is real in a subtle unmanifest form, but it becomes perceivable when the different aspects of this world *combine*. Individually, they are all unmanifest or unperceivable.

The universe is created when the different unmanifest parts start mixing or combining. Prior to this mixing, the world exists materially, but there is no experience. The creation of the universe is therefore not the creation of matter itself; it is rather the creation of experience.

Can Biology Be Based on the Nature of the Soul?

Published Date: 2017-07-21

Introduction and Overview

In Vedic philosophy, the soul has three properties—*sat* or consciousness, *chit* or meanings, and *ananda* or pleasure. These three aspects of the soul are also reflected in matter and pervade throughout the body—the parts of the body are due to *chit*, the functions of each of the parts is due to *sat*, and the purpose associated with the functions of the parts is due to *ananda*. Thus, even the world around us is a reflection of the soul (as parts, functions, and purposes). However, because everything combines these three, therefore, we tend to think that the part is itself the function, and the function is itself the purpose. This article discusses the differences between these three aspects of the soul, and its implications for biology.

The Hierarchy of Objects

The aspect of the world easiest to observe is that it comprises material objects. These objects are produced from elementary concepts, and they hence constitute complex concepts. The elementary concepts combine in a hierarchy, to create an inverted tree of meanings, quite like sentences are constructed from words, and the grammar of combination forms a tree structure.

As you observe the higher and lower parts of this tree, you find a pattern. The higher nodes are the "bigger" or "macroscopic" objects, while the lower nodes are the "smaller" or "microscopic" particles. For example, the bigger node is an elephant, and the smaller nodes are the elephant's body parts—tail, stomach, legs, ears, etc. The smaller is connected to the bigger, although the bigger is logically prior to the smaller because it is the higher node in the tree.

If the higher nodes are not perceived (because they are more abstract and hence not amenable to sense perception), then the elephant is not seen. We could still perceive the "tail", "stomach", "legs", etc. and therefore think about the elephant quite like the proverbial blind men, who only see the individual body parts, and call them "cylinder", "sphere", "line", etc. Without the detection of the elephant (even without the existence of the body parts), the body parts themselves would not be considered parts of the single body. They would just be modeled as independent and unrelated objects.

The Part-Function Separation

Of course, in just describing the body parts, we haven't fully described the body because each part of the body also has a unique function, which isn't yet known. For example, the hands can hold, the legs are used to move, the stomach helps digest food, the head is employed in thinking, etc. The functionality is an additional appellation of the body part due to which the part acquires a *role* in relation to other parts. The parts are different from the roles, because a part can perform another part's role. For example, hands can be used to move, and the legs can be used to hold. While a part cannot perform every other part's functions (the hand cannot think) some parts can perform other's functions. That ability, however, entails a separation between the *ability* in the part and the *function* it is used for.

This idea is easily understood in case of an organization that has functional departments such as engineering, marketing, sales, human resources, finance, legal, manufacturing, etc. quite separate from the people who are employed in these departments. You can describe the organization as comprised of people—which are parts that you can see. You can also describe the same organization as divided into functional roles—which are not observable as parts, but become apparent in *activities*. Some people could potentially work in multiple departments, while others can only do one function. But the key point is that due to job mobility the person is not identical to the role.

The distinction between part and function has been the topic of much debate in biology because many biologists contend that the part is itself the function, and because the parts often perform different functions, although not every part can do every function. The different functions are manifest when a part comes into interaction with another part to which it wasn't previously interacting. Therefore, new functionality is not a magical property of the part that we don't see otherwise. It is rather a property that always exists but is only manifest when we put a part into interaction with a previously non-interacting part. In that sense, we an say that the part has a new role in the system.

The problem for the biologist is that they cannot *observe* the functions as *objects* because the functions are always subject to the interaction between specific parts. Each new type of interaction potentially brings a new function. And yet, since all parts don't always interact with all other parts, there can be potentially new functionality in the system. The flaw in biology lies in the thinking which originated in classical physics: that all parts in the universe always interact with all other parts. Therefore, the function of a part is always given exclusively by the part itself. This premise is falsified when all parts don't always interact with each other, and the evidence of that falsification is atomic theory where the *agency* of interaction—called the 'field'—is *quantized* which means that the interactions are never simultaneously but *sequenced* in a particular order (which current atomic theory is unable to predict, because the order is a 'choice').

The problem is akin to the well-known fact that a workman's tool can be used in many different ways, in relation to different objects. The tool is therefore different from the *function* it performs, because bringing the tool into interaction with another object involves a choice, which can be empirically observed but it cannot be empirically explained because we cannot observe this choice as material object. The materialist claims that since we cannot see the choice objectively, it must not exist. The problem with such a view is that the function of the part changes in relation to different parts and by changing this relation we can produce new behaviors not previously seen in the part.

The Hierarchy of Roles

Again, this is seen in organizations where competition between the divisions creates problems, although the individuals might be competent if they were afforded a better environment. If we applied the object-like thinking, then we would blame the people in each division (because we can see them) but not focus on defining their roles in such a way that they can cooperate rather than compete. Just being parts of a larger system doesn't mean that the parts cooperate with each other. The dysfunctional parts need not be faulted if the head was tasked to digest food, the stomach was required to move the body, and the hands were mandated to think. There is a proper role for each part, and while we can know which role is suitable for which part, it is not always necessary that he part is indeed involved only in that role.

The hierarchy of roles also constitutes a tree of functionalities in which the higher node supervises the functions of the lower nodes. However, the functional hierarchy is separate from the physical hierarchy (of parts and wholes). The same part can be used in different ways, and thus the relation between part and function varies.

All living entities perform the same basic functions—eating, sleeping, mating, and defending—but the body parts employed in these functions might be different, and the functions themselves might be executed differently. For example, some animals use claws to defend, others use teeth, while others use poisons. The differences in the functions are produced by the functional hierarchy, while the parts used for functions involve mapping the material parts to the material functions. They are two separate hierarchies but they are also combined in the body.

When consciousness leaves the body, the body stops functioning, even though you can still perceive the body parts such as head, legs, hands, stomach, etc. The reason is that the function is always separate from the parts and the relation between the part and the function varies even during this lifetime. However, since we don't *perceive* the functions as *objects*, we cannot see how the function is an additional property of the part, not reducible to the parts.

The Hierarchy of Purposes

When the body parts are functioning, we must also ask ourselves about the purpose of this working. Why do living entities want to live rather than die? Why do we consider life better than death? And why do some people begin to prefer death over life? The key purpose of life is pleasure or enjoyment. We prefer life over death when there is abundant pleasure, and we prefer death over life when there is too much suffering. The pleasure of the soul is called *ananda*, which is embedded in matter as its purpose.

Every part of the body affords some or other pleasure, and the desire for pleasure pervades the body, and ultimately constitutes the purpose. The pleasures of the senses (eyes, skin, tongue, ears, and nose) are well-known. However, there is also pleasure is the senses of action. For example, some people enjoy running, others enjoy working with their hands, while yet others derive great pleasure from talking, sex, or defecation. The mind enjoys thought, the intellect enjoys analysis and judgment, the ego enjoys creating goals, and the moral sense enjoys the production and consumption of moral values. Body parts like the stomach create pain and suffering when hungry, and satisfaction and pleasure when full. There is much rejuvenation in the body through stable breathing and circulation, just as there is suffering.

If the desire for pleasure was killed, then the body parts could function, but there would no incentive for them to function. To keep the body incentivized, there is purpose embedded in the body as pleasure and pain. Unless we overcome this desire for pleasure, the body parts have to be kept functioning. However, just as there is a mapping between body parts and their functions, similarly, there is a mapping between the bodily functions and their associated pleasures. The simple act of touching another person can mean paternal, fraternal, or conjugal pleasure. Similarly, you can look upon a beautiful person with admiration, wonderment, or lust. The cognition of beauty is quite different from our *disposition* towards that beauty.

How the Soul is Reflected in the Body

Every part of the material body is simultaneously comprised of the three aspects—structure, function, and purpose. Take your brain, for example. It is comprised of different regions, which are in turn comprised of molecules, which are in turn comprised of subatomic particles. Due to this composition, we can say that my brain has a frontal lobe, a parietal lobe, an occipital lobe, etc. This constitutes the structure.

But the parts of the brain also play a role or function due to which some parts become vision, while other parts become speech, and yet other parts become motor control. This designation of the parts constitutes the functional feature of the consciousness.

Each part can also create a pleasure associated with a body part and function. For example, I can say that I enjoy music—where the pleasure is tied to the ears and the surrounding which provides the music. The pleasure associated with the part and function constitutes the purpose.

Each part of the body has some function, and each function has some purpose. These three aspects are mixed in such as way that we could be forgiven for thinking that the parts are themselves the function, and the function is itself the purpose. And yet, they are separate because they constitute different concepts.

Consciousness and Conflicts

The *evidence* of their difference comes from *conflicts* between them. For example, if the part of my brain that performs the function of motor control worked exactly the same way all the time, then I would never spill water while pouring it into a glass. If the part of my brain that performs the function of auditory cortex worked the same way always, then I would never hear incorrectly. Similarly, if my tongue (part and function combined) always had the desire for tasting the same thing, then I would never require to eat more than one dish. And if my ears (part and function combined) always desired the same sound, I would not need a second sound.

The difference between *sat*, *chit*, and *ananda* is evidenced from the fact that they can conflict. The evolution of the molecules in my brain can be observed easily. However, what can't be observed easily is that the *role* played by different parts of the brain is also evolving over time, which means that there isn't necessarily a fixed brain part for seeing, hearing, tasting, or touching, although in most people the function is performed roughly in the same place. It is now well-known through neuroscience that it is impossible to isolate a function to a specific part, although we can still speak about some typical areas of perception in the brain.

The Study of the Body in Biology

Anti-evolutionary biologists recognize a difference between the body parts, and the role they perform in the body. These are respectively called *structure* and *function*: the material hierarchy of parts is the structure, and the job performed by each part is called the function. The mystery is that the same kinds of cells and molecules make up most parts of the body and yet these parts *behave* differently. The material parts are like an actor playing different roles in a drama. Similarly, even if the structure and function are fixed—and the parts *can* function in the same way—they may not, because the part now has a different intent, purpose, goal, or desire.

We are able to observe the material body and its structure, but we are unable to observe the *functional* and *intentional* states, which are also material, just not the *structural* matter. This idea generates much debate in biology because scientists don't understand that there are three basic categories—originating from *sat*, *chit*, and *ananda*—and science studies matter corresponding to *chit* but cannot perceive the reality corresponding to *sat* and *ananda*. The reason is that *sat* and *ananda* are role and goal, which are overtly "subjective" while *chit* as concepts includes material objects and thus appears to be "objective". Physical concepts are incapable of anything subjective. And therefore they are completely incapable of dealing with *sat* and *ananda*. Physical concepts can, however, reduce a world of varied meanings to a few physical properties. In that sense, physical concepts can (within limits) describe *chit*, but not *sat* and *ananda*.

Biology is therefore incomplete because it requires three constructs to describe the embodiment of the *sat-chit-ananda* soul in the body, but we have only one—*structure*. People sometimes ask: Can you prove the existence of the soul scientifically? The short answer is that yes we can prove, and the proof is that *structural* matter is inadequate to describe scientific phenomena. The structure has to be complemented by two other kinds of matter—*function* and *intention*. With these three kinds of matter, we can talk about *structures* that perform *functions* for some *intents* or goals. Without the function and intent, the structure is incomplete, and the reason is that the soul has three aspects but science captures only one and that too incompletely.

The denial of the soul therefore translates into a scientific problem where we are trying to reduce the material body to molecules, and in that process we ignore the *function* and *intention*, which too are material, just not the molecules. Even the molecules have to be described as symbols of meaning—which means that they exist as *possibilities* converted into observables (the well-known Quantum Measurement Problem). But even if we provide a semantic theory of atomism, biology would still be incomplete without the study of function and intention.

Free Market Economics vs. Capitalism

Published Date: 2017-07-28

Introduction and Overview

Free market economics is about competition between businesses, and it operates under the assumptions of a *closed* system in which wealth can be redistributed, but the total wealth must remain constant. Capitalism is the contrary idea that the economy is an *open* system in which wealth can be infused, in order to create a net growth for the economy. The wealth infusion is carried out by the wealthy using a business model that is stripped of risks, and the lender is certain to gain wealth over time, making the rich get richer and the poor poorer.

This article discusses how free markets are different from capitalism; in the former, wealth is constant although it can be redistributed by competition, but in the latter an illusion of growth through borrowing is perpetuated to surreptitiously take wealth from the borrower. The post also discusses the Vedic economic system and how it reconciles economic growth with altruism, contrary to the modern economic system where altruism doesn't exist..

The Nature of Closed Systems

Consider a predator-prey ecosystem comprised of lions and deer. If some lions develop a larger appetite but the deer do not change their rate of reproduction, then as the lions eat more, the jackals may have a problem finding enough food. The jackals might then eat many insects, which would then reduce the pollination in the plants, thus decreasing plant population, which then reduces the population of the herbivores, which then impacts the food supply for lions. Ultimately, as the food of the lions decreases, their population must also reduce.

Conversely, if the lions start eating less deer, then it will cause the deer population to increase, and jackals may suddenly find an abundant supply of deer which was previously not seen and they will now replace the lions as the primary carnivores. However, now we will find an increase in the insect population that the jackals were previously consuming, which then pollinates the plants more, thus increasing the food for the deer and thereby the deer population, and ultimately the quantity of food available for the lions, thereby increasing lion population.

The moral of the story is that if the lions eat less deer, then there can be more lions, keeping the total consumption and production constant. Conversely, if the lions eat more deer, then the total number of lions must reduce, while the total consumption and production remains constant. This is a peculiar property of closed systems in which the total energy remains constant, although the energy can be *redistributed* among the producers and the consumers differently.

The Stability of Markets

This stability is a fundamental premise underlying the study of market economics which supposes that the total production and consumption in a market remains stable, although it can be redistributed. On one hand, therefore, we can assume market determinism because the patterns of consumption and production are stable. On the other hand, we must always allow for an instability in the market as the production and consumption shift to different actors.

Assume for the moment that I'm addicted to alcohol consumption, but I make a successful attempt at quitting alcohol. My quitting alcohol, however, doesn't stop the producers from continuing their alcohol production. Therefore, when I stop consuming, there is a small amount of surplus alcohol in the market, which makes it easier to obtain the alcohol.

Typically, as the alcohol inventory builds up, the providers or resellers will slash prices, prompting others who desire to drink alcohol to increase their consumption, which compensates for my quitting. As time passes, and the demand reaches its original levels, the prices go back to where they were before. In effect, after a short blip, the system returns to its original state such that the same amount of alcohol is produced, although consumed by one less person.

If a large number of people quit at once, the prices will drop suddenly but the production of alcohol would not change. In fact, in most cases, producers compensate for their lower margins by producing higher volumes and pushing more product into the market to crash the prices and gain market share. Thus, a competition arises and those who can produce more efficiently take the market share from those who are unable to produce the product as efficiently.

Owing to these factors, it is now standard practice to think that the market of demand and supply is stable, but the producers and consumers can be different. We are able to successfully "impersonalize" economics by removing the actors, while just studying the transactions. Thus, all industries "size" the market—the total consumption—before one starts production. The belief is that the market size is independent of the individual produces and consumers. Even if one person changes their habits, there is sufficient demand to shift from one consumer to another. Businesses relying on such market trends care little about individual consumers.

Competitive Dynamics in the Marketplace

Under the veneer of market stability is the instability arising from market competition in which actors try to grab a greater share of the production or consumption from other actors. If the production by one actor increases, it must cause one of the following three outcomes: (1) the existing producers retaliate by slashing prices, causing the new producer to go out of business, returning the system back to its original state, (2) the increased production causes a fall in prices, causing the smaller producers to go out of the production and dividing the share of the bigger producers, settling the system into a new state with realignment, or (3) an oscillation in the system is created where the share of production moves from one actor to another.

All these alternatives assume that the demand remains constant during this redistribution, although there could be similar reversals, realignments, or oscillations in the consumptions of different consumers too. So long as the demand is constant, and there is ability in the system to produce, the economic system remains stable as a whole, although within that system there can be continuous competitive activity to grab the share of production or consumption.

We commonly call this competitive activity 'market driven economics' in which producers and consumers are free to grab the share from each other keeping the total size of the market constant. Economists try to measure the size of the market and call it Gross Domestic Product or GDP, which signifies the total value of all the transactions that occur in a system.

Flaws in the Concept of Economic Growth

The GDP increases as the total value of the transactions grows, and every economic system tries to maximize their GDP—indicating an increase in production and consumption. As we have seen above, a closed system cannot grow by itself; it can only redistribute production and consumption among the actors. Then how can we ever think of growing the GDP?

This is where economics supposes that the economic system is not *closed* but rather *open*. While you can only redistribute energy in a closed system, you can *infuse* more energy into an open system. It is supposed that this infusion can be achieved if we inject *capital* into the system. The premise is that by injecting capital into the system we can increase the GDP.

One school of thought claims that if the producers had more capital at hand, then they will produce more, but the problem is that even if the producers do produce more, the consumers still don't have the extra capital, and they cannot consume the production. Therefore, giving more capital to the producers does stimulate the production but it doesn't increase the GDP because the consumers don't have the money to buy the products. Giving more capital to the producers is called Supply-Side Economics because it tries to increase the GDP by stimulating the supply.

The opposite approach to the GDP increase says that instead of stimulating the supply, we must stimulate the demand, and this approach is therefore called Demand-Side Economics because it tries to dole out capital to the consumers, so that they can start spending, thereby raising the demand, hoping that the producers will then respond to the demand with greater production. Unfortunately, higher demand itself doesn't mean higher GDP, because the producers don't have the capital at hand to increase their production—e.g. more equipment and factories.

The Outcomes of Capital Infusion

The GDP can increase only when consumers and producers simultaneously have disposable capital which generally turns out to be false because typically only those who have the capital can obtain more capital since they have the capacity to return that capital. Those who lack capital generally have a harder time finding the capital because the capital infuser considers them a risky borrower and hence not a prudent investment.

Furthermore, even if both consumers and producers have disposable capital, there is no guarantee that both consumers and producers have an equal amount of spending and investment in the same commodity. For example, if a producer borrows capital to create new kinds of beds but the consumers want to spend their spare capital on curtains, then both demand and supply side of the equation would be frustrated. If the infused capital invigorates different commodities on supply and demand sides, the outcome of the infusion would be uncertain. Since there is no way to guarantee that the capital is invested by both consumers and producers in the same commodities the outcomes are always uncertain. When the curtain consumer wants to spend their capital but there isn't additional supply of curtains (because the producers are investing in beds) it leads to price rise for curtains, which then appears as growth in GDP although no real growth is involved. Likewise, the bed producers lose their capital because the consumers don't want beds. Ultimately we see a growth in GDP due to increased curtain prices and a loss in capital due to bed investment. It makes people think that there is growth in GDP although if we look at the economy holistically there is a net loss in capital due to the infusion and yet the curtain prices have gone up, which means you now require more capital to acquire curtains. Thus, on one hand, capital is being lost and on the other more capital is required.

Also, having more capital at hand doesn't necessarily mean increased spending; people could just decide to save all the capital for the rainy day, keeping the GDP unchanged. Those who save the capital now obtain a lesser interest on their saving because there is abundant supply of capital which forces a drop in interest rates. On the whole, the return on the capital is lost, which means that ultimately some capital has been lost, because the return on the capital would be higher if it were invested in a genuine business.

Finally, as you infuse more capital, there may also be capital flight from one system to another. After all, the system is now *open* which means that capital can both enter and exit. Thus, as capital is being infused at one end, it could be leaking at the other end, entering a different system, where the same kinds of possibilities noted above apply.

The Pretentiousness of Economic Growth

Given the tremendous uncertainties and adverse consequences of capital infusion, it is surprising that lending and borrowing money has become the *de facto* process for stimulating growth. It is impossible to explain this trend except for recognizing that those who already have substantial capital encourage others to borrow by advertising the hope of economic prosperity. If the borrower is successful in returning the loan, the lender gains from the interest on the loan. If the borrower fails in returning the loan, the lender grabs the collateral assets backing the loan, extracting a bigger return on investment.

For example, in the housing bubble, some people successfully paid their loans with interest, giving profits to the banks. However, those who failed to repay the loans, lost their houses, *after* they had already paid a percentage of the loan. In such cases, the bank got back the house, along with the capital that the borrower had already paid to the bank. The housing crises created a problem because the banks could not sell the houses due to a massive oversupply of the houses. But, on a somewhat smaller scale, the banks would have been the net gainers—taking interest from the diligent borrowers, and the house plus interest from the defaulting borrower.

The successful borrowers think that they are able to buy a house with a loan, but they actually pay (over time) a price far greater than the value of the house—the difference being the bank's profit. The borrowers who default on the payments lose not just the house but also their hard earned wealth given through previous repayments. If the economic system had no inflation—e.g. the house prices were not growing—there would be no economic incentive to buy the house given these extreme risks. The borrowing therefore has to be incentivized by inflation—created easily by infusing capital.

Capital infusion creates a self-perpetuating illusion of growth, that begins in price rise, which gives the impression of quick profit, which motivates borrowing with the idea that the borrower will gain from the loan, and the net result of this borrowing is that the borrower parts with greater value than the assets they procure. The lender loses only if there is massive default on returns, but even then it obtains disproportionate control over the borrower's assets. If the lender can maintain its power over the economic system, there is simply no scenario in which their capital would not increase over time.

The Crimes Underlying Money Lending

Every business opportunity involves a finite amount of risk; we nominally suppose that the greater the opportunity, the greater must be the risk. Money lending, however, is a business without risks. If a borrower is successful in repaying his loans, then he has returned the capital with a profit. If he fails in returning the loan, he will lose the collateral which was used to guarantee the loan; the collateral is always assessed at rates lower than its true value, which means you lose *more* by failing to repay. The business model of lending is designed to pass all the risk to the borrower, while the lender always reaps the rewards. This cannot constitute a legitimate business because in this activity the lending party has no risks, and they are hence bound to continually grow over time.

People generally think that stealing is a crime, because their wealth is taken directly by someone who did not previously own it. They don't realize how borrowing is wrongdoing by which their capital is taken. In the case of borrowing you seem to be *receiving* money rather than *giving* it away. How can you be a loser if you are receiving money? That's the complicated illusion created by "economic growth" in which a person, organization, society, or country is enticed to borrow with the prospect of growth, and no matter what you do, you give back far more value than you borrowed. You think that you are growing, but actually the wealth is being redistributed—from the borrower to the lender.

Economy should be viewed as a *closed* rather than *open* system which never grows as a whole, although there can be wealth redistribution. Therefore, if you take more, someone else will have less. There is simply no scenario of *net growth*. When we understand that the system is closed, then we can see that the more you borrow, the more you lose control of your life to the lender. In fact, capital infusion is the primary reason for inflation which makes even those who are not borrowing poorer just because others are borrowing. Systemic borrowing is therefore an unmitigated social disaster.

The premise of economic growth is an illusion perpetuated by the moneyed class by telling others to borrow money. The net effect of borrowing is not *growth* but *redistribution* of wealth. Effectively, the system behaves not as an *open* system in which wealth is infused from the outside, but as a *closed* system in which the wealth is redistributed by lending.

The Problem of Growing Debt

Capitalists have sold the idea of economic growth to the whole world. They tell people how their miseries can be solved if only they borrow money. Governments all over the world are busy finding ways to borrow, and banks all over the world are busy trying to lend money. The more you borrow, the more the lender profits. As time passes, and you keep borrowing, your debt mounts to a point where all your income will be used to repay the interest on the debt. That is the point at which you have been bought by the lender; you have no freedom of choice, and you have to do exactly what the lender tells you to.

It is amazing that this simple wisdom can be easily understood by a child, but it is overlooked by societies and governments who are busy accumulating debt, losing their autonomy to lenders, and becoming their slaves where they and their future generations will be forced to work simply to repay their debts to the lender and they cannot regain their autonomy until this debt is repaid. While some people seek conspiratorial reasons for this state of affairs, I would argue that the conspiracy is far deeper than imagined thus far: it is embedded in the very theory and practice of capitalism, which foregoes the questions of economic stability and propagates the illusion of economic growth.

The Question of Equal Opportunity

I'm sure many of you may be thinking—if I don't have the capital, and I cannot borrow the capital, then how can I grow? The short answer is this: if you don't have capital, then work hard, earn the capital, and save it so that you can invest *your* capital into your development.

If one looks into the past, there was a moneyed class but there was no lending. What can the moneyed class do with their money? They will obviously keep spending their money to lead a luxurious lifestyle which means that their wealth will decline over time. To retain their wealthy status, they have to create a business, employ other people, compete with the other businesses, by which their wealth distributes to the rest of the society.

The workers—who begin by not having any money—offer their services to the businesses created by the moneyed class and gradually accumulate wealth which they can now invest in creating their own business. This is their legitimate path of upward social mobility. This is a longer path—in fact, it may involve a few generations to yield substantial upward mobility—but it is a path of social stability. You receive from your employer a fair return on your work, or you work for another fair employer. The free market system ensures that you are free to work for an employer of your choice, the moneyed class is forced to invest their money into a business in order to maintain their wealth, and this investment then creates the employment for those who do not have the money to create a business.

Free Market is Not Capitalism

We must realize that 'free market economy' has little to do with 'capitalism'. The free market system only talks about redistributing the resources in a system through fair and honest competition. The capitalistic system on the other hand talks about infusing capital from a lender to a borrower in order to surreptitiously redistribute the borrower's wealth to the lender. There can be free market economy even without capitalism. In fact, as capitalism grows, the market becomes less free because every borrower gradually loses their wealth to the lender, and the lenders become ever more powerful.

When the free market system is confused with capitalism, then the moneyed class invests not in legitimate businesses but in *lending* money. Whoever borrows their money falls into the illusory growth trap while the lender profits from everyone's borrowing—whether they win or lose. By stopping borrowing, people can force the lenders to become businessmen and under the free market system their wealth will naturally distribute to the society.

Private Lenders Fuel Government Borrowing

The biggest lenders today lend to the governments who are obligated to return the borrowing by exerting taxes on the citizens. In other words, the government borrows, and the citizens pay on their government's behalf. The citizens have no power to make the borrowing decision, but they are obligated to repay the debt acquired by the government through taxes. Unless the country and the government itself disappears, the lender is guaranteed his profitable return through taxes applied on the citizens.

Normally when citizens take a loan, they invest it into useful activities—e.g. a house, education, healthcare, leisure, security, etc. But when nations borrow money, most of it is spent in worthless activities—e.g. waging wars, destabilizing other nations, and having the loan disbursed to a few rich contractors. Thus, the citizens seldom receive the benefits of the borrowed wealth, although they receive the full burden of the loan repayment. The lender gets back their money with profits, and the preferred contractors see a significant rise in their wealth as they receive the lion's share of the money borrowed through a loan, which the poor now have to repay through taxes. National lending is therefore a scam by which the lender and a few rich contractors steal wealth from the poor.

Recycling Stolen Wealth as Loans

If you lend some wealth to others, you have a shorter supply of wealth, and your capacity for lending is reduced until the borrower repays their debt with interest. It means that in the normal scenario, a lender will have to pause their lending unless the borrower repays.

But this never happens for national borrowing because the money provided by the lender is passed (through the government) to the favored contractors who put the money back to the same lender from whom the wealth was originally disbursed as a loan. This completes the cycle of money rotation in which the lender gives a loan to the government, which passes the wealth to the contractor, which then puts it back into the kitty of the lender.

From the lender's perspective, even though capital was disbursed—which is yet to be officially repaid by the government—the lender has already received all the wealth back through the contractors. Thus the lender never runs out of capital because whatever he lends comes back to his coffers, enabling him to lend even more, while the debt of the governments and citizens keeps piling. The preferred contractors are therefore an essential part of this cycle because they have to put the money back to the same lender to enable the lender to perpetuate the incessant cycle of government borrowing.

The preferred contractors after receiving the bulk of the government loan, invest it into the schemes that offer loans to the citizens. Obviously, the citizens are drained from the excessive taxes, and often need to borrow capital. Most of the capital in this personal lending comes from the huge wealth amassed by the private contractors through banking fronts. The process works like a thief who steals your money and then returns it back to you as a high-interest loan. In this process, the stealing is done by the government, and the loans are fueled by the wealthy contractors through banking fronts. The people only see the banks and the government while the original lender and the contractors who ultimately profit from the government borrowing remain hidden. Thus common people never understand the cyclic flow of money and how they are being cheated.

With every iteration, the poor work hard and part with large portions of their earnings either via taxes or interests on loans—both of which end up either with the government lender or the wealthy contractors. In this scheme, the government, the lenders, and the contractors have to only ensure that the common people have enough wealth to keep the cycle of taxation and interest going because through this cycle their coffers keep growing. All the hard work of the people is drained dry by taxation and interest.

Paper Money is Used to Fuel Borrowing

If the token of wealth exchange were minted in gold and silver, then the natural scarcity of gold and silver in nature would entail a naturally short supply of currency as well. That short supply would mean that currency will always maintain its value. Since you cannot magically create currency out of nowhere (e.g. by printing paper currency) there would be no inflation. When there is no inflation, the rate of interest on a borrowing would be near zero. When the rate of interest is so low, nobody will put their money in a bank because the banker cannot return a good rate of interest, and executing a business is far more profitable. If the banks cannot acquire people's money, then they cannot lend.

The moneylender needs the ability to pump money into the economy, which means that money must be in abundant supply and it cannot be a scarce commodity like gold or silver. By pumping money, there is inflation. With that inflation the lender can charge a higher rate of interest from the borrower, and entice the people who have the money to deposit it with him for interest. As money is deposited, more money can be pumped. This creates a self-perpetuating cycle of money rotation through which the lender profits.

Paper currencies are used to fuel lending, which leads to price rise, which enables a higher rate of interest, which entices people with money to deposit it with the lender, which then enables the lender to fuel more lending, thus resulting in cyclical price rise, higher interests, more depositing, and then more lending, by which the lender profits.

The Vedic Economic System

In the Vedic social system, there are four classes—the intellectuals, the rulers, the businessmen, and the workers. The businessmen are wealthy; they invest their wealth into a legitimate enterprise, compete with the other businessmen under the free market system, and employ the workers, thereby passing some of their wealth to others. There is simply no concept of lending money to the worker so that he can start his own business, while the lender earns interest without doing any actual work or taking any risk.

In the Vedic system, only the businessmen pay taxes, because they are the wealthy class. There is no concept of "income tax" levied on the intellectuals, rulers, and workers. In other words, the wealthy bear the cost of government and its functions. That is all the more reason for them to not simply preserve their wealth and enjoy it, but actually invest into legitimate businesses. If they did nothing, they will gradually fall into the worker class.

Social organization therefore exerts a pressure on the wealthy too: if you want to maintain your status, you have to run a business and employ other workers, and you are required to pay taxes to the government (as opposed to others who are not). In return you receive a peaceful environment where you can compete on fair grounds. You can never reach a state of self-perpetuating wealth because as you get wealthier, you have to share a bigger burden of the state taxes, to maintain your wealth you have to employ a greater number of people, and bear the burden of running a much larger business. There are natural checks and balances in being rich that encourage you to be prosperous and yet prevent you from gaining an inordinate amount of control over society or its individuals.

The central difference in the Vedic system is the complete lack of a banking system which is used to collect other's wealth, and then use that wealth to lend to others. The Vedic system also relies on using a scarce commodity—e.g. gold or silver—to create currency, which acts as a natural deterrent against banking the money with someone else. The government controls the economy in two ways—(1) maintaining a scarce currency to keep inflation to zero which means lending is not incentivized, and (2) exerting taxes on the wealthy so that they are incentivized into investing their wealth into a business, rather than lending.

Morality and Economic Growth

The Vedic system doesn't mean everyone is wealthy, but it means those who are wealthy will pay for the running of the state, and they will redistribute their wealth by investing into legitimate businesses or risk decline over time. When you are wealthy, you can afford to let go of some of your wealth—and by letting go of this wealth, the rich contribute to the society and thereby accumulate good *karma* by which they become wealthier. In other words, the recipe for richness is not accumulating money, but giving it away.

Karma operates on *value* rather than *money*. The value of money for a poor person is high, and the value for the same money for the rich person is low. Therefore, when a rich person gives away wealth, he parts with little value, but creates greater value for the poor. This is called good *karma*. The return for this *karma* is also through value, which means that the rich person will obtain as much value as they created for the others. Since the value of wealth for a rich person is relatively lesser, a lot more money is required to attain the same value. In short, you give little money to the most needy in order to create greater value, then you receive the same value, which means far greater money for you.

Thus, the law of *karma* entails that by giving away money, you *grow* your money, because as you create value for others, the value returns back as greater money. For a small investment, you obtain greater returns, and this entails continual growth. The Vedic model of economic growth is hinged on charity rather than accumulating wealth. In this model, we don't measure physical assets—e.g. money—but the *relative* value of that asset to the person involved in the transaction. We normally call that relative value *meaning* of something. For a poor person, a small amount of money *means* a lot (relative to a richer person), and *karma* operates on that *meaning* rather than the physical asset itself.

Economics and Moral Altruism

Since modern economy is based on materialism, where people look at the money rather than the value, it has condoned the accumulation of wealth. There is, however, a different kind of materialism in the Vedic system based on the relative value of money rather than money itself. The foundations of this economic system lie in seeing meaning as reality and the laws of nature are therefore described in relation to meanings rather than things.

The system therefore encourages charity instead of lending. It tells people that the money that you give away is not money lost, but by giving away wealth to the most needy you create a lot more wealth for yourself. Wealth therefore naturally flows from the rich to the poor, and this process is itself the method for economic growth. Thus, in the Vedic system, there is no lending; the rich will either voluntarily give away their wealth, or at the very least offer interest free loans to the most needy. There is a conflict between modern economics and altruism because economics advocates profit over charity, but in the Vedic system even the most selfish rise in society by performing the greatest charities. By understanding this system we can not only correct the evils of money lending, but also lay a firmer foundation for the idea of economic growth based on meanings.

The Six Systems of Vedic Philosophy

Published Date: 2017-07-30

Vedic knowledge comprises the four Vedas (Rig, Yajur, Sāma, and Atharva) with their numerous *Samhita*, 108 *Upanishad*, 18 *Purāna*, *Mahabharata*, dozens of *Tantra* texts, and so forth. The above texts, however, are not exhaustive; for example, they don't contain meticulous details on astronomy, linguistics, grammar, logical reasoning, life sciences, architecture, economics and government, music and art, and so forth. The Vedic texts are also so expansive that it is difficult for anybody to even read all the texts in one life, let alone comprehend their meanings, or their ultimate conclusion. Considering these problems, the Six Systems of Vedic Philosophy were devised to (1) provide a detailed explanation of the key Vedic ideas, (2) present philosophical ideas separate from stories for academic development, (3) apply the Vedic knowledge to practical matters, and (4) complement Vedic texts with the works of other teachers who were followers of the Vedic tradition, but whose voice may have been left out of the Vedic texts. This post discusses the relevance of the Six Systems of Philosophy both for understanding the Vedic mainstream, as well as for how their approach can be the mainstay of academic activity.

Understanding the Six Systems

By far the best known of the six systems today is *Vedānta*. It has become popular because people lost the ability to read and understand expansive books, and there was a need to summarize the conclusions of Vedic philosophy in a succinct form for the common man. The term "Vedānta" literally means the "conclusion of knowledge". It deals with the nature of reality beyond the phenomena, the questions of how this reality produces the phenomenal world, how the living entity enters the phenomenal world, and how he can get out of the miseries of the present world. Vedānta is the attempt to condense extremely vast and complex ideology into simple and accessible conclusions.

Once we understand the conclusions of knowledge, obviously we have to do something about it. That something involves a *practice* which we commonly call "religion", *dharma*, etc. What is our *dharma*, duty, or practice, given that the conclusion of all knowledge is given by Vedānta? What should the common man and woman do, after they understand the conclusion? What is the best method for exiting the life of temporary happiness or suffering and attaining eternal happiness by transcending material existence? The inquiry into these questions is called *Mimānsa*. Unlike the *Vedānta* school which is preoccupied with the theoretical questions of the nature of reality and our entanglement, the *Mimānsa* School is preoccupied with the pragmatic practice of religion, and how by the realization of reality one can become freed of the material entanglement.

To transcend the material world, we have to understand how the material world binds us into the repeated cycle of birth and death through *guna* and *karma*. We cannot solve a problem unless we know what the problem is. Vedānta tells us how we entered the world, but what keeps us bound to the world? To understand our bondage we need to know the nature of matter and how it creates the living body. This gives rise to two further schools of philosophy called *Sāṅkhya* and *Yoga*. The *Sāṅkhya* school deals with the study of material elements including the sense objects, the senses, the mind, intellect, ego, and morality, the nature of time, the material desires of lifetimes, and how these elements are organized hierarchically into a tree-like structure from abstract to detailed.

The *Yoga* school incorporates the understanding developed in *Sāṅkhya* and extends it to the understanding of the living body, including the working of the *prāna* or life force, how the soul is covered by its past habits called *guna*, which create the consequences of actions called *karma*, which lead to the transmigration of the soul in which *prāna* carries the soul from one body to another. *Yoga* philosophy deals with the different types of material coverings such as the gross body, the subtle body, and the causal body, and how the life force energizes all these bodies. It concludes that since the life force takes the soul from one body to another, by understanding the life force and learning to control it, the soul can transfer itself into the desired type of body, or become free of all bodies.

By and large this covers practically everything given in the Vedic texts, but the philosophers of yore were not satisfied simply by enunciating the different types of bodies and various types of material elements. They wanted something even more fundamental and rigorous. Thus arose two more schools of philosophy called *Nyāya* and *Vaiśeṣika* which deal with logical argument and atomism respectively. The idea was simple: the world is comprised of atoms which are combining according to rules of logic, and therefore we have to find the most fundamental atoms and the laws of their interaction.

Nyāya and *Vaiśeṣika* correspond to what we call "science" in modern times. *Nyāya* is the fundamental principles of reasoning, which are formalized as logic and mathematics today. *Vaiśeṣika* corresponds to what we call physics in modern times. The goal of these two systems of philosophy was to construct the most parsimonious foundations to describe the working of the material world. Since material nature in *Sāṅkhya* is built from three modes, one of the key goals of *Vaiśeṣika* was to describe how the three modes of nature combine to produce complex "atoms" such as *paramānu, anu, dvīanu, trisarenu,* etc. Since reality is conceptual, the rules of combining these atoms were the rules of logic by which simple concepts were combined to create complex concepts.

Philosophy, Science, and Technology

The six systems of philosophy are paired together into three couples: (1) *Vedānta* and *Mimānsa*, (2) *Sāṅkhya* and *Yoga*, and (3) *Nyaya* and *Vaiśeṣika*. Of these, *Vedānta* is the most philosophical because it deals with the highest conclusions which are all transcendental to the material world; the material world only enters this system in the attempt to explain the soul's fall down and suffering. *Mimānsa* is also philosophical because it deals with the question of the ideal method for liberation. It recognizes the existence of many processes, *dharma*, or religious practices. But which is the best of them? We could call *Mimānsa* "comparative religion" because it recognizes the possibility of many paths to liberation and yet undertakes the analysis by which we know the best path.

Yoga is more pragmatic as it deals with the details of rituals, mysticism, mind and body control, meditation, the performance of day-to-day duties, deity worship, etc. The term "yoga" is today nearly synonymous with physical exercises, but the term had a very broad connotation in Vedic texts due to which there were many kinds of *yoga* such as *karma-yoga, jnana-yoga, astanga-yoga*, and *bhakti-yoga*; by perfecting these practices one could obtain extraordinary powers and good life, besides transcending the world. In that respect, the can be considered "technologies" by which one lived a worthy and useful life.

Sāṅkhya, *Vaiśeṣika*, and *Nyaya* deal with the structure of the world, the material elements that make up conscious experience, their fundamental constituents, and the laws by which the body evolves; these systems can be said to constitute a "material science".

Over the past several centuries, the *Vedānta* system has expanded considerably while the other systems have gradually declined. For example, much of the philosophical knowledge in *Mimānsa* that compares the different processes of practically leading a moral life, the foundations of *karma* and *dharma*, and the theories underlying social, economic, and political morality have disappeared. What remains is a rudimentary analysis of Vedic *mantra* and how to perform some rituals using them. *Mimānsa* is today erroneously equated with *hermeneutics* or the process of interpreting the meaning of texts, when in fact its original purpose was defining the nature of *dharma* or right and wrong.

Similarly, the understanding of *prāna* in the body, how this *prāna* carries the will of the soul, and how it carries the soul from one body to another is now largely lost in the *Yoga* system. What dominantly remains is *asana* and *pranayama* or bodily exercises and breath control. Similarly, *Sāṅkhya* as a system of philosophy practiced today is not only out of touch with the *Sāṅkhya* system as described in the Vedic texts, but also far more primitive, when as a system of philosophy we would expect it to be far more detailed.

Finally, *Nyaya* and *Vaiśeṣika* as systems of reasoning and proof have have been almost completely lost except for some preliminary understanding of the different kinds of proof or *pramana*. The connection between these systems and the other four systems is now almost never visible and therefore it is impossible to see how they are "theistic" philosophical systems, let alone how they were expansions of Vedic ideology. Finally, as much of this knowledge has been lost, whatever remains is so primitive that it cannot present a viable alternative to modern mathematics and physics.

The Neglect of the Six Systems of Philosophy

Vedic knowledge at present lies neglected. Not only is the number of people studying it declining, but the deeply scientific nature of this knowledge is also not known. For most people, Vedic texts are synonymous with "Hinduism", which is then equated with the caste system, idol worship, and many other misconceptions. Even those who read the Vedic texts sincerely, only make feeble attempts to understand the philosophy, and have no inkling of its profound scientific nature. In fact the parts that deal with the nature of the material world, the nature of space and time, the atomism that builds the macroscopic world, and the laws by which the atoms combine are completely ignored.

While *Vedānta* as a system of philosophy has expanded over the last several centuries due to the works of *Shankarāchārya*, *Madhavacharya*, *Ramānujacharya*, *Nimbārkacharya*, and others, a systematic exposition of the differences between their philosophical positions is also presently missing. Most people are occupied not with understanding the nature of the Absolute Truth, but with petty ritualistic differences. Even the *Advaita* philosophy of *Shankarāchārya* is confused with the *māyāvāda* philosophy of 20th century "reformers" of Hinduism who never fail to underwhelm the great tradition.

With such a sustained neglect of the intellectual, philosophical, and academic traditions, we can hardly be surprised if the Vedic system is today considered to be on par with many other religions where such traditions either never existed, or only existed in far more primitive forms. How can people be attracted to Vedic knowledge when its best "marketers" fail to highlight its greatest strengths?

The Importance of the Six Systems

We must view the Six Systems of philosophy as a hierarchy that begins in the ultimate conclusion or Vedānta, which then spawns a practice and duty called *dharma*. This *dharma* includes not just ritual and worship (which are only one part of the *dharma*) but conducting a moral society organized on the basis of the *Varṇāśrama* system.

The understanding of this system involves the pragmatic knowledge of how society must be organized, how the economy should be managed, and how the political class must govern society. We make a grave mistake when we limit *dharma* to meditation, *mantra* chanting, or deity worship, because this only constitutes a small fraction of our daily life. When the rest of our life—e.g. earning, social interactions, political system, and leisure—are out of sync with *dharma*, then the above mentioned limited notion of *dharma* has fewer benefits. The scope of *Mimānsa* is not the analysis of *mantra* but the analysis of *dharma*, which in the broadest sense comprises the *Varṇāśrama* system.

The life of *dharma* in turn depends on the understanding of material nature, the principles of healthy living, how the mind and body are connected, how the intellect controls the mind, how the intentions control the intellect, and how everything is subordinate to the moral principles or *dharma*. In short, just knowing that we have to lead a life of *dharma* isn't enough. We must know how *dharma* expands into intentions, intellect, mind, senses, sensations and then sense objects. This understanding of nature is called *Sāṅkhya* and *Yoga* by which we understand body, sense, mind, and other controls.

While a philosophical understanding of *Sāṅkhya* and *Yoga* can take us far into the process of *dharma*, ultimately one needs a rigorous science in order to convincingly answer difficult questions. Philosophy, unfortunately, is the victim of innumerable misinterpretations. Since it deals in the most general and accessible concepts, it appears amenable even to the most uninformed minds. But in their hands, philosophy only becomes a playground of idea-twisting and needless hair-splitting.

Philosophy becomes wasteful without the rigorous methods of proof. The systems of *Nyaya* and *Vaiśeṣika* were therefore preoccupied with the problem of proof. Without such rigorous methods, there can be no scientific understanding because it becomes impossible to weed out the false interpretations and twisted ideologies without rigor.

Academic Rediscovery of Vedic Knowledge

Today we have a range of surviving work from the different schools of *Vedānta* but the other five systems of philosophy comprising the practice of *dharma*, the scientific basis of this *dharma* in the principles of material nature and the transmigration of the soul, founded on the rigor of conceptual analysis and reasoning are missing.

The future of Vedic knowledge depends not just in knowing the ultimate conclusions but also on the science by which we arrive at the conclusions. In other words, we need not just the system called *Vedānta* but the other five systems too. They may or may not be called by the same names, but their importance is unquestionable. Only when all these six systems of philosophy are understood can we claim to see the Vedic system scientifically.

Since the *Acharya* of the past few centuries have primarily focused on the enunciation of *Vedānta*, the other systems that deal with the scientific basis of the *Varṇāśrama* system, the theories of material nature, and the logical basis of reasoning and proof are at the present missing. The job of academic inquiry lies in establishing the other five systems of philosophy pursuant to the highest conclusions of *Vedānta* philosophy.

This task might seem difficult, but it is not impossible, simply based on the fact that Vedic texts did not primarily deal with the substance of the other five systems even in the past; at best the practice of *dharma* was cursorily described in texts such as *Manu Smṛti*, the basic categories of matter along with some high-level descriptions of the living body were presented in some *Purāna*. Based on these texts, later sages and seers were able to generate the other five systems of philosophy. The six systems have been called *āstika* or "theistic" not because they directly *originated* in the Vedic texts themselves, but because they were *derivative theories* based on the ideas often found in the Vedic texts.

There is no reason why a similar effort in modern times cannot substantively rediscover a new science that presents a rigorous explanation of the material world using which society can be organized morally to practice *dharma* by which people can become happy in the present life and transcend the repeated cycle of births at the point of death. We just have to look at the six systems for the inspiration that such a feat could be accomplished.

DOES PRAYER ALLEVIATE SUFFERING?

Published Date: 2017-07-31

Nearly every religion employs the idea of prayer, and most people view prayers as a way to alleviate their suffering. If such a thing were possible, it would encourage the sinner to continue sinning and use prayer to be pardoned. Conversely, if such a thing were impossible, then the skeptic could ask: If God can take away my suffering, then why doesn't He? Is He too weak to take away the suffering or is He not kind enough to pardon my sins? Both alternatives present problems, and this post discusses why sometimes prayer works, and other times it does not. It also discusses the purpose of prayer, which is not to remove the external causes of suffering, but the internal attitude that creates it.

The Legend of Queen Kunti

Mahabharata describes that when *Kunti* was still a maiden, she was given a *mantra* by *Durvasa Muni* to call upon any demigod and ask them for any benediction she desired. Just to test the efficacy of the *mantra*, *Kunti* called upon *Surya* and was astonished to find that he arrived. Even though *Kunti* did not want any benediction, *Surya* gave her a son—*Karna*—promising that she would remain a maiden even after the childbirth. *Kunti* subsequently used the same *mantra* to obtain three more sons—*Yudhiṣṭhira* from *Dharmaraja*, *Bhima* from *Vayu*, and *Arjuna* from *Indra*. Indeed, she also helped her co-wife *Madri* to obtain two sons—*Nakula* and *Sahadeva*—from the twins *Ashvni Kumara*. Technically speaking, her sons were not conceived with her husband *Pandu*, and yet they were called *Pāndava*.

One could argue that if these sons were not born, then there would be no battle of *Mahabharata*, and hence they were the cause of the deaths of hundreds of thousands of soldiers. But, ironically, their birth was caused through a *mantra*, which we might call a prayer to the chosen demigod. Clearly, then, the prayer appears to produce results which would have otherwise deemed impossible. Since *Kunti* is the cause of their birth, does that make her responsible for all the deaths subsequently?

The problem seems even more confusing because Lord Kṛṣṇa tells *Arjuna* in Bhagavad-Gita that the warriors on the battlefield of *Kurukśhetra* had already been killed by Him, and *Arjuna* only had to become the *nimitta* or the instrument of destiny. If the actions of *Pāndava* were instruments in the death of *Kaurava*, then were *Kunti's* actions only instruments in the birth of *Pāndava*?

We must understand that the birth of the *Pāndava* was inevitable. Similarly, it was *Kunti's* destiny to bear children, although her husband was not capable of conceiving those children. Therefore, nature arranged the encounter with the demigods for the birth of these children. Similarly, the *Kurukśhetra* war was predestined and *Kunti* wasn't responsible for causing the war. When Lord Kṛṣṇa says that all the warriors have already been killed by Him, and *Arjuna* is only an instrument, it means that their deaths are inevitable, although *Arjuna* can become the mechanism of *Kṛṣṇa's* will on His command.

The Action of Karma

These are good illustrative examples through which we can understand why the worship of demigods doesn't cause that which is not already destined, although the demigods can be asked to directly provide what is otherwise achievable through other means. For instance, *Kunti* could have had her sons through her husband, but she got them through the demigods because she had the requisite *karma* for the bearing those children, but her husband did not have the *karma* to conceive them.

This is important because people think that the worship of demigods will give us something that is *not* already in our *karma*, or that their worship can be used to contravene *karma*. Under such a view, many people imagine that their worship is like a prayer that alleviates their suffering when the fact is that the demigods can only give to the worshiper what is already in their *karma*. If that *karma* is not being achieved directly through the means directly visible to a person, then a demigod can intervene directly to fill that gap. But the demigods cannot contravene the dictates of previously created *karma*.

This means that prayer may not yield the desired results, if that prayer requests relief from suffering, when a person's *karma* has destined them to suffer. God doesn't pardon a living entity's *karma* because if such pardoning actually worked, then there would be no need to punish anyone; all living entities could just go on sinning and offer prayers requesting to be pardoned. A living entity's sins cannot be pardoned just because he or she "confesses" to the sin, and/or prays for forgiveness. The person has to be punished according to the laws of nature, because the moral system has to be fair and just.

How Paramātma Helps the Soul

Nevertheless, *karma* isn't just producing adverse circumstances; it is also responsible for the abilities in our senses by which we can counteract the circumstances. Just as adverse circumstances and disabilities cause us to suffer, similarly, conducive conditions and abilities are also created by *karma*. When one is undergoing a bad situation, there may be simultaneously the possibility of counteracting this situation by the conducive conditions and abilities that are also manifesting at the same time. However, unlike the adverse situations that are forced, the conducive conditions and abilities are not forced. That is, one is not required to spend the capital of good *karma* in counteracting the effects of bad *karma*.

When we pray to God or the demigods, and they appear to cancel the adverse effects of previous bad *karma*, they are only consuming the good *karma* which was otherwise lying unused. Similarly, upon prayer, we might obtain the intellect and be reminded of our abilities and opportunities by which we can counteract the adverse situation, or even surpass it. These "magical" effects of prayer are not magical at all, nor are they counter to the moral laws of nature. They are simply methods of fulfilling our desires by consuming the good *karma* to counteract the bad *karma*. This counteraction is possible only when the good and the bad *karma* are fructifying simultaneously. If only bad *karma* fructifies, then it would be impossible to counteract its effects. This means that sometimes the prayer appears to work, and at other times it doesn't. The underlying mechanisms for both the situations is the same.

God Helps Those Who Help Themselves

Paramātma can provide the intelligence to take what is available or possible in a given situation over and beyond what you are automatically receiving. God's inspiration is like pointing the correct door to open to take the reward. It is within my reach, and I am entitled to it.

But I may not have the intelligence to see how what I desire is entirely within my reach—i.e. that what I want is behind the door and I have to open the door and take it. *Paramātma* tells us from within which door should be opened.

Thus it is said "God helps those who help themselves". The God in question here is *Paramātma*. He can help us if we desire the help, and are prepared to make the effort. However in so helping *Paramātma* is not violating the law of *karma* or pardoning the sins of the soul. Instead, *Paramātma* is pointing a path in which a person can counteract their bad *karma* with good *karma*. For example, if you are suffering from a disease which you are unable to cure through conventional medicine, then *Paramātma* may give an inspiration from within—"why don't I try alternative medicine?" And sometimes when you make the attempt, you actually cure the disease, provided you have the *karma* to do so.

Similarly, if you don't have the necessary *karma* and yet you desperately want to do something to achieve it, then *Paramātma* will also take away the intelligence—i.e. give false ideas. Due to these false inspirations, the soul is misled into dark alleys where he wastes his time trying to achieve the impossible. Both remembrance and forgetfulness thus arise from the *Paramātma*.

Misunderstanding Regarding Prayer

Most people arrive at erroneous conclusions regarding such inspiration. First, they might think that God gave them the inspiration by which a disease got cured, so God must have "pardoned" my sin, when the fact is that two instances of *karma* got cancelled. Second, they might attribute the inspiration to their own intellect and claim the credit for it; for example, when God inspires scientists to search in a certain direction, the scientists attribute their successes to their own intellect, and not to God's inspiration. No scientist has stood up and said that he would have never found the answer were it not for God's inspiration. We don't understand how God is giving us answers to help us enjoy our *karma* when we only have a strong intention (in the ego) but no ideas (in the intellect) on how to fulfill them. God can appear as a new insight in the intellect to fulfill the intent in the ego. Third, some people erroneously conclude that if a particular solution worked for them in the past, then it will work for others too; for example, if I'm able to cure my diseases using alternative medicine, I might think that everyone should be able to cure their diseases in this way. The problem is that we forget that what allows us to cure (or not cure) is *karma*. Internal inspiration (from *Paramātma*) or external guidance (from our friends or family) can work only when there is requisite *karma* to allow us to cure the problem.

Paramātma is not helping us overcome the sins. He is just helping us use our own *karma*. God responds to prayers, but only by letting you tap into your own bank of *karma* in case you are unaware that you have a bank account of *karma* from which you can draw at the moment. If you don't have a bank account that can be drawn from, then God will not respond to prayers seeking a pardon. Similarly, He will not inspire you if you don't pray, even if you have the bank account from which you can draw. In that sense, God's response to prayers is not in violation of natural laws. It is an act of reminding the soul that his suffering can be mitigated by consuming the medicine he is carrying in his pocket.

Spiritual Life Depends on Good Karma

Anyone who has taken a casual interest in astrology knows that there are periods in which you can make significant advancement in spiritual life—this advancement pertains to new realizations either coming because of external triggers or due to internal inspiration when the soul seeks to find answers to difficult questions—which help us decrease our material desires and increase our purification. Anyone who has come to spiritual life can go back in time and look at the possibilities entailed by their horoscope and they will find favorable influences driving them towards greater knowledge.

All our encounters are arranged by *karma*, and when suitable *karma* arises we can meet the right kind of person. However, whether we are inspired to listen to such a person, and whether we continue that engagement, often depends upon us: the *karma* may still allow us to engage, but our desires may not. As our desires change, *Paramātma* also changes His stance: He stops inspiring us in spiritual life, and starts inspiring us in materialistic activities. This is the nature of *karma*: it affords us both kinds of encounters with spiritual and materialistic options, so that we can prefer one over the other. If we forego the *karma* of an encounter with a spiritual person, then that *karma* remains dormant; it is still in our bank, and it exists like a medicine we keep in our pockets while suffering the disease.

Abuse and Betrayal in Spiritual Life

Even when a person comes to spiritual life, their *karma* doesn't end. Owing to this, even spiritualists can suffer in ways worse than the suffering of the materialists—which often prompts them to go away from spiritual life. Stories of abuse and betrayal are legend in all religious institutions and much of the problem is due to the shock we experience in having been abused or betrayed by a person who isn't expected to do so. We must realize that *karma* is blind. It acts as betrayal or abuse when it has to, regardless of how much we trust the person who abuses or betrays. Clearly, if you don't trust the person, the same betrayal would have a smaller effect on you—because you already expect something to happen—than if you have placed a huge amount of trust in the abuser. The events of abuse or betrayal can be the same, but their effects on us can be different based on our trust.

This doesn't absolve the abusers from heinous actions; on the contrary, by indulging in such actions, they are misusing their position far more, and the repercussions would therefore be far greater. Nevertheless, the victims must understand that abuse and betrayal are results of previous *karma*. That bad *karma* is delivered through someone they trust spiritually doesn't absolve the perpetrator from future consequences, but because *karma* is blind, it doesn't care how much you trust the person who abuses or betrays you. Our trust is therefore independent of the abuse and betrayal; the fact that we trust the wrong person is a lesson to be learnt on how to determine trustworthy people.

The pain of such abuse can only be dealt with through knowledge. First, we must separate the events from their psychological effects; the objective events are due to *karma*, but the psychological effects are due to our trust. Second, we must recognize that trust is our individual responsibility when we are grown, and the responsibility of the elders, parents, or guardians, when we depend on them; all these parties may be implicated in creating the illusion of trust, when none should have existed. Third, even though one might deserve suffering due to previous *karma*, the perpetrators—especially when in positions of responsibility and acting heinously—ensure a very prolonged period of personal suffering. Retribution cannot be the solace for one seeking advancement, but retribution is nature's law.

God's Pardon in the Bhagavad-Gita

Towards the end of Bhagavad-Gita, *Kṛṣṇa* says to Arjuna:

> *sarva-dharman parityajya*
> *mam ekam saranam vraja*
> *aham tvam sarva-papebhyo*
> *moksayisyami ma sucah*
>
> *Abandon all varieties of religion and just surrender unto Me. I shall deliver you from all sinful reaction. Do not fear.*

The verse appears to indicate that if one surrenders to God, He will take away all the sinful reactions, i.e. bad *karma*, which then seems to directly counter all that we have said above. And yet, we also know for a fact that even those who have surrendered to God are sometimes seen to suffer adverse material conditions. What is then the nature of God's pardon, and when does it apply or not apply?

This verse should be read as a whole, and not piecemeal. In the verse, *Kṛṣṇa* says that *Arjuna* should abandon all varieties of *material* duties and just surrender to Him. Now, when we normally abandon our material duties, there is negative *karma* naturally created. For example, if you are working in a job and you don't do your job correctly, there is adverse *karma*. However, when you neglect your job *because* you are serving God, there is no negative *karma*. For instance, you might not adequately perform your job duties because you are spending most of your time reading *Kṛṣṇa*'s pastimes. In such a situation, when the person has surrendered to God and prioritizes His service over material duties, *Kṛṣṇa* assures *Arjuna* that He will free such a person from adverse *karma*. In other words, there is material *dharma* or duty, and there is an even higher *dharma*—service to *Kṛṣṇa*. When material duties are neglected to perform this higher *dharma*, there is no adverse *karma*. This is not a blanket freedom from all *karma* created by the person in the *past*. It is rather freedom from *karma after* you have surrendered to God.

This verse becomes confusing only when we think that God gives freedom from all *karma*—including *karma* acquired from previous lives and previous activities—when *Kṛṣṇa* is only alluding to the *karma* that is created by the neglect of material duties in lieu of surrender and service to Him. *Kṛṣṇa* assures *Arjuna* to not worry because it is commonly feared that neglecting our duties leads to adverse *karma*.

Does Guru Take Away Karma?

It is said that Jesus suffered the sins of his followers. Śrīla Prabhupāda also mentioned that the *guru* takes a disciple's sins. But if we see the lives of spiritualists, we can often find them suffering—diseases, betrayal, disrespect, etc. In what sense does the *guru* take away the sins if the followers are still suffering? Furthermore, how can the *guru* take away the sins when God Himself doesn't do so?

The short answer is that the *guru* takes the *karma* of the disciple in the same sense that *Kṛṣṇa* promised to free *Arjuna* from *karma*—it is freedom from the *karma* arising due to dereliction of *material* duties when this neglect manifests due to the service of *guru*. More than anything, it points to the fact that whenever we neglect our material duties, adverse *karma* is created. The reprieve from this *karma* is not universal; it is rather very specific and for the cases when we follow the *guru's* instructions.

The idea that Jesus took everyone's sins (even from the past) just because they accept him as their teacher is therefore false. Jesus took (and will take even in the present) a person's sins if they truly follow his teachings even when the teachings appear to contradict the edicts of society. For example, the society might enact laws that force you to lie, cheat, or kill, and you might think that it is your duty to abide by such laws but the fact is that if you truly follow Jesus you can disobey the social laws and Jesus will take the adverse *karma*. You might appear to disobey your authorities, and you may be even punished for doing so, but that punishment comes as the result of previous *karma*, and not from the dereliction of duty. The *karma* produced by the dereliction of duty, when that duty is against the teachings of Jesus, would be taken by Jesus. In that specific sense, Jesus can take away the sins on your behalf, because he is instructing you to follow his rules.

The fact is that when we accept employment from someone we are obliged to follow his command because that person compensates us for the services rendered. The material *dharma* therefore tells us to obey our employer. But a discriminating person might realize that their employer is not honest, and they may therefore decide to ignore his commands. Since the person is still being paid by the employer, there is—technically speaking—a dereliction of duty, and therefore there must be bad *karma*. However, when this neglected duty is pursuant to moral principles, then the *guru* takes the adverse *karma*.

The True Purpose of Prayer

Our suffering—in Vedic philosophy—is an outcome of two things: *guna* and *karma*. When we are suffering, the *karma* constitutes the adverse circumstances and our inability to counteract it. But we still have the free will to interpret the adverse situations in different ways: (1) we might blame the situation for our suffering, (2) we might blame ourselves for having landed in the situation, and (3) we might recognize that the suffering is inevitable and it we must be cautious about the law of *karma*. These reactions are respectively in the modes of *tamas, rajas,* and *sattva*. When we blame our situation we get frustrated and suffer even more. When we blame ourselves for having landed in trouble, we have a better attribution of responsibility but it is only partially true because we don't realize that the situation was inevitable. Only by attributing suffering to past *karma* is our reaction completely true.

This tells us that the situation is not always in our control but the *interpretation* of that situation can be changed by choice. Our suffering is only partly due to the circumstances. Most of the suffering is due to the inner frustration, fear, and anger at the situation. Even when we cannot change the situation, we can overcome the frustration, fear, and anger, and apply our intellect—in conjunction with prayer—to find the best counteraction for the situation. If we have the requisite *karma*, then we might be able to counteract the situation through intelligent action. But even if we cannot change the situation, there can be substantial reduction in suffering simply by changing our attitude towards the situation.

Knowledge of *karma* therefore comes handy in reducing the fear, anger, and frustration, which then quietens the mind and allows the intellect to find the best possible mitigation. If we also pray to God, then He can provide an answer by which we can overcome our situation, provided there is requisite *karma*. Ultimately, we have to bear out all the *karma* from the past, but a lot of the bad *karma* can be counteracted against the good *karma* if we have the knowledge and use it intelligently.

In that sense, by praying to God we can become *almost completely* free of suffering even when we have a considerable pile of *karma* because we are able to intelligently counteract bad *karma* against good *karma*, and when this counteraction fails we are not angry, frustrated, or fearful. These are tactical solutions to the problem. Ultimately, however, we have to stop creating good or bad *karma*, by surrendering to *Kṛṣṇa*. For the intelligent devotee, therefore, life can be almost free of suffering if he accepts *Kṛṣṇa* as the controller without foregoing his own sense of responsibility.

The purpose of prayer is to help us find answers by which we can apply our intelligence to trade off good *karma* against bad *karma*. The purpose of prayer is also to focus our mind on God so that we are free of the interpretations under *tamas* and *rajas*, which will help us overcome fear, anger, and frustration. Finally, the purpose of prayer is to realize that our free will is limited and therefore held accountable as opposed to God who is totally free and hence His actions have no counter reactions. These are valid uses of prayer, but the idea that by praying we can destroy our past sins is false.

Universalism and Personalism in Science

Published Date: 2017-08-01

Introduction and Overview

The laws of nature in current science are mathematical formulae that predict the behavior of objects deterministically, which precludes any role for choice and morality in nature. Therefore, if nature permitted choices, how would we reconceive natural laws? In Vedic philosophy, the law is a *material entity* called a *role* which defines the *expected* behaviors but doesn't preclude choice. The interaction between choice and expectation creates a consequence, which moves the actor into new roles. There is determinism as far as the outcome of the choice-expectation interaction is concerned but the determinism is based on the *local* conditions or *role* without precluding choices. The current contradiction between choice and determinism in science is actually reflective of a mistaken notion of material reality and its laws. This article discusses how natural laws can be reconceived compatible with the existence of choices.

The Cartesian Origins of Anti-Materialism

Descartes gave a specific definition of matter, which has been employed in science ever since. The definition was that matter is *res extensa*, which means that it is extended in space, and therefore has a spatial location. By implication, all ideas were *res cogitans* or outside space, and hence they were not constrained to a specific object. The mathematical laws of nature are such ideas; they span more than one object. By definition, they must be non-material.

If something is universal, then it must be non-material because material objects are local. Given that science seeks universal laws, which must apply to all material objects, and we cannot imagine something material that exists in two distinct objects, the natural conclusion must be that mathematical laws which apply to all objects must themselves be non-material.

The origins of anti-materialism exist in Cartesian philosophy which separated the mind from the body. Most materialists today presume that if they reduced the mind to the brain, then we would get rid of this inherent anti-materialism. The fact, however, is that by such reduction they will never be able to reduce ideas because ideas—by definition—span multiple objects. If you reduce an idea to an object, then you lose the ability to see the commonality between objects.

Therefore, if we take materialism to its logical conclusion, then we must also lose the mathematical laws, because the laws (as ideas, formulae, propositions) would be reduced to a specific object, which would entail that they can only be applied to the specific object to which they are reduced. That entails a collapse of science because there would be as many laws as there are objects, which then means that each object is a unique law unto itself, and we cannot subsume the behavior of that under a universal law that spans more than one object.

The Pragmatic Problems of Reduction

Anti-materialism in science exists as mathematical laws that go across all objects. We cannot perceive such a thing by the senses because the senses can only see particular objects, not something that is common between the objects. The human mind is capable of perceiving that commonality and in that sense it perceives what the senses cannot.

The mind can never be reduced to matter precisely due to this problem because if such a reduction were indeed possible it would mean the collapse of mathematical laws and indeed all concepts which span more than one object. The world, upon such reduction, would only be *particular* objects, without the ability to see the *commonalities* across objects.

You could no longer use words like table, chair, color, red, sweet, bitter, because they are found in many objects. You could not even use words like energy, momentum, mass, charge, spin, rotation, spin, etc. because they are also general ideas which can be applied to many objects. In fact, come to think of it, you cannot use any word, because they all denote ideas, and ideas must be illusions—reduced to specific objects (e.g. words)—which means that you cannot believe that the word 'apple' *means* a concept "apple". You can just hear 'apple' and say 'apple' but there can be no conceptual appellations attached to this sound beyond the sound itself.

The reduction of the mind to matter entails an irrevocable collapse of language as the bearer of meanings. Similarly, it also entails the collapse of science whereby the formulae of science describe multiple (or all) objects. By reduction, mathematical laws would just be blots of ink on paper and while you can sense and write these blots, you cannot call them laws that apply to other objects or representative of something that is common across objects.

Science Depends on Anti-Materialism

Whether or not the mind can be reduced to matter is beside the point. The point is that if a reduction were possible there would be absolutely no meaning and symbolism. For example, you cannot use money to buy goods because money is no longer a symbol of meaning—e.g. value of things. Money is just a piece of paper, and the numerals printed on that paper are just squiggles, and you cannot associate any meaning with the paper—e.g. as a token of exchange.

I would be shy to deny that such a world is possible, but I would be confident to assert that it is indeed the world of animals. Animals don't read books, they don't buy goods using money, and certainly animals haven't pioneered scientific theories and technological innovations. The animals have sensations, by which they eat, fight, mate, and survive. The conceptual faculties, which are so pronounced in the human beings, aren't as evident in the animals.

Therefore, the reduction of mind to matter entails the reduction of humans to animals whereby the humans must also discard their conceptual, linguistic, and symbolic abilities by which they see commonalities between things which is then used to formulate *descriptions* using words, and as language develops we can talk about universal laws of nature that span all objects. In so far as animals don't have pronounced symbolic abilities, the reduction of mind to matter would produce a glaring empirical contradiction—that we have non-animal faculties.

The Problem of Epistemology

The separation of mind from matter was incomplete in Cartesian philosophy because it did not tell us how the two interact. I'm not just talking about how *we* think, but the general problem of epistemology in which to know the world means to *attach* ideas to things, or see a particular thing as part of a larger *class* of things. What makes us say that something is a table or chair, granting that there is a world of ideas (comprising ideas of table and chair) and there is a world of things (comprising objects which could potentially be called tables or chairs)?

The problem manifests in science too where conceptual properties like energy, momentum, mass, charge, etc. have to be *measured* using an instrument. The mind-body problem in science appears as the *choice* of a particular instrument used to measure a property. The instrument is physical but it produces a conceptual output—namely the value of a *property*—by which the object becomes a part of a general class of things, and we then attach ideas to things. The big question is: How do we attach the physical world to a general concept using an instrument? Such instruments are analogues of that hyphen that conjoins the body with the mind.

In science, the mental concept—e.g. heat—is objectified into a measuring *instrument* and all other objects are then *compared* to this instrument which now becomes the *standard*. This process is much like converting the idea of a 'car' into a real car, and then calling that real car as the first, the ideal, and the standard bearer for all other cars. Once you identify a standard, you have objectified the idea into a thing, and subsequent measurements will only involve comparisons between objects, by which we can *infer* that other objects have the same property, and then we can put all these objects into the same class, attached to the idea.

The Choice of Measuring Standards

But, how do we create the *first* instance of an idea? How do we *choose* an instrument as the standard for the idea such that all other objects would be described in *relation* to it?

For example, when a hot object touches our skin we typically feel the sensation of burn but science cannot measure the extent of burn as a measure of heat. Therefore we *choose* to not measure heat by its burning effects but by its ability to cause an *expansion*. Liquids expand better than solids, which makes for a convenient process of measurement, and mercury happens to be a liquid metal which then serves as a suitable expanding material used for heat detection.

This gives rise to the thermometer that employs mercury to measure heat. But mercury expansion is only one manifestation of heat, and not the most obvious one at that. Yet, we pick that as the standard for heat, just because we find it very *convenient*. We must realize that in picking the thermometer as the standard for measuring heat, we are not talking about heat itself (as an idea) but one instance of one of the many *effects* of heat—i.e. expansion.

But how do we know that the thing that causes the mercury to expand is heat? Clearly, in the case of other substances, expansion could be caused by push and pull forces rather than heat. So, the idea that heat causes mercury to expand involves not just the observation of expansion but also the touching of the hot object to realize that it is actually hot—i.e. it can scald the skin.

The fact is that the thermometer is not experiencing heat; it is undergoing *expansion*, which is different from the scalding of the skin. And yet, we suppose that the *same* cause is involved in creating both effects—scalding and expansion—so it really must be the same thing. In other words, through our mind we have already made a connection that has no sensual basis because there is nothing common between scalding and expansion, but we mentally make that connection, which then leads to the idea that the thermometer measures heat.

The Cause and Its Effects

Our assumption here is that there is indeed something called *heat*—a concept. But this concept has different *effects*—e.g. expansion and scalding. The concept called 'heat' is thus the cause, and it can branch into more than one effect. The fact that we only perceive the effects—i.e. expansion and scalding—and never the concept 'heat' itself entails that we are using heat to explain the effect. Such a premise is created mentally because every time there is scalding there is expansion and vice versa, so we can say one of them could be a *sufficient* condition for the other to occur. But since expansion is not the cause of scalding (and vice versa), both of them are simply *effects* of a deeper cause—heat—which we can never perceive by the senses.

Geometrically, we can represent this fact as an inverted tree in which 'heat' is the 'root' and 'expansion' and 'scalding' are branches emanating from the root. We cannot see the root, but we can see the branches. And yet, we mentally connect the different branches and claim that since scalding and expansion go together, they must emerge from the same root cause. And since they are produced from the same root, therefore, thermometer can be used to measure heat, because it measures at least one of the observables—expansion—which is an *indication* of heat.

The key point is that science doesn't measure heat. It rather measures the *effects* of heat. There are several indicators—or effects—and we pick one of the effects for convenience. We suppose that the cause can potentially have many effects, which are branches emanating from the root, although we can only see the branches by the senses, and the connection between the separate branches—essential to postulate the existence of the root—is made by the mind.

If we discard the mind, there would just be individual effects such as scalding and expansion. There would be no reason to suppose that they are indeed caused by the same reality because the fact is that we never perceive the reality itself although our conceptual and scientific inclinations want to reduce the variety of the world into a parsimonious theory of nature. That theory involves going from the branches to the root, although we cannot perceive the root. If we reduce the mind to the body, there would be no root other than branches and hence no knowledge. We could experience scalding and expansion but we could not say these are due to *heat*.

The Structure of Science

The world is structured like an inverted tree; this is not something we have recognized thus far, but it is something that is pervasive in all attempts at knowledge that go from contingent and detailed to abstract and imperceptible. As we rise higher in this tree, we get farther and farther from sense perception, but we also obtain a better and better ability to reduce our unique concepts by which we can unify even more diverse phenomena in the same theory.

To see the world as an inverted tree, we must acknowledge that the branches of the tree emanate from the root, which means that *heat* precedes scalding and expansion, but we can never see heat itself, only its effects. Therefore, there is an imperceptible reality that exists prior to the perceivable phenomena. We can think about this reality and speculate on its nature, but we cannot sensually perceive it. Scientific advancement means the access to such inaccessible realities beyond sense perception. The observable phenomena are *effects* of the causes, and a scientific theory is that which describes the causes. So long as we can connect the branches to the root in a theory, we can say that the imperceptible reality *causes* the perception. But nobody can truly claim if that is indeed true, because we are unable to *see* that reality itself.

Our conviction of the truth of a scientific theory is therefore not based on empirical tests. The conviction is rather based on the *breadth* of phenomena that the theory can explain. For example, if the postulate of heat can explain scalding, expansion, glowing, cooking, etc. then our concept is far more robust than if it only explained one phenomenon. Ultimately, only a concept that explains *all* phenomena can be considered irrefutably robust and therefore *true*. But there is no way we can be sure that our theory indeed explains all the possible phenomena, because of practical limitations in which our senses are limited to a few perceptions. This then gives rise to the need to *empirically confirm* the reality of the concept. Clearly, since we cannot see the general things by the senses, we need another mode of perception by the mind itself. We have to suppose that the only way we can advance in science is if the ability in the mind to perceive generalities was indeed treated on par—if not better—than sensual perception.

Material vs. Efficient Causes

This approach to perception alleviates the problems entailed by mind-body dualism and its current alternative—materialistic reduction—because we realize that the mind and the body interact through a *connection* that instantiates an unperceivable cause to perceivable effects. The cause itself can become perceivable through perceptual advancement in which the ability to see generalities (which cut across many objects) is "higher" than sense perception. Such perception corresponds to the ability to see heat through many possible phenomena such as expansion, scalding, glowing, etc. Or, to the ability to see that many objects are cars.

But this approach to perception also leads to a new problem, namely that we have to ask ourselves why, when, and how the unperceivable becomes perceivable. This conversion corresponds to the process of the tree growing from the root to the leaves. Since the root can exist even when the leaves don't, it is not enough to say that the leaves are produced from the root. We must also identify the *cause* that converts the root into the leaves.

This obviously requires a separation between two kinds of causes—e.g. the heat which can be called the *material cause* of scalding, and an *efficient cause* which causes heat to convert into scalding. The distinction between material and efficient causes becomes necessary when we recognize that perception is produced from the imperceptible reality because we are now talking about two distinct things—(a) something that exists materially prior to perception, and (b) something that converts that materially existent thing into a perceptible thing.

We could say that the mind is the material cause and scalding is a material effect, but the *connection* between them is the efficient cause. Reduction forgoes the conceptual nature of the cause, and thereby confuses the cause with the effect, not realizing that the same cause can have many effects, as that cause is brought into interaction with other causes. Dualism recognizes the conceptual nature of the cause but is unable to make the connection between cause and effect and therefore suffers from the mind-body interaction problem. The additional cause—the efficient cause—addresses the problem of dualism and tells us that it is not enough to have heat in order to produce scalding. Rather, we must put the heat in contact with my hand to produce the effect of scalding. If the same heat is put in contact with mercury the effect is expansion.

The efficient cause therefore answers the question of *which* object is put in contact with heat, and this involves a *choice*. Even though the material reality—e.g. heat—exists conceptually, its conversion into a phenomena such as scalding or expansion is not predetermined without this choice. Scalding is produced when the conceptual reality called heat is brought into interaction with another conceptual reality called my skin. The efficient cause is that which brings my skin in contact with the heat, and thereby produces the observable effect of scalding.

Particles and Fields in Modern Science

In modern science, the distinction between material and efficient causes exists partially as particles and fields—the particles are the material cause while the fields are the efficient cause. The difference is primarily that in classical physics we also supposed that the efficient cause involves no choice. Thus, whether a given reality—heat—will cause the mercury to expand or the skin to scald is predetermined. This assumption has now failed in atomic theory where we cannot predict which phenomena will be caused by the given reality and when.

Physicists are baffled by atomic theory because they continue to think in terms of the material cause alone and don't recognize the existence of the efficient cause owing to the legacy of classical physics. They are unable to realize that the 'field' that puts two objects into interaction with each other is no longer the classical field which simultaneously causes all objects to interact with each other. In other words, according to classical physics, if heat exists then it must affect the mercury and my skin simultaneously because the field exists everywhere. Atomic theory forbids this idea because the field is now 'quantized' which means that it *can* exist everywhere but in *fact* it only exists in one place. Hence, the *possibility* to exist everywhere is called the 'field' while the fact that it exists in only one place is called the 'particle'. How that possibility of existing everywhere is converted into the fact of existing in one place is unknown.

The short answer to this quandary is that the field doesn't exist everywhere; it is rather the efficient cause that makes two conceptual objects interact to create a phenomena. Therefore, the existence of heat will not automatically cause the mercury to expand unless the heat is 'emitted' from the source to the destination, and this emission can't be predicted in current physics because we have never incorporated an understanding of efficient causes, which are responsible for putting together two objects into interaction. In other words, not every object interacts with every other object in the universe. Rather, some objects will interact with other objects, which will then be able to 'perceive' the presence of each other. The 'field' is nothing but that physical entity which makes one object feel the presence of the other object *specifically*.

Theorizing the Nature of the Efficient Cause

This is the point at which Vedic philosophy becomes relevant. In this philosophy, reality has three aspects called *sat*, *chit*, and *ananda*. The *chit* is the conceptual reality, which produces the hierarchical tree-like structure from abstract to detailed; in other words, our minds and bodies are due to *chit*. We have also called this reality the *material cause* because it exists as objects; some of these objects are conceptual and imperceptible while other objects are perceivable.

The material cause is incomplete and cannot produce experience unless complemented by two other causes—corresponding to *ananda* and *sat*—which we can call *desiring* and *deserving*. These are also called *guna* and *karma*, and I have collectively called them the *efficient* cause.

In simple terms, two conceptual objects (material cause) are brought in contact with each other due to a combination of desiring and deserving; for the senses of knowledge, the deserving is more important and we can desire from the available options that we deserve, but for the senses of action, the desiring is more important and they decide which of the deserving will be employed. Setting aside the details and nuances of this process, the key point is that the material cause is by itself inadequate unless *combined* with the efficient causes (two of them).

The *sat* creates relationality—it puts us in relation to the world. We commonly call this relation 'consciousness' by which our experience is *directed* towards an object. But *sat* is not just a transcendental concept; it also has a material counterpart by which an object can *potentially* interact with other objects. The *ananda* is the cause of choice—it allows us to pick from the available options in the world through which the potential becomes perceivable.

Sometimes, the options are so limited by our circumstances that our desires can only choose from the available options. At other times, the desires are stronger and they can change our circumstances. Therefore, sometimes *sat* dominates *chit* and *ananda*, and at other times *ananda* dominates *sat* and *chit*, while at other times *chit* dominates *sat* and *ananda*. At all times, *sat*, *chit*, and *ananda* must be combined to create an experience, which means that there is always some material reality, there is always a desire, and there is always some deserving. If these three are separated, there is no experience; experience is produced by their mixing.

The Role of Consciousness in Science

The terms *sat*, *chit*, and *ananda* are three aspects of the soul. In the material world, the same three aspects are reflected in matter. We can describe matter based on the nature of the soul, incorporating the understanding of *sat*, *chit*, and *ananda* in science, contrary to the present attempts of trying to divorce matter from the nature of the soul. Such a study is not in the least 'unscientific'; in fact it would be called upon only to solve those problems that current materialism cannot solve. And it involves no 'transcendent' factors per se.

The distinction between efficient and material causes needs an observer-centric view of the world in which a 'field' is not universally pervasive because this 'field' is *quantized*. The quantization of the field means that there are specific relationships between objects which this field instantiates. The world is not an illusion that simply manifests out of the field and disappears into it. Rather, the world is real material objects that exist imperceptibly as concepts. When these objects are put into contact with each other by the field, they are seen.

There are hence two distinct approaches to employing consciousness into science. The impersonalist approach claims that because observations are popping out of possibility and disappearing into that possibility we can suppose that the possibility is the ultimate ground of experience, and the observations popping out of the possibility are ultimately illusions. We can identify the possibility with 'consciousness' and the popped out illusion 'matter'. Ultimately we conclude that consciousness is reality and the material phenomena are illusions.

The personalist approach rejects this interpretation and claims that the world is not an illusion and it really exists. But what we see is not just because that thing exists but also because we are put into contact with that thing. Each observer comes into contact with different things and science is the ability to predict which things the observer will contact based on what they deserve and desire; the missing ingredient in atomic theory is how to explain who contacts what.

Personalism vs. Impersonalism

The two approaches are as different as chalk and cheese. In the impersonalist approach the observers are ultimately an illusion created from the universal possibility; they pop out and they pop back in from that possibility, and they mistakenly imagine that their individuality is real. The temporariness of the atomic phenomena is therefore indicative of the temporariness of our individuality because we must identify our individuality with the material body.

In the personalist approach the observers are eternal but the interactions between these observers and the material objects are temporary; everything therefore exists at all times, but everything is not *perceivable* at all times. The temporariness of the material experience has to be explained by an additional efficient cause which is a material reflection of the *sat* and *ananda* of the soul.

When the personalist approach is adopted, both the individuality of material objects and the individuality of the soul are reinstated. This allows us to both do science (because there are individual objects) and practice religion (because the soul is eternally individual). In the material experience, the desiring and deserving are incompatible due to which the desires are often frustrated and we are forced to experience what we don't desire. But in religion the desiring and deserving become compatible which we means we only experience what we desire and what we desire is always available. The principles of *sat*, *chit*, and *ananda* don't disappear in either case; the difference is that these are conflicting in matter and consistent in transcendence.

The study of matter is thus non-different from the study of the soul, because the material dynamics are described as the conflict between the material counterparts of *sat*, *chit*, and *ananda*. The analysis of this conflict leads us to the need for consistency in which what we desire, what we deserve, and what we perceive in reality are not conflictual but consistent.

The Expansion of Material Ontology

Current material science only speaks about material *reality* but the personalist approach adds two more categories—desiring and deserving. The material experience is therefore not caused by a material reality alone; it is rather created from the conflict between desiring, deserving, and reality. In that respect we have to expand our ontology from one thing to three things. The material reality exists independent of my desiring or deserving, which means matter is objectively real. But the material reality doesn't produce an *experience* unless it is combined with the desiring and deserving, which means that the observer is not permanently bound to matter. The material experience is therefore the outcome of *combining* three things, and the process of this combination is the essence of the complete scientific explanation of the world.

Conversely, in the impersonalist approach there is one thing—possibility—so how it becomes an experience can never be explained except by supposing that this conversion occurs randomly. This has, historically speaking, been the central burden of oneness because they cannot explain the origin of experience, even if we grant the illusion of the material experience.

Since experience is produced from the mixing of reality, desiring, and deserving, there is an additional need to explain the cause of this mixing in order to create experience. Since there is a time when they are mixed and a time when they are unmixed, *time* becomes the cause of mixing or unmixing, which are then the origin and the end of the universe. The personalist ontology is broader than the impersonalist ontology, but that is because it recognizes the reality of both individual observer and individual object, besides the reality of both material and transcendent experiences. The impersonalist rejects the individuality of both the observer and the objects, besides rejecting the reality of both material and transcendent experience.

Of course, when we present the problem in this way, it appears that the questions of reality are ultimately metaphysical and there is no way to decide if one is better than the other. However, science can play an important role here because it presents a problem of explaining and predicting and there are two kinds of answers to this problem: (1) there can be no better prediction and explanation because this is indeed the reality, and (2) there can be a better explanation and prediction if we expand our ontology. In that sense, the impersonalist approach can be considered *incomplete* although it is never *inconsistent.* The personalist approach instead presents an alternative that is both *complete* and *consistent.* The criterion of selection is therefore not simply a metaphysical preference, but an objective and rational choice.

The Universal and Local Laws

When the 'field' puts everything in contact with everything else, the laws of nature are universal. However, when the 'field' puts a specific set of objects in contact, then the laws of nature are *contextual* to that relation. In simple terms, the laws are contingent on the specific *role* that an object plays in relation to another object, and the law of nature is normative. That is, the role prescribes the expected behavior, and the consequences of the action are decided by whether the action conforms to the expectation. In other words, when we go from universalization to contextualization, we change the determinants in the law from universal to contextual.

The material world is objective and universal; it exists as the tree-like hierarchy of gross phenomena produced from subtle reality, when the efficient cause acts upon the subtle. However, the efficient cause (*guna* and *karma*) is contextual and not universal. This basically means that you can study the material objects in a third-person universalist way, but why you see a particular object (and not other objects) can only be explained in the first-person way. The material cause is the universalism and the efficient cause is the personalism.

Time acts differently on the material and the efficient causes. On the material cause, time acts to create the material objects regardless of the individual observers. On the efficient cause, time acts to manifest the desiring and deserving which combine with the reality to experience it. Thus, the objective evolution of the material world is independent of all observers. But the subjective experience of this world by individual observers depends on the respective observers.

We can thus speak about two kinds of laws—universal and contextual. The universal law is the objective evolution of the material world. The contextual law is that each situation has different expectations and the same action has different consequences in different roles. This contextuality is the *personalization* of science from the prior impersonalism. The personalist ideology entails not just a philosophical preference in viewpoint. It also entails a new type of law in nature, and by proving the truth of such laws we can conclude the truth of personalism.

Economics and Reductionism

Published Date: 2017-08-13

The Cost of a Chair's Design

Profits require that the whole must be greater than the sum of the parts. For example, half a chair is not half price of the full chair; most times you cannot sell two halves of a chair separately, or price them separately, even when you assemble the chair yourself from packaged parts. Similarly, the price a carpenter will charge for a chair is necessarily greater than the cost of the parts that make up the chair. In that sense, the whole cannot be reduced to the parts because the price of the whole is necessarily greater than the costs of the parts. If we equated prices to costs, there would be no economy because nobody will find that proposition *profitable*.

The inability to reduce prices to costs means that the whole is priced based on the costs of the parts, but there is always something extra in the whole beyond the parts. The act of putting the parts together is itself very valuable, and this combination exists independent of the parts.

This viewpoint can be understood only when the whole is *separately real* from the parts and is *added* to the parts in order to *organize* them. It requires us to conceive a chair as a "design" that exists even when the object embodying the design does not. The design is in fact logically prior to the observable object that embodies it even though we cannot see it as an object; the design, rather, exists as an *idea* and it forms the basis or ground on which the chair is built.

The price that the carpenter charges for the chair includes the cost of the visible parts and the cost of the invisible design, and what it took to convert the design into a visible object. The price is greater than the cost of the visible components because the price includes the invisible. Unless we recognize the reality of the invisible, we cannot conduct economics.

The Value in the Citizens and Government

The economic system is like the chair in which the total value is greater than the value of the parts. The total wealth of the economy is greater than the wealth held by all the individuals and corporations, because the additional wealth is with the government which taxes the citizens and businesses. Like the value of the chair is not fully in the parts, similarly, the value of the economy is not fully in the citizens and corporations. The government is the idea or design of a society—which is independent of the economic activity and yet designs that activity.

By virtue of designing the economic system, considerable amount of value is held in the government, and the government needs this wealth to maintain and improve the economic system. However, the government doesn't become part of the economy by holding this value, just as the idea chair is not one of the chair parts, and yet it co-exists with the chair. The difference is evidenced in the fact that the government taxes the citizens but not itself. The government can escape taxation only when it is situated outside the economic system.

The Inverted Tree of Economic Value

The chair is a part of a room, which is part of a building, which is part of a city, and so forth. Just as the price of the chair is greater than the cost of its parts, similarly, the value in the room is greater than the value in the sum of the parts, the value in the building and city is greater than the sum of their parts. As more and more levels of organization are embodied in a system, a greater amount of value is produced in the system. Just as the chair exists as an idea prior to its parts, similarly, the room, the building, the city, and the nation existed as a design before their parts. The whole doesn't reduce to the parts because it existed logically prior to the parts.

These ideas can only be understood when we describe space as an inverted tree in which the higher nodes are like trunks from which branches, twigs, and leaves emanate. The concept chair, is higher than the chair parts, the concept room is higher than its parts, the building design is higher than the bricks and wood in the building, and the laws of the government which provide the blueprint for the working of the economy are higher than the economy itself.

Hierarchy Creates Increasing Value

All societies are based on some foundational ideas—e.g. the moral values of humanity and the purpose of life. The ruler of the land converts these ideas into *laws* which the governmental machinery—e.g. military, police, and bureaucracy—enforces to ensure that the society conforms to the ideas. Based on such laws, the cycles of production and consumption are created in the economy via businesses. And finally there are employees that work in a business.

There is additional value in the business (possessed by the business owner) than in all the workers in the business put together. There is additional value in the country (possessed by the ruler and the government of the state) than in all the businesses put together. And there is additional value in the ideas (possessed by the intellectuals who guide society with moral values) than in the government which controls the businesses. This produces a hierarchy of value in which the workers relinquish some value for the business owner, the business owner relinquishes some value for the government, and the government relinquishes some value by financing the intellectual and moral activity.

Based on the relinquishing, a tree of value is produced across four levels of organization in a society—intellectuals, government, businesses, and workers—due to which the business cannot be reduced to the workers, the government cannot be reduced to the businesses, and the intellectual activity cannot be reduced to the government. This tree of value constitutes an abstract conceptual model of the society that is both necessary and sufficient.

Concepts Exist Unperceivable

In this hierarchical model, we cannot perceive moral values that create the foundation of society. Similarly, the laws that the government creates to administer society are conceptual entities. The business organization is a conceptual entity which is given a legal status as an individual with rights and duties under the government. And each business creates rules for its employees. The moral principles, governmental laws, business incorporation, and employment rules, are all conceptual. Each of the higher concepts can produce the lower concepts, and different people are involved in this conversion. These people then become the four tiers in organizing a society.

The activities of these people provide *evidence* for the existence of the concepts, and by this evidence we can *perceive* moral values, governmental laws, business entities, and employment rules. That doesn't mean that these ideas are created only at the point of empirical manifestation. We must rather conclude that these ideas exist independently of observation but they are observable when a person with a life force coverts them into recognizable activity.

For example, the moral values can exist, but the society at large cannot automatically become moral unless these moral values are expressed in the actions of moral person. The laws of economic governance can exist but they would not be realized until the government enforces them through a legal, law enforcement, and bureaucratic machinery. A business can remain incorporated but its existence of paper cannot be perceived unless the business transacts with other businesses. And the laws of worker employment can be well-defined but they won't be evident to anyone unless employees follow them. People convert ideas into activities, and without the life force in their body we can have ideas but no evidence of the existence of such ideas.

How is Semantics Related to Religion?

Published Date: 2017-08-14

Seven Steps to the Knowledge of God

Before we can understand the nature of God, we have to understand the nature of the self or the soul. The soul is identified as the triumvirate of eternity, knowledge, and happiness. In the material world we seek knowledge and happiness but they are temporary. So, the distinction between matter and soul begins in the eternity of the soul. God becomes relevant as the object of eternal knowledge and happiness, only when the soul is itself eternal. If life is simply the temporary material body—which obtains temporary knowledge and happiness—then there is no need for God. From the standpoint of inquiry, therefore, the question of the eternity of the soul is prior to the existence of God. We can also say that we must know that we are not the body before we can understand the nature of God.

The proof of the eternity of the soul rests on reincarnation. Most people think that reincarnation is the rebirth of the soul in a different form of life in another time and place, but in Vedic philosophy there is rebirth at every moment. The process by which a soul is born into a new body is the same process by which the person changes bodies in this life. For example, if you walk across a room, the *same* body isn't moving. Rather, the soul is continually stepping into a new body. Therefore, the process is called *changing* bodies rather than *moving* bodies. The term "reincarnation" thus has a broader significance—it is the substitution of the theory of "motion" in modern science; the soul is eternal not just because it is born into new bodies after this body is dead, but because it is continually being born into new bodies. If we have to prove the eternity of the soul, we have to describe how the body is not moving, although the body is changed.

The process of the change of bodies is mediated by *karma* in Vedic philosophy. *Karma* is the abilities and opportunities accorded to the soul; of these, the body is the ability to perform some actions, and when this body comes in contact with other bodies it has new opportunities. The soul chooses which abilities to enact and which opportunities to use. So the world exists as a *possibility* from which the soul selects. But these possibilities are themselves created as a consequence of previous actions—i.e. *karma*. In order to describe how the body is changing, we have to describe the process of *karma* creation.

Karma is produced through *judgments* of *right* or *wrong*. If we have to explain *karma* we have to first explain *judgments*. Why is this a problem? Judgments have become a problem because we have conceived of matter as particles and waves which do not judge. Some religions therefore add judgments as God's decisions based on His commandments. But note that we just said that to prove God we need to prove the soul, to prove the soul we need to prove reincarnation, to prove reincarnation we have to prove *karma*, and to prove *karma* we need judgments. So we are trying to prove the existence of God and we cannot assume God in that proof—in order to avoid circularity. Instead, we have to prove the reality of judgments in nature itself: nature has to determine right and wrong.

For nature to determine right and wrong there must be *contextuality* in nature because right and wrong are contextual to time, place, and role of a person. What is right action for a soldier is not the right action for a civilian; what is right action for a parent is not the right action for a child. In other words, we cannot define right and wrong universally. The laws of moral judgment cannot be universal as the laws of modern science are. There has to be something materially unique in the time, place, and role based on which nature can judge. This requires us to discard universality in favor of contextuality and entails a fundamental revision of the notions of material nature in science where all locations in space, all instances in time, and all relationships between individuals are viewed uniformly. Ultimately it means that the laws of modern science based on the uniformity of nature must be false; we have to find new laws of contextuality. The contradiction between religion and science is rooted in the issue of universality vs. contextuality.

Many people have a problem with discarding universality because they imagine that if laws were contextual then there would be as many laws as there are contexts. What good would science be if it could not use the laws to predict every situation because we have to first know the situation before we can understand the laws? This is where it is important to understand the distinction between cause, effect, and consequence. Modern science deals only in cause and effect, and employs universal laws. This universality can continue. However, the moral *consequence* of the action is not universal. An object never interacts with everything else in the universe—as modern science postulates (e.g. the mass of an object exerts a force on every other object in the universe simultaneously). Rather, an object only interacts with *some* objects at any given time. Therefore, we can distinguish between the visible outcome of an interaction (cause and effect), and the moral consequence of that interaction caused by a judgment (cause and consequence). For a judgment to be possible, there must be intention in the action. We cannot say that a person is wrong if that person did not know what he was doing and had no intention. This means that even the causal interaction must be *intentional*: e.g. a particle must be directed toward a destination with the aim and purpose to collide. Classical particles are famously compared to billiard balls, but anyone who has seen a game of billiards knows that the balls are hit intentionally to collide with other balls to put them into pockets. There is foreknowledge and intention even in the collision of billiard balls.

Moral judgments rest on a prior knowledge of reality, and knowledge requires a conceptual ability by which in knowing the apple I don't become the apple. If we were all automatons which interacted with a limited set of objects without *knowing* what those objects were there would be contextuality but no judgment. In order to judge a soldier, the soldier must be able to distinguish the enemy from the friend. In order to judge a parent, the parent must be able to distinguish their children from other children. In short, knowledge and meaning are properties of the objects involved in limited interactions.

The Seven Steps Summarized

We can recapitulate the above seven steps succinctly as follows:

To prove the existence of God we have to prove the eternity of the soul

To prove the eternity of the soul we have to prove the reality of reincarnation

To prove the truth of reincarnation we have to demonstrate the truth of *karma*

To prove the truth of *karma* we have to provide evidence for judgments

To prove the reality of judgments we have describe the world contextually

To prove the reality of contexts we need the reality of knowledge and intention

To prove the reality of knowledge, we have to imbibe meanings in matter

Contexts appear in the fact that no object interacts with all other objects at once—which has been the cardinal cornerstone of modern science—based on which *universal* laws of nature were postulated. If all objects don't interact with each other simultaneously, then the question of which objects interact at any given time itself presents a new problem. The answer to that problem is *karma* which is produced as a consequence of previous actions. These interactions create an observer's abilities and interactions and because each interaction is produced individually, we don't see everything at once.

The succession of our abilities and interactions constitutes the succession of bodies: we are *changing* bodies with each interaction, and some changes are small while others are large. However, since all interactions are instantiated discretely, all bodies are discrete. Thus, the *same* body doesn't move into a new state. Rather, we acquire a new body at each instant. To explain the succession of such bodily experiences—the "trajectory" in space—there must be something that *joins* the discrete states, and that thing which establishes the *continuity* cannot be matter because matter is always discrete.

The soul emerges as a necessity in science to establish continuity when matter is always discrete because the soul *connects* the discrete states into a trajectory or continuous experience. This continuity can never disappear because if it disappears it would be discrete again. In that sense, the soul is a non-material entity. Once the eternity of the soul is understood, then we can speak about why the soul is suffering—which then requires us to add pleasure and pain to the material categories. God becomes a necessity only after the soul's eternity is established, as the path to eternal happiness. The soul is eternal even without God, but the soul is not eternally *happy* without God. However, before we can speak about eternal happiness, we have to first speak about the soul's eternity itself.

Why I Emphasize the Study of Meaning

My emphasis on the study of meaning—as the path toward the knowledge of God—is deeply grounded in the Vedic notion of the world where the soul transmigrates due to *karma* which is a natural law based on the moral judgment of our actions, and that judgment is impossible without imbibing contextuality, which then necessitates the existence of knowledge, which then demands meanings.

We first know the world cognitively and cognition requires meanings. Once we know the world then we act in the world knowingly such that our actions are liable to judgments. We cannot impose a moral judgment if the actor is ignorant about what he is doing. For example, if a policeman just shoots the bullet and has no idea what that bullet is going to hit, there can be no judgment of the action. In order to judge an action, there has to be foreknowledge about what the person is doing. Therefore meaning is the prerequisite for a moral judgment. The moral judgment is the prerequisite for *karma*, which is the necessity for transmigration, which it the precondition to understand the eternality of the soul, which is the qualification to realize the reality of God. This gives us the aforementioned hierarchy.

The conflict between religion and science did not begin in the rejection of God. It rather begins in the misperception of matter—as something that exists objectively but is incapable of *knowing*. This illusion about matter was created by Descartes when he separated mind from matter, and made matter incapable of knowing. Once matter cannot know, then there cannot be judgments on the activities of matter. If we cannot judge matter, then there cannot be morality and contextuality. A variety of false conceptions of nature follow from here—namely that the universe is uniform, that all objects interact with each other simultaneously, that the laws of this interaction are universal, etc.

The misconceptions are therefore not with regard to the soul and God. They are primarily about the nature of material reality. At least, they originate in the study and description of matter. Which is rather fortunate because we can stop the debate about the reality of the soul and God and discuss whether all objects interact with each other always, whether the universe is uniform, and if the laws are universal. Many of these problems are now directly appearing within mainstream science.

The Connection to Modern Science

Contextual interactions are now seen in atomic theory because the "field" through which an object interacts with other objects is *quantized*, which means that objects no longer interact with all other objects at once; rather, they interact with other objects one by one, and present atomic theory is unable to predict the order of these interactions. In other words, we now have the evidence of contextuality in science but this contextuality stands in contrast to the universalism prevalent in classical physics.

The reason we can never predict the order of interactions using a universal law is because the order is contextual. Now, this contextuality presents deep problems for physicists because they tend to think of reality as quarks, leptons, and photons. What could be contextual about these particles?

The short answer is that the contextuality is in the *macroscopic* objects, not in the quarks and leptons. In other words, quarks and leptons don't interact with other quarks and leptons. Rather, the absorber of radiation interacts with the emitter of radiation, quite like our eyes see the apple. The contextuality comes from the whole eye and the whole apple, not from the quarks, leptons, and photons. To express this contextuality, we have to describe the interacting objects as eyes and apples.

If eyes and apples were fully reducible to their constituent parts, then the parts would act independently without any contextuality. At worst we would need to formulate separate rules for the order of quarks, leptons, photons, etc. The fact that we can never formulate any universal laws predicting the order indicates a demise of the idea that apples and eyes are reducible to their constituent parts.

We have to now reinstate the *reality* of apples and eyes, use that as the context of the quark, lepton, or photon interaction, and the order of events can then be judged based on that context, which then produces the consequence of the quantum of action (called *karma*), which then produces new contexts. In other words, we have come to the end of the road as far as reductionism is concerned. We have to now imagine how the macroscopic wholes are *conceptual* objects, though not *sensual* objects.

The reality of concepts makes knowledge possible. Through that knowledge we know what we are doing. Since we know what we are doing, we can be morally judged by nature's laws. Once that judgment is performed, a consequence is created. Through that consequence, a new kind of body and interaction is produced. And through such bodies and interactions experiences are created. The soul passes through the succession of these experiences enjoying and suffering but it doesn't realize that it is different from the material body that keeps changing. Without that realization there is no need for religion. In that sense, the first step is understanding the conceptual ability. Once that issue is solved then we can speak about the successive issues, all the way to the knowledge of God.

The Four Legs of Dharma

Published Date: 2018-01-02

Introduction and Overview

The word 'dharma' means *duty*. In the Śrimad Bhāgavatam, dharma is described as a 'bull' who stands on four 'legs'—austerity, cleanliness, truthfulness, and kindness. These principles, also called 'the four pillars of dharma', are common to all aspects of human life, including that which is not directly associated with a 'religion'. Indeed, 'religion' in the Vedic context is simply one's duties associated with one's *role*. The roles, however, are hierarchical and a person is simultaneously in multiple roles. The duties associated with the highest role—in relation to God—are called 'religion'. Other duties, which are lower in the hierarchy, include one's social duties such as 'father', 'employee', 'student', etc. The four legs of dutifulness are associated with both lower and higher duties. This article discusses the meanings of these four 'legs' of dutifulness.

The First Leg of Austerity

Austerity—in the simplest sense—means 'hard work'. It is the act of self-abnegation to achieve some goal. All of us understand that to get something, we must work. Austerity is the trouble that the mind and body have to undertake to achieve the goal. Now, typically, the body and the mind are not accustomed to austerity because the senses and the mind desire *pleasure*. Hard work can mean denying that pleasure in the short-term to achieve something that will yield pleasure in the long run.

Owing to the innate need for pleasure in the senses and the mind, a person may be driven by short-term thinking: "let me do what I need to do right now for my happiness, and I will think about the long-term problems later on". When a person is dominated by short-term thinking, he or she becomes controlled by the urges of the body and the mind, and doesn't realize that he or she is different from them.

To force the body and the mind to prepare for the long-term

happiness, one may have to sacrifice the short-term happiness. This sacrifice ultimately depends on the realization that the soul is eternal, and even though some short-term sacrifices may be made, the eternity of the soul implies that there would be sufficient time later on enjoy the fruits of this sacrifice. When a person doesn't believe in the eternity of the soul, he or she feels that their life will be wasted in sacrifice because after death there is no pleasure. Prioritizing the long-term happiness therefore appears to be risky: we might spend the majority of our life sacrificing our happiness, and since death will be the end of all pleasure, we gain nothing in the end. Hence, austerity is possible only when one is convinced of the soul's eternity.

Austerity also requires *will power*, or what we call *free will*. The urges of the body and the mind can be overpowered but we must exercise the force of will power to achieve that mastery. Since the body and the mind are material, and always changing, the bodily and mental tendency is always to think of the short-term pleasure: "I will enjoy this now, and when things change, then I will enjoy something else later". Some people hence interpret the "live in the present" exhortation to naively mean the focus on the short-term and immediate pleasures. To think for the longer-term, one has to master the art of will power (long-term thinking) over the urges of the body and mind (short-term thinking).

By exercising that will power, one realizes that he or she is different from the body and mind, and while the body and the mind keep changing, the ability to exert that will force remains unchanged. Thus, most people with weak will power claim to be helpless against the material forces, and since they are unable to control their body and mind, there must be no soul or free will in this world. This is a symptom that they haven't developed their will power and don't exercise it, and hence they succumb to the short-term pleasure urges. We might also note that the realization of free will is not uniform across everyone. Quite specifically, one has to *use* the will power to realize that we have it. The more we use the will power—to prioritize the long-term happiness over the short-term urges—the more we understand how the soul is different from the body and the mind. As a result, not everyone has free will; if we don't use it, we lose it. But the potential for using it and finding it always exists.

Austerity is the act of using the will power to discover that we have will power, so that we can use it even more in the future, until we have complete mastery over the body and the mind.

Why is this a 'leg' of *dharma*? The fact is that when we face our duties and responsibilities, we are often compelled to think of the long-term vs. the short-term. Should I do the bare minimum to get past the day, inflict the minimum amount of pain on the body and the mind? Or should I take my role seriously for the long-term, and understand that sacrifices in the short-run will yield results in the long-run?

Most people prioritize the short-term over the long-term. They want quick results for their effort, and if those results are seen to be distant or non-existent, they become demotivated and stop working. Due to lack of effort, the results—which could have been achieved in the long-run through austerity in the short-run—are not seen over the long run. A person who prioritizes the short-term happiness goes through a vicious cycle of seeking their short-term pleasure, but as time passes even the short term happiness in the future depends on the sacrifices for the long-term made in the past. Since the delay between hard work and subsequent gratification seems large, the motivation to make that effort is generally weak, which means that the short-term happiness is again prioritized. By always prioritizing the short-term pleasure a person loses the will power to take pain in the short-term, and hence even the short-term pleasures disappear over time (because they depended on past sacrifices).

To practice *dharma* or duty, one must begin thinking about the long-term over the short-term. Pain in the short-term must be accepted if it means long-term happiness. Austerity therefore doesn't mean eternal suffering. It means *temporary* sacrifice for eternal happiness. The practice of austerity naturally increases the soul's will power, and hence the detachment from the mind and body. Hence, in Vedic texts, *tapasyā* or austerity is a dominant means for self-realization. However, every step of our life involves the short vs. long term thinking question, and hence the question is perennial.

The Second Leg of Cleanliness

The word 'clean' is normally identified with hygiene and sanitation—e.g. taking bath, wearing clean clothes, washing our food before consumption, etc. But 'clean' also means systematic and organized. For example, we might say that "the room looks clean" not just because it has been swept and mopped but also because the things in the room seem to be organized and orderly. Cleanliness appears in our lives through systematic and organized working. Some people do their work systematically—step by step, following a clear process, designed to achieve a result, even if it means delayed gratification, because the results of following that systematic approach are predictable and certain.

It's noteworthy that cleanliness depends on a longer-term thinking because to do things systematically, we have to invest time, energy, and effort into creating that system, bringing that discipline in our activities, and ensuring that we don't break the regulations of process and procedure in order to 'quickly' achieve results. If a person prioritizes the short-term urges, he would be tempted to quickly get to the finish line to achieve fast gratification, and hence shortcuts would be taken. The result of these shortcuts is that outcomes become fault-ridden, unpredictable, and patchy.

Of course, when we work unsystematically and produce an unclean outcome, we have to expend further effort in cleaning it up. If the urge for getting to a clean state is very high, then under that urge a systematic way of cleaning and fixing the situation would be avoided. So, we employ an unclean process to clean up things, and the result is further clumsiness, clutter, and disorganization. Now, we are caught in the vicious cycle of uncleanliness: we did not do the work systematically the first time, and we are now under the pressure to clean it up, but the pressure motivates us to pursue short-term outcomes and quick-fix solutions, which then leads to more uncleanliness in the effort to clean up the mess created by previous uncleanliness. As a result, the mess is never cleaned up. It becomes more and more convoluted and complex, and over time all our energy is spent in clean-up operations.

With an unsystematic way of working, we appear to make rapid progress in the initial stages, but over time we become paralyzed by the disorganization—most of the time is spent just apply patches to the leaking bucket that was haphazardly put together under an urgency to produce something like a bucket. The pressure to clean up things remains high, so the systematic process is never followed, and all the energy spent in cleaning creates more clutter. To clean up, we not only have to institute processes and procedures, but these in turn rest upon prioritizing the long-term over the short-term. Hence, if there is no patience—based on the longer-term benefits of working systematically—then processes will be broken, and the net result is stagnation as more energy is continually invested to clean up.

As this stagnation becomes a way of life, people become demotivated with their work, and give up the desire to clean up. They keep applying patches to give the appearance of progress, but internally they lose the conviction that they are doing something meaningful. Over time, they must become more cynical about the prospect of progress, and this cynicism is depicted today in cartoons such as Dilbert where the entire workplace is permeated by the need for short-term results, overlooking a systematic way of working, producing unsatisfactory results, and an endless cycle of patchwork.

Cleanliness is a 'leg' of *dharma* because it means that we might crawl like a tortoise initially but we outpace the hare who runs fast in the beginning but is stagnated thereafter. The moral of the hare and tortoise story is that the benefits of systematic progress outstrip those of discrete and discontinuous activities, if only we can believe in the benefits of the long-term over the short-term.

The Third Leg of Kindness

Kindness is the opposite of selfishness, and to be kind means to be unselfish and cooperative. Kindness depends on humility, which comes from self-confidence. Conversely, selfishness is the symptom of inner weakness, which prompts a person to remain selfish and fear their self-preservation. Under that fear of survival, a person forgets that all relationships are based on trust, and that trust is quickly broken by selfish actions. When the trust is broken, other people stop cooperating and we become even lonelier in life, and our inner weakness and fear is exacerbated, prompting a vicious cycle in which weakness leads to selfishness, which then leads to breach of trust, which then leads to more fear.

Kindness is a symptom of internal emotional self-confidence. When a person works hard (is not afraid of austerity) and works systematically (is not afraid of discipline) he or she naturally develops confidence, and with that confidence comes kindness. With kindness emerge strong relationships based on mutual trust, and with that trust, we can rely on others to reciprocate our kindness.

The emotionally weak cannot be kind because they are always worried about self-preservation. Kindness to them appears too risky, because by being kind they fear being cheated by others. That fear of being cheated prompts people to be selfish. But if we are always selfish, then we must expect selfishness in return. If we are prone to manipulate other people, then we must expect manipulation from others. Emotional weakness hence leads to selfishness, which turns into subversive manipulation of others, but over time others understand our nature and become uncooperative. The kind person brings out kindness in others, but the selfish person causes others to become selfish. The irony is that selfishness is the symptom of weakness, and if we are already weak, we need the support of strong relationships. If we break the trust via selfishness, then we also break the relationship and we are now left even lonelier. However, most weak people don't realize that their selfishness is the cause of their loneliness, and that weakness to selfishness to loneliness constitutes a vicious cycle.

When a person is confident, he or she becomes less egoistic. They are able to treat criticisms objectively as areas of improvement, rather than as an affront on their individuality. Confidence therefore brings humility, whereas weakness breeds egoism. Those who are egoistic are not confident. They are in fact weak to the point of being unable to handle criticism, make improvements, become more confident as a result of those improvements, and become humble as a result of confidence. They remain stuck in their weakness, acting selfishly out of their fear, which manifests externally as ego, but eats a person from within because that ego hinders a person's self-correction leading to improvement.

In the material world, no relationship is perfect. However, long-lasting relationships require a person to be receptive to change—making the necessary corrections. If a person has flaws, but remains adamant about those flaws, he or she imposes the adverse outcomes of their flaws on others. The person on the receiving end of those flaws suffers only to the point where their own kindness can take them. Beyond that point, they stop tolerating the flaws, by moving out of the relationship, or fighting it, because they are unable to bear the burden of the other person's flaws being inflicted upon them.

Kindness means that I am willing to fix my problems and make the life of others—living or working with me—less painful. We must realize that a flawed person is a burden on other people, and they may bear that burden only if they are kind toward others. Kindness means not just giving something valuable to others. It also means that taking out the pain of our own personality problems which make other's life difficult. Correcting one's flaws is the preliminary form of kindness. Once this kindness is perfected, then people want to trust and seek our help. That's when we can expand our kindness toward generosity—i.e. offering our time, energy, and abilities to further their goals. Therefore, charity is a much advanced form of kindness, but the preliminary form of kindness is self-correction.

Sometimes people perform charity—e.g. offering others money and time—but don't want to fix their personality problems. Their charity is a masquerade for selfishness: they pretend to help others to show their superiority over them. That selfishness is eventually seen as the person supposedly "helping" others is found helping himself while destroying others. It is the inverse of kindness, but masquerades as kindness, and cannot be considered one's duty. The preliminary duty one has is fixing one's personality problems. Without fixing those problems, charity and kindness are another form of show business.

The Fourth Leg of Truthfulness

Once we have become kind, we can offer help to others. But what kind of help is that going to be? Should that help expand their short-term thinking, support the practice of unsystematic and patchy work, and spread superficial charity in order to appear to be kind to others? Or should it be the dissemination of truth—however harsh and painful—that reinforces long-term over short-term thinking, exhorts the person to work in a systematic and disciplined manner, and points out personality flaws so that they can be corrected? By truth we mean the latter rather than the former.

It is said that truth is harsh, and truthfulness is therefore painful. It is easier to appeal to a person's short-term gratification, support their wrongdoing in order to achieve that pleasure, and pretend to have a relationship that exchanges short-term gratification as motivation for their work. It is much harder to tell the truth that enlightens a person about their real long-term happiness, which then leads to a systematic and organized practice with predictable results, while challenging a person to fix their personality problems as the primary purpose of having a relationship with the others.

Indeed, when one begins telling the truth, he or she also faces criticisms. To continue speaking the truth, one must have the requisite kindness, which in turn depends on the previous two legs of *dharma*. Most people are deterred by that truth-speaking—because it makes life uncomfortable—and seek refuge in self-preservation. Such self-preservation sometimes goes in the name of not 'offending' or 'hurting' other's emotions and feelings, but it is primarily motivated by keeping oneself happy. By avoiding to speak the truth, one breaks the kindness and austerity legs of *dharma*. He or she might maintain good relations with others, find his support reciprocated, besides popularity. But he or she has failed to perform the expected duty in exchange for pleasantness, happiness, and peace. Leo Tolstoy writes in his book *War and Peace*: "All that is necessary for evil to triumph is for good men to do nothing".

When truthfulness is spoken as a leg of *dharma* the implication is that harshness may be involved. That harshness is, paradoxically, kindness, because only by speaking the truth can illusion be mitigated. It requires austerity because by speaking the truth, one might get into trouble and therefore one must be prepared to sacrifice short-term interests for a long-term fulfillment. And harshness is often necessary to drive out laziness in life to enforce a discipline by which life's goals can be achieved systematically. The quest for truth is not easy. It involves not only questions about what reality is and how we know it, but also the ability to *accept* the truth even when it becomes unpleasant to one's life.

Truthfulness requires detachment. Those who rely on deception might seem successful, prosperous, and loved by others, and our desire for these things often prevents us from speaking the truth. The acquisition of truth also depends on detachment because then we can see things as they are rather than as we might want them to be. Truthfulness and detachment are therefore always connected to each other as *jñāna* and *vairāgya* because without detachment our 'knowledge' is biased.

The Progression in the Legs of Dharma

Since we can count the four legs of *dharma*, we can also ask: In which order should we count? The Vedic texts describe that the four legs of *dharma* are dominant in the four ages or *yuga*. The time called *Satya-yuga* dominates in austerity—i.e. voluntarily inflicting suffering on the body and mind to detach the soul from the material world as well as develop the power of will that separates the soul from the body. The time called *Tretā-yuga* dominates in cleanliness—it involves the strict performance of elaborate rituals (processes and procedures) without mistakes. The time called *Dvāpara-yuga* dominates in kindness by performing charity and fixing one's personality flaws because intense austerity and elaborate rituals are very hard to achieve for most people. Finally, in the age called *Kali-yuga* truthfulness is the dominant form of religiosity because charity, rituals, and austerity are very hard to perform.

Of course, the relative predominance of one of the legs of religion doesn't mean the non-existence of the others. But the fact is that when the body and mind are weak, they cannot tolerate severe austerities. If we are unable to perform complex tasks in a systematic manner, then the performance of *yajña* would be filled with violations and mistakes. If most people are poor and struggling to survive, charity is very hard and limited to a few rich people.

In the present age of *Kali-yuga* even truthfulness declines, and speaking the truth leads to quarrels. To avoid those quarrels, most people want to keep quiet, or offer false support to the misguided. At the bare minimum, therefore, truthfulness in this age means self-criticism through honest introspection. We may not offer honest guidance to others, but at least we must be honest with ourselves. We may not be able to teach others the truth, but at least we must learn the truth ourselves. Bringing oneself out of delusion, false hopes, and misapprehensions about one's real state in life is our *duty*.

We can be assisted in this duty by other teachers, but the fact is that a teacher who offers the truth plainly may be disliked and challenged—making his or her task much more difficult—forcing them to recoil from their kindness, austerity, and cleanliness, because these are not easy anyway. The net result of such delusion partially impacts the teacher; but it greatly impacts the students themselves.

Dharma therefore doesn't mean 'religion' in all cases. It does, however, mean 'religion' when the person is involved in the highest duties (which override all other duties). As Lord Kṛṣṇa says in the Bhagavad-Gita 18.66: "Abandon all varieties of *dharma* and just surrender unto Me. I shall deliver you from all sinful reaction. Do not fear", the lower *dharma* or duties can be discarded in favor of the higher *dharma*. As a result, austerity, cleanliness, kindness, and truthfulness can also be discarded if it pleases the Lord. But that rejection is generally rare and perilous, and it must be taken only under the guidance of a teacher who knows how to override the lower *dharma* with the higher *dharma*.

As a general principle, one must aspire to maintain all the four legs of *dharma*. But if all four cannot be maintained then one must try to the least bit of sacrifice to the minimum number of legs to *dharma* for the shortest period of time. If we are not able to even do this, then we must at least practice truthfulness. If truthfulness toward others becomes impossible, then at the bare minimum honesty with oneself is essential. The worst form of *adharma* is self-deception, which leads to the deception of others, and over time to unkindness (instead of kindness), uncleanliness (instead of cleanliness), and hedonism (instead of austerity).

Honesty toward oneself is asking the basic questions of life and accepting their answers. The questions are: Who am I? Why am I here? What should I be doing? What am I doing? The answers are: I am an eternal spiritual particle, I am here to realize this nature, I should be trying to realize this nature, but I am (probably) not doing enough to fulfill the mission of life. If we can't do this, we have already violated the principle of truthfulness, which is the main principle for Kali-Yuga, and after that, all other principles of *dharma* will be violated. Being dharmic is not about blowing a trumpet. It is about following these principles.

The Contradictions of Being

Published Date: 2018-02-16

Introduction and Overview

Even as choice and responsibility are essential features of any moral conception of human life, they often present a paradox when the three aspects of the soul—pleasure, ability, and responsibility—are differentiated and what we enjoy becomes different from what we are capable of, and what we are capable of becomes different from our duty. The article discusses the resulting conflicts and how they are solved.

The Inner Contradiction in the Soul

The desires or choices of the soul are produced from the *ananda* of the soul, and they constitute the judgment of good. The sense of responsibility is produced from the *sat* of the soul, and it constitutes the judgment of right. The abilities of the soul are produced from *chit* and they constitute the judgment of truth or reality. The three aspects of the soul—*sat, chit,* and *ananda*—often conflict. Sometimes you want to fulfill your duties but you don't have the ability. Sometimes you have the ability but it is not your duty. And sometimes you have the ability and it is your duty but you don't enjoy it.

The inner conflicts in the soul have to be resolved; this is done through prioritizing. One of the three—*sat, chit,* or *ananda*—will become dominant and the others will be subordinated. However, different aspects may dominate at different times, thereby overturning the prioritization. Through this dominant-subordinate relation, the contradiction is temporarily solved; one aspect wins and the others then become subordinate. However, the conflict will likely return again at a later time.

Common examples of such conflicts are visible every day. For instance, sometimes desire rules over ability and opportunity—e.g. I can digest milk, and I have the opportunity to drink milk, but I hate milk; so, despite milk being available, and my ability to digest it, I'm not going to drink it. At other times, opportunity rules over desire and ability—e.g. I want to drink milk, and I have the ability to digest it, but I have no access to milk; therefore, my desire and ability are meaningless because the opportunity determines the final outcome. Finally, sometimes ability rules over opportunity and desire—e.g. I want to drink milk, and I have access to milk, but I have a bad stomach due to which I can't digest milk; now, my desire and opportunity are futile because the final outcome is determined by my ability.

The State of Perfect Balance

When the three aspects of the soul are perfectly balanced, then what gives you pleasure is identical to what you are capable of, which is identical to your duty. The state of balance is called self-realization in which the soul is capable of fulfilling himself, has the duty to satisfy the self, and enjoys that product of that ability and duty. This is not very straightforward, as it might seem at first sight.

Imagine living alone in a forest where in order to eat food, you must be capable of cooking, and must cook for yourself every day. Some day you might be bored of eating the same thing; you may desire to eat something different but you might not be able to cook that food either because you don't know how to make it, or the raw ingredients are not available. Now the inner balance is disturbed: you desire something that you are not able to cook. Or, you might get bored of cooking every day and want a break; the inner balance is disturbed: your sense of duty is conflicting with your enjoyment.

The State of Mutual Balance

When this sense of balance in the soul's self-awareness is disturbed, typically, the soul will seek other souls. For instance, he might say: Today I don't want to cook, can someone else cook for me? Or, that I want to eat something different, but I don't know how to make it; can someone else make it? Now, the soul emerges out of his self-absorption because an inner conflict has been created, and to overcome this conflict, the soul needs to associate with other individuals. Typically, this would mean that he enters a society of individuals which is functionally divided into roles: each person doing their job.

He again finds a balance because he can now get the things he wanted through the relationships he has established in exchange for some other things he has to offer. His sense of duty is modified to include service to others, and as long as he is satisfied with the food he is getting there is no conflict.

The balanced state is easily regained if one can limit one's desires to what is possible within the available situation, with the current capabilities. In effect, the *sat* or situation dominates, the *chit* or ability is applied within the situation, and *ananda* or pleasure is subordinate to that ability. This requires minimization of one's desires, and subordinating them to whatever is available. Of course, the soul may enjoy using all his abilities and the *chit* now dominates; this *chit* now may want to change the situation or *sat* in order to find the most fulfilling environment for expressing one's abilities to the fullest, and the happiness is subordinated to the primary aim of fulfilling one's ability expression.

In this way, there are six possible dominant-subordinate relationships with three facets of the soul. In each case, a disturbance in the inner balance will drive one toward their destination where their inner balance is restored because the external situation is compatible with the inner state.

The State of Continual Change

This stability is predicated on the assumption that the priority between the three facets doesn't change. But as we saw before, different aspects can dominate at different times. Sometimes you let your desires drive you to a new situation, sometimes you subordinate your desires to the situation, and sometimes you want to change the situation to fulfill your desires. Each such change involves an internal imbalance, and it drives the soul to change its relationships, abilities, and desires.

Apart from the fact that *sat*, *chit*, or *ananda* can dominate the other at different times, each of these three aspects has many subdivisions, and they can also become dominant and subordinate. The *chit* for instance, is six qualities of knowledge, power, beauty, wealth, fame, and renunciation; there are as many types of responsibilities (*sat*) as there are types of relationships; there are as many pleasures (*ananda*) as there are unique types of emotions. Each of these create further conflicts. You may not be sure if knowledge is always better than beauty, or power is more important than wealth. You may not be sure if you should always prioritize love over anger, or anger over love. And you may not necessarily know if it is always better to be a father and take responsibilities for your children, or you should also sometimes be a child and act unreasonably in relation to a father. Given all the possible internal contradictions, the soul can try to be everything—changing his or her state in order to resolve all the contradictions.

Stability and Instability in the Soul

It should be apparent that the prioritization between *sat, chit,* and *ananda*, and the subsequent prioritization between the various subdivisions of each, constitutes a *choice*. Stability in life means that you don't change your priorities and choices; that particular form of choice and prioritization becomes your eternal personality, and you choose a personality in order to avoid instability.

The opposite of that choice is confusion. You don't necessarily know what you want; you try different things, you don't feel satisfied, and therefore you keep changing the prioritization and personality. The material world dominantly comprises this continual change where the soul is unaware of its true nature, and doesn't know what to prioritize. Remember that this prioritization is unique to the soul; so there is no universal prescription for what kind of personality one must be. In that sense, the soul has to discover its true nature and identify the state in which he wants to be. Unless this choice is made, the soul remains conflicted among various alternatives. Sometimes he prefers one personality and at other times he wants something else. The material world represents this confusion about the true nature of the self: the soul goes from one situation to another, and is hence is never fully satisfied.

Clearly, if you prioritize *sat* over *chit* over *ananda*, you will seek a person who does the same. A person with different priorities will lead to conflicts. Similarly, if you prefer knowledge over beauty, someone else who prioritizes beauty over knowledge will cause a conflict. Thus, as the soul comes into contact with other beings—who are equally confused about their priorities—a myriad conflicts are created. The soul trying to solve its inner conflict becomes insensitive to the conflicts in others.

As a result, one person hurts another, and receives retribution, which then changes their personality, which leads to further confusion, internal conflict, which then drives more external conflict. In this way, the ignorance about the nature of the self leads to a cycle of conflict and change. The hallmark of the material world is that any internal conflict generally leads to external conflicts; indeed, even if you were stable in your understanding, someone else who is internally conflicted can trouble you.

The Resolution of Contradictions

The inner contradictions are resolved by prioritization—something is dominant, and something else is subordinate. The external contradictions are resolved by complementarity—when you want to be the seeker someone can be the sought, but if you decide to reverse the role, then you can find the complementary reversal. The stability of the external relationships depends on the internal stability, and the internal stability depends on identifying one's true personality or prioritization.

The choice of prioritization creates internal consistency, but it leads to a sense of *incompleteness*. After all, you could have prioritized something else, been a different person, performed different kinds of actions, and enjoyed in different ways. However, since you have made a choice, you have precluded other choices. You have become a particular type of person, to the exclusion of other persons. What if you are not totally satisfied being one type of person, and you desire multiple personalities?

You may not be hurting others, and hence there are no consequences of your actions on others. However, your choices still have consequences: if you make a particular choice, you preclude the other choices. If you choose a particular persona, you preclude the other persona. Now you are driven not by internal inconsistency, but a sense of incompleteness: How can I make the other choices?

The Four Worlds of Personalities

We can thus see that in the material world a person is ignorant about their persona and hence shuffles between numerous personas one after another. He can discard the variety of personas and just decide to create a perfect balance in himself by being with himself. But if this is not too satisfying then he can identify a fixed personality in relation to other persons. The internal inconsistency is solved but an incompleteness exists, which the soul can solve by acquiring more than one persona; different personas are visible in different relationships, and you seem like a different person in each relation.

Vedic texts identify these situations as the material world, *Brahman*, *Vaikuṇṭha*, and *Goloka*, respectively. The material world constitutes the ignorance of one's personality. In *Brahman* one attains a complete balance in the self. In *Vaikuṇṭha* one has a fixed persona, in relation to everyone. In *Goloka* the soul has many personas which are visible in different relationships to different souls. In each case, the soul seeks an answer to his inner conflicts—in changing their persona with the changing material situations, being a fixed person in relation to oneself in *Brahman*, being a fixed person in relation to all persons in *Vaikuṇṭha*, and being a different person in each of the different relations in *Goloka*.

The drivers can be either internal inconsistency or even a sense of inner incompleteness. As your sense of incompleteness grows, you acquire more personas, and express them via more relationships. But you could be totally satisfied with internal consistency and a specific universal persona.

Multiple Personalities in a Person

We normally think that each person has a unique personality, when the fact is that in the material world our personalities are changing continually—even in relation to the same person. Thus, sometimes you are polite with your friends and spouse, sometimes you laugh and please them, and at other times you are cold, rude, or detached from them. Similarly, a person may have multiple personas which are expressed in different relationships. Thus, you might be cold and detached with outsiders, but you might be warm and loving to people at home (or vice versa). You might be aggressive at the workplace, but submissive with your spouse (or vice versa). Modern personality theories don't understand this fact very well. They conjure a universal persona for the person, disregarding subtle or manifest changes that occur with time, places, situations, relationships, and even specific other personalities.

Similarly, men express one kind of personality in the presence of other men, and a different personality to women. You may have one personality for friends, and another one for colleagues. You may have one persona with your parents, and another one with your siblings, or your children. By donning multiple personas and realizing them through different relations, you feel more complete. As long as you don't change your persona in relation to the same person, they will find you consistent.

Consistency and Completeness

The material world is full of inconsistencies. We don't necessarily know what person we truly want to be. Should I be the strong and angry person who conquers the world, or should I be the loving and caring person who nurtures the world? As you look at other people, you tend to change your mind. Similarly, as you meet with success and failure in your endeavors you change your mind. The material inconsistencies are created because we change our minds, and the other person—to whom we are in a relationship—hasn't changed. We also compete with each other to take the other person's role disrupting their existing relationships. Both of these situations create *competition.*

The position of *Brahman* removes this competition, because there is no one else other than the self. So you are not going to compete with yourself, try to disrupt yourself, or change in relation to yourself.

The position of *Vaikunṭha* brings cooperation. You are now with other persons, and your personality is well known to everyone. You take on a role—consistent with your universal persona—and relate to everyone according to that persona. Your personality doesn't create competition because you are not changing your persona, and you are not trying to take over someone else's position. Everyone is situated in their respective position, and they are able to live with mutual respect and cooperation.

The position of *Goloka* goes beyond cooperation; you realize that a universal persona is not enough and you desire multiple personas and then multiple relationships to realize these persona. Many of these personas are hidden until they are manifest in a new relationship. Or, the persona may be so unique to a relationship that it is only exposed to a particular individual and unknown to everyone else.

The competition of the material world, the consistency of *Brahman*, the cooperation of *Vaikunṭha*, and the completeness of *Goloka* are all possible features of the soul and can be understood by the soul. If and when the soul realizes his properties, these types of worlds become automatically visible.

A Brief Guide to My Books

Published Date: 2018-02-26

Over the years as I have written many books, and new readers often want to know where to begin, how to proceed systematically, so that understanding them would become easier. Implicit in this request is the problem that the books are not easy reading, especially if you don't read them in order. While I try to summarize the relevant ideas at the beginning of each book, that summary might sometimes be breezy, and if you are not used to the novelty, then the rest of the reading can seem harder. With that problem at hand, this post describes a progression from one book to another. These books were not necessarily written in that order; sometimes I leapt forward, and then came back to plug a gap. Due to that back and forth, there is some repetition in different books, which I think is good because the only way to familiarize oneself to a new way of thinking is to go over it multiple times. I might also note that the books have more than what I outline below, but this is a summary of the progression.

Gödel's Mistake – The Role of Meaning in Mathematics

Overtly, this book deals with some fundamental paradoxes in number theory and computing theory, and discusses their significance. But covertly this book is about the three modes of nature of *Sāṅkhya* which manifest as *manas* (concept), *prāna* (activity), and *vāk* (objects). The book deliberately never discusses *Sāṅkhya* directly because the goal is to derive the above said distinction from problems within mathematics. The book shows how numbers are sometimes concepts (ordinals), sometimes activities (programs), and sometimes objects (cardinals). The inability to distinguish between these three types of numbers leads to numerous paradoxes with mathematics, which the book discusses.

The lesson of these paradoxes is that we must describe numbers—and hence everything that uses mathematics—in terms of the three categories (concepts, activities, and objects). If we use only one category—e.g. objects, or cardinal numbers, as science does at the present when it describes the world as quantities—then it can be *consistent* but *incomplete* (because the other two categories are missing). But if we try to reduce any category to any other category, we end up in a contradiction. Thus, the three categories are necessary and sufficient in order to make mathematics consistent and complete.

How the three categories of numbers co-exist and combine forms the biggest outstanding problem of modern mathematics, and the book illustrates that the solution to this problem is to describe a theory in which *concepts* are converted by a *process* into an *object*. In mathematical parlance, concepts are *sets*, processes are *functions*, and objects are *quantities*. There is a long tradition in mathematics that treats sets and functions also as objects, which constitutes a category mistake and creates paradoxes.

This reduction arises due to a materialistic view in which the world is only objects, and ideas and processes must therefore be reduced to objects. The book shows that unless this category mistake and the resulting reduction is corrected, mathematics will be either inconsistent or incomplete.

Quantum Meaning – A Sematic Interpretation of Quantum Theory

If you have followed the thesis of the previous book, it should be evident that if processes are used to convert ideas into objects, then these objects must be treated as *symbols* of the ideas. Objects are not therefore meaningless entities; to every object we must attach a meaning. In the everyday world, we identify these objects as tables, chairs, cars, houses, etc. which are things, but they are also symbols of ideas denoted by the same word. Philosophers—owing to the use of the same word—have tried to reduce ideas and processes to things, which, as we saw above, is a category mistake.

Just as mathematics is inconsistent when this reduction is carried out, and incomplete if the other categories are disregarded, a similar problem must appear in a physical theory too. The theory must be incomplete if we don't induct ideas and processes, and inconsistent if we reduce one to the other. This book shows how the problems of current atomic theory mimic those of mathematics above.

The most prominent example of quantum incompleteness is probabilities and it arises when we treat objects as things instead of symbols. You can measure symbol probability in a text but you won't be able to predict the word order because the order is semantic but probabilities are physical. We might say that the *effect* of word order is empirical, but the *cause* of that symbol order is not empirical.

Quantum theorists have shown that if we try to predict symbol order using additional 'hidden variables' we end up in a logical contradiction. In one sense, there is nothing hidden because the symbol order is empirical. And yet, that symbol order is not a physical object. Thus, the quantum problem is identical to the problem in mathematics—if we ignore ideas then we get incompleteness but if we reduce ideas to objects then we get inconsistency. Therefore we need three categories (idea, process, and objects) two of which exist in physics already: the 'process' is *bosons*, and 'objects' are *fermions*. But without the ideas to which a process is applied to make things, processes and things remain probabilistic.

All standard interpretations of atomic theory try to explain away the probabilities as a feature of reality, or hope that these will one day be replaced by determinism. This interpretation instead shows that neither is probability a feature of reality, nor will it ever be replaced by determinism. However, it can be replaced by the three modes of nature in which things are symbols of ideas, produced by a process.

Sāṅkhya and Science – Applications of Vedic Philosophy to Modern Science

If you followed the thesis of the previous book, you would have noticed that there are effects that can be *perceived* by the senses but they cannot be *explained* by what the senses perceive. We noted one such effect, namely, the meaning that creates the order of words, but it is not the only effect.

Sāṅkhya describes multiple levels of deeper realities beyond the mind: these are called *intellect* (which judges the truth), *ego* (which judges the goodness), and *mahattattva* (which judges the rightness). If the mind's existence creates the problem of word order, then others must have effects too.

The effect of intellect is that only logically consistent meanings can exist together because they affirm each other's truth. Inconsistent meanings cannot coexist; they will be pushed apart. Therefore the *truth* of the meaning causes aggregation and disaggregation, and having seen the effects caused by meaning, there must now be effects caused by truth. This effect can be explained by treating the *intellect* as a cause which seeks consistency among propositions. The modern explanation of 'attractive' and 'repulsive' forces as the cause of molecules and chemical reactions must now be replaced by the idea that these molecules are produced in the process of creating semantic *consistency.*

This theory of aggregation will explain some chemical reactions but prove inadequate because other reactions are caused by *incompleteness*. This is because after a consistency is created, we need to preserve what we have and provide what we lack. That which lacks is the incompleteness and manifests as desire. And that which is considered irrelevant is the fullness which manifests as revulsion. Both hinge upon a *purpose* which causes a change. In order to explain this change, we need a new property called the ego in *Sāṅkhya*; it creates *purpose* that looks like attraction and repulsion but it is neither a physical force, nor semantic consistency. Why does an already consistent system expand, at the risk of destabilizing itself? This needs a new explanation caused by incompleteness.

Then we will find situations in which reactions don't occur even when both desire and its object are present. This is the counterpart of the fact that just because you desire things you see, doesn't mean you get them. Similarly, sometimes reactions will occur fortuitously without incompleteness, which is the counterpart of the fact that often we get things without desiring them. We are still talking about motion, but now the explanation needs morality and the consequences of previous actions which sometimes prevent the fulfillment of desires, and at other times deliver results without such desires.

The existence of mind, intellect, ego, and morality can thus be made relevant to the discussion of the behavior of atoms and molecules, successively bringing insights from within the observer to explain what lies outside. This is the new philosophy of science in which introspection, rather than sense perception, is the method for the advancement of science, even for physics and chemistry.

Moral Materialism – A Semantic Theory of Ethical Naturalism

We have talked a lot about the nature of matter so far. Now we will talk about the interaction between matter and the soul. The central problem here is *free will*. It conflicts with the idea of *determinism* in science, which is needed in order to predict the future state of the universe. If this state is determined by my free will then I could (based on morality) predict my future, but not the universe's future.

This book discusses a reconciliation of free will and determinism in which the world is like a drama whose script is fixed in advance, but the actors in the drama are yet to be decided. The script defines the events but it doesn't determine the *actors*. Since the script is predefined, you can deterministically predict all that will happen in the universe—past, present, and future—and yet you cannot predict who will do what. The universe is *what* (will happen) deterministic, but who (will do it) indeterministic.

As we established the properties of the individual experience semantically, we now talk about the universal space and time semantically. Both are hierarchical and closed. Hierarchical space means that the boundary of your house constitutes a space, which is embedded in the boundary of the space demarcated by a city, and so forth. Space is not flat and open; there are imperceptible boundaries which create effects, which cannot be explained without the hierarchical view. Hierarchical time means that a faster clock exists inside a slower clock, like seconds are within hours, hours are within days. Thus, the entire universe is closed, and it evolves cyclically. This structure can be described as a tree.

There are thus two kinds of laws in this space and time. The first is the cyclic creation of *events* of the drama. The second is that which connects the events into *trajectories*—individual life stories. Both laws are predictive; the former says what will happen, and the latter defines who will do it.

Trajectories are drawn *after* the events are defined, which means that individual action cannot change the course of the universe. Rather, individuals will grab the roles from the available ones, and if you vacate a role then someone else will take it. Thus the universe has a fixed destiny but individuals can choose their own destiny. The interaction of these two laws constitutes the crux of this book.

Signs of Life – A Semantic Critique of the Theory of Evolution

It was important to establish the idea that the universal evolution is independent of individual evolution, because it leads us to a different understanding of the evolution of species which is caused by changes in cosmic events rather than the random mutation and natural selection of individual bodies.

The evolution of species is caused by the changes to the roles being created in the cosmic drama and the individual living entity is simply an actor in that drama, not the cause of the drama itself. Thus, some species will automatically appear and disappear at different times, quite like the king and queen in a drama go backstage to allow other scenes to be enacted before they return to the stage. Given that the drama is cyclic, just because you don't see the king and queen on the stage doesn't mean they have ceased to exist. The roles of king and queen—the different species—exist permanently. And yet they become visible or invisible at different places and times, due to script of the drama.

Thus all species are eternal, and yet they appear and disappear. Indeed, there are patterns of this evolution shared with the evolution of ideas, cultural evolution, the rise and fall of civilizations, boom and bust in the economy, the changing of seasons and weather patterns, and many others.

A crucial factor in each of these cases is that the system is *closed* and each closed system oscillates in certain predefined *normal modes* like a drum which can produce many sounds depending on where it is hit. The cause of such cycles is outside the system—like a hand that hits the drum to trigger a new vibration—and individuals in the system cannot create a new cycle, but they can participate in a cycle. The book presents flaws in the idea of individual change causing macroscopic change, through theories and examples drawn from physics, mathematics, computing theory, game theory, etc.

Uncommon Wisdom – Fault Lines in the Foundations of Atheism

We started by discussing the problems in mathematics; we then took it to a discussion of issues in modern physics; we then discussed how this paradigm will be extended into chemistry; we then talked about the separation between individual experience and cosmic events, describing the nature of space and time; we used this foundation to discuss the flaws in evolutionary theory. Every foundational idea in modern thinking—reductionism, materialism, relativism, determinism, and evolutionism—was critiqued in the process, showing how science needs to think differently than it has so far.

We can now use this foundation to critique atheism, as this book does. Materialism is false because even to explain physics and chemistry we need to invoke mind, intellect, ego, and morality. Reduction is false because ideas and processes are required in addition to material objects. Determinism is true, but not in the sense that we conceive it—i.e. as the contradiction of free will. Evolutionism is false because the individual actions (mutations and selection) don't influence the macroscopic change; rather macroscopic change creates the avenues in which individual actors can participate. Relativism is wrong because an absolute space and time creates macroscopic change independent of individual changes. Atheism therefore is an ideological dogma that has no foundation in real science.

As we saw above, even to explain sense experience we have to delve deeper into the recesses of the observer. But if a person is not introspective themselves, then the insights of an introspective person can be used to formulate new theories although the non-introspective person will not perceive the new reality sensually (because it can only be observed introspectively). Thus we can talk about an epistemology in which faith in the words of perceptually advanced individuals are used as springboards of intuition but reason and experiment are used to verify these intuitions in science. This process is akin to accepting a password from one who knows it, and then verifying if the password works correctly.

Reason and experience are useful in verifying the password, but faith is useful in discovering the password if we don't know it. In that sense, revealed knowledge is valuable source of passwords, *in lieu* of our own perceptual advancement because we haven't yet looked inward.

Emotion – A Soul-Based Theory of Its Origins and Mechanisms

Once we have rejected evolution, set aside the challenges of reductionism and determinism, and demonstrated the use of introspection in the progress of material science, we can now begin looking at the question of meaning and purpose in life by understanding the nature of the soul.

The soul in Vedic philosophy has three aspects—*chit* or cognition, *sat* or relation, and *ananda* or emotion. These three are also the judgments of truth, right, and good, respectively. In the material world, the judgment of right appears in the moral sense, the judgment of good in the ego, and the judgment of truth in the intellect. The judgment of truth operates on meaning in the mind, those meanings are derived from sensations, and the sensations are produced from the material objects.

Individually, relation, cognition, and emotion are incomplete; we can experience them in a first-person manner, but we cannot see their effects in the third-person manner. Therefore, the three must combine, although when they combine, one of three dominates while the others become subordinate. This dominant-subordinate relation changes with time, as a result of which sometimes we prioritize our duties, at other times our desires, and then at yet other times the nature of reality.

The three aspects of the soul are often internally inconsistent, and in the material world this inconsistency drives the soul to prioritize different things at different times. This model of the soul can be used as the paradigm for change in the material world; that change includes the shifts in our personality, and the transmigration of the soul through bodies. The model is also useful in formulating a theory of the body in which three aspects must be balanced in order to maintain health.

It means sometimes emotion dominates cognition, and at other times cognition overpowers emotion. Sometimes we do things as the situation demands, and other times we bend the situation to our demands. Attaining this balance by allowing different aspects to dominate at different times is the essence of choice. But we are also *expected* to use this choice correctly, which means different things can dominate at different times, places, and situations. If choice is used as expected, then we can be happy; if this choice is misused or its effects are not understood then we become unhappy.

Six Causes – The Vedic Theory of Creation

If the nature of the soul within this world is understood, then we can also ask how the soul enters this world, why the world is created, and how it is created. These questions require us to go beyond the soul into the nature of God, the relation between the soul and God, and between God and matter.

Every living entity has a need to know itself and express itself. Like an artist who creates a work of art in order to express his personality and then admires this work as a reflection of his persona, similarly, both the soul and God create to express their personality and by that expression know themselves. The power of action is used to externalize the personality, and the power of knowing is used to internalize it.

But these powers are inert in themselves unless there is a *motivation* to express and know. That motivation can further be divided into three parts—the idea to be expressed and known, the desire to express and know that idea, and the judgment if that expression and knowledge is appropriate.

The activity of expressing and knowing, together with the three aspects of internal motivation are collectively called *thinking, feeling, willing, knowing,* and *acting*. These are the five primordial stages of creation, which require an explicit understanding of the creator as a *person*. The product of God's thinking is *pradhāna*, the product of His feeling is *prakriti*, the product of His willing is *mahattattva*, the product of His knowing is *ahamkāra*, and the product of His acting is *prāna*. Once *ahamkāra* and *prāna* are created, the rest of the process of universal creation follows as described in *Sāńkhya*.

This book discusses six kinds of causes; God who stands prior to the process of creation is the *personal* cause; the five steps through which He creates a primordial reality are the *efficient* cause; the senses, mind, intellect, ego, and morality are the *instrumental* cause; the material elements that these senses perceive, understand, judge, desire, and value are the *material* cause; the result of the contact between the instruments and the objects is forms which constitute the *formal* cause; and the combination of these into living, breathing, and working systems through *prāna* is the *systemic* cause.

This constitutes the *philosophy of creation* in Vedic texts. Greek philosophers had conceived of four causes—formal, material, efficient, and final; to this, we add instrumental and systemic causes, and both God and soul are the final cause or the purpose for which the universe exists. This is a convenient method to understand Vedic creationism for those who have prior familiarity with similar attempts in Greek philosophy where matter was only one of the four causes. Taking a broader approach to causality makes for a more comprehensive view of the universe.

Mystic Universe – An Introduction to Vedic Cosmology

Now that we have the philosophy of creation, we can talk about the actual universe. This is a complex book because it deals with many complex problems, namely flat vs. round earth, linear vs. cyclic time, clock time vs. conscious time, geocentric vs. heliocentric models, higher vs. lower planetary systems, heaven and hell, the invisible mountains, rivers, oceans, and islands, the motion of the planets and their effects on human lives, and finally the role of understanding cosmology in astrology.

If this wasn't enough, there are also conflicts with modern cosmology regarding distances to different planets, the existence of multiple galaxies (which are rejected in Vedic cosmology) and multiple universes (accepted in Vedic cosmology, but not understood in modern cosmology). Problems of a Big Bang stemming from cosmic microwave radiation, the problem of dark energy (which causes a faster expansion) and dark matter (which must slow the expansion), exotic objects such as black holes and supernovae, and why everything we know from modern science is only 4% of the universe.

Tackling all these questions becomes possible only when we have a profound understanding of Sāṅkhya, how it changes the structure of space and time into a tree, how causality in this tree-like space and time is different, and why atomic problems entails that light never travels in space although there is remote and non-local causation which indeed takes a finite amount of time that we currently attribute to travel rather than change. The book covers these at some length because if these are not grasped then everything else in cosmology would appear to be meaningless. All these constitute the *theory* of matter (space, time, matter, causality) before we understand the *model* of the universe.

Cosmic Theogony – The Personalization of Nature

Whereas the previous book delved into the structure of the universe, but did not discuss the personalities which rule over these places, this one delves into the personalities. It discusses why there are 12 signs of the zodiac, 28 star signs, 15 phases of the moon, and how each of these are individually personalized as different types in nature. With this understanding we can also talk about the origin of the solar, lunar, and sidereal calendars.

Based on this we discuss Vedic Theogony—the 36 demigods that control the entire universe. These demigods are representations of a trinity—*Viṣṇu*, *Shiva*, and *Brahma*—due to which sometimes the trinity is taken out of the 36 demigods and only 33 demigods are considered in the Theogony.

The purpose of this book is to describe how nature is *personalized* through the control of higher living beings, which means the laws of nature are *normative*. They are like laws of society; they can be broken, but they are followed due to moral imperatives. The planets move in their orbits not due to gravity but because demigods perform their duties under the direction of *Viṣṇu, Shiva,* and *Brahma.* Our contact with material objects is also mediated by the influence of demigods, which is a new type of causal model in which a demigod delivers our *karma* or destiny based on our material desires.

Once this model is known, then we can understand how the worship of the trinity of *Viṣṇu, Shiva,* and *Brahma* led to the worship of sun, moon, and stars, which then morphed into three religious ideologies—polytheism, monotheism, and monism—which dominate all over the world today. These ideologies carry numerous shades of the sun, moon, and star worship from the past, as well as the ideas of the trinity noted above. These might appear to be conflicting ideologies but they are not; they stem from the three aspects of the soul, as the trinity represents the three features of the soul.

Based on the understanding of the soul, and its representation in the trinity, we can conceive of a religious universalism, in which polytheism, monism, and monotheism are progressive ideas about religion; they were part of a single system earlier, but were split into conflicting ideologies as the understanding of the soul, and its progressive journey of realization was forgotten.

The Yellow Pill – Conceptual Basis of the Varna System

The term "Yellow Pill" derives from the popular designation of socio-economic-political positions by names like the "Blue Pill" (surrender your individuality to the system), "Red Pill" (fight the system to get your individuality), "Green Pill" (replace the current system by a new one), etc. This book introduces the reader to the Vedic socio-economic-political ideas. The book has dedicated chapters that deal with economic, social, and political ideas.

In the cacophony of ideologies, the discussion about the moral purpose of life and how it is achieved through society is missing. This book hopes to fill that gap; it talks about how society cannot be organized without a transcending purpose, and when such a purpose exists, the conflicts between competition and cooperation, government and business, the individual and the system, are resolved.

It discusses a social model that is neither left-wing nor right-wing, and yet brings the benefits of both systems. This system is based on the ancient theory of Varna or four classes described in the Vedic texts. The book discusses the foundational ideas of this system in the context of modern social, economic, and political theories showing how stability is more important than growth, how localization is more important than globalization, and how a society organized hierarchically based on merit is better than one where everyone pretends to have equal rights.

The Balanced Organization – The Surprising Science of Non-Living Organisms

After critiquing the principles of modern sociology, economics, and politics in the last book, this book formulates a theory of society as an organism. In Vedic philosophy, society is compared to a "body", with different classes in the society being identified with hands, legs, head, belly, etc. But what kind of "body" is it? It clearly is not a living person. By "body" we mean a functional structure comprised of many parts that perform different roles and duties. There are many such types of non-living "organisms": cultures, organizations, businesses, etc. which exist in their environment, such nations, government, economy, etc. These "organisms" compete, survive, and evolve, but what are the mechanisms of this dynamics? This book identifies three dominant mechanisms: (1) the dynamics within the organization, (2) the dynamics or an organization in an environment, and (3) the dynamics of the environment itself.

Each of these mechanisms is then described as being based different kinds of conflicts such as that between the functional divisions and hierarchical levels within an organization, between organizations in a marketplace, and between markets within an economy. Conflicts don't have a permanent resolutions; they are resolved by choices of compromises. Since a compromise is a choice, the choices are constantly reversed to change the dominant-subordinate patterns in conflict resolution. The structure of the conflicts, the types of compromises, and how they evolve over time, then become the basic mechanism of organizational, societal, and economic evolution.

This book extends the Vedic ideas about the nature of the body, specifically, that it is the competing forces of *kapha*, *pitta*, and *vata*, and 'health' involves their balance, while 'sickness' involves their imbalance. All bodies are known to change their patterns of *kapha*, *pitta* and *vata* dominance several times a day, and constantly through the lifetime of an organism. This model of biological evolution is illustrated through the evolution of organizations, which are clearly not 'living' in the sense that they don't have a mind. The book therefore mutually illuminates the nature of the bodily evolution as well as how the principles of this evolution are independent of living beings.

Is the Apple Really Red? – Ten Essays on Science and Religion

This is a short book, relative to the others, and probably the best starting point for a reader who is unfamiliar with Vedic philosophy. It comprises ten short essays that cover the entire gamut of ideas ranging from the understanding of matter in Sāṅkhya philosophy, to the conflict between free will and determinism, to the nature of life and why the modern evolutionary account of evolution is wrong.

There are discussions about how God creates the universe, and why He is both transcendent and immanent. Finally, there is a discussion about common misunderstings about Vedic philosophy, such as its apparent polytheism which is shown as subsidiary to monotheism, how we must understand deities and rituals, and how miracles are not spiritual but advanced material capabilities that do not contradict the laws of nature.

The book emphasizes how the personal nature of God is important to understand the origin of meanings, pleasures, and relationships in this world, rather than considering them as 'illusions'. Notably, impersonalism and voidism decry the material world as an illusion–i.e. it simply doesn't exist. The book shows how matter exists but is temporary, and the material world is rejected not as an illusion but because it is temporary.

Western Questions, Eastern Answers – A Collection of Short Essays

In between conceptualizing, writing, and publishing the books, I had occasion to post many blogs, which were sometimes driven by questions from readers, sometimes served as overview of the books, and at other times discussed topics that are not yet covered in any of the books. Over time, as I write more blogs, the growing content will facilitate a series of books that collect the essays in a chronological order.

Given the nature of blogs, the subject matter is not topically organized as in the case of other books. However, these blogs are generally complementary to the content in the above books. It is impossible to fit every type of question into the books, without elongating them significantly. The blogs serve as answers to point questions. They often revisit the background material covered in the books, and sometimes point to the books or other blogs, in case the reader is interested in delving deeper into the topics covered in the blogs.

Each volume of this series contains about 30 essays, and we plan to issue new volumes every year, or whenever there is adequate amount of content to form an additional volume.

Happiness is a Choice

Published Date: 2018-03-03

I used to think that happiness is caused by other people, situations, and things. If only they would just behave, I would be happy. As silly as it sounds, it is indeed a deep-seated belief in each one of us. I have now realized that happiness is a *cause* rather than an *effect*. When I am unhappy I gravitate toward the useless things—e.g. news, economics, entertainment—hoping that these things will make me happy but they make me feel worse. When I'm happy I gravitate toward writing, teaching, and meditation, which make me happier. Thus, my unhappiness brings more unhappiness, and my happiness increases my happiness. Under happiness, I have an optimistic view of the world; when I'm unhappy the same things are seen pessimistically. Therefore, I now hope not to *get* happiness, but to *choose* happiness. This post shares some insights on this choice.

Chant and Be Happy

The Hare Krishna movement is famous for popularizing the slogan "Chant and Be Happy". Simple and effective. But probably too cryptic. It gives the impression that *if* you chant you will *become* happy. That's quite simple, and everyone can do it. You don't have to change your dress, leave your job, family, or religion, in order to chant. You simply chant, wherever and however you can. Given the simplicity, why *isn't* everyone chanting? And why isn't everyone who is chanting also happy?

Those who have tried chanting realize that the mind takes you on fantastic journeys while chanting. The tongue may be uttering, but the mind is elsewhere. You try to bring the mind back to the sound again and again. On some days, concentration is easier—those are the days when you are *happy*. On other days—when you are *unhappy*—concentrating becomes very hard.

So, "chant and be happy" means that the tongue is pronouncing the words, and the mind is *happy* in order to concentrate on the sound. If the mind is disturbed, then the tongue may utter the sounds, but the mind would be on its own planned and unplanned expeditions. If the mind is even more disturbed, then even the tongue doesn't want to utter the sound. In short, "chant and be happy" doesn't mean that you chant and you will *become* happy. It means that you have to utter the sounds *happily*.

Concentration is an *effect* of your happiness. Consequently, inability to concentrate, or inability to chant, are consequences of your unhappiness. To chant and *become* happy, you have to chant *with* happiness. If you are happy to begin with, then chanting enhances your happiness. If you are unhappy during chanting, it will not have any effect, and you will probably stop chanting.

A Labor of Love

All of us are familiar with the fact that if you don't enjoy doing something, then you do it poorly.

If you are an unhappy cook, then your bread may be burnt, vegetables may be half-cooked, there may be excess salt or spices, and the disproportionate ingredients will cause the food to taste terrible. The happiness in your heart cannot be experienced by others. But happiness has an empirical effect—the food you cook is tasty. Despite the fact that you cannot experience my happiness, you can *know* whether I'm happy simply by *tasting* my cooking. When the cook is happy, a subtle quality is created in the food. That quality also makes one who eats that food happy. Conversely, simply by eating the food that is cooked with unhappiness will also make you unhappy.

This is true for every kind of work. You can tell from the *quality* of the work whether the person was doing a labor of love, or a labor forced by circumstances. The same goes for chanting. If you are happily doing it, then you will also be attentive. Conversely, if the mind is not attentive, then chanting is like forced labor; we are calling God, but we are not happy while doing it. Thus you can measure your spiritual advancement yourself by just asking—how attentive is my mind while chanting?

Choosing Happiness Instead of Sadness

Since my concentration depends on happiness, happiness is a self-fulfilling prophesy. If I begin chanting happily, then by chanting I will beget more happiness. Conversely, if I begin chanting unhappily, my mind will wander, I will not enjoy the activity, I will probably leave it half-hearted, and then I will feel guilty about the entire process—lack of concentration, resulting in cessation of the activity, resulting in unhappiness. Both happiness and unhappiness thus become self-fulfilling prophecies.

Realizing that these are self-fulfilling prophecies is a breakthrough in life, because then you don't do things in order to *become* happy. You rather do them *happily*. In short, we have to find a way to remain happy by choosing happiness over unhappiness, so that we can do our work happily. If I have chosen unhappiness, then my work is not going to make me happy; I will quickly stop working. Work will make me happy when I am doing it happily; positive feeling begets more positive feeling.

The Genesis of Unhappiness

The *Śrimad Bhāgavatam* describes the birth of *Rudra* from *Brahma* as an anxious child. This anxiety is born when *Brahma* creates his four sons—*Sanaka*, *Sanandan*, *Sanātana*, and *Sanatkumār*—and asks them to create progeny. These advanced souls are not interested in begetting any children, which causes *Brahma* to become angry, and *Rudra* is born from between *Brahma's* eyebrows.

> *SB 3.12.6— On the refusal of the sons to obey the order of their father, there was much anger generated in the mind of Brahmā, which he tried to control and not express.*
>
> *SB 3.12.7— Although he tried to curb his anger, it came out from between his eyebrows, and a child mixed blue and red was immediately generated.*
>
> *SB 3.12.8— After his birth he began to cry: O destiny maker, teacher of the universe, kindly designate my name and place.*
>
> *SB 3.12.9— The all-powerful Brahmā, who was born from the lotus flower, pacified the boy with gentle words, accepting his request, and said: Do not cry. I shall certainly do as you desire.*
>
> *SB 3.12.10— Thereafter Brahmā said: O chief of the demigods, you shall be called by the name Rudra by all people because you have so anxiously cried.*

Rudra is the incarnation of anxiety in this universe. The moment He is born, He cries asking for His name and place. These *names* are called *vāk* and they represent material objects. Similarly, the *place* of these objects, in relation to other objects, constitute the *meanings* of the material objects. In other words, the anxiety represented by *Rudra* is to worry about material objects and their meanings.

Common examples of such anxiety include ruminating about what someone said and what they meant. Why did they say this? What do they mean by it? What do they want to achieve? These meanings are—if one understands *Sāṅkhya*—expressed at many levels beginning with the mind. The mind contextualizes the meaning from sensations; the intellect judges the truth based on the context; the ego perceives the intentions of the person uttering that contextualized truth; and the moral sense (called *mahattattva*) decodes the moral values of the person—right and wrong—from the utterance.

Affliction of the Rudra Mindset

It's noteworthy that this anxiety comes due to fear and frustration; we are afraid that the objects and their meanings are going to cause us harm, or our plans of success will be frustrated. Fear is the enemy of happiness. If I am happy, then I will not worry about who said what, what they meant, what others want to do, what is going to happen; or if I think about these things then I will come out with positive and constructive interpretations.

We commonly think that unhappiness is the outcome of reasoning about worldly events. But that is not true. The reasoning is itself dependent on the state of unhappiness or happiness. If I am happy, then I will give the world a positive interpretation—even if I reason—which will enhance my happiness. If I am unhappy, then all the reasoning is simply going to increase my anxiety because in the unhappy state I will only find more problems by viewing the world pessimistically. Reasoning is a slave to our emotional state. We have to therefore *choose* a positive emotion *before* reasoning.

Rudra is born out of *Brahma's* anger, and He is depicted as a crying child. When we are afflicted by the *Rudra* mindset, we act like angry children—crying due to frustration, and desiring to placate this anxiety. *Brahma* also designates many places for *Rudra* as described in the following verse.

SB 3.12.11— My dear boy, I have already selected the following places for your residence: the heart, the senses, the air of life, the sky, the air, the fire, the water, the earth, the sun, the moon and austerity.

All these places are afflicted by anxiety, fear, and unhappiness. The most prominent among them is the heart, but it also afflicts the senses, our breathing, digestion, etc. Due to this anxiety, we will move around rapidly or become stationary because the sky is afflicted. We will gain or lose weight because water is afflicted. We will may burn too brilliantly or lose our sheen because the sun is afflicted. We may become hedonistic and lazy or indulge in flattery and deceit because the moon is afflicted.

Adopting the Brahma and Viṣṇu Mindset

The *Brahma* mindset is more constructive than the *Rudra* mindset. Under this mindset, we desire to create positivity as an outcome of our actions; *Brahma* for instance wants to expand the population and asks his sons to do so. This is the mentality of a positive thinker, but as noted in the case of *Brahma*, the positive thinker quickly falls prey to negative thinking when their desires are frustrated.

The *Viṣṇu* mindset is instead one of detachment and self-satisfaction. You can do things like *Brahma* does—e.g. to expand the population—but failure in such projects will not make you unhappy. You may also desist from projects that are likely to be mixed with success and failure, or perform them without regard to the outcomes. Under the *Brahma* mindset, there is positivity prone to turn into negativity. Under the *Viṣṇu* mindset, there is unmitigated positivity due to detachment. In other words, under the *Viṣṇu* mindset, we are able to give a positive interpretation even to adverse situations.

These are hence called the influence of *tamo-guna* (negativity – represented by *Rudra*), *rajo-guna* (positivity which can turn into negativity – represented by *Brahma*) and *sattva-guna* (positivity that stays – represented by *Viṣṇu*). Only under *sattva-guna* we permanently remain constructive.

The Nature of Choice

Given a particular world of objects, their interpretations are varied. Each interpretation emphasizes some parts of the world, and neglects others. These sensations become foreground and background and the meaning is produced from ranking their priorities. This prioritization of what we experience is entirely our choice. The happy person will ignore another person's insult, and an unhappy person will magnify it. The positive things in life will thus take a back seat relative to the unhappy things.

Our choice is simply the selection of an emotional state. As we practice the choice of happiness, the world remains unchanged, but our *prioritization* of the things in the world changes. What comes to the foreground and what remains in the background constitute our *focus*. As we change our priorities due to happiness, the half-empty glass begins to look half-full, because fullness is foreground.

There are innumerable examples of these foreground and background visual experiments, which are used to judge your interpretive process. In a black and white picture, for example, if the dark parts are foreground for you then you are prioritizing the negativity over positivity. Similarly, if the white parts are foreground and the black parts are background then you are prioritizing positivity over negativity. A lot can be judged about a person simply by asking them about what they see in a picture. This method has therefore been used by psychologists to understand a person's mental state.

Interpretation in Sāṅkhya

The Vedic texts describe that the universe originates in *pradhāna* which is the soul imbued with desire for material happiness. Then it chooses a particular definition of happiness called *prakriti*. From that definition of happiness emerges a moral sense or what we consider right and wrong which is called *mahattattva*. From that moral judgment we arrive at goals and purposes called the ego. From such goals emerge beliefs of truth called the intellect. From such beliefs emerge thoughts in the mind, from the thoughts emerges the need to create empirical evidence for ideas in the senses, the need for empirical evidence transforms into the properties such as taste and smell called *tanmātra*, and once these properties have been formalized then the material objects are values of properties.

Objects are numbers—e.g. 10—but *tanmātra* (material properties) make it mass. Now, the "mass is 10". Then senses act as the standards of measurement, and the property kilogram is appended—now we have "mass is 10 kilograms". The mind then says that this heavy object is a chair. The intellect judges the cognition to be true or false based on memory recall of similar experiences from the past. The ego then says this is *my* chair and I aim to use it. The *mahattattva* says that sitting on my chair is morally acceptable (sitting on someone else's chair may need a prior permission). Finally, *prakriti* says that I'm happy because I am doing morally acceptable things.

It is a fact of life that even the morally decrepit morally rationalize their actions; a serial killer may therefore claim to be doing 'God's work' by purging the world of other 'sinful' people, which is morally good in his view. There is hence always a morality in the process of acquiring happiness; the morality may just be very perverted.

If you were unhappy to begin with, then your moral sense will disown the world considering it a waste of time. The ego will then experience revulsion at the ownership of a wasteful thing. The intellect will suspect the truths and beliefs—"Is this really a chair?" The mind will then produce an alternative interpretation—"this is not a chair; it must be something else". The senses will change the standard definition of a chair in order to stop perceiving a chair, where one was seen previously. The *tanmātra* will be modified to disregard the properties that lead to the chair perception. And objects will then not reveal the properties which were previously visible to a happy perspective.

The Three Modes of Nature

Our emotional state alters everything from moral values to thoughts to sense perception to objects. Unhappiness thus not only changes our experience, but it also causes diseases in the body. Likewise, happiness not just alters our perception, but it also makes the body healthier. These emotional dispositions are our *prakriti*; from the subtle emerges the gross. The subtle takes priority, which means that if you have a negative feeling, even positive situations will seem problematic. Instead of seeing opportunities in these situations, we will perceive suffering and disaster in them.

Thus a fearful person sees a snake in a rope, and a confident person sees a rope in a snake. The cause of this change lies in our *prakriti* or what makes us happy or unhappy. If our *prakriti* is dominantly in *tamo-guna* we will be naturally prioritizing the negatives over the positives. If our *prakriti* is dominantly *rajo-guna* we will prioritize positives over negatives. However, under the influence of *sattva-guna* we see the world as it is, and we are neither afraid of the negatives nor attracted to the positives.

As our *prakriti* is modified—from *tamo-guna* to *rajo-guna* to *sattva-guna*—we become addicted to permanent happiness, which means rejection of *tamo-guna* or negativity and *rajo-guna* positivity that can lead to negativity. Fixing on *sattva-guna* is hence called *śuddha-sattva* or 'pure' goodness.

The Elevation of Happiness

Now that we understand how everything is caused by our sense of happiness, we can ask: What is the *ideal standard* for happiness? The *prakriti* is imbued with three modes, so there is happiness in the mode of *sattva*, *rajas*, and *tamas*. Wallowing in self-pity—e.g. that I'm a good guy caught in a bad situation—is an example of happiness in *tamo-guna*. You get the satisfaction of being the good guy who is exempt from trying harder because the situation is so pitiable. Similarly, indulging in self-pride—e.g. that I'm so great that I conquered all the situational adversities—is an example of happiness in *rajo-guna*. The happiness in *sattva-guna* is doing the work, without self-pity or self-pride.

It is a mistake to think that a person with a negative outlook is unhappy. It is more appropriate to think that the person afflicted by negative emotions is enjoying a different type of emotion. Unhappiness is only caused when there is a conflict in the emotions—e.g. that I want to have a positive outlook but I have a negative outlook; I want to enjoy the happiness of those with the positive outlook but I'm not able to enjoy it due to my own negative outlook. We must thus distinguish between negative outlooks (which can be a source of happiness) from unhappiness (caused by emotional conflict).

The problem is that the happiness in *tamo-guna* and *rajo-guna* are *temporary*. Which means that I cannot forever wallow in self-pity, nor can I always indulge in self-pride, because either situation will be disrupted. Only the happiness in *sattva-guna* is permanent. Therefore, a person who is in *tamo-guna* or *rajo-guna* and claims to be happy is only happy *sometimes*. At other times, he is unhappy.

This gives rise to the necessity of elevating our happiness from *tamo-guna* to *rajo-guna* to *sattva-guna*. If happiness in *rajo-guna* and *tamo-guna* were permanent, there would be no necessity for elevation. Therefore, negativity needs to be given up because it is temporary. You cannot forever enjoy self-pity because sometimes the situation will get better and in order to enjoy that improved situation we must feel self-pride. Similarly, if you are feeling self-pride right now, the situation will get worse and you will be forced to feel self-pity. Due to this change, both modes create an emotional conflict and unhappiness. To be permanently happy, one has to adopt the mode of *sattva-guna*. The argument for *sattva-guna* is not happiness vs. unhappiness. It is rather permanent vs. temporary happiness.

Permanence Needs Change in Prakriti

The soul is eternal and therefore it seeks permanent happiness. And to find that happiness, it has to change its *prakriti*—namely the *kind* of happiness it seeks. The happiness of self-pride and self-pity will be temporary, and therefore a new kind of happiness has to be sought which is permanent. This happiness must become a *habit* and owing to habituation *prakriti* is called *nature*. It is material nature, but it is also *our* nature, or personality comprised of likes and dislikes.

The nature of *sattva-guna* is eternal, but those of *rajo-guna* and *tamo-guna* are temporary. The soul therefore has to *choose* a type of happiness that can be stable. Once this choice becomes a habit, then the person always perceives the world just as it is, and is neither attracted nor repulsed by it. We can say that *sattva-guna* is the mode in which the soul acquires *objective perception.* In every other situation, the perception is colored by the observer who modifies the foreground and background.

Beyond the Happiness of Sattva-Guna

Sattva-guna is the beginning of happiness, but not its end. An even higher form of happiness is produced from a new kind of bias in which everything connected to God is sought and prioritized and everything disconnected from God is ignored and deprioritized. Of course, ultimately, nothing is disconnected to God. However, some things are more relevant than others. A devotee of God therefore develops a *bias*—after attaining an *unbiased* position from a material standpoint.

God is Himself biased; namely He puts certain things in the foreground and other things in the background. Material nature as a whole is on the background; God is said to have His *back* towards it; His *front* toward the spiritual nature. The devotee of God develops the same priorities as God. In the material world, such a devotee keeps material nature in the background and spiritual nature in the foreground; in the spiritual realm the background totally disappears and the foreground remains. The materialists on the other hand keep spiritual nature in the background and material nature in the foreground, and for many materialists the background simply doesn't exist; they imagine that the foreground they can perceive (material properties) does not have any spiritual basis.

Happiness and Relationship to God

The soul is manifest from the *chit-śakti* of God, which represents His "I have" ability. As a result, the soul is said to be *part* of God (quite like we say the body *has* a hand, the hand *has* fingers—which represent the whole-part relationship). However, these parts can be either on God's front or His back (i.e. in spiritual or material natures respectively). As the soul moves from the back to the front (or vice versa), his *relation* to God is altered. This relation is called *sat*—or the soul's awareness. By moving to the back, for instance, the soul becomes unaware of God and pretends that He doesn't exist. As this relation is altered, a different kind of happiness—called *ananda*—is derived from it. The driver of this change is the quest for a different type of happiness, which pushes the soul from the back to the front.

Factually, God is aware of both His front and back, so God never forgets the soul even if the soul tries to forget God; rather God honors the soul's desire to go behind God's back to do things as if God did not exist. This is a mischievous type pleasure and the soul can never be free of fear and guilt of being caught in his act. That fear and guilt are automatically created by the material nature or *prakriti*.

The guilt is that no matter what you prioritize you have deprioritized something else; the burden of this choice is overwhelming, and the soul always seeks to reverse the effects of this prioritization. The guilt associated with every choice in the material world causes the cyclic change in choices. In the material world, for example, a working mother feels guilty about neglecting her children, and a stay-at-home mom feels guilty about not realizing her potential. This is due to the dualism of the material world. In the spiritual nature too there is guilt; since I focused on something, I neglected other things. A devotee experiences this guilt and is humbled by it. He considers himself not doing enough.

Happiness and Guilt

The difference between material and spiritual guilt is that in the material world a working mother will indeed neglect her children, but in spiritual nature whichever part of God you serve every other part is equally well-served because when you choose one part, someone else will automatically choose another part. This is the philosophy of cooperation in which all the opposites are prioritized, although by different persons. The men feel humbled by women as they are not taking care of children, and the women are humbled by men because they are not working outside. This humility is the product of guilt, rather than pride, and under this humility there is unceasing cooperation between all.

Material guilt is real but spiritual guilt is imagined. Material guilt dampens our desires, but spiritual guilt strengthens our desires. Material guilt causes us to oscillate from one extreme to another because each person is isolated and individualistic and needs to do opposite things by themselves (the isolation is because once the soul turns away from God, each person considers themselves the center of the world). Spiritual guilt compels us to cooperate rather than compete and be stridently fixed in our work, but humbled by other's contribution. Guilt is the source of unhappiness here, and freedom from guilt is accepted as salvation. But beyond the material guilt is another kind of guilt that enhances happiness. The soul has the choice of happiness—material guilt, freedom from guilt, or spiritual guilt.

When this desire for happiness is altered, different things are automatically visible or invisible. In that sense, choice simply means the choice of happiness. I titled this post 'Happiness is a Choice'. However, having reached this point, I will modify the claim somewhat: 'Happiness is *the* choice' because once this choice is made, everything else gradually changes through a successive domino effect.

Did We Land on the Moon?

Published Date: 2018-03-03

According to a Gallup poll, about 6% of Americans believe that man never went to the moon; they endorse conspiracy theories in which these landings were supposedly staged in a studio. This post is not about such conspiracy theories. I will discuss why we cannot go to the moon, although we can have the *experience* of going to the moon, based on a *fractal* space in which there is a 'moon' within the earth (because the whole is represented in the part), but it is not the real moon. I will discuss how fractal space is evidenced in *Sāṅkhya* when space is described as a tree rather than a box. Since modern science treats space as a box rather than a tree, we can *interpret* the arrival on the earthly moon to be the arrival on the real moon—assuming such a journey is undertaken. Thus, regardless of whether the moon landings were staged or not, we cannot go to the real moon, but we could go to the moon within the earth space. To understand the real moon, we will have to revise the model of space from a box into a tree.

Fractal Geometry

A fractal is a picture in which the parts are self-similar to the whole. Therefore, as you zoom into the picture, you rediscover the same whole through a scaling transformation. However, clearly, the picture you see by zooming in is not the same as the picture you see as you zoom out.

Such pictures were originally discovered in the study of *non-linear* systems in which a variable is referenced in the computation of that very same variable. A classic example of such a computation is the *Mandelbrot Set* which is computed by using the following equation:

$$Z = Z^2 + C$$

Clearly, you cannot solve this equation as a polynomial. However, you can use discrete mathematics to solve such equations, which means that these are always solved via *incremental steps.*

$$Z_{N+1} = Z_N^2 + C$$

The incremental process is that the N+1th iteration of the variable Z is computed based on the Nth iteration. The result of such a process can be compared to an artist who draws an outline and then fills in the details. The details are *within* the outline, and yet they mimic the outline itself. To count the points in this space you cannot go from left to right, top to bottom as if the space were *linear*. You have to rather count *hierarchically* such that the whole picture is the first object, which is then subdivided into parts, and each part is then further subdivided into subparts. This process of counting constitutes a hierarchical geometry because the whole is counted ahead of the parts. However, given the legacy of reductionism in modern science, we don't call this *hierarchical*; we call it a *fractal.*

Examples of Fractal Geometry

Our everyday world is replete with the use of fractal geometry, which is quite counterintuitive because modern science treats space linearly. For instance, our ordinary notions of space are hierarchical; when you send a letter to a person, the address includes a country, a state, a city, a street, a building, and then a person. When the mail is routed to the destination, it is first forwarded to the country, then a state, then a city, then a street, then a building, and finally the person. The mail service zooms out from the sender (from person to building to street to the city to state to nation) and then zooms into the receiver (nation to state to city to the street to the building to person). This is quite unlike ordinary motion in linear space in which we suppose that the object goes directly from one place to another.

Of course, even when a letter is sent from a source to a destination, it goes hop by hop, and therefore it has a trajectory. However, the individual *locations* on this trajectory are not in the *linear space*. For instance, there is a post box in a building that is 'lower' than the city post office, which is 'lower' than the state post office, which is 'lower' than the national post office, and so forth. Thus, from a physical viewpoint, the letter appears to move in a linear space, however, the points in that space have higher or lower designations relative to each other, and the letter first goes upward and then downward.

Similarly, when you send an email to john@doe.acme.com the email server first finds a registry for all .com addresses. This registry then forwards the mail to acme.com, and when the email reaches the acme.com email server, this server will resolve a sub-domain called doe.acme.com. When the mail reaches doe.acme.com server, it will locate the mailbox of john and post it into that mailbox. The email goes hop by hop, but it starts at the top (.com) and descends downward (to john@doe.acme.com). When John responds to this email, his email server will append the name 'doe', create the 'from' address as john@ doe, and forward it to the mail server for acme.com which will append its name and create the full address of john@doe.acme.com. Now, the email is moving upward before it will go downward.

This hop by hop forwarding is quite like a post office stamping the mail on receipt. Typically, on international mail, you can see multiple stamps on the envelope through which you can know the succession of post offices the letter passed through.

Internet addresses are also defined hierarchically. An IPv4 address for instance involves a hierarchy of 4 numbers—A.B.C.D—in which A is the highest level designator and D is the lowest level. With IPv6 addressing (which has 128 bits instead of 32 bits for IPv4 addresses) the number of levels increases. When packets are forwarded on the internet, the packet routers *summarize* the routes; in other words, they send the packet upward toward a router that advertises the route for A.0.0.0/8 (meaning that only the first digit of 8-bits is considered significant) and then downward to A.B.C.D.

Note that in these cases, it is possible to have an address A.A.A.A which means that each digit in the address can be repeated at any *level* of addressing. Therefore, it is not sufficient to know a single-digit—e.g. A—in order to route the packet; we have to rather know the number's *position* in the hierarchy, and this position is itself defined hierarchically. Thus, A may be the first, second, third, or fourth *byte* in the address. If you don't know the position of the byte, you cannot forward the packet.

Fractal geometry is thus all-pervasive in our world. I just gave examples of snail mail, email, and internet addresses. It constitutes a very *efficient* system of motion because each building only needs to know the *city* post office rather than all the post offices in the world. The city post office similarly needs to only know the state post office, and the national post offices only need to know other national post offices. Hierarchy makes motion very efficient, which is why everyone uses it.

However, modern science doesn't treat motion in this manner because particles move *directly* from one destination to another, kind of like people carrying packages to each other in a village where they don't need the assistance of a post office because the package can be carried directly. The model of motion in modern science is the extension of the model of communication in a village. When the system gets very large this communication model fails, and a hierarchical model has to be adopted.

Hierarchy Produces a Tree

All hierarchical addressing systems are organized like a tree. Below is an example of the internet domain name hierarchy. This is not a novel idea because all systems of classification are organized as trees.

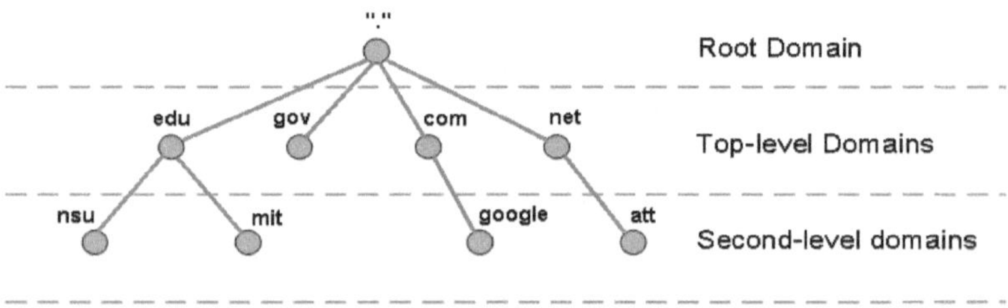

The novelty is that when hierarchy is used for *addressing* then motion doesn't occur *directly* between the leaves of the tree. Rather, the moving object has to go up and down the tree. For example, if an email is sent from MIT to Google, then it will find the lowest node in the hierarchy that connects to Google. In this case, it might be the mit.

edu server sending to a root server, which then forwards it to the .com server, which then forwards it to the google.com server.

Straight-line motion is forbidden in a tree. This means that if light were a particle moving according to hierarchical addressing, then it will not go directly between the leaves of the tree. It will rather go up and then down the tree. The path of light would seem to be *curved* (as we now understand through relativistic space-time bending) but the *reason* for this bending would be entirely different. In particular, the cause of this bending would not be matter (as we postulate right now) but the hierarchical nature of space itself in which light doesn't move linearly because space is itself hierarchical.

Our Brain is a Fractal

Using this understanding of light and space, we can now formulate a theory of perception in which light from an object goes up and down a tree (whose higher nodes are not always known to us) but when the light is received by an observer, a new *leaf* is added to the tree that looks just like the object outside but this time it is actually in the brain. Cognitive scientists call this the *mental representation* of reality in which there is a real object outside but its *representation* is created within the brain.

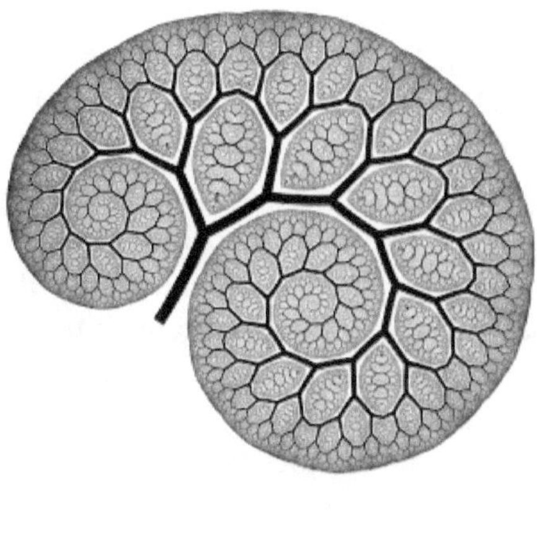

Clearly, the mental representation is *contextualized* against your prior beliefs, which means that the higher branches in the tree constitute prior acquired information, which you already believe to be true, while the new reality is *added* as a leaf to the existing knowledge. Accordingly, if the new information is inconsistent with previous knowledge, then this leaf would be shed from the tree as an illusion or mistake. If, instead, the new knowledge is consistent with the previous knowledge, then the leaf would be assimilated as part of the growing tree.

The addition and removal of knowledge will constitute the 'change' of the brain where additional neurons are added or older neurons are removed. As the person gets older, or under degenerative diseases like Parkinson's, new neurons are not created while the older neurons are lost. As a result, the person loses their long-term memory gradually (because the old neurons are being destroyed) and has a difficulty in forming new memories (because new neurons are not being created). We can liken it to a tree in autumn that is gradually shedding its leaves.

Clearly, when we form a picture of the world in our brain, the picture is not as detailed as the reality, but that *abstract* picture is created as a *detail* of our brain. Thus, *physically* the picture is detailed, but *semantically* it is an abstraction of reality. Everything we have ever experienced and which we remember exists as a memory in our brain, but obviously, the brain is much smaller than the world we have seen. Thus, the world outside is also real inside, but these two worlds are different.

The Representation of Reality

If you were an electron microscope looking at a brain that is, in turn, perceiving an apple, you will see the *representation* of the apple inside the brain, but you won't be seeing the apple itself. And if you simply look at the individual molecule that represents the apple in the brain then you will find no similarity to the real apple because you will only see a molecule. To *convert* that molecule into the perception of an apple, you have to traverse the entire hierarchy up and down. In other words, you have to correlate the individual molecule corresponding to the perception of the apple to practically every other molecule even to understand that the molecule denotes an apple.

If you simply look at an individual neuron or molecule you can never know what it *means*. The meaning is created by correlations to the other branches and leaves on the tree. If we don't perform that correlation, then we will only see a neuron or molecule but it cannot be *interpreted* as an apple. You can say that you have the sense perception of the brain molecule but you have no grasp of what the molecule *means.*

The net effect of the interaction between the apple and the brain is that there is a *representation* of the apple in the brain. Similarly, there is a representation of the brain in the apple. My looking at the apple not only changes my brain, but it objectively alters the apple itself. The act of looking is an act of impregnating the apple with a representation of myself, while the apple has been impregnated in me. Thus, in the act of knowing, both knower and known are modified. This fact is commonly experienced when people realize that they are being stared at even though they are not looking at each other directly. It is because both objects are modified in the act of seeing.

Understanding Fractal Cosmology

We have so far discussed the hierarchical nature of fractal geometry. We saw its application in everyday notions of motion—e.g. in sending letters, emails, or packets over the internet. We saw how perception has to be modeled in the same manner. In different ways, we are simply talking about the structure of space which gives us the necessary background to understand the travel to the moon.

The moon and the earth are interacting objects. Due to their interaction, there is a part of the earth that *represents* the moon, and there is a part of the moon that *represents* the earth, quite like there is an apple representation in me and there is a representation of the self in the apple.

If we try to observe the *effects* of the existence of the apple from within the brain, we can study the apple representation in the brain. It won't be the real apple, and yet there will be something that corresponds to the apple that we can observe. An electron microscope can thus 'go' to the apple inside the brain, but it won't be going to the real apple. Similarly, when it sees the representation it won't interpret it as an apple unless the representation is correlated to everything else in the brain.

Our landing on the moon is like the electron microscope seeing the apple representation in the brain. It is not the real moon, and yet it looks like the moon as its representation. Loosely speaking, we could say that the moon we see is the 'ambassador' of the real moon. It appears to have the qualities of the real moon, and yet it is not the moon.

The Meaning of the Earth Planet

We normally think that the earth planet is just the land and water surface of a globe. But in fractal geometry, the earth is much bigger; apart from the surface of the globe that we can perceive, it includes every other planet, galaxy, and star that we can see from the *earthly viewpoint*. If the earth is a trunk of the tree, then all these planets from earthly perception are branches, twigs, and leaves *of* earth.

The real planets and stars are different; we have no access to them through our sense perception. However, if we correlate and understand everything in the sky then we can understand that the earthly moon is actually a *representation* of the real moon, like an external apple is represented in the brain. Thus, by 'earth' we don't mean the surface of land and water. We rather mean everything that can be *experienced* using this body and all the instruments that we can build on this planet. In short, 'earth' is to be defined as a collection of possible experiences, of which land and water are parts.

Sāńkhya and Vedic Cosmology

Vedic cosmology provides this type of description of the universe in which space is modeled as a tree rather than a box. An individual planet has a 'size' from the most zoomed-out view. But, given that the entire universe is represented in each part of the universe, you can keep zooming in within that space and discover the entire universe from that perspective. It won't be the real universe, but it will be an impression of that universe that you can see. Indeed, the universe exists inside each body as a representation. Thus, living entities on different planets can see the entire universe from their planet, but it's all within the 'space' of that planet. They are looking *down* from their vantage point on the inverted universal tree where they see other planets as twigs and leaves *of their planet* rather than branches and trunks of the tree emanating above their planet.

Each planet, therefore, has a sense of *self* and *others*. The surface of the earth constitutes the 'self' of the earth, and all the planets that we can see from earth constitute the 'other'. This idea is described in *Sāńkhya* as *ādiatmika* or self and *ādibhautika* or other. The planets such as the moon and the sun that we see from our earthly vantage point are not the real planets; they are just the *ādibhautika* representations of the real sun and moon.

Similarly, in the brain, there is a core part called the *amygdala* which constitutes the emotional center of the brain because it denotes the sense of self; if this self is 'attacked' then fear is created and it is responsible for the fight or flight responses in the body. Similarly, happiness is created when this 'self' is mollified. The rest of the *cortical* brain holds the representations of the external world—visual, auditory, tactile, etc. Thus even within the brain, there is a self-center and places for 'others'. Descartes, while formulating the mind-body interaction postulated that the pineal gland (which also lies in the center of the brain like the amygdala) was the seat of the soul. He was right in a sense because the center of the brain represents the 'self' although it is not the soul; similarly, the parts of the brain surrounding it represent the 'other'.

The Model of the Atom

The same fractal approach to space can be used to understand the nature of atoms such as oxygen, carbon, etc. The *nucleus* of the atom is the real atom or the *self* which we can call the *ādiatmika*. The electrons surrounding this nucleus are *ādibhautika* or representations of other realities in the 'world' of the atom. These electrons correspond to the other nuclei and the nucleus sees the effects of other atoms through such electrons. It knows its 'world' through the representations of the 'external reality' that exist within its own space.

In one sense the atom is only the nucleus. But, the 'world' of the atom is significantly larger than the nucleus as it contains electrons too. Typically, the atoms (including the electrons) are 100,000 times larger than the nucleus. If this were used to estimate the size of the earth-space relative to the earth globe then the earth space would be 100,000 larger than the earth globe. The diameter of the earth globe is about 8000 miles, and by such an estimate, the earth space will be 800 million miles in diameter.

We might note that the diameter of the earth-space is a measure of the size of the *fractal* space, not *linear* space. The diameter of the circle is a circle limit such that the circle is bound but you still can never reach the boundary. The extremities of this circle represent the farthest galaxies and stars we can perceive. They are not that far if we look at the earth space from the outside, and yet they *appear* to be very far from within the earth space. A satellite sent to the extremities will take billions of years to reach its destination, giving the impression that these are very far, although they are within earthly space.

When we view the electrons of an atom representing an external reality, then the addition or removal of electrons becomes a counterpart of our *perception*. Thus, more electrons (which create a negative ion) correspond to an interaction with more nuclei. Similarly, fewer electrons (which create a positive ion) correspond to an interaction with fewer nuclei. The 'electrovalent bond' between two atoms is then the counterpart of a unilateral perception—i.e. one nucleus 'sees' the second nucleus, but the second nucleus doesn't. The 'covalent bond' between atoms is similarly a counterpart of both nuclei seeing each other as a result of which atomic theory models them as 'sharing' electrons. If we understand the deeper levels of perception in Sāṅkhya then we can also understand why these chemical bonding models are useful in some cases but inadequate in others.

The Universe of Virtual Realities

If we understand space linearly as we do right now in modern science, then the moon we see is the real moon, and if we happen to go to this moon then we have to go to the real moon. If however, we understand space hierarchically according to Sāṅkhya, then the moon we see is simply a *representation* of the real moon, and even if we go to this 'moon' we haven't truly gone to the moon.

The question of lunar travel, therefore, is a scientific question, but not quite the current science, which is based on a model of communication suitable to a small village. When this model is extended to the entire universe we arrive at erroneous conclusions. Similarly, when the understanding of matter is divorced from the understanding of the observer we make erroneous conclusions.

Each planet has to be treated as a combination of reality and virtual reality. What we can see, touch, taste, smell, and hear on this planet is reality. But the things in the sky are virtual reality. We can know about the reality outside the earth space by looking at this virtual reality. This virtual reality also exists, like the apple exists in the brain as a representation. And yet, it is not reality itself. Therefore, we cannot go to the real moon through moon expeditions because the moon we will go to is within earthly space. To treat the objects in the sky as virtual reality, we need to understand how matter becomes a symbol that references some reality but it is not the object being represented.

The Arithmetic of Concepts

Published Date: 2018-03-17

In all religious philosophies, God is the original person, Who creates all else. If we were to count things, then God would represent 1. In Vedic philosophy, additionally, all that is created is also a *part* of God, Who is then described as the complete truth. In effect, since God is the complete truth, everything that follows is a *partial* truth. Similarly, since God is the original truth, everything that follows is a *relative* truth compared to the original truth. The partial truth represents a *fraction* of God, and the relative truth represents an *order* or *succession* among the fractions, which can be counted as 1, 2, 3, etc. Two ideas—(1) that God is the origin, and (2) God is the whole truth—can thus be used to construct a theory of natural numbers and fractions, which this post discusses. Once this foundation is established, then we also talk about other types such as complex and irrational numbers. This post discusses how a new understanding of numbers can be built based on God's existence.

Philosophical Background

The Invocation of Sri Īśopaniṣad

The first verse in the *Sri Īśopaniṣad* presents a paradox which, if understood, can open a new thinking about numbers. The invocation states the following.

oṁ pūrṇam adaḥ pūrṇam idaṁ
pūrṇāt pūrṇam udacyate
pūrṇasya pūrṇam ādāya
pūrṇam evāvaśiṣyate

Śrīla Prabhupāda provides a devotional translation to this verse here. But I will provide a more literal translation to the above verse below, before returning to the devotional translation in a subsequent section.

That is complete. This is complete. From the complete emerged another complete. After the complete emerged from the complete the remainder is certainly complete.

This verse presents a paradox because if you remove something from another thing, the remainder must *reduce*. It is supposed that the thing being removed is a *part* of the whole, and if that part is taken out then the whole should have become incomplete. Then how do we understand this paradox?

The Addition and Subtraction of Knowledge

Suppose you know Newton's three laws of motion, and I then tell you about the first law. The information I provide you doesn't add to your knowledge as you already knew the three laws. By adding the knowledge of the first law to the preexisting knowledge of the three laws, the total knowledge is unchanged. If the knowledge of three laws is X and the knowledge of one law is Y, then

$$X + Y = X$$

Magic has happened. This equation is possible in the case of concepts. When you have a more complete concept, a partial concept doesn't add to the more complete concept. Rather, the complete concept is like a big box, and you just put the incomplete concept like a smaller box inside that bigger box. Ultimately you still get the bigger box as the more complete concept.

Now, suppose that X means "full knowledge", and you add "full knowledge" to that "full knowledge". The conclusion applies again. We replace Y by X.

$$X + X = X$$

Since full knowledge doesn't add to itself, we can move X to the other side:

$$X = X - X$$

If adding X to X gives us X, then subtracting X from X must also leave X as the remainder. This is precisely what *Īśopaniṣad* says in the invocation. You take out complete from the complete and the balance is still complete. How does it happen? You impart your complete knowledge to someone and by such imparting, your knowledge is not reduced. You still have complete knowledge, and the other person also has complete knowledge. That's how X – X = X. Again, remember, we are talking about concepts.

This idea is partially encompassed in the union of sets where adding the same set to itself doesn't add to the set, and X U X = X. But subtraction from the set removes elements from it. Therefore, the set theory construal is incomplete because the subtraction from the whole leaves the whole reduced.

God is the Completion of Knowledge

The Vedic texts describe that God is the completion of knowledge. When He imparts His knowledge to others, He is not reduced. And yet a world is created from that knowledge. Similarly, when this material world is absorbed back into God's person, all the knowledge remains within God from where it can emerge again. *That* is complete and *this* is complete; from complete emerges the complete. Now that we have a grasp of the literal translation above, we can appreciate Śrīla Prabhupāda's devotional translation.

> *The Personality of Godhead is perfect and complete, and because He is completely perfect, all emanations from Him, such as this phenomenal world, are perfectly equipped as complete wholes. Whatever is produced of the Complete Whole is also complete in itself. Because He is the Complete Whole, even though so many complete units emanate from Him, He remains the complete balance.*

Śrīla Prabhupāda's translation combines the *Īśopaniṣad* verse with one additional fact, namely, that the complete is the Personality of Godhead. My explanation adds another fact to it namely that the complete person is also the fullness of knowledge because He imparts and expands His knowledge into everything else. This method of bringing additional ideas to explain a particular verse has been used by *Ācharyas* especially when the meaning of the verse may present a paradox not easily understood by everyone.

The Creation of Parts from the Whole

We are dealing with an anti-reductionist paradigm in which the parts are not *combined* to build the whole. Rather, the whole is *divided* into parts. In order to create the parts, the whole must *precede* the parts. This idea is presented in *Śrimad Bhāgavatam 1.3.28* when fullness *expands* into subsidiary forms.

ete cāṁśa-kalāḥ puṁsaḥ
kṛṣṇas tu bhagavān svayam
indrāri-vyākulaṁ lokaṁ
mṛḍayanti yuge yuge

All of the above-mentioned incarnations are either plenary portions or portions of the plenary portions of the Lord, but Lord Śri Kṛṣṇa is the original Personality of Godhead. All of them appear on planets whenever there is a disturbance created by the atheists. The Lord incarnates to protect the theists.

This verse further adds to the *Sri Īśopaniṣad* invocation noted above and identifies that the complete is *Kṛṣṇa*. The conclusion is described after enumerating various incarnations such as *Nara* and *Narayana, Kapila, Rishabhadeva, Narasiṃha, Vāmana, Vyasadeva,* and so forth. In other words, while the aforementioned forms are parts, there is a *complete* form which is the source of these manifestations. Accordingly, these are subsidiary forms who are classified into three categories—*aṁsa, kalā,* and *puruṣa.*

Three Kinds of Expansions

There is deeper philosophical significance to these subdivision forms which I will briefly discuss. My forthcoming book Cosmic Theogony discusses this at greater length. The basic idea is that God has three aspects—*chit, sat,* and *ananda*—which manifest as *part, function,* and *purpose,* respectively. (If you are interested in this topic, I would suggest reading the book Emotion).

The *aṁsa* are the *parts* of the whole and manifest from *chit*; the *chit* has 24 primary divisions which manifest as 24 incarnations in this world (described prior to noting that *Kṛṣṇa* is the origin of all – SB 1.3.1 to 1.3.27). These 24 incarnations are as follows: (1) *Ādi Puruṣa,* (2) The Four *Kumara,* (3) *Vāraha,* (4) *Nārada,* (5) *Nara,* (6) *Narayana,*

(7) *Kapila*, (8) *Dattatreya*, (9) *Yajña*, (10) *Rishabh*, (11) *Prithu*, (12) *Matsya*, (13) *Kūrma*, (14) *Dhanvantari*, (15) *Mohini*, (16) *Narasiṃha*, (17) *Hayagriva*, (18) *Vāmana*, (19) *Parshurama*, (20) *Vyās*, (21) *Rāma*, (22) *Balarama*, (23) *Buddha*, (24) *Kalki*. Within the spiritual creation too, there are 24 *Viṣṇu* forms described as follows in the purport to SB 2.2.8: (1) *Puruṣottama*, (2) *Acyuta*, (3) *Narasiṁha*, (4) *Trivikrama*, (5) *Hṛṣīkeśa*, (6) *Keśava*, (7) *Mādhava*, (8) *Aniruddha*, (9) *Pradyumna*, (10) *Saṅkarṣaṇa*, (11) *Śrīdhara*, (12) *Vāsudeva*, (13) *Dāmodara*, (14) *Janārdana*, (15) *Nārāyaṇa*, (16) *Hari*, (17) *Padmanābha*, (18) *Vāmana*, (19) *Madhusūdana*, (20) *Govinda*, (21) *Kṛṣṇa*, (22) *Viṣṇu-mūrti*, (23) *Adhokṣaja* and (24) *Upendra*.

Aside from these 24 forms is the fullness called *Kṛṣṇa* described in *Śrimad Bhāgavatam 1.3.28*. Similarly, *Sāṅkhya* philosophy describes 24 elements with the soul as the 25th element. There is hence a similarity between the two: the 24 incarnations of *Kṛṣṇa* are partial expressions of the 25th form; quite like the 24 elements of *Sāṅkhya* are partial expressions of the soul's *chit* or cognition. This *chit* is divided into 3 parts called *ādidaivika*, *ādibhautika*, and *ādiatmika*. The 24 *Sāṅkhya* elements include *ādibhautika* and *ādiatmika* but not the *ādidaivika*—which constitute the demigods.

As a result, the *Sāṅkhya* elements are 24 but the demigods are only 12. These 12 parts are called *Aditya* and are represented by the 12 signs of the zodiac. 12 forms are also marked on the body by applying *Tilaka* at 12 places—they are called *Keśava, Nārāyaṇa, Mādhava, Govinda, Viṣṇu-mūrti, Madhusūdana, Trivikrama, Vāmana, Śrīdhara, Hṛṣīkeśa, Padmanābha, and Dāmodara*. These 12 forms are included in the above 24 forms, but the other 12 forms are left out. We can understand that for God, we are *ādibhautika* and the other 12 forms are *ādidaivika* as God Himself. The forms that we mark on our body are the *ādibhautika* forms; by marking the *ādibhautika* on our body, we are spiritualizing the body and making it God's known.

God is both *ādidaivika* and *ādiatmika* from His perspective. Therefore, if we look at the world from God's perspective, there is only *ādibhautika* (the world) and *ādiatmika* (God Himself) denoted by the 24 forms. But if we look at things from our perspective, then there are 24 elements of *Sāṅkhya*—which denote *ādibhautika* (objects other than God) and *ādiatmika* (our body)—in addition to the 12 *ādidaivika* representing God. Owing to this fact, the 24 elements of *Sāṅkhya* can be compared to the 24 forms of God as they embody the *ādibhautika* and *ādiatmika* of God, quite like the 24 elements of *Sāṅkhya* embody the *ādibhautika* and *ādiatmika* for the soul.

The 24 forms are incredibly important not just as the study of matter (as many people may accept) but also as the study of God Himself. They should be regarded as meaning forms and the world as the byproduct of combining these elementary meanings to create complex meanings. The study of the 24 elements of *Sāṅkhya* is almost identical to the study of the 24 *Viṣṇu* forms and incarnations. Nevertheless, it is a scientific study where the form of the meaning is treated as a personality. It is not 'material' science because God's meaning is reflected in matter.

The *kalā* constitute the divisions of *purpose*, or pleasure. They are manifest from *ananda* and have 16 parts which are expressed as the 16 phases of the moon called *ṣoḍaśa-kalaḥ* in *Śrimad Bhāgavatam 5.22.10*. Of these 16, the first part is the fullness of happiness, and the other 15 are subdivisions of that fullness. Therefore, while we speak about the 16 parts, we often express only the 15 parts. Our happiness is totally subjective; that is, it doesn't depend on material objects or a demigod. The happiness is created by our reaction to the surroundings, and demigods can help us change the surroundings but not to make us happy or unhappy. Owing to this, the spiritual advancement of the soul is considered more important than the material prosperity—i.e. changing the circumstances. Hence, happiness is not divided into *ādidaivika*, *ādibhautika*, and *ādiatmika*. However, happiness has an associated gender (male and female). These are also represented as rising and falling forms of happiness. Thus, the 15 parts of the moon are doubled to create a lunar month of 30 days. Of these, half the days denote rising moon and the other half a setting moon. In this regard, we might note narrations in the *Purana* regarding how *Chandra* was originally a male but then became a female and then stayed as male for 15 days and female as 15 days.

Kṛṣṇa as the embodiment of all varieties of pleasures is said to be the personality comprised of 16 *kalā*. In the *Tantra* system the *Sakti* who represents this pleasure in the material world has 16 different forms beginning with *Pārvati*. In several places (e.g. *SB 3.11.40*) the material energy is described to have 16 different aspects. These 16 forms of pleasure are enjoyed through 4 different relationships (child, master, lover, and friend) owing to which the 16 pleasures are also divided into 4 parts, thereby creating 64 *kalā* according to *CC Madhya*

24.289 – 24.231. When *Kṛṣṇa* studies with *Sāndipani Muni* he masters these 64 *kalā* which are then described as 64 different art forms employed for enjoyment.

The meaning of *sat* is awareness or relation to other things. This awareness has 8 parts—the first being self-awareness. The other 7 parts of awareness are expressed at different levels in a hierarchy. These levels are morality, ego, intellect, mind, senses, sensations, and sense objects. Each type of awareness helps us connect to something else at a deeper or shallower level. These 8 forms of awareness are taken by the 8 *puruṣa* forms. These forms constitute the coverings of each universe, and are described by *Kṛṣṇa* as *prakriti astadha* or the nature with 8 parts. These 8 parts are sometimes called Earth, Water, Fire, Air, Ether, Mind, Intelligence, and Ego, but they are not the same as the elements of *Sāṅkhya*. The significance of these elements is that in the innermost part of the universe, one can obtain all the 8 levels of experience, but in successively outer coverings of the universe, one type of experience would be missing. Ultimately, one would be left only with self-awareness.

We noted 4 types of relationships earlier, and these divide the 7 lower parts of awareness to form 28 divisions of awareness. When these divisions of awareness are combined with the three modes of nature—*sattva, rajas*, and *tamas*, three parts of the universe are created—28 *Nakṣatra* or all the stars under the mode of *sattva*, 28 *Naraka* or hells under the mode of *tamas*, and 28 divisions of planetary systems (14 planetary systems divided by 14 oceans and islands) under the mode of *rajas*. This is the summary of the Vedic cosmology discussed in Mystic Universe.

The division by 8, 16, and 24 are described in the *Śrimad Bhāgavatam*. The confusion is that the same words are used to describe each of these categories. For instance, among the 8 elements are Earth, Water, Fire, etc. The same is the case with the 16 elements, and the 24 elements. This leads to confusion about their true nature especially if we disregard the 8 and 16 divisions as being already subsumed under the 24 elements of *Sāṅkhya.*

> *SB 3.11.40. This phenomenal material world is expanded to a diameter of four billion miles, as a combination of eight material elements transformed into sixteen further categories, within and without, as follows.*

SB 3.11.41. The layers or elements covering the universes are each ten times thicker than the one before, and all the universes clustered together appear like atoms in a huge combination.

This confusion can be cleared by understanding that 8 forms are created from *sat,* 16 forms from *ananda,* and 25 forms from *chit,* of which the first form denotes self-awareness, fullness of pleasure, and fullness of cognition, respectively. Together these form 49 categories, and God is the 49th category. Beyond these 49 categories is *śakti* which constitutes the 50th category, and represents the logic or rationality of the world. We will see later how there are 8 such types of rationalities and worlds, each of which divides into 3 parts. These three parts of material rationality are represented by three *puruṣa* called *Karanodakaśāyī, Garbhodakaśāyī,* and *Kṣīrodakaśāyī.* In the material world, additionally, there are two other principles associated with material rationality (we will discuss them later) which embody time and *karma,* and they are represented by *Saṅkarṣaṇa* and *Śeṣa.* Thus, the 50th category called *śakti* has 5 parts denoted by a separate form.

All these 50 categories constitute a *typology,* which as we will see later creates the alphabets of the *Sanskrit* language. If we can understand the forms of God, then we can understand the meaning of alphabets. In that process, we will also understand how all meaning is created in order, due to which this meaning can also be counted as numbers. The type, alphabet, form, and number are identical; they are all manifest from the three features of the soul, which is originally embodied in *Kṛṣṇa.* Once the basic pattern of creating parts from the whole is understood, then the same pattern is used to subdivide the previously created parts. As a result, now, we get even more numbers (fractions), although the succession of divisions appears as additions (we will discuss the reasons for this shortly). They constitute the basis of language, objects, and numbers. The study of numbers is identical to the study of language, meaning, and God's forms.

In the case of demigods, the 12 divisions of *chit* are called *Aditya,* the 16 divisions of *ananda* are called *Rudra,* and the 8 divisions of *sat* are called *Vasu.* Together they form the 36 gods of which the first person is a representation of *Viṣṇu, Shiva,* and *Brahma,* respectively. If we keep the above said trinity aside, then Vedic texts speak about 33 demigods. The system of demigods therefore also reflects the same typology, with the exception that the *Aditya* are 12 instead of 24.

The understanding of this typology is the essential preliminary step required to understand everything else. As mentioned earlier, *Cosmic Theogony* discusses these types.

The Construction of a Tree

Just as the whole divides into parts, the parts subdivide into further parts. This successive subdivision produces a 'tree' in which the whole is the root, and the smallest parts the leaves and fruits. The successive emanations from the root are *fractions* of the whole, and yet they can be ordered and counted. In several places in Vedic texts a tree of diversification from the origin is noted. The same idea is described in *Śrimad Bhāgavatam* as rivulets from a source of water after completing the narration of various incarnations.

> *O brāhmaṇas, the incarnations of the Lord are innumerable, like rivulets flowing from inexhaustible sources of water. (SB 1.3.26).*

The analogy is different than a tree, but the essential idea of branching is the same. However, while we use the analogy of trees and rivulets, we must remember these are *analogies*. We don't expect to see a real tree or river. The reality is that the root is the *whole* the branches are the *parts*. We should keep this hierarchical picture of whole-part in mind, while also remembering that the hierarchy of such divisions creates a tree-like structure.

How Addition Becomes Subtraction

Since the whole is the complete, the diversities are created by *removing* something from the complete to create *parts*. Unlike reductionism, where things have to be *added* to create the whole, here they are removed from the whole. This removal is represented by the negation called *māyā*.

Māyā hides parts of the whole such that only the part of it is visible; the successive steps of hiding appear as *additions* to the tree but they are in fact *subtractions* from the whole. Thus with additional branches it seems that the tree is growing but in reality parts of the whole are gradually hidden. Thus, we have to think of the operation of addition as the operation of subtraction from the whole, because what is being added to the whole is *negation* or *māyā* which hides some aspects of the whole to create parts.

Owing to this fact, a 'chair' is an object in its own right, separate from the 'legs' of the chair which are created by hiding some parts of 'chair'. In one sense, the 'legs' were *added* to the chair. But in reality the legs are manifest by hiding parts of the full chair. The hiding comprises *opposites* or *duality* due to which you can have a left and right leg of the chair. Therefore, the leg also has the full chair in it, although the leg is itself not the full chair (because parts of the whole are being hidden in order to create the part). Thus, God as the whole is in everything, but everything (created by hiding different aspects of God in order to create the parts of the whole) is not equal to God.

The Role of Māyā

The process of hiding the whole leads to a problem that is often a source of confusion. Is God being covered by *māyā*? Or is *māyā* covering *our* vision of God? If *māyā* were covering God, then God would gradually become ignorant about His own self through this covering. If instead *māyā* covers the soul, then the soul gradually becomes ignorant of God. It is not hard to guess why Vedic texts say that *māyā* covers the soul's *vision* of God.

Māyā covers the three aspects of the soul, creating the soul's goggles through which he sees. In this seeing, the soul is always seeing God, and yet because of wearing the goggles he only sees the parts instead of the whole. Now that the whole is missed from the vision, the parts are misinterpreted as being independent things. Furthermore, the soul gets so absorbed in the vision that he forgets that he is different from the thing he is seeing.

The situation is like that of a fan at a rock concert. When he sees the rock star playing the guitar, he imagines himself to be a rock star and starts acting just like the rock star. The fan pretending to be the rock star is an imitation of the real rock star. It is unreal as the fan is not the rock star. In another sense it is real because there is indeed a rock star. The actions of the rock star are not the illusion; the fan's identification with the rock star is the illusion.

Yoga-Māyā vs. Mahā-māyā

God is the rock star and the soul is a fan of that rock star. Sometimes the soul remains a fan and appreciates the rock star. But sometimes the soul imagines himself to be the rock star. These two are called *yoga-māyā* and mahā-māyā, respectively. In the vision of *yoga-māyā* the soul has the identification with the thing he is seeing (as he is absorbed in seeing), but the whole is not missed in the vision. As a result, the soul sees the whole and identifies with a part. Through that identification and vision he becomes a part of God. In *mahā-māyā* the soul identifies with the part but doesn't see the whole. So he thinks he is the body and that body exists independent of God.

Both are called *māyā* because the function of *māyā* is to create parts from the whole. The soul naturally identifies with a part and considers it his identity. The crucial difference is only that the vision of the whole is missed in *mahā-māyā* and the vision of the whole is present in *yoga-māyā*.

In order to pretend to be a rock star, the fan has to forget a deeper level difference with the rock star, and just see some superficial similarities like both having the same body parts. The fan will ignore the fact that the rock star has friends, relatives, duties, property, commitments, and personality different from the fan. After forgetting many differences, and remembering only the superficial similarities, the fan pretends to be the rock star.

Unity and Diversity in a Tree

Since both *mahā-māyā* and *yoga-māyā* are trees, the unity is the root of the tree, and the diversity is the many leaves on the tree. In *mahā-māyā* only the leaves are seen while the deeper level branches and the root are ignored. The deeper realities are the unity in the diversity. When they are ignored, only the diversity is seen, while the unity is forgotten. Therefore, any knowledge that reveals the whole even through gradual steps constitutes a spiritual path. *Mahā-māyā* is the vision in which the universe appears to be comprised of individual particles which are operating independently. *Yoga-māyā* is the vision in which the unity is seen along with the diversity. Therefore, the full hierarchy from leaves to root is visible. In this vision, things do not move independently; they are rather *controlled* by the deeper level reality, and ultimately by God.

When the deeper level reality is missed, then the theory of nature by which motion is controlled is not understood. One speculates on the theory that controls nature, and there are many possible speculative theories, which seem to work temporarily but fail in other situations. This working and failure constitute our ignorant lives in which an incorrect theory sometimes works and gives us happiness, but at other times this theory fails and then we become unhappy. When the theory fails we try to change it. Similarly, when we are unhappy, we are compelled to revise our view of the world.

A crucial part of this theory is the nature of the self; from that self-identity springs the understanding of the world around us. If the true identity is not found, we keep inventing new ideas about the self and the world—i.e. pretending to be different rock stars. In each case, the illusion is broken; just dressing up like the rock star doesn't make one a rock star. This pretention thus leads to change in pretension. However, if one is situated in the true identity then the changes to personal identity also cease to occur.

Fundamental Principles of Counting

Cardinal and Ordinal Counting

When the tree expands into branches and leaves, we begin counting the tree from the root. The root is the first element in the tree, so it denotes 1. As successive branches come out of the tree, they are designated as 2, 3, 4, etc. In effect, the *complete* at the start is designated by 1 and all the fractions that follow are the successive numbers. This presents a confusion because in one sense they are fractions and not whole numbers, and yet they are *ordered* or sequenced as if they were whole numbers. To understand this paradox, we need to distinguish between ordinals and cardinals.

Numbers are defined in two ways—cardinal and ordinal. Ordinal numbering is represented by the words *first, second, third, fourth,* etc. Cardinal numbering is denoted by words such as *one, two, three, four,* etc. The parts of the whole are fractions as cardinals and sequenced as ordinals or whole numbers. There is no paradox between describing the same thing as a fraction and as a whole number if we remember that the fraction is a cardinal and the whole number is an ordinal. Thus, we can interchangeably call the whole numbers as fractions or vice versa as long as we remember this distinction.

A curious property however arises when we note that the arithmetic operations—when performed on ordinals—produce different results. For example, when 1, 2, 3, 4 are ordinals, then 1 + 2 = 2, because the addition says: *add a second element to first.* The result of addition is that you get a second element beyond the first. Thus:

1 (ordinal) + 2 (ordinal) = 2 (ordinal)

Conversely, when 1, 2, 3, 4 are cardinals, then 1 + 2 = 3, which is the more familiar type of addition. It says, *add two elements to one element* due to which we now get three (cardinal) elements. Thus:

1 (cardinal) + 2 (cardinal) = 3 (cardinal)

This distinction is very important because—as we noted above—the same thing is a fraction (cardinally) and a whole number (ordinally). Therefore, in principle, we can replace the entire mathematical description of the world (which is presently based on cardinals) to a description based on ordinals. That will not *refute* the validity of the cardinal addition, but the successes of the cardinal addition will also not *contradict* the truth of the ordinal system. This is very important because it means that everything in mathematics can be replaced by an ordinal arithmetic without disproving anything in modern cardinal mathematics. There can be an alternative description of the world based on ordinal arithmetic without disproving cardinal usefulness.

Based on the cardinal-ordinal distinction, we can revisit the addition operation we discussed at the start of this post. The whole or the complete is the original object, which is designated as 1. Since nothing else exists right now, we can only add 1 to itself, which is like adding complete knowledge to itself, and it only produces the same complete knowledge. Therefore, 1 + 1 = 1. Remember we are talking about ordinal (first) here. Adding first to first gives us first. Similarly, when the complete expands into the other completes, we are talking about subtracting the original from the original, and the balance of subtraction is still the original complete. Therefore, 1 – 1 = 1. Clearly, if '1' denoted a cardinal then the familiar rules of addition and subtraction will apply (1 + 1 = 2, and 1 – 1 = 0). The crucial point is that the first element can never be removed, indicated by the fact that 1 – 1 = 1. Thus, you cannot go *prior* to the root of the tree, and 0 is not *before* 1. Logically, you cannot assert the origin to be void. The paradox in *Sri Īśopaniṣad* is thus mathematically equivalent to the claim that the origin is not void.

The Meaning of Zero

Now, if 0 is not *before* 1, then where is it? If we cannot get to a zero before 1, then it would appear that we cannot also go to the negative ordinals such as -1, -2, -3, etc. That is both good and bad. It is good because if negative ordinals were possible then there would simply be no starting point in the process of counting because we would have to start counting at -∞ which cannot be defined as an ordinal. It is also bad because if we cannot get to 0 then we cannot get to negative numbers which would mean they are unreal, when the fact is that negative directions in space are denoted by opposites such as east and west. Therefore, we need to get the reality of 0 and that of negative numbers, without claiming that $1 - 1 = 0$. This requires a different approach which—as we have seen previously—can be easily understood if we describe 0 as a cardinal and view it as the smallest fraction.

Remember that we are dividing the whole into parts, and those parts are fractions of the whole. Therefore, if we took that division to its logical conclusion, we will get 0, and it won't be a 0 *before* 1. It will be a 0 that follows 1 after the successive application of hiding parts of the whole. Effectively we are saying that the whole (1) is not created by summing up the smallest parts (0)—which is what modern mathematics tries to do when it constructs *length* by adding up infinitesimal points. We adopt the opposite approach in which the *length* is divided into smaller and smaller parts and the limit of that division (the smallest obtainable part) represents 0. This 0 is not actually an infinitesimal point. It is the *smallest* part of the whole.

To better understand this idea we need to discuss the three modes of nature called *sattva*, *rajas*, and *tamas*, in conjunction with two other ideas—*everything* and *nothing*. Let me illustrate these with the example of colors, and then we will try to formalize this understanding logically thereafter.

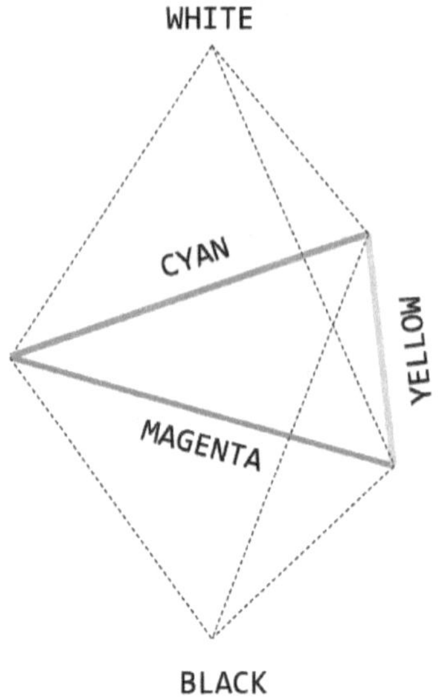

The color *white* represents *everything*; it is the complete color, because it contains all other colors. This complete color is divided into three parts—*yellow, magenta*, and *cyan* (loosely called yellow, red and blue). When all the colors have been removed from white, we are left with *nothing* denoted by black. If you are familiar with color schemes, then 4 colors (cyan, magenta, yellow, and black) are used for printing on a white paper. Each color *hides* the background white, and if everything is hidden, then the result is black, which (from the standpoint of colors) constitutes hiding all the colors.

These five categories are sometimes called *pañca-tattva* and sometimes the five deities of *Vaishnavism—Narayana, Vasudeva, Saṅkarṣaṇa, Pradyumna*, and *Aniruddha*. These are not merely theological topics; they are in fact the basis of expanding, distinguishing, and counting. Counting here simply means the succession of things emanated from the original Absolute Truth.

The color white denotes *śuddha-sattva* or 1. Yellow is *sattva*. Then *magenta* is *rajas*. Then *cyan* is *tamas*. Finally, the negation of white is black; it denotes 0. It is obtained when everything in the whole has been hidden. If hiding is achieved in atomic steps, then the last step in hiding produces 0. We can thus equate 0 with the last step of hiding, and the result with total obfuscation. White and black are opposites.

And yet, we are not using positive and negative numbers to denote these opposites. Rather, we denote the positive by 1 and its negation by 0. The reason is that the absence of light is darkness. You just remove all the light and you are left with darkness. Once you attain total darkness, you cannot take more light out of that darkness.

Therefore, we can talk about opposites like light and dark, but darkness is simply the *absence* of light. You cannot ever get beyond that absence and imagine something darker than complete darkness. The same holds true of opposites like hot and cold. You remove all the heat and you get cold, but you cannot make it any colder. Therefore, there are opposite directions in space and yet in the examples above the negation is simply 0. With this process we have established the reality of 0, but in the act of doing so we also have seemed to imply that negative numbers are impossible.

The Reality of Negative Numbers

These negatives are found in many types of concepts. Take the example of money. If you have the fullness of wealth then we can denote that by 1. If we remove all the wealth, then we get 0 which is poverty. But there is a state beyond poverty—that of *debt,* where you don't have any money and instead you *owe* someone money. The money you have in debt is *negative* money. Similarly, we can have fame and if fame is removed we will get anonymity. But beyond anonymity is disrepute and to escape from disrepute, anonymity would be progress. Similarly, there can be knowledge and if this knowledge is removed then we get ignorance. But beyond ignorance are false beliefs where you deny reality or believe in something that doesn't exist.

Thus, there are certain cases—e.g. light and dark—where removal of light is itself darkness, and you can't go beyond that absence of light. But there are other cases—e.g. knowledge, fame, wealth, etc.—where removal leads to ignorance, anonymity, and poverty, but it is not as bad as falsity, disrepute, and debt. We have to understand how both scenarios are real.

The short answer is *māyā* which *hides* some parts of the whole and thereby *reveals* some other parts. The hidden parts are negated and the revealed parts are asserted. The *prāna* or *śakti* that hides represents the negation while the *vāk* which is revealed through such hiding denotes assertions. These respectively constitute the negative and positive numbers. We might say that the negatives are being added to the whole to subtract from it. Owing to the successive application of negations—which in turn produce the assertions, the negatives and positives must be alternated.

Masculine and Feminine

The positive represents the masculine and the negative, the feminine. The positive is the whole, and the negative is the restriction on the whole. The whole is the *manas,* the restriction on that *manas* is *prāna*, and the product of restriction is another positive called the *vāk.* The restriction creates a boundary for choice; things within the boundary are possible and things outside the boundary are impossible. Things within the boundary constitute our *freedom*; things outside that boundary are forbidden. Choice is an assertion within the boundary and what lies out of bounds is the negation. We make the choice *after* we know the possibilities. Therefore, the assertion *follows* the negation. Possibility is *feminine* and choice is *masculine.*

The female is superior to the male because she asserts boundaries on the male. The male is superior to the female because he chooses within the bounds. The basic need in a female is to control; the basic need in a male is to be free. When a male exists without a female, he sees infinite possibilities but without a constraint he is unable to make a choice; the male languishes in indecision. Restriction *accelerates* choice; if the alternatives are limited by the female then the male chooses something definite over the endless possibilities. By that choice he becomes something real instead of an unlimited potential. A child is an unlimited potential; he could be anything. But as the child grows up, it has to sacrifice that unlimited possibility to be some definite reality. The process of growing up involves association with a female. The female that restricts a male's choices accelerates a choice. Both enjoy in that combination because the male chooses something definite over mere potentiality, and the female restricts the potentiality to something definite. The choice is masculine and the restriction is feminine.

The language used to define the restriction is different from that used to describe the choice because the restrictions are what lies outside the boundary and choices are what lies inside the boundary. The choices are *relative* to the boundary which means two complementary methods have to be employed in order to describe the choice. For instance, you can say that a certain choice was the *best* choice given the circumstances. Therefore, even to define the ideal, we need the definition of all that is possible. As a result, all masculine forms of God are coupled with a feminine form because the masculine represents choice and the feminine denotes possibility.

The Yin-Yang Principle

Since the whole is successively restricted, there is an alternating cycle of restriction and assertion. The picture below expresses this fact in which the left side negates the complete and as this negation proceeds, the right side denotes the successively reducing parts of the whole. Thus, the progression from 1 to 0 involves successive restrictions and revelations.

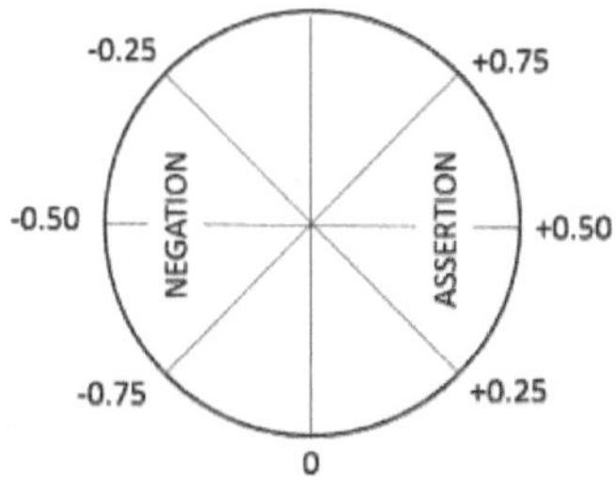

Now we have the reality of positive and negative numbers; these are simply fractions lying between 1 and 0. There is no ordinal 0 prior to 1. There is only a cardinal 0 which follows 1. There is no ordinal -1 which is prior to 1 because there is no ordinal 0. But, we can talk about positive and negative fractions *if* we allow for a *cardinal* negative that subtracts from the cardinal 1. At the bottom of this expansion is the cardinal -1 which represents complete constraint on the choice, and hence freedom is completely denied. The extent of this negation is equal to the extent of the whole, which means that you can deny the existence of the whole truth but nothing beyond that can be denied, because that denial constitutes the negation of everything.

Owing to the successive application of the negation to create an assertion, and the alternating nature of the male and female, the tree can also be described through the yin-yang picture in which the yin is the dark part that negates and yang is the light part which is revealed. Once something has been negated, something is still left asserted. Therefore, within the negation denoted by the dark, there is a circle of white. Similarly, whatever is left asserted will subsequently be negated. As a result, within the assertion denoted by white, there is a circle of black. It is not a coincidence that these black and white parts are called feminine and masculine respectively.

Care must be exercised in distinguishing between the opposites everything and nothing which lie at the top and bottom respectively and are denoted by white and black respectively, and assertion created from the negation which exist in the middle. In the above example, the masculine and the feminine have been denoted as white and black which is inaccurate. An accurate symbol of the feminine is magenta, and that of masculine is yellow and cyan.

The Logic of Three Parts

There is often confusion between the *śuddha-sattva* denoted by white and *sattva* denoted by yellow. Similarly, there is confusion between *tamas* denoted by cyan and nothing denoted by black. This confusion can be cleared when we look at the full spectrum of colors. It can also be cleared logically. If choices are represented as the selection between alternatives A and B, then white represents the category called *both* while black represents the category called *neither*. Each globe in space exists in between the logical extremes called everything and nothing; the top of the globe represents everything and the bottom represents nothing.

At the top of the universe, choice means *both* or *everything*. Similarly, at the bottom of the universe, choice means *neither* or *nothing*. These appear to be logically non-permissible from the middle but they become possible when we recognize that they were split from an originally unified state. Similarly, the rejection of all alternatives at the bottom becomes possible when you cannot make out the difference between the two. We will see shortly that this inability to make choices is caused by the inability to distinguish, which is caused because the 'distance' between things reduces to a point much smaller than the cognitive ability in the observer to make a distinction.

In conventional dualistic logic, two extremes—everything and nothing—are mutual opposites. In between everything and nothing lies *something*. This something is comprised of three aspects, which are called the three modes of nature. Thus, everything built from the three modes of nature is *something*; we cannot call it everything and we cannot say it is nothing. Each something embodies an *idea* or *manas*. The thing is *vāk*, and by embodying the idea it becomes a symbol of the idea, produced from the idea by a process or *prāna*. Therefore, the same word can denote the idea, process, and thing, although they are not the same. The concept is yellow. The activity or process is magenta. And the object that embodies the concept is cyan.

The Role of Concepts and Logic

In modern science we see objects, but we don't recognize the reality of concepts and processes. Without the existence of concepts, and their unique implications to arithmetic, we won't have a hierarchical tree structure. We don't need to deny the objects; we must realize that this objectivity is the last step in production; the first two steps are concept and process. The concept is the entity that is being hidden and the process is selecting the part to be hidden. The result of that process is that we see a part of the whole.

The part that we see as an object is an *effect* of the concept and the process of hiding. In that sense, *vāk* is less relevant to the explanation relative to *manas* and *prāna*. We might also say that *vāk* is the final empirical evidence that the process has been completed. It is required for empirical verification but it is totally irrelevant from the standpoint of explanation.

The irrelevance of *vāk* arises as the same empirical evidence can be produced by taking a different whole and hiding different parts in it. For instance, your vision of a square object can be created from hiding different parts of a triangle and a circle. Just because you see a square doesn't mean you know how it was created. However, if you know the whole and the process of hiding, then you will know the outcome to be empirically measured. In that sense, the science of objects (i.e. modern science) can be completely replaced by a science of concepts and processes. Modern science sees squares and thinks that they are real. A new science will say that some part of a circle was hidden to create a square. Both can be empirically confirmed but the latter is more powerful because you can keep the same reality (*manas*) and apply a different process (*prāna*) to see something else.

The Ideal Thing

The modern notion of numbers came from set theory. A set is an *unordered* collection of objects, which means that you can *claim* that there are N objects but you don't know which object is *first, second, third,* etc. For that claim to be substantiated, you have to actually order them from 1 to N, which means that the number of objects in a set is known only after ordering.

Ordering requires concepts and processes. For instance, if you have a collection of horses which you call the set 'horse', then to order the objects in that set you would typically begin with the *best horse* as the first member of the set, the next best horse as the second member of the set, and so forth. In this act, you need to know two things—(a) the definition of horse which identifies the ideal horse as the concept of 'horse', and (b) and a comparison procedure by which the ideal is compared against the other non-ideal horses.

In simple terms, you need to establish an *origin* of the set which constitutes the ideal horse, and a *metric* from the origin which identifies how far an actual horse is relative to the ideal horse. If the origin and metric have been defined, then ordering is straightforward, and once ordering has been done then we actually know how many objects exist, which leads to the *number* of members in the set. In essence, a set by itself cannot tell us how many members it has; we need to add a *geometry* with an origin and a metric in order to distinguish and order the members in the set before counting them.

Thus, we require three things to count—(a) origin, (b) metric, and (c) objects. The first is the definition of the ideal horse, the second is a process of measuring horses, and the third is the actual horse. To know an individual object, we must know the origin and metric prior. These three things are known in *Sāṅkhya* as *manas* or concept, *prāna* or process, and *vāk* or object.

The Absolute Truth

When set theory talks about collections, it speaks of the *complete* before counting. To actually count, we need three additional things as noted above. The first of the three things is the *ideal thing*. There is a difference between the collection of all horses and the first *ideal* horse—origin. *Śrīla Prabhupāda* explains this idea in the introduction of *Śrimad Bhāgavatam* as follows:

The conception of God and the conception of Absolute Truth are not on the same level. The Śrīmad-Bhāgavatam hits on the target of the Absolute Truth. The conception of God indicates the controller, whereas the conception of the Absolute Truth indicates the summum bonum or the ultimate source of all energies.

The *Absolute Truth* is the complete, or what mathematicians call the 'set' of all things. However, *God* is the first member of this set, or the ideal thing which becomes the origin in relation to which all subsequent things are measured. Thus, there are two ideas—(1) everything, and (2) the ideal thing. The ideal thing is the first member of everything, but everything is logically prior to the ideal thing. Therefore, *Śrimad Bhāgavatam* is speaking about *everything*. Theologically, *Kṛṣṇa* is everything, and *Balarama* is the ideal thing. *Balarama* is the first manifestation from *Kṛṣṇa* which means the ideal thing manifests from everything. Since *Kṛṣṇa* is everything, He has darkness as everything includes the dark side. *Balarama* as the ideal thing is yellow.

The Mechanism of Counting

The ideal horse has the same three aspects. It is a definition of the ideal, which constitutes the *manas*; it measures against itself which is the *prāna*, and it is the instantiation of the ideal which is *vāk*. When only the ideal exists, then *manas, prāna*, and *vāk* are not *separated* as the definition, process of measurement, and the object being measured are the very same thing. As successive objects are manifest, then we know that the first object is *manas*, the second object is *vāk*, and the relation or distance between these two objects is *prāna*. The three modes were inseparable in the ideal object and they are separated when subsequent objects are created.

The ideal object by itself combines *manas, prāna*, and *vāk*. But, when we speak of the ideal in relation to the subsequent objects coming from the ideal, then it is only *manas* because the other objects are *vāk* and their relation to the ideal is *prāna*. In this way, God is described to be fully satisfied in Himself, and yet He engages in relationships with other persons.

Every successive object is also a combination of *manas, prāna*, and *vāk*. It embodies an idea, which becomes the origin of subdivisions, in relation to which the subdivisions are located. In this way, each thing is a combination of *manas*, *prāna*, and *vāk*, and yet they are organized hierarchically.

Finite vs. Infinite

Everything is inexhaustible. However, *parts* of everything are *finite* and can therefore see an end. This idea can be expressed very simply by saying the tree has *infinite* branches but each of the branches of the tree is itself *finite*.

A universe is a branch and it is finite. But there are infinite universes. Therefore, we can say that the full thing is unlimited, and yet each part of that thing is limited and has an end. The soul is also a branch of the tree. Since the branch is finite, the soul can know the path to God. The soul cannot, however, know all the branches. In that sense, while the soul can know the complete, he is not *omniscient*. The difference between the soul and God is that the soul knows one branch and God knows all branches.

Different Classes of Numbers

The Reality of Fractions

All positive and negative numbers are defined between 1 and 0. However, the whole numbers only represent the order among the fractions. Fractions are therefore real, and negative numbers are also fractions. The fraction is defined in relation to the whole; i.e. we can say how *small* the fraction is relative to the whole. Now, we can map the natural numbers to fractions. For instance, 2 can be mapped to 1/2, 3 to 1/3, 4 to 1/4, etc. As the natural numbers get larger, the fractions get smaller, but we can never reach 0 through the successive subdivisions. In that sense the limit of natural numbers—infinity—is equivalent to the limit of fractions, namely 0. While infinity is unbounded, zero is bounded. If you were asked to go till infinity you will not know the destination. But if you have to go to zero you will at least know the destination even though you can never reach it.

In one sense, therefore, even the present universe is infinite because you can never reach the boundary. And in another sense, the universe is finite because there is a definite boundary of the universe. Therefore, when we say that each branch is finite, we simply mean that it is *bounded*.

This idea is clearly demonstrated by Zeno's Paradox in which you start from 1 and head towards 0, but there are infinite steps because you subdivide the steps to the destination through fractions. If the distance between 1 and 0 was indeed infinitely divisible, then you can never reach 0 (which is what Zeno argued) because there are infinite steps to that destination. In modern mathematics this is sometimes called a *bounded limit*; to reach it infinite steps are needed even though there is a definite boundary.

The Problem of Missing Fractions

Through this method of mapping natural numbers to fractions, we miss out on many fractions. For example, we cannot reach 2/3 = 0.666 through such a method because 1/2, which is the first fraction in the list, is 0.5, and it is already smaller than 0.666. Similarly, 4/9 = 0.444 is smaller than 1/2 but larger than 1/3. The conclusion is that there are many *more* fractions between 1 and 0 than all the natural numbers. Therefore, if this universe were *countable* as 1, 2, 3, etc. and it began in 1, then many numbers will never be possible. This now constitutes the problem of missing fractions.

This is however not a real problem because we are counting *within* a branch, but there are infinite branches. A fraction such as 2/3 can be understood if the numerator denoted the order of the *branches* while the denominator denoted the fractional part of that branch. To allow for this, we will have to allow for infinite branches (as we saw above) and yet each branch having a limiting end in 0. This would mean there is no location called 2/3 in the first universe, because that location exists in the second universe.

1	DEPTH WITHIN A BRANCH								
BREADTH OF BRANCHES	1	2	3	4	5	6	7	8	9
	2	3	4	5	6	7	8	9	10
	3	4	5	6	7	8	9	10	11
	4	5	6	7	8	9	10	11	12
	5	6	7	8	9	10	11	12	13
	6	7	8	9	10	11	12	13	14
	7	8	9	10	11	12	13	14	15
	8	9	10	11	12	13	14	15	16
	9	10	11	12	13	14	15	16	17

We can see how *everything* is 1 because it is the first thing, and all the other things that follow are considered fractional parts of that whole. Thus, everything represents both cardinal and ordinal 1. Thereafter, there is the ordinal 1, which is a part of the whole, but the ideal part. From this ideal part we proceed horizontally and vertically. The vertical process creates the non-ideal from the ideal, and the horizontal process creates subparts of the ideal and non-ideal parts. The vertical process is creating numerous branches of the tree, and the horizontal process sub-branches of each branch.

Both contribute to the fractionalization of the whole—the horizontal process changes the numerator and the vertical path changes the denominator. As a result of applying these two processes we obtain all the fractions.

Cantor's Diagonal Argument

In 1891 Georg Cantor produced a similar (though not identical) argument depicted below. Let's look at the similarities and the differences.

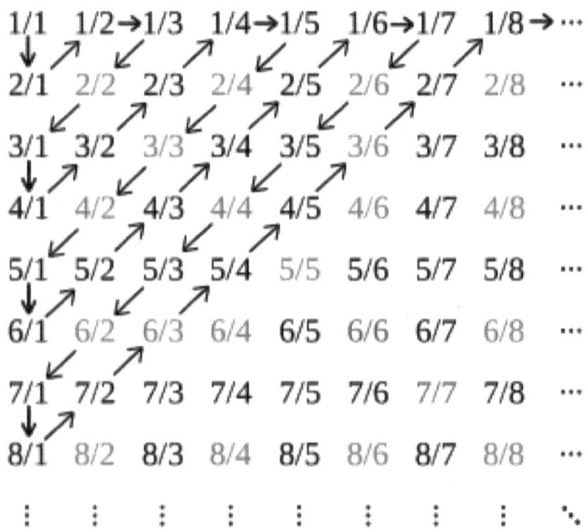

The point of Cantor's argument was that all the rational numbers can be sequenced in an order, and thereby 1-1 mapped to the sequence of natural numbers. He claimed that the set of rational numbers has a *size* equal to the set of natural numbers. This seems rather unintuitive because we know that there are many fractions between any two natural numbers.

In Cantor's argument this problem rears its head because each number—such as 1—if viewed cardinally is counted infinite times: 1/1, 2/2, 3/3, etc. Similarly, 2 is counted infinite times as 2/1, 4/2, 6/3, etc. In effect, all the whole numbers are counted *infinite* times. Similarly, all the fractions are counted infinite times—e.g. 1/2, 2/4, 3/6, etc. So, the list above is $\infty * \infty$ for cardinal numbers. Similarly, each natural number creates an infinite fraction (numerator and denominator), so it is also $\infty * \infty$ although the whole number infinite is contained in the infinity of the fractions.

Cantor's claim was that all these numbers can be *counted* like infinity, so in a weird sense of sizing the set, collectively they have the same 'size' as ∞. Cantor then showed that the irrational numbers (e.g. π) were uncountable and therefore had a bigger size—2^{∞}. Clearly it turns out that 2^{∞} would be much bigger than $\infty * \infty$, but this is a distinction that can wait for a bit.

A Precise Definition of the Tree

To address the problem of including the same fraction many times, we have to say that 1/2 is actually different from 2/4. The number 1/2 is the second member of the first branch, while the number 2/4 is the fourth member of the second branch. In other words, while 1/2 and 2/4 are fractions of the whole, they are in different places on the tree. Similarly, all the branches are parts of the complete whole. While the members of the branches are denoted by using numerator and denominator, to depict all the branches as parts of the complete whole, we need a third *level* that denotes the whole.

This is eminently possible if we use the triad of *manas*, *prāna*, and *vāk*, wherein the whole is the original *idea*, each branch becomes the *metric* relative to the whole (which denotes the numerator), while the individual parts on a given branch become the individual *objects* distinguished using that *metric* (which represents the denominator). The diversification of the root would then be a consequence of defining multiple metrics which produce many branches, and then many leaves on each branch.

We can now give a very precise definition to the tree. There is a whole which we call its root. Then we have many individual metrics which are used to divide this root. Then we have the individual objects produced as a consequence of this division of the whole using the different metrics.

Atomism to Time and Operations

Since *manas*, *prāna*, and *vāk* are hierarchical, as we traverse this hierarchy from top to bottom, the ideas, methods, and objects get smaller. The incremental reduction constitutes the march from everything to nothing. There is a limit to this reduction which constitutes *atomism* of ideas, methods, and objects. Depending on the scale employed, atomism may be attained quickly (if the scale is large) and slowly (if the scale is small). The variety in the universe depends on how small the scale is. If we measure something with a foot, we get more feet than if we measure with a meter.

Accordingly, the universe is larger when our scale of measurement is small, and smaller when the scale is large. Each of the branches of the tree can be viewed as a universe; the growing order in the universe implies the use of successively smaller scale, and therefore the successive universes are also larger. A smaller scale means a greater capacity to zoom in, but a limited capacity to zoom out. A larger scale means a limited capacity to zoom in but greater capacity to zoom out. Thus, in the universe with larger scale, it is easier to see the big picture and harder to see the detailed picture. Conversely, in the universe with the smaller scale, it is easier to see the detailed picture but much harder to perceive the full reality.

The present universe is described as the smallest universe, which means it is the first in the order of universes, and therefore has the largest scale of measurement. Using this largest scale, it is easier to know the whole (which is why the universe will appear to be the smallest). In this universe, it is harder to know the smallest possible atomic reality because the senses are 'blunt' instruments to measure atoms. But the same senses can understand the whole reality much better. In other universes, they can understand the atomic reality much better, but it is harder to know the whole truth.

The Universe is a Half-Empty Glass

The universe in Vedic cosmology is described as half filled with water and the other half is planets floating like particles in the air. The planets are *vāk*, the air is *prāna*, and planets hang like light bulbs of a chandelier from a roof called *manas*. But this is half the universe, which comprises all the possible ways in which the whole can be hidden to create individual objects. Not every method of hiding is however real at all *times*. For instance if you see some empty land, there is possibility that it can get a building in the future. Similarly, a place where there are buildings can become an empty ground later.

All the elements of the tree can be counted, but they are not always *visible* which means these branches are not occupied by any soul. Time causes them to manifest and unmanifest. If there are N individual possibilities, then there are 2N *combinations* of possibilities, which are manifest slowly over time. The lower half of the universe constitutes the 2N *irrational* numbers (as we discussed from Cantor's theorem earlier), and each such number represents the state of the entire universe at a given *time*. You can imagine a glass half full from which one particle of water evaporates every moment and creates the entire visible universe. The very next moment, the particle condenses and goes back into the lower half and a new particle evaporates.

There is hence a cycle of rainfall and evaporation inside the half-empty glass. When we reach the point *we* call 'nothing' we have reached the limit of spatial division. Beyond this is a world of irrational numbers, equal to all the *combinations* in the upper half. These numbers are real, but *we* cannot perceive them because knowing each such number is equivalent to knowing the complete state of the universe at any given *moment*.

Space and Time Trees

The upper half of the universe represents locations in space and the lower half represents instances in time. Both space and time are hierarchical, so the bottom half is also like a tree in which the higher nodes represent larger spans in time while the lower half denotes parts of these larger time spans. The universe is spherical, which can be understood to indicate that the time tree is upright while the space tree is inverted. Thus in the time tree the lowest element represents the entire duration of the universe, whereas the lower nodes in the same tree represent smaller time durations.

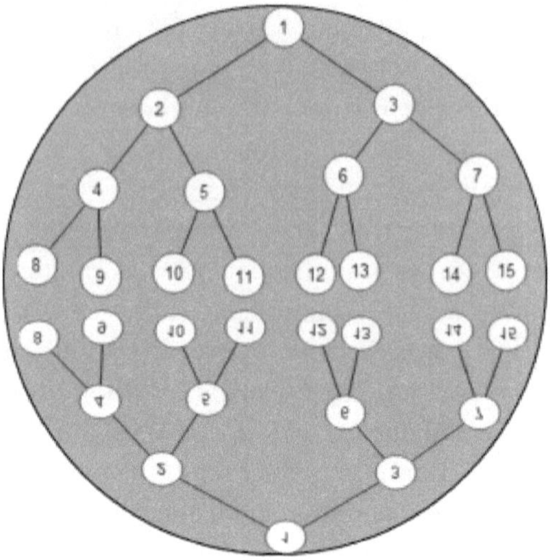

The entire past, present, and future of the universe are therefore real. But *we* cannot *experience* this past and future unless we have a sense perception capable of seeing beyond the countable individual objects. The view from top to bottom represents all the things that will ever exist at any given time. The view from bottom to top denotes all things existing at any given time. By knowing both we know the extension and duration of the universe.

Sub-Structure in the Tree

So far I have depicted the tree simply—a single inverted structure. The real structure is like a *Christmas tree* with many tiers called planetary systems. It comprises a central 'stem' or the *axismundi* from which many individual stems protrude. As one descends downward, more of reality is hidden. Similarly, as one goes outward even more reality is hidden. Therefore, the path of advancement is *inward* and *upward*—inward on a single plane, and then upward through the higher planes. This model is remarkably similar to the nerves coming out of the spinal cord in the human body.

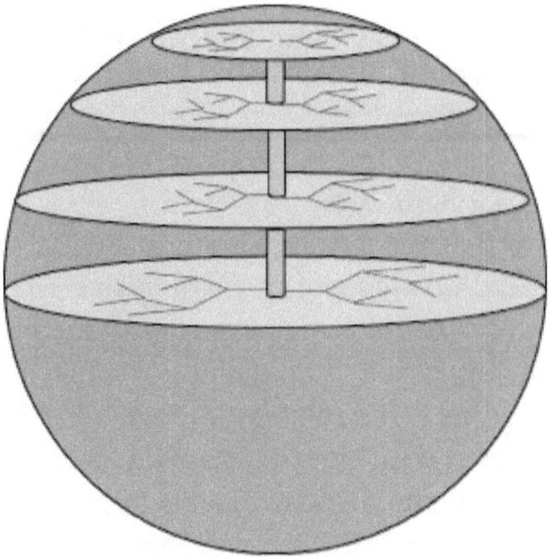

Śrīla Prabhupāda writes in the purport to SB 3.26.34: Form rests in subtle existence in the sky, and internally it is perceived as the veins within the body and the circulation of the vital air (emphasis mine). This idea allows us to see the planetary systems as analogues of chakra in the body, the number of petals in the chakra representing the number of divisions of the space. While the yoga system speaks about the 7 upper chakra because the goal of the system is to rise, Vedic cosmology speaks about 7 upper and 7 lower planetary systems. Correspondingly there are 7 lower chakra, which together constitute the 14 levels corresponding to 14 planetary systems. Mystic Universe discusses the division of flat plane at greater length.

Varieties of Number Types

Students of number theory know that mathematicians classify numbers into many classes such as Triangular numbers, Square numbers, Pentagonal numbers, Hexagonal numbers, Heptagonal numbers, Octagonal numbers, Nonagonal numbers, Decagonal numbers, Dodecagonal numbers, etc. There are many kinds of integer sequences such as the Fibonacci numbers. The different levels of hierarchy in the tree can be thought of as corresponding to some unique number types, which may include the above mentioned types or other types that have not yet been discovered.

These worlds will be mathematically describable but quite different in their properties from each other because they will correspond to different number types. A detailed study of these number systems, and organizing them along a hierarchy, will constitute a hierarchical number theory, which will also give us an understanding of the differences in the different tiers.

The Use of Complex Numbers

The flat planes that we see above are not *physical space* because each of *sat, chit,* and *ananda* can be further divided into two parts—knowing and acting, denoted by the senses of knowledge and action. Factually the division is only within *chit* but it can also appear in *sat* and *ananda.* Thus there are roles of knowing and acting, objects of knowing and acting, and purposes of knowing and acting. The hierarchy in a tree looked at simplistically is just two dimensions—vertical height and horizontal plane. But the horizontal plane has to be further divided into two dimensions—knowing and acting.

This plane needs complex numbers as each object has two features—it *is* some properties and it can be *used* in certain ways. A knife can be used to cut and pierce, and a saw can also be used to cut, while a needle can be used to pierce. If we change the properties perceived by the senses of knowledge (e.g. hardness and sharpness) we also change the uses to which the knife can be put to (e.g. cutting and piercing). However, changes to other properties (e.g. color or smell) may not change the use of a knife. Knowing and acting are hence correlated but they are not identical. Similarly, a plastic knife may be useful in cutting butter, but not in sawing through wood.

Mystic Universe discusses this correlation between the two properties at greater length, and uses them to describe the subdivision of a flat surface into many subparts which correspond to different types of objects and the different uses they can be put to. These divisions correspond (in Vedic cosmology) to different body types which look different and can be used for different types of activities. The body has two kinds of senses (of knowledge and action) which perform individual functions. These two types of senses are unified by the mind which is able to hold both the concepts of knowing and acting. The flat surface is a mental or conceptual plane, not a sensually perceivable surface. The property of this plane is that if you add two numbers you are performing two operations—translation and rotation. This is unlike natural numbers where addition simply translates the number.

The imaginary part of the number is action. As you apply the same action repeatedly, the object returns to its original state, which means that actions rotate the object. Why does this happen? The reason is that we created the object by hiding different parts of the whole. As we perform actions on this object, that action simply hides another part and reveals a different part. This hiding and revealing can happen at various levels (due to hierarchy) but all change appears to be rotation because there are finite number of aspects of the whole which are being hidden and revealed. The situation is like throwing a dice or tossing a coin. Depending on how many 'faces' a thing has (based on how small we divided it) each action will reveal one face.

A complex number combines *prāna* and *vāk* or action and thing; it says that the object was produced by a process, but it could have been produced by another process. This becomes important when you want to know the location in space and how one reached that place (because you could have used other paths to reach the same place). In hierarchical space, the element on the tree is the place, and the branch connecting it to the higher element is the path. You can never have more than two paths to a destination and hence two numbers are not needed. The confusion arises in flat space as we only see the leaves and by looking at them we don't know which branch they are connected to. As a result we suppose that they *could* be connected to any branch. Complex numbers are simply saying that there is an element and there is a connection to the *center* of that space (which constitutes the higher node). A complex number forces a hierarchical view of the world because you have to represent a *path* along with an *object*. It is a caricature of hierarchy and if one employed hierarchy this caricature would not be needed.

The Creation and Destruction of the Universe

We noted earlier how the tree expands when the whole is covered partially creating *fractions* of the whole. We also discussed at the beginning how adding partial knowledge to the whole knowledge doesn't change the whole, and since the addition of the part doesn't increase the whole, the removal of the part also doesn't reduce it. Thus, during the creation of the universe, some form of *śakti* is used to expand the universe. This *śakti* originally existed in the whole as its *prāna* and constituted the *full* knowledge of the whole. However, as the *śakti* divides into smaller parts, the whole is also known and represented partially thus causing the expansion of the tree. Similarly, as the *śakti* merges the parts into the whole, the entire creation is terminated.

The creation and dissolution of the universe don't change the whole because they are created as parts without dividing the whole itself, and they are merged back into the whole without adding anything to it. Thus the whole is unchanged by creation and dissolution of the universe. The change is entirely caused by *śakti* which constitutes a *method* of knowing the reality.

Mathematics and Conscious Experience

The Philosophy of Perception

Manas is the seer, *prāna* is the process of seeing, and *vāk* is the seen. The original seer is one. But there are many methods of seeing due to which many visions are seen. *Yoga-māyā* and *mahā-māyā* are two methods of seeing that create two visions. The soul is also a method of seeing that produces a vision. These are respectively also called *bahiranga-śakti, antaranga-śakti,* and *taṭasthā-śakti.* These three methods of seeing are like mirrors in which God sees Himself. The result of that reflection is an image *inside the mirror* and the seer can perceive what is within the mirror. Thus, God enters inside the soul as His own reflection in the mirror. And then God appreciates His own reflection as it is being reflected in the mirror.

Sri Chaitanya calls the soul a mirror when He exhorts the soul by asking for *cheto darpan mārjanam,* or to clean the mirror such that God can be reflected in this mirror. Here, *chitta* is the soul, *darpan* is the mirror, and *mārjanam* is the cleansing of the mirror for reflection. By comparing the soul to the mirror and its cleansing as the process of spiritual reinstatement, spiritual life is succinctly summarized as the path in which the soul reflects an image of God by holding up a mirror to Him for His self-perception.

The Description of Dṛṣṭa and Dṛṣya

In this process, the real seer or *dṛṣṭa* is God and the reflection in the soul is the *dṛṣya* or vision. However, the reflection is also within the soul, because that reflection is precisely what God sees. Therefore, the soul is also a *dṛṣṭa* because he creates the vision of God within himself. Similarly, the material world is the reflection of God inside *bahiranga-śakti,* and the spiritual world inside *antaranga-śakti.* They are different processes of seeing; they see the same object but create a different picture. The reflected object and the seer of that object are the same entity—God—and the process of seeing is simply an instrument for God's seeing. This instrument has the same three properties as God, and yet the instrument is meant for God's use.

The rock star is reflected inside the fan. The rock star sees that reflection and says—that's me! The ideal fan sees the same reflection and says—that's you! The material perversion is that the fan sees a reflection of the rock star in himself and says—that's me! The soul has the ability to see himself (instead of God) and that vision of self-consciousness is true, but it is not God's vision. The ability to have the self-vision and God's vision are truth. The ability to impute God's vision on the self is false. In that sense, the material world where the fan considers himself the rock star is an illusion. However, there is indeed a rock star so only the identification with reality is the illusion.

The personal image of the rock star is *ādibhautika*, the self-image formed in the process of perception is *ādiatmika*. Similarly, when the rock star sees the fan enjoying, he has a vision of the fan called *ādibhautika* and the self-image of the rock star in relation to the fan is *ādiatmika*. Under *yoga-māyā* there is a distinction between the self and the vision, but under *mahā-māyā* this distinction is blurred. In *mahā-māyā* there is a separate *ādidaivika* which connects the rock star and the fan, but in *yoga-māyā* this person is always visible as the root of the tree and hence everything is known in relation to *ādidaivika*.

The Use of Logic in Creation

The *śakti* represents the different ways to know the whole. However, remember that this knowing is dividing the whole into parts. We can say that it is knowing by *analyzing* the whole into its various parts; the whole is known to the self, but the parts of the whole are not known unless the whole is analyzed. This analysis is like saying that I have wealth worth millions but whether this wealth is held in property, gold, cash, or land is not known. The purpose of *śakti* is to detail how all the wealth is actually held, and there are many ways to convert millions into property, gold, cash, or land. In one sense, *śaktianalyzes* the whole into parts. In another sense, the parts are being created from the whole by applying a process of measurement on the whole. In yet another sense, the whole is only taking stock of itself.

Logic is the fundamental tool for analysis, and the division of the whole into parts is the outcome of analysis. The *śakti* or *prāna* thus acts as *logic*, analyzes the whole into parts like cutting up a picture into a jigsaw puzzle. There are *infinite* ways in which the picture can be cut-up, each of which constitutes a branch of the whole which presents the act of detailing the whole into parts. There are hence infinite *śakti* each creating a different branch; each branch is a different jigsaw puzzle of the same picture.

The Genesis of Logic

We can divide the infinite representations of the whole into 8 distinct classes if we understand that the division of the whole into parts is a *choice* and this choice is a property of the soul. The basic mechanism of choice is that the three aspects of the soul are often in conflict, and the conflict is resolved by creating a hierarchy or a dominant-subordinate structure. Sometimes emotion dominates cognition and cognition dominates relation. At other times, this order is changed. Based on the dominant-subordinate patterns, 6 personality types are created, which the book *Emotion* discusses at greater length. Then there are two other personality types—(1) where we know we have choice but we don't use it, and (2) we believe we have no choice and hence we don't use it. The former is called *oneness* and the latter is called *nothingness*. The former accepts choice but rejects its use; the latter denies choice itself. The denial of choice is also a choice. Oneness, nothingness, and the 6 personality types create the 8 fundamental types of choice. To divide the whole into parts, we must employ these 8 methods.

When choice is denied or not used, the whole is not divided into parts but it can still be experienced as emptiness and fullness, respectively. The same reality is thus expressed in two ways which correspond to *Brahman* and a destination of voidism or emptiness pursued by the Buddhists. Far more interesting uses of choice involve the prioritization of the three aspects of the soul which represent right (*sat*), good (*ananda*), and truth (*chit*) and the prioritization creates 6 types of choices, logic, methods of division.

In the material world, truth is subordinated to good, which means that truth is relative to our goals; we choose the goals, which helps us choose the beliefs, and those beliefs confirm/deny the truth. However, the good is subordinate to right; which means that I have to choose the happiness within the bounds of my role; I cannot enjoy by violating my duty. This is well-known as the dilemma between choice and responsibility and becomes the cause of *karma*: if you violate your duties to enjoy you will have to suffer. This structure of choice is reflected in matter when the moral sense is placed higher than ego or desire, which is higher than intellect or beliefs. In essence, *sat* dominates over *ananda*, and *ananda* dominates over *chit*.

Now imagine another type of world in which truth dominates over desire and desire dominates over duty. The truth would indicate all that exists. We will perceive this truth which would then lead to a desire within us. Whatever that desire is, it then becomes our duty. For example, in such a world, you could walk into a fashion store where the clothes displayed are the truth. As you look at these clothes you develop a desire for them. But desire fulfillment is now your duty, which means that you can rightfully take whichever clothes you like and walk out of the store, without paying for them in return, because you are just performing the duty of fulfilling your desires and if you don't desire to pay the shop owner any money then you are not morally obligated to do so because your duty is whatever you desire. Does this sound illogical? It is not illogical to imagine such a world, although it is not the logic of this world. Vedic texts describe that there are worlds where you can take whatever you like without having to pay for it in return, because there is no moral obligation above and beyond the fulfillment of desire itself.

Therefore, the logic of that world is different from that of this world. In this world, duty rules over desire and desire rules over truth. In another world, desire can rule over duty, and duty can be ruled by truth. In effect, what we call *śakti* is simply choice of how we decide to order the three facets of the soul. When the soul is in the material world, he has to prioritize duty over enjoyment, and enjoyment over truth; this prioritization is reflected when morality is higher than ego and the ego is higher than the intellect. However, in other worlds—governed by different logics—the order can change.

Of course, this doesn't deny the possibility that you could have a different *personality* that prioritizes truth over good and good over right in this world. But it is not the ideal personality within the material world because you will often neglect your duties in order to pursue enjoyment. Similarly, you might sometimes deny that you have choice, or accept that you have choice but refuse to use it, and remain in an indecisive state. The soul is however not independent of the world; the world is governed by a particular type of logic and the soul has to follow that logic too. If he desires a different logic, then he has to finish the pending business of this logic—the balance of accounts—and then go to another world. All these worlds can be described logically because logic is a choice, and choice is a property of the soul which is used to resolve the inner contradiction between *sat*, *chit*, and *ananda*.

The above 8 methods of seeing the same reality constitute the different worlds, of which the entire material world is just one. The whole truth is *manas*, the type of logic is *prāna*, and the world created by that logic is *vāk*.

The Three Principles of Logic

Material logic is defined as a set of three rules—identity, non-contradiction, and mutual-exclusion. The identity in material logic is the counterpart of *sat*, which creates the "I am" of the soul—the soul enters a 'role' such as parent, employee, citizen, etc. Then, non-contradiction constitutes the *chit* which creates the "I have" of the soul—the soul gets a body comprised of parts which are also logical opposites (e.g. front and back, head and foot) and yet these opposites are separated by space as different locations and parts. Finally, mutual-exclusion constitutes the *ananda* of the soul which creates the "I want" of the soul—the soul develops desire and need for pleasure, owing to which choice becomes a necessity and you cannot rule out all the alternatives. If you are presented with vanilla and chocolate ice creams, then non-contradiction means you cannot choose *both* at the same time, and mutual-exclusion means you cannot choose *neither* of the alternatives. Once both and neither are rejected, you must choose one. This choice may not be compatible with your identity—i.e. your role—and if there is inconsistency between the role and the choice, then a *consequence* will be created.

Effectively, you must make a choice (not choosing is not an alternative), and you must choose one alternative (choosing everything is not allowed), and whatever you choose will be *compared* to your identity. In modern logic, identity is defined as the truism 'A is A' which is to say that you can never deny your identity or claim something contrary to that identity. This is an erroneous claim because the choices you make may be incompatible with your identity, when that identity is defined not as your personality but as a *role*. The fundamental question is: What is identity? Is the identity of an entity defined by itself (which would mean that the object is independent of other objects)? Or, is the identity of something defined in relation to the original thing? In modern logic 'A is A' entails that my identity is defined by me, and hence I can never contradict myself. That is false on two grounds. First, my identity is defined in relation to others (e.g. parent, citizen, employee, etc.). Second, I can contradict myself in the future; or I can make self-contradicting statements right now: "This sentence is false".

Thus, the fundamental problem in modern logic is the rule of identity which is used to supposedly create a *consistency* when the fact is that we are often inconsistent with ourselves. We are also—as the conflicts and wars of this world suggest—often contradicting others. To understand this inconsistency we have to go back to the issue of internal contradictions in the soul. The *ananda* or the desire of the soul makes a choice out of competing options. However, this choice is not necessarily compatible with our role or duty. Identity is true when our choices are subordinated to the role. However, the identity rule fails when the choices are incompatible with the role.

Everything in logic changes when this incompatibility has to be accounted for. For instance, the concept of moral consequence emerges when choices are incompatible with our duty. This moral consequence changes our role (e.g. as a punishment) and even more incompatibilities may then be created between what we want and what our situation or role will allow.

Modern logic views the world as one big consistent reality disregarding the fact that meaning is created through opposites. This error exists in the principle of non-contradiction where everything in the universe must be consistent, which entails the rejection of meaning created by opposites.

Thus out of the three principles in modern logic, two of them are patently false. The failure of non-contradiction represents the resurrection of meaning, and the failure of identity denotes the idea of moral consequences based on the interaction between choice and role. Even the third principle of mutual-exclusion—which leads to choice—is presented as a necessity but it is not necessary because choices are based on goals, and by discarding goals and the quest for happiness we can in fact stop making choices. Thus, every fundamental principle in modern logic is flawed—partially or completely. The rejection of meaning and morality is ensconced in modern logic itself.

The rule of non-contradiction must be modified to mean that while opposite alternatives will exist in the universe (and hence the universe as a whole is logically contradictory), I cannot choose the contradictions simultaneously. I may choose them one after another, or different persons may choose them simultaneously. The former entails that non-contradiction is subject to time (because contradictory choices can be made at different times) and the latter means that non-contradiction is subject to space (because contradictory choices can be made by two separate individuals simultaneously). The universe as a whole—and by that we mean different souls—can be logically inconsistent with each other, but I am not allowed to make opposite choices because I can only be situated at one place at one time. Violating that principle requires me to be present at multiple locations simultaneously and that is forbidden because the soul is atomic. Non-contradiction therefore follows from the atomicity of the soul, just as the necessity for choice follows from the desire for happiness which compels one to make choices.

Once this new foundation of non-contradiction is grasped, then we can speak about the problem of identity—namely that my choices as a human can be incompatible with my role as a citizen. My identity is the role—e.g. a citizen. In Vedic philosophy this is also called *Svarūpa* (*sva* = self, *rūpa* = form), and the *Svarūpa* is defined in relation to God as a relationship (e.g. of a servant or friend). Being situated in that identity simply means that my choices are compatible with my role. If that identity is broken, then I make choices inconsiderate of my role. A moral law must now apply. This moral law is not like modern scientific laws presented as *formulae*, which in turn assume all of mathematics and logic. Rather, morality is a *logical principle* and it emerges from the fact that *ananda* is subordinate to *sat* which means that my desires can be subordinated by my duties, but my duties cannot be subordinated to my desires. In simple terms, we must always do our duty even if we don't like it. Not doing so constitutes the violation of the *identity* principle. If I enjoy my duties, then the contradiction between *ananda* and *sat* is resolved. To live free of *karma* therefore one has to perform their duties *happily*.

Modern logic is necessary, but the above mentioned logic is *normative*. Its individual principles can be violated—e.g. that I may not do my duty—but logic as a whole is necessary because violation creates consequences. Thus, every principle in logic is not always upheld. However, collectively logic is always upheld. The core principles of logic—namely identity, mutual-exclusion and non-contradiction are purely normative and not necessary. That is, we are *expected* and *supposed* to be logical according to these core principles but we can act illogically—that illogical action is our *free will*. The subsequent fall-out of this illogical choice is necessary and not normative. That is, the moral consequence is not just something that is supposed to happen; it is necessary, which means that it will always happen.

To the above three core *normative* principle of logic, therefore we can add a fourth *necessary* principle which we can call the 'action-reaction' principle. This is a universal principle which depends on the *gap* between the choice and the role and effected when the normative identity principle is violated. Then the reaction to the action doesn't act immediately, so we must add a fifth necessary principle called 'delayed-action' that delivers the consequence of a previous normative violation after a certain gap in time. The action-reaction principle is a feedback loop, and the delayed-action principle causes this loop to cause oscillation which manifests as various cycles.

In modern mathematics theorems are eternally true, and applicable to all times and places, and to describe *change* we have to separately *compute* the laws of nature, which requires a computer to calculate the outcome, which in turn needs some material system, which must in turn be governed by some logic, which also needs to be computed on a computer governed by logic, *ad infinitum*. Logic and mathematics don't explain how things are changing because they never describe how logic and mathematics is computed. The system we describe above is self-computing. We don't need a law which is then computed assuming input data. Rather, our choices are the input data and moral consequences are the output which again drive the input. In one sense, the driver underlying this logical system is our choice; it is not electricity or material force, and as long as the choices exist, the system can keep running forever. Therefore we need only one idea to describe why nature works perennially—namely that the soul is eternal. When the soul leaves the body, the bodily computer stops working gradually, because the logical system was being fed by choice and their consequences.

The Five Principles of Logic

Thus, we can define the scope of logic as the following 5 principles:

- The principle of the eternal possibility of choice,
- The principle of individual non-contradiction,
- The normative principle of identity,

- The action-reaction principle,
- The delayed-action principle.

The principle of mutual-exclusion is called 'choice' above. The principle of non-contradiction is matter. The identity principle represents God because the soul's role is defined only in relation to God. The principle of action-reaction is called *karma*. And the principle of delayed-action is time. This the scientific-logical framework in which we need to think of a new logic—it is representative of five key ideas—soul, God, matter, time, and *karma*. This logic has normative and necessary parts, and it is free from the contradiction between necessity and choice. Similarly, logic is also self-sufficient because it doesn't need an external computational device to find an outcome. The principle of mutual-exclusion or choice is itself the computer.

Clearly, the last two—*karma* and time—arise when the principle of identity is broken. If these principles were upheld, either because the morality was subordinated to desire or truth, or because one enjoyed their duties in the material world, the last two principles will cease to be operative. This cessation is the *logical* explanation of salvation by which one can exit the material logic. That exit is not a denial of logic; it is entirely within material logic, and it is also supported by alternative 'transcendental' logics.

These five principles are embodied in this world as the five *prāna* or 'forces'. In some transcendental worlds (beyond the material world and different from the places of *oneness* and *nothingness*), only three of the above five principles will exist, and we can call them three divisions of *śakti*. In the realms of oneness the principle of *śakti* is understood but not differentiated into separate principles. In the realm of nothingness, *śakti* is not used. In that sense, the different worlds are different because of different *śakti*. The material world is also working according to logic, with two differences. First, this logic is different than stated in the modern understanding. Second, the logic is itself the force that drives the universe, so we don't need a computer to emulate that logic, which in turn needs some operating logic, etc.

The *prāna* is divided into five parts called—*prāna*, *apāna*, *samāna*, *udāna*, and *vyāna*. The power of *prāna* is the power of choice or what we call mutual-exclusion by which we must make a selection. To live means to make choices, and therefore *prāna* is the essence of life; it manifests in the body selecting—e.g. in accepting food, inhaling, and hearing. The power of *apāna* represents individual non-contradiction; which means that if I select X then I must reject its opposite. This power manifests in the various excretory processes in the body. The power of *samāna* is the principle of identity by which we compare the choice against the role to find a compatibility; it is said to be the 'digestive' power by which the consumed food is reconciled by the digestive system. The power of *udāna* is the creation of a consequence if an incompatibility is found; this power manifests in our urge to speak because we are unable to hold the contradiction within ourselves. The power of *vyāna* is the motion or change caused when the consequence manifests; it the main cause of the transmigration of the soul, or any kind of motion.

Two Kinds of Restrictions

Once logic has been created, to reason, we must also create *symbols*. The role of *śakti* now changes from defining the type of logic to defining the origin, metric, and objects. Quite specifically, we move from doing logic to doing mathematics, thereby introducing space, time, and objects. Due to the change in role, *śakti* is now called *prakriti* or the creatrix. *Manas*, *prāna*, and *vāk* act again, but this time *manas* is the ideal object, *prāna* is the metric or relation to this ideal object, and *vāk* is the individual objects.

There are hence two kinds of *prāna*. The first *prāna* is *śakti* which creates one of 8 types of logics based on the nature of choice of the soul. We discussed this *śakti* in the previous section. Then there is the *prāna* which produces the negation or hiding thereby creating a manifest tree from a root. The latter form of *prāna* is also called *prakriti* in contrast to *śakti*. The *śakti* is also a type of negation in the sense that it creates a world in which only certain types of choices are idealized. The material choices for instance dominate in *sat* and subordinate *chit* and *ananda*. Subsequently, this restriction on choice is used to further restrict the complete truth by creating smaller parts of the whole truth such that the choices are further restricted until we get to the bottom of the universe where there is no choice—only determinism.

Logically Sizing the Universes

We must note that the ideal object can be defined only after the logic of the world has been defined. For instance, in the material world, since morality rules over desires, an ideal person is one who controls His desires through principles of morality. Since morality is defined by austerity, truthfulness, cleanliness, and kindness, the ideal person will embody renunciation, knowledge cultivation, restrictions on sexuality, and charity to others. In a different world, the definition of the ideal person will be different. The ideal person may for example simply play instead of working hard, may indulge in deception instead of being truthful, have numerous amorous partners instead of abstinence, and be competitive instead of being kind.

Sakti and *prakriti* are successive stages of the same power. In the spiritual world, *Hara* is *śakti* and *Ramā* is *prakriti*. In the material creation, similarly, *Pārvati* is *śakti* and *Durga* is *prakriti*. We can say that *śakti* is the power that controls the entire material creation (all the universes) and *prakriti* is the power that controls a single universe. The region outside all the universe is described as a material 'ocean' but it has no material objects. It is the domain in which *sat* is higher than *ananda* and *ananda* is higher than *chit*. Entering this domain means a soul wants to enjoy but also be morally responsible. Entering a particular universe, on the other hand, means giving a definition to morality—e.g. how many values constitute the ideal morality? Similarly, how many pleasures are to be considered primordial? Likewise, defining how many unique concepts are sufficient to form a complete theory?

These definitions provide the number of *directions* in space. When the space represents cognition, then the number of directions in space represent the number of fundamental concepts necessary to form a theory. When the space represents pleasure, then the directions denote the fundamental pleasures of life. When the space denotes relations then directions denote the basic types of moralities and duties within the society. Vedic texts describe that the present universe is the smallest, and the planar surface in this universe is fundamentally divided into four directions called—East, West, North, and South. Due to this fact, there are four basic moralities (austerity, cleanliness, charity, and truthfulness), four basic types of roles in society (*Brahmana*, *Kshatriya*, *Vaisya*, and *Sudra*), four basic divisions of time into ages (*Satya*, *Tretā*, *Dvāpara*, and *Kali*). Similarly, there are four kinds of pleasures of life, namely, eating, sleeping, mating, and defending; life as a whole is divided into four phases—*Brahmacharya*, *Grihastha*, *Vānaprastha*, and *Saṃnyāsa*. Finally, the space of concepts needs minimally four basic concepts; those familiar with atomic theory will know that these four concepts are energy, momentum, angular momentum, and spin. Life is also modeled as 4 primordial goals—*dharma, artha, kāma,* and *moksha.*

These divisions are unique properties of this universe, but they don't apply to other universes. In other universes, there are more divisions of society, more stages of life, more distinct moral values, more basic types of pleasure, more properties are necessary to formulate a theory, and life has more goals. The smallest universe is the *simplest* because it involves the least number of divisions. *Cosmic Theogony* discusses in greater detail the basis of this division by 4. The basic reason is that there are 4 kinds of relationships (one-to-one, one-to-many, many-to-one, and many-to-many) which create *dharma.*

Space can be divided into more and more directions if the 'many' in the above relations is treated as 2, 3, 4, etc. In the smallest universe, all these distinctions are collapsed, and hence 'many' includes 2, 3, 4, etc. However, the successively larger universes will divide the same plane by 8, 12, 16, or more parts. Then the same material elements will be divided into a greater number of parts, and the same pleasures will be further divided into a greater number of pleasures. The smallest universe is defined by the 4 directions because they constitute the simplest meaning of 'many'—i.e. it includes everything greater than 1. In the next larger universe, we can separate out the relations of 1 and 2, and use 'many' to denote 3 and above. In the next higher universe, there will be separate relationships for 1, 2, and 3, and 'many' will be used for 4 and beyond. Each universe therefore simply redefines the meaning of 'many' and thereby expands gradually.

The Significance of Four Directions

We saw above how the smallest universe has four directions, and the ideal must therefore have four facets. The meaning of the ideal having many facets is that these facets can be self-contradictory. For example, in this universe both truthfulness and kindness are moral values, but they can easily conflict. Thus if a killer asks you of the whereabouts of a person who he intends to kill, should you demonstrate truthfulness and tell him about the person's location, or should you show compassion and lie about the person's location in order to mislead the killer? If compassion were always superior to truth, then you could save all criminals out of compassion by lying to the police. If truth were always superior to compassion, then being truthful to a killer and telling him of the whereabouts of the person he intends to kill would be morality. Thus, truth and kindness are often contradictory moral values; you cannot practice them always as they are going to conflict. In such cases, you must prioritize them—e.g. compassion over truth, or vice versa.

The ideal situation is one in which all the four moral values are present, which lies at the *center* of the space. As we move out of the center in any of the four directions, we will find truth without compassion, or compassion without truth. This indicates how the *imperfect* is created from the *perfect*. The combination of truthfulness, cleanliness, austerity, and kindness is perfect; however, parts of that are imperfect. The world appears to have evil, and this evil is created from good. The method of creating evil is simply to take parts of the good in isolation which is achieved by moving away from the center. Now, if we embody truth and neglect compassion, the fact that compassion is missing can be *construed* as cruelty. Similarly, if we show compassion and neglect the truth, the fact that truth is missing can be *viewed* as cheating. As we saw earlier, the missing ingredient can be regarded as the *denial* of the ingredient. As more things go missing, more and more of the ideal can potentially be denied. As a result, some truthful people will argue *against* compassion, while other compassionate people will argue *against* truth. They forget that both positions are not ideal because the ideal lies not at the edges or even in the middle of the flat space, but its center.

As we move out of the center, we increase our distance from the ideal. This is commonly seen in many religions where compassion may be advocated but truth may be neglected. Alternately, one may be compassionate to some and cruel to others; truthful in some cases and deceitful in others.

The Creation of the Alphabet

The *chit* comprises of six qualities: knowledge, beauty, fame, power, wealth, and renunciation. The *chit* is also divided into acting and knowing, which are also called *prāna* and *vāk*. As we saw earlier, the *prāna* acts as negation and the *vāk* as assertion; they are respectively the feminine and masculine. The 12 divisions of the zodiac represent the six qualities of *chit* in both assertion and negation. This completes one circle, and the circle represents knowledge and action, assertion and negation, masculine and feminine. The 12 divisions of the zodiac, however, constitute the *ādidaivika* portion of *chit* which becomes the controller or administrator of cognition or *chit*.

The *chit* also divides into *ādiatmika* and *ādibhautika* or knower and known, which are the administrated parts of cognition or *chit*. The known reality is represented within the knower as a symbol of reality, which means that there is a real thing externally and there is a representation of the known in the knower. The known thing and its representation are not identical, as a result of which we must distinguish between the reality and its knowledge, although the real thing is also knowledge (if it is completely known). Thus, aside from the fact that the whole is itself dividing into parts to create the various knowns, the knower is also looking at the known through different relationships or perspectives in order to obtain a subset of the knowledge. Owing to this separation, there is a further distinction by the knower and known, which doubles the number of divisions from 12 to 24.

Then the 16 types of pleasures are enjoyed through the 8 levels and the 24 divisions of each knower into *ādiatmika* and *ādibhautika*. The sum of these categories—8 + 24 + 16 = 48—constitute the elementary alphabets in terms of which everything has to be described. Aside from these are two other categories—the *śakti* and God—which make a total of 50. God is the ultimate male and His *śakti* is the ultimate female. As seen above, this *śakti* is the five-fold logic, which binds God into a cosmic 'egg' restricting His choices.

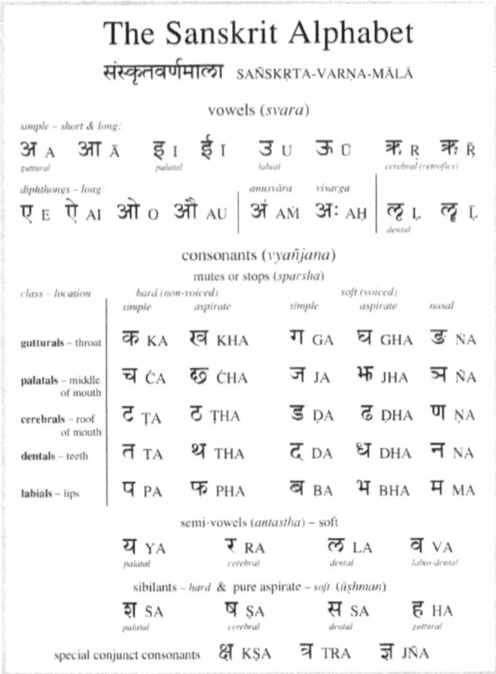

Out of the 50 alphabets, 25 alphabets represent the 24 elements of *Sāńkhya* and the 25th alphabet represents the whole truth. These 25 elements are represented by the 25 consonants in *Sanskrit*. As we have seen above, this pattern of 25 categories was seen previously in the 24 transcendent forms and the 24 incarnations in the material universe, followed by *Kṛṣṇa* as the complete whole. The 24 elements of *Sāńkhya* are therefore not just material elements. They are actually semantic categories or divisions of *chit* which constitutes all that can be known and done by the conscious observer.

The 16 forms of pleasure are denoted by the 16 vowels. The 8 types of awareness are represented by the 8 semi-vowels and sibilants. This makes a total of 49 alphabets. Finally, *śakti* as the logic which restricts the remaining 49 categories is the 50th alphabet. This *śakti* is originally three principles of identity, non-contradiction, and mutual-exclusion which are represented by the 3 conjuncts. But in the material world, there are two additional principles of time and *karma* represented by श्र and ळ. If we keep the 5 divisions of *śakti* aside, then the alphabet has 50 letters. If these divisions are included, then the alphabet has 55 letters. For the sake of our discussion, we will restrict ourselves to the 50 alphabets. In the *yoga* system, 48 of the 50 alphabets are represented in the 6 lower *chakra* and the top *chakra* represents God and His *śakti* or the union of male and female. Therefore even if we understood all the material categories we would have obtained only 48 out of the 50 principles. Our knowledge will remain incomplete because the most essential two alphabets of language represent God and His *śakti*.

The *ādidaivika* or demigods represent this symbolic structure partially. They oversee the 8 roles, and 16 pleasures, but out of the 24 they only comprise the 12 divisions of *chit*. As a result, the demigods are 8 + 12 + 16 = 36, which are manifested from *Brahma*, *Viṣṇu*, and *Shiva* respectively. If these three deities are excluded, then the total count of demigods becomes 33. The 36 deities of the material world are divided into 8 *Vasu* (manifest from *Brahma*), 12 *Aditya* (manifest from *Viṣṇu*) and 16 *Rudra* (manifest from *Shiva*). Their enjoyment is in controlling the connection between knowers and knowns. Like *Kshatriya* in the material world control the economic activity between producers and consumers, similarly, the demigods are the *Kshatriya* of the universe. They are not producers and consumers directly.

Over and beyond the demigods and the three deities from whom they are manifest, there is the ultimate male and female of the material world called *Param-Shiva* and His consort *Pārvati*—She is the *śakti* or logic of this world who restricts the male—*Shiva*—to behave according to Her dictates. Her rules constitute the rationality of the material world. The combination of *Shiva* and *Pārvati* creates the other 48 categories and 36 demigods. Together, 48 and 36 constitute the 84 principles of creation, which become the basis of the 8,400,000 lakh species of life that pervade different parts of the universe.

The crown *chakra* is also called *sahasrāra* or the thousand petal lotus obtained after time and *karma* are removed from the logic. The 8,400,000 lakh species on the other hand are created with these principles. This is probably an indication that each logic principle creates a 10-fold division because the entity without time and *karma* is said to have 1,000 divisions and the one with those divisions has 100,000 divisions. This is a topic for further investigation when we delve into the nature of logic in a separate post.

The Nature of Mathematics

The collection of alphabets and the logic employed to combine them into sentences constitutes the scope of 'mathematics'. It is contiguous with matter, conscious experience, and even religion, because its alphabets are based on the division of the whole into parts and ordering the parts in relation to the whole. Current mathematics (because it only considers cardinals) describes the world in a materialistic way—it views things as independent objects rather than parts of a whole, and then the whole is constructed by aggregating the parts. However, the same 'mathematics' (when it is seen as the parts of the whole) will mean logic and alphabets and will create cognition, relation, and emotion—the three facets of the soul under the influence of a particular type of logic which constitutes the material world. This is not the only possible logic, as we have seen above, although the alphabets remain unchanged. By studying the material world, therefore we can discover the alphabet, and its governing logic. Then we can retain the alphabet and employ a different logic based on the understanding of the soul. Thereby emerges a new kind of world that looks just like this world because it embodies the same alphabet, and yet it employs a different logic. That logic entails a different type of choice.

The problem of counting is identical to the problem of perception, discrimination, and ordering. Some fundamental ideas regarding counting are altered when the first object is the complete object, and everything is defined as a part of the whole, in relation to the whole. A fundamental feature of this division is that the whole itself cannot be cut up into parts, because the origin of counting would then be lost. Instead, we have to create the parts, without dividing the whole itself into parts.

This is then the philosophy of mathematics—a whole is divided into parts. The method of this division is logic (called *prāna*), and the results of the division are alphabets (called *vāk*). Once the division has occurred and the alphabets have been created, then the second-order function of logic is to create their combinations. These combinations are nothing other than further subdivisions. *Karma* and time play a role in the combination or subdivision—*time* creates the combination and *karma* pushes a soul into the combination. As a result of time and *karma* the combinations are experienced.

The alphabets are symbols of meaning, and those meanings are subdivisions of relation, cognition, and emotion. By using an alphabet that mimics the properties of the soul, we begin to understand a language that can explain everything in experience. This experience is different everywhere; in particular, the material world is identified by a different logic, and each universe is defined by a different scale of dividing, which then produce different alphabets. By adding more letters to the alphabet, the language becomes more complex but that complexity is useful in describing nuances missing in the smaller universes. By removing letters, language is simplified, and the nuances are removed. Thus, a universe with more alphabets will afford a finer subdivision of relationships, a more refined division in concepts, and more variety in pleasure. These are also counterparts of the *coordinate reference frames* we use to describe nature. Reference frames are not arbitrary. Each universe is a different frame, which means that if you tried to a more elaborate language you will not be able to experience the associated subtleties there.

As these divisions are increased, we get different universes. As these divisions are successively applied in a hierarchy we get smaller parts of the universe. The part-whole relationship is the geometry of space and time. There are two crucial insights in this philosophy. First, we need to understand how logic is a choice created from inner contradictions in the soul. Second, we need to know how that logic creates the ideal embodiment of the logic by choosing the directions in space in order to create the alphabets.

Our conscious experience is seeing a world around us comprised of places, times, things, and situations—i.e. geometry. Our unconscious existence is the logic that precedes the above said geometry. By understanding the different kinds of logics we can know the different philosophies of life. By knowing the different geometries we can describe different worlds based on these philosophies of life. The scope of logic and mathematics are thus different, but they are successive progressions in analyzing the complete truth.

EPILOGUE

The essays in this collection are not ordered logically or topically. They are only a snapshot in time—essays written between April 2017 and March 2018. The chronological ordering makes an interesting reading for quite different reasons than a logical or topic ordering: you get to see how the mind has been preoccupied with different ideas over time.

While thinking about combining all these posts into a book, I did not imagine that I had so much material to make a long book; the result is therefore a pleasant surprise. Having done this once, I am tempted to do it over and over: compiling the chronological posts every few years into a book, making it easier for people who prefer to read books rather than posts online to have easy (even offline) access to this material.

If you have comments about this material, or ideas about how to improve the content, or suggestions on the kinds of posts you would like to read in future, please do not hesitate to contact me through my website.

www.ingramcontent.com/pod-product-compliance
Lightning Source LLC
Chambersburg PA
CBHW050011170726
48282CB00025B/356
9789385384202